Why the West Fears Islam

Culture and Religion in International Relations

Series Editors:
Yosef Lapid and Friedrich Kratochwil

Published by Palgrave Macmillan:

Dialogue Among Civilizations: Some Exemplary Voices
By Fred Dallmayr

Religion in International Relations: The Return from Exile
Edited by Fabio Petito and Pavlos Hatzopoulos

Identity and Global Politics: Theoretical and Empirical Elaborations
Edited by Patricia M. Goff and Kevin C. Dunn

Reason, Culture, Religion: The Metaphysics of World Politics
By Ralph Pettman

Bringing Religion into International Relations
By Jonathan Fox and Shmuel Sandler

*The Global Resurgence of Religion and the Transformation of International Relations:
The Struggle for the Soul of the Twenty-First Century*
By Scott M. Thomas

*Religion, Social Practice, and Contested Hegemonies: Reconstructing the Public Sphere
in Muslim Majority Societies*
Edited by Armando Salvatore and Mark LeVine

Beyond Eurocentrism and Anarchy: Memories of International Order and Institutions
By Siba N. Grovogui

The Public Sphere: Between Tradition and Modernity
By Armando Salvatore

*Civilizational Identity: The Production and Reproduction of "Civilizations" in
International Relations*
Edited by Martin Hall and Patrick Thaddeus Jackson

Civilizing Missions: International Religious Agencies in China
By Miwa Hirono

*Civilizational Dialogue and World Order: The Other Politics of Cultures,
Religions, and Civilizations in International Relations*
Edited by Michális S. Michael and Fabio Petito

Why the West Fears Islam: An Exploration of Muslims in Liberal Democracies
By Jocelyne Cesari

Why the West Fears Islam

An Exploration of Muslims in Liberal Democracies

Jocelyne Cesari

First published in 2013 by
PALGRAVE MACMILLAN®
in the United States—a division of St. Martin's Press LLC,
175 Fifth Avenue, New York, NY 10010.

Where this book is distributed in the UK, Europe and the rest of the world,
this is by Palgrave Macmillan, a division of Macmillan Publishers Limited,
registered in England, company number 785998, of Houndmills,
Basingstoke, Hampshire RG21 6XS.

Palgrave Macmillan is the global academic imprint of the above companies
and has companies and representatives throughout the world.

Palgrave® and Macmillan® are registered trademarks in the United States,
the United Kingdom, Europe and other countries.

ISBN: 978–1–403–96953–8

Library of Congress Cataloging-in-Publication Data is available from the
Library of Congress.

A catalogue record of the book is available from the British Library.

Design by Newgen Imaging Systems (P) Ltd., Chennai, India.

First edition: July 2013

10 9 8 7 6 5 4 3 2 1

Contents

List of Figures   vii

Acknowledgments   xi

Introduction: Shari'a, Burqa, and Minarets; What Is the Problem with Muslims in the West?   xiii

1   Muslims as the Internal and External Enemy   1

Part I   In Their Own Voices: What It Is to Be a Muslim and a Citizen in the West   21

2   Islam: Between Personal and Social Identity Markers   29

3   Multiple Communities of Allegiance: How Do Muslims Say "We"?   49

4   Religiosity, Political Participation, and Civic Engagement   71

Part II   Structural Conditions of the Externalization of Islam   81

5   Securitization of Islam in Europe: The Embodiment of Islam as an Exception   83

6   How Islam Questions the Universalism of Western Secularism   107

7   Salafization of Islamic Norms and Its Influence on the Externalization of Islam   129

Conclusion: Naked Public Spheres: Islam within Liberal and Secular Democracies   139

Appendix 1   Focus Group Description   147

Appendix 2   Focus Group: Moderator Guidelines   151

Appendix 3   Draft Survey of the Civic and Political Participation of German Muslims   155

Appendix 4   Berlin Survey Description (January 2010)   179

Appendix 5   Survey of Surveys   221

Appendix 6   Master List of Codes   225

Appendix 7   Trends of Formal Political Participation   227

Appendix 8   European Representative Bodies of Islam   239

Appendix 9   Islamopedia: A Web-Based Resource on
               Contemporary Islamic Thought   241

Appendix 10   Major Wanabi Organizations in Europe   245

Appendix 11   Salafis in Europe   249

Appendix 12   Fatwas From Salafi Websites   255

Appendix 13   Data on Religiosity and Political Participation of
               Muslims in Europe and the United States   305

Notes   317

Bibliography   355

Index   375

Figures

1.1	Muslims in the West are seen as both the internal and external enemies	1
2.1	"How strongly do you identify with your country and your religion?," United Kingdom	30
2.2	"How strongly do you identify with each of the following?," US Muslims	30
2.3	"How strongly do you identify with each of the following?," US Protestants	31
2.4	"Is religion important in your daily life?," France	32
2.5	"Is religion important?," United States	32
2.6	Religious levels, Germany	38
2.7	"Never attended a religious service," Germany	44
2.8	"Attend a religious service at least once a week," United States	44
3.1	Trust "a fair amount," across 11 European cities	68
A7.1	Voted in last national election (2005), United Kingdom	228
A7.2	Voted in last national election (2007), France	228
A7.3	Voted in last national election (2005), Germany	228
A7.4	Voted in last national election (2006), the Netherlands	229
A7.5	Registered to vote, United States	229
A7.6	Informal participation, Germany	229
A7.7	Informal participation, France	230
A7.8	Informal participation, the Netherlands	230
A7.9	Informal participation, United Kingdom	230
A7.10	Informal political participation, Paris	231
A7.11	Informal political participation, Berlin	231
A7.12	Informal participation: Volunteer time, United States	231
A7.13	Informal participation: Given to charity, United States	232
A7.14	Muslims who voted, Paris	233
A7.15	Muslims who voted, Berlin	233
A7.16	Muslims who voted, Rotterdam	233
A7.17	Muslims who voted, Marseille	234
A7.18	Registered to vote, Protestants	234
A7.19	Registered to vote, Catholics	234
A7.20	Registered to vote, Jews	235

A7.21	Registered to vote, Muslims	235
A7.22	Registered to vote, Mormons	235
A7.23	Registered to vote, other Christians	235
A7.24	Political alignment, France	236
A7.25	Political alignment, the Netherlands	236
A7.26	Political alignment, US Muslims	237
A7.27	Political alignment, US Protestants	237
A7.28	Political alignment, US Catholics	237
A7.29	Political alignment, US Mormons	238
A7.30	Political alignment, US Jews	238
A13.1	Non-Muslims who have an unfavorable view of Muslims	305
A13.2	Non-Muslims who have an unfavorable view of Muslims, Spain and Germany	305
A13.3	Non-Muslims' perception of Muslims' loyalty, France, Germany, and Britain	306
A13.4	Being less expressive about one's religion is necessary for integration, France, Germany, and Britain	306
A13.5	"How strongly do you identify with your country and religion?," France	306
A13.6	"How strongly do you identify with your country and religion?," United Kingdom	307
A13.7	Consider themselves Muslim/Christian before their nationality, United Kingdom	307
A13.8	Consider themselves Muslim/Christian before their nationality, Germany	307
A13.9	Consider themselves Muslim/Christian before their nationality, France	308
A13.10	"How strongly do you identify with each of the following?," US Catholics	308
A13.11	"How strongly do you identify with each of the following?," US Jews	308
A13.12	"How strongly do you identify with each of the following?," US Mormons	309
A13.13	"Is religion important in your daily life?," United Kingdom	309
A13.14	"Is religion important in your daily life?," Germany	309
A13.15	Religiosity in the United States	310
A13.16	Never attended a religious service, the Netherlands	310
A13.17	Never attended a religious service, France	310
A13.18	Weekly mosque attendance	311
A13.19	Identifying as Moroccan/Turkish/Iraqi first and then Dutch, Amsterdam	311
A13.20	Identifying as Moroccan/Turkish/Egyptian first and then American, Boston	311
A13.21	Confidence in institutions, France	312
A13.22	Trust in elections, United States	312

A13.23	Trust in the FBI, United States	312
A13.24	What do you consider yourself first?	313
A13.25	Formal political participation, Berlin survey	313
A13.26	Informal political participation, Berlin survey	313
A13.27	Confidence in institutions, Germany	314
A13.28	Confidence in institutions, United Kingdom	314
A13.29	Trust in the military, United States	314
A13.30	Attended mosque at least once a week, United States	315
A13.31	Attended mosque at least once a week, the Netherlands	315
A13.32	Attended a religious service at least once a week, United States	315

ACKNOWLEDGMENTS

This volume is the product of the Islam in the West (IIW) Program research activities during the period 2005–2010, made possible by the institutional support of the Center for Middle Eastern Studies at Harvard University directed at the time by Stephen Caton and the Groupe de Sociologie des Religions et de la Laicite (GSRL-CNRS) in Paris directed by Jean-Paul Willaime and Philippe Portier.

My participation to the Challenge Research Program directed by Didier Bigo from 2005 to 2009 was also very beneficial to the implementation of the survey. The support of John Slocum at the MacArthur Foundation allowed us to organize focus groups among American Muslims as well.

The cooperation with Dalia Mogadeh at the Gallup Institute gave me the opportunity to access the Gallup data on American Muslims.

My research has also profited from my position as Minerva Chair at the National War College in 2011 and 2012.

I owe special thanks to my colleagues Ron Geaves, Johan Meuleman and Riem Spielhaus who coordinated the focus groups discussions respectively in London, Amsterdam and Berlin.

The list of students and young scholars who made possible the organization of more than 60 focus groups in Paris, London, Berlin, Amsterdam, and Boston is too long to acknowledge them by names, but I thank you all.

Lisa Baughn, Terra Dunham, Bethany Kibler, Amanda Garrett, Ashley Anderson, and Aline Longstaff worked enthusiastically and zealously with me on the long process of data analysis.

The dedication of the wonderful Euro-Islam team has also been precious in making the Euro-Islam.info website a powerhouse for information and data on Islam in Europe and the United States from which I have benefited tremendously in the writing of this book.

Many colleagues have provided stimulating feedback on my work in its different stages: Bryan Turner, Jose Casanova, Nillufer Golle, Dalia Mogadeh, Jennifer Hochschild, Nancy Ammerman, Wendy Cage, Jennan Reid, Denise Helly, and Stephen Caton.

Finally, wonderful research assistants Aline Longstaff, Lisa de Bode and Michelle Nellett have put long hours in the finalization of the manuscript.

INTRODUCTION: SHARI'A, BURQA, AND MINARETS; WHAT IS THE PROBLEM WITH MUSLIMS IN THE WEST?

The integration of Muslim immigrants has been on the political agenda of European democracies for several decades. However, only in the last ten years has it specifically evolved into a question of civic integration closely related to religious identity. In the 1960s and 1970s, the socioeconomic integration of immigrants with a Muslim background was the primary focus of academic literature,[1] but with the emergence of the second and third generations, the interest has shifted to political mobilization.[2] Beginning with the Rushdie affair in the United Kingdom and the hijab affair in France from 1989 to the present, the spotlight has moved to the legitimacy of Islamic signs in public space, such as dress code, minarets, and halal foods. As a consequence, controversies surrounding the visibility of these signs have steadily grown. Controversy is not merely a disagreement about divergent points of view, but is about fundamental differences (or at least perceived as such) about the principles and norms that regulate the common life of individuals sharing the same time period. Such fundamental divergences cannot coexist in the same public space, because they convey exclusive and binary visions.

Consequently, headscarves, mosques, and minarets are increasingly seen as a rejection of Western democratic values or, even worse, as a direct threat to the West. During the 2006 campaign to ban minarets in Switzerland, posters from the Egerkinger Committee[3] displayed a woman in a burqa standing next to minarets that were rising from a Swiss flag and pointing to the sky like missiles. Such a perception of Islam in the public sphere has reached the United States as well through the ongoing shari'a debates, discourse on Islamic radicalization in jails, and the ground zero mosque controversy in the summer of 2010.

Islamic signs are not only ostracized in public discourse but are also controlled and restricted through multiple legal and administrative procedures in an attempt to "civilize" or adjust them to fit Western political cultures. In April 2011, the French government enforced the ban on wearing the niqab, which was overwhelmingly approved in 2010 by the French legislature. Other countries like Belgium have followed the French path in 2011 and 2012. The most recent addition to the long list of outcast Islamic signs is circumcision. In June 2012, a judge in Cologne, Germany, outlawed circumcision on the grounds that it causes "illegal bodily harm." However, because of the amplitude of protests from both Jewish and Muslim groups in Germany and beyond, there was a political reaction leading to the swift adoption by the Parliament in December 2012 of a law permitting nontherapeutic circumcision to be practiced under certain conditions.[4]

This cultural struggle is also fought on the Muslim side. Salafism, a specific interpretation of Islam in stark opposition to Western values and cultures, advocates many practices such as gender segregation and rejection of political and civic engagement that are deemed as efforts to fight the impurity of the West. This particular brand of Islam is one of the most visible, widespread, and accessible interpretations, and thus gives the illusion to both Muslims and non-Muslims that Salafism is the true Islam.

In sum, an essentialized West and an essentialized Islam are fighting each other and in so doing reinforce one another. The "burqa versus the bikini" opposition often used by both Islamophobes and Muslim fundamentalists encapsulates this sense of profound incompatibility that relates to politics, lifestyles, and, most interestingly, women's bodies.[5] On the one hand, for most Westerners, the burqa symbolizes the total denial of freedom and gender equality. On the other hand, for fundamentalist religious voices, the burqa symbolizes a woman's dignity and her devotion to family values, as opposed to the bikini seen as an objectification and degradation of the female body. Such stark oppositions are of course extreme but, at the same time, reflect the "either or" approach, in which most of the discourse on Islam is currently trapped. The German president, Joachim Gauck, involuntarily illustrated the milder version of this binary opposition when he said that Muslims can live in Germany but that, unlike his predecessor (Christian Wulf), he does not think that they can be a part of Germany.[6]

One major consequence of such a polarized mindset is to mask the sociological reality of Muslims. In fact, a striking gap exists between the image of Islam as it is constructed in binary public discourse and the multifaceted reality of Muslims across countries and localities. For example, the dominant assumption is that visible Islamic identities in the West are inversely correlated to their civic and political loyalties, while there is empirical evidence that contradicts such an assumption. In other words, the "Muslim" has become the invisible man (and woman) of western societies, like black or Jews used to be. In this context, invisible does not mean hidden or undetectable. In fact Muslims are in plain sight and highly scrutinized. It rather refers to people incapacity to see the reality of Muslims of flesh and blood with their "inner eyes"[7] or what Martha Nussbaum calls respect and sympathetic imagination.[8] Taking up this intriguing invisibility, this book is a unique and unparalleled effort to make sense of this disjuncture between what Muslims do and the political construct of the "Muslim problem."

Such a project is unprecedented for several reasons. First, the data presented in this book are the result of five years of collective research conducted by the Islam in the West Program (IIW) at Harvard University,[9] funded by the European Commission, the MacArthur Foundation, and the Carnegie Corporation. This research concerns the different aspects of the Muslim presence in Western democracies: policy-making analysis, empirical surveys, content analysis of political and religious discourses, and mapping of existing knowledge on the sociological and political reality of Muslims in European countries and the United States. It is, therefore, a unique holistic synthesis of the most significant knowledge on Muslims in Europe and the United States, combined with a production of original data.

Second, it is based on premier research among lay Muslims in Europe and the United States to assess their religious and political practices. Under the auspices of the Harvard-based IIW program, focus groups were conducted in Paris, London, Berlin, Amsterdam, and Boston between 2007 and 2010. In each of these five cities, 12 focus groups were organized, with the result that 500 Muslims of diverse ethnicities, nationalities, generations, education levels, and genders participated. Third, the results of these focus groups were analyzed in the broader context of preexisting quantitative data on Muslim political and religious behaviors produced over the last ten years in different European countries and in the United States. In this regard, this book is the first systematic and comparative review of the existing knowledge about Muslim political behaviors and religious practices in western European countries and in the United States (presented in chapters 2, 3, and 4). This review concerns *only* structured surveys and pollings but has been informed by the wealth of knowledge provided by the abundant qualitative sociological and anthropological literature on Muslims in Europe and the United States.

Fourth, it is also the first systematic assessment of forms of global Islamic thinking that influence Western Muslims (chapter 7). This assessment was made possible through a systematic review of Islamic guidance on the Internet that was made accessible in an online web resource at islamopedia-oneline.org.

Fifth, it is based on a rigorous analysis of policy making and political discourse since 9/11, gathered through several research projects in the IIW program and its Euro-Islam network.[10]

By combining these different sources and materials, this book challenges many disciplinary boundaries from sociology to political science. For this reason, it may appear "heretic" to all disciplines. Its ultimate goal is to unveil the social and political mechanisms at work in the binary opposition between Islam and the West, in which many Muslims and non-Muslims are locked. Such an exploration cannot rely on one set of explanations because this binary opposition works at different levels from discourses to social attitudes and policy making.

These different levels are interpreted in the overall framework of the symbolic integration of Islam. Symbolic integration refers to the creation of symbolic "boundaries" that places a religion or ideology, in this case Islam, either inside or outside the national identity discourse. These boundaries can determine whether or not a particular culture is included or excluded from societal norms. More specifically, this book looks at the issues at stake in the externalization process, as well as the different protagonists at work, such as state actors; intellectuals; transnational religious actors; and Muslims of different groups, ages, and genders. For some of these individuals, their legitimacy to be engaged and visible in the public space rests on the outcomes of these conflicts over symbolic integration, including Islamists and women who wear the hijab or burqa.

Therefore, the main question of this book is, "How are the symbolic boundaries that place Islam 'outside' created or reinforced?"[11] For example, certain social groups may have full citizenship rights but will still be located outside of what Jeffrey Alexander (1993) calls the "national community."[12] Members of national communities tend to firmly believe that the world, which notably includes their own nation, is filled with people who either do not deserve freedom and communal support or are not capable of sustaining it (in part because they are immoral egoists). Members of national communities do not wish to include, protect, or offer rights to such persons, because they conceive them as being unworthy, amoral, and, in some sense, even "uncivilized."

To be clear, this is not another book on policies toward Muslim immigrants in Europe or the United States nor a book on Islamophobia. A wealth of literature already exists on these very issues. For example, in the domain of policy making toward immigrants, multiple surveys discuss demographics, political opportunity structures, international crises, media salience, level of government, courts, institutional and legal heritage, ethnic origin, and administrative rationality or "governementality."[13] Islamophobia has been addressed in a growing number of books that present the main features of the anti-Islamic discourse and discriminations against Muslims in specific countries as well as the actors involved in this discourse or practices.[14]

The goal of this research is to combine the results of these existing studies with a less common examination of the collective norms and values that underlie the current public discourse an policies vis-à-vis Muslims.[15] These collective norms and values or what Theodore Lowi calls "public philosophy" shape the social perceptions regarding Muslims and Islam.[16] The aim is therefore to unmask the ideas, values, imagery, and emotional attachment that political actors tap into in order to build ideological arguments, such as the ones surrounding rejection of minarets, the burqa, or shari'a. These idioms have a longer-term, more anonymous, and less partisan existence than ideologies. When political actors construct ideological arguments for particular action-related purposes, they invariably use or take account of available cultural idioms, and those idioms may structure their arguments in partially unintended ways.[17] It is important to note that the polarization of Islam and the West come also from Muslim actors such as Salafis who convey globally similar idioms but invert the positive and negative value.

In addition, these same norms are not operating in or playing out in similar ways across Europe and the United States. To the contrary, this book illustrates that the political cultures or cultural idioms of each country are quite decisive in shaping public norms and repertoires of legitimacy even though the different discourses may appear the same from a distance. Specifically, this book shows that secularism is central to the European debates about Islam, while in the United States, the main issue is security in the post-9/11 context. Of course, there are variations in the secular discourse across European countries. Some have argued that the issue in the UK or the Netherlands is related to multiculturalism rather than secularism (see, for example, Tariq Modood[18]). But despite these different contexts, our research shows that what is at stake everywhere are the challenges brought by Islam to two major secular principles: private vs. public and collective vs. individual rights (chapter 6). Additionally, even if the fierce anti-shari'a campaign in the United States can also be interpreted as a challenge to secularism, we will show in chapter 5 that it is primarily motivated by security issues and is not the result of a crisis of American secular principles.

Finally, our focus on symbolic integration is not limited to public discourse but includes policy making that affects Muslims, such as immigration, citizenship, urban development, education, and the legal status of religious practices (chapter 5).

Layout of the Book

A cursory review of public opinion surveys and political discourse in both Europe and the United States over the last decade highlights the main arguments that put Islam and Muslims outside the civilized space of the West (chapter 1).

This externalization will be contrasted with the empirical reality of Muslims by presenting the results of our focus groups (Part I, In Their Own Voices: What It Is to Be a Muslim and a Citizen in the West—chapters 2, 3, and 4).

It will then analyze three main structural conditions that shape and solidify the symbolic boundaries between the West and Islam: the international context of the war on terror, the crisis of secularism, and the global visibility of Salafism (Part II, Structural Conditions of the Externalization of Islam).

The first factor is the ongoing securitization of Islam since 9/11 that is common to both Europe and the United States. Securitization refers to processes by which Islam is seen as an existential threat to European and American political and security interests and thereby justifies extraordinary measures against it. The consequences of this "emergency" mentality on the day-to-day management of Islamic practices are analyzed in chapter 5. The second factor is related to different versions of secularism that tend to render illegitimate all religious signs, especially Islamic ones, from public spaces. It also includes the political issue to reach a balance between groups' rights and individual rights as illustrated by the cartoons crisis and the shari'a debate (chapter 6). The third factor concerns the globalization of the Salafi trend, which over the last 30 years has become one of the most visible and widespread religious interpretations of Islam across the West and beyond (chapter 7).

There are of course other significant structural causes that contribute to the externalization of Muslims, notably the increase of social inequalities, the weakening of the welfare state, and the pauperization of the low middle classes. Specifically in Europe, where Islam is associated with post–World War II migrations, the externalization of Islam and Muslims is part of the overarching neoliberal transformation that has reshaped immigration and integration policies.

However, our goal is not to add to the already abundant literature about the socioeconomic reasons for the discrimination of immigrants or minorities. It is instead to tackle a question that this literature does not address: Why are the changes in these policies increasingly justified in cultural rather than political terms?

Arguably, these three factors—securitization, secularism and Salafism—could also be interpreted as effects rather than causes of the deficit of symbolic integration. However, our research shows that each of them exists independently of the presence of Muslims in the West, therefore, influencing the perception of Islam rather than being a consequence of this presence. For example, securitization is present not because Islam is already seen as the enemy, but because specific and extraordinary international conditions have built or rebuilt Islam as the external enemy. The specific nature of European secularism has also created a number of crises related not only to the visibility of Islam but to other religions as well. Moreover, the significant presence of a transnational, anti-Western interpretation of Islam deepens the perception of Islam as a religion that is impossible to integrate.

The accumulation of these three factors creates and reinforces the symbolic boundaries between Islam and the West. This book argues that even in the case of successful socioeconomic integration, as is the case for American Muslim immigrants, some of these factors heavily influence the integration process of Muslims and cast them as outsiders. Even more interestingly, the externalization of Islam and Muslims is not influenced by the reality of social and political behaviors of Muslims across countries, which actually shows integration in progress.

CHAPTER 1

MUSLIMS AS THE INTERNAL AND EXTERNAL ENEMY

The study of national symbolic boundaries addresses the ways citizens engage in the exclusion of some groups from the national community.[1] National community is embedded in institutions and practices that are concerned with the "moral regulation of social life."[2] As such, it includes in traditions, rituals, texts, discourses, and collective memories that reinforce and construct symbolic boundaries around the national community.[3] Symbolic codes are the underlying common constituents of these cultural practices that divide the world into those who are "citizens" or "friends" and those who are "enemies."[4] Symbolic boundaries are thereby constructed around the "national community" both internationally and intra-nationally. For example, enemies do not only reside outside of the territorial confines of the nation-state but may also lie within, reflecting the "internal structure of social divisions," as well as particular national myths, narratives, and traditions.[5] It is therefore possible to create a two-dimensional typology of symbolic boundaries within the national community: friends/enemies and internal/external. Through boundary-maintaining processes, social agents are located in one of four cells, which are internal friends, internal enemies, external friends, and external enemies (figure 1.1).[6]

Perception of Islam and Muslims	Description
Internal enemy	Muslims cannot or will not integrate. Islam is incompatible with Western values (freedom/equality). Islam is incompatible with national values (history/customs/language).
External enemy	Islam is the main cause of international terrorism. Muslims maintain external allegiances that endanger national security.

Figure 1.1 Muslims in the West are seen as both the internal and external enemies

In the case of Muslims in Western Europe, the construction of symbolic boundaries is influenced by several factors: immigrant background, socioeconomic status, and ethnic origin. In this regard, Muslims are at the core of multiple social processes related to the economic changes since the 1970s, as well as the expansion of the European Union and the redefinition of migration flux. In contrast, Muslims in the United States are not as central to socioeconomic evolution or immigration policies because they neither constitute the majority immigrant group nor belong to the lower economic classes. For these reasons, immigration debates have not been Islamicized in the United States.[7] Similarly, terrorism remains at the margins of immigration and social concerns. Although, in the aftermath of the Boston Marathon bombing of April 15, 2013, some political actors attempted to explicitly link repression of terrorism with immigration reform, due to the fact that the perpetrators of the bombings entered the United States as political refugees. In Europe, by contrast, the association of Islam and immigration has led to a tightening of immigration laws specifically targeting migrants from Muslim countries. This does not mean, however, that the war on terror has not permeated American immigration policies and increased procedures of control.[8]

In this regard, the difference with Europe is notable where the categories of "immigrant" and "Muslim" overlap. The reasons for the conflation between Islam and immigration lie in the specific post–World War II history of Muslim presence in Europe.[9] Most Muslims are immigrants (and vice versa), or have an immigrant background, and are currently estimated to constitute approximately 5 percent of the European Union's 425 million inhabitants. There are about 4.5 million Muslims in France, followed by 3 million in Germany, 1.6 million in the United Kingdom, and more than 0.5 million in Italy and the Netherlands. Although other nations have populations of fewer than 500,000 Muslims, smaller countries such as Austria, Sweden, and Belgium have substantial Muslim minorities for their respective sizes. In general, these populations are younger and more fertile than the domestic populations, prompting many journalists and even academics such as Bernard Lewis[10] to hypothesize that these numbers will become even more significant in the future.

The majority of Muslims in Europe also comes from three regions in the world, which determines the course of future immigration. The largest ethnic group is Arab, comprising approximately 45 percent of European Muslims, followed by Muslims of Turkish and South Asian descent. The groups are unevenly distributed, based on each European nation's immigrant history. In France and the United Kingdom, for example, Muslim populations began arriving from former colonies in the middle of the twentieth century, leading to a predominately North African ethnic group in France and a South Asian migrant population in the United Kingdom. In contrast, the Muslim community in Germany began with an influx of mainly Turkish "guest-workers" during the postwar economic boom. Although immigrants currently arrive in Europe from all over the world, the countries with established Muslim populations tend to attract more people from the same ethnic background. Among current European Union member states, only Greece has a significant indigenous population of Muslims, residing primarily in Thrace.

Another feature of European Muslims is their relatively low socioeconomic status.[11] As immigrants, the majority of European Muslims came with very low labor skills from underdeveloped nations. This reality, combined with the low standards of education and fewer job opportunities, explains the poor economic performance of immigrant Muslims. Furthermore, across Europe, Muslim immigrant populations are often concentrated in segregated, urban areas, which are plagued with delinquency, crime, and deteriorated living conditions. Additionally, the high density of immigrants from one ethnic group in specific areas raises the question of separatism and ghettoization. In the Netherlands, for example, almost all of its 850,000 Muslims live in the country's four major cities of Amsterdam, Rotterdam, Utrecht, and the Hague, where they make up 30 percent of the population overall.

In the United States, the perception of Islam as the external enemy can be traced back to the Iranian Hostage Crisis (1979–1981) and became more acute after the end of the Cold War and 9/11. Additionally, in the aftermath of 9/11, Muslims have also been seen as internal enemies due to the fear of homegrown terrorism. In Europe, 9/11 and, most significantly, several home grown terrorist attacks such as the Madrid bombings (March 2004) and London bombings (July 2005) have had a far-reaching and multifaceted effect on Muslims. Policies that range from immigration laws to integration, multiculturalism, and State accommodation of Islamic practices have changed in the post-9/11 political terrain.[12] The growing fear of home grown terrorism has driven the linkage of security and immigrant integration policies, and this linkage is increasingly connected not only to malevolent outsiders but also to disaffected groups and individuals inside European states.[13]

As a result, many European intellectuals and public figures have endorsed Samuel Huntington's "clash of civilizations" to make sense of these social and political challenges. They typically view Europe as a contested continent wherein Western civilization is in conflict with religious fundamentalists bent on eradicating modernization and hard-won freedoms.[14] In such a struggle, tolerance and respect for religious differences are considered weaknesses that may be exploited by the enemy. "The intensification of this "civilizational self identification"[15] has been exacerbated by the candidacy of Turkey to the European Union, which is seen as an existential threat to European identity.[16]

The liberal ideology is the vehicle of choice to articulate these "civilizational" concerns, mainly because since World War II the ethno-cultural or "racial" wording has been associated with the Nazi notion of civilizational superiority based on biological differences.[17] The demise to a certain extent, of racial and nationalist discourses have, therefore, led to an emphasis on liberal values in defense of national identities. Hence, immigrants who express religious or cultural values that are not part of this liberal narrative cannot be included within the boundaries of the national communities.[18]

This ideological approach is typical of what Trefidopoulos calls "Schmittian liberalism,"[19] which justifies coercive state power to protect the values of liberal societies from illiberal and putatively dangerous groups:

> This type of liberalism shares nationalism's commitment to the defense of the community's core identity, but differs from traditional nationalism in that the values constituting this identity are liberal and progressive, rather than conservative and traditional. That is, identity liberalism is dedicated to defending the liberal state's core principles against real and perceived threats from illiberal and perilous immigrants. As such, it is not simply a new brand of old-style xenophobia, but rather a consciously liberal response to the challenges of cultural pluralism that seeks to distinguish itself from its primary competitor: liberal multiculturalism. Schmittian liberals reject liberal multiculturalism because it endorses negotiation, compromise, and a willingness to accommodate groups whose religious beliefs and cultural practices may diverge from those of the majority.[20]

Consequently, these "Schmittian liberals" frame the problem in existentialist terms and advocate aggressive integrationism to justify policies that might otherwise be seen to contravene liberal principles of toleration and equality.

In this renewed focus on enlightenment, Islam and Muslims make the perfect enemy both inside and outside European nations. Historical reasons make this externalization understandable by a vast majority of citizens because Muslims and Islam have been the typical others of Europe for centuries not only in historical narratives but also in popular culture.[21]

More specifically, Europe has built its modern political identity in opposition to Islam. In the mirror of enlightened Western elites struggling for equality and democracy, the Ottoman Empire was the other.[22]

In this sense, Islam is a "topos" that is continuously activated at different moments in European history from colonization to post–World War II immigration. The post-9/11 era adds concerns on pluralization of societies and security, therefore, exacerbating and resurrecting the mentality of an "us versus them" where Muslims are "them."

Homo Islamicus and His Multiple Embodiments

For several centuries, Islam has played the role of the "other" in the Western psyche. Of course, Muslims have never been the sole "others" of the West: for instance, China, Africa, and aboriginal populations were also constructed in this way.[23] Moreover, this construction was not always negative:

for example, some forms of Orientalism focusing on eroticism were often favorably contrasted with the puritan West.[24]

From these multiple facets of the Muslim other, one specific trend emerges: the Western self-definition based on the concepts of progress, nation, rational individual (such as the myth of Robinson Crusoe), and secularization that was built in opposition to Muslim worlds.[25] In other words, the liberal modernist story at the heart of Western modern identity has adopted Islam as its foil in order to create itself. Such mirroring can be traced back to the Ottoman Empire's political domination of Mediterranean lands during the eighteenth century. Europe's relationship with the Ottoman Empire gradually established the East-West dichotomy that had a decisive impact on the eighteenth- and nineteenth-century world politics. The distinction of East and West was more than a product of religious differences; it was a reflection of political defiance. "The orientalization of the Orient," as Edward Said deemed it, was the primary effect of a European cultural crisis linked to the advent of modernity, which defined itself against the Ottoman neighbor.[26]

This binary vision of Islam versus the West has long-lasting effects beyond the formation of European modern polities. For example, this divide has been seen as the primary cause of the post–Cold War international crises. In this sense, the clash of civilizations is a reactivation of the West versus Islam dichotomy.[27] The idea of a monolithic Islam, which is at the core of the clash of civilizations, is the same idea (as the pre–Modern Europe self-defining moment) that leads to a reductionism in which conflicts in Sudan, Lebanon, Bosnia, Iraq, and Afghanistan are viewed as stemming collectively and wholly from Islam.[28]

The construction of Islam and Muslims as the enemy within liberal democracies takes place in this preexisting environment, though with its own specificities related to different domestic political situations. In these circumstances, Islam plays a dual role—as the internal enemy, represented by Muslims who are living within the territorial boundaries of the nation, and as the external enemy, represented by foreign Muslims who are perceived as military or political threats. The following sections briefly document the position of Islam and Muslims in both these roles by presenting significant declarations of public leaders, events, and public opinion surveys that corroborate the continuous "otherization" and externalization of Muslims in the West.

The systematic examination of these sources indicates a persistent linking of Islam to un-civic behavior and terrorism inside and outside European countries and the United States. As an internal enemy routinely associated with immigration and waves of change both irreconcilable and inimical to national values and identities, Muslims, regardless of their nationality, are fixed as a foreign presence. This external depiction of Muslims is best seen in the widespread public rhetoric depicting them as "strangers in our midst."

Public opinion polls and surveys also portray a mixture of seemingly inconsistent, but ultimately telling, expressions of reluctance and fear. While Europeans largely view Islam and Muslims as holding different values than Europeans, they are hesitant to specifically attribute negative labels to Muslims. Across the board, the surveys indicate that Muslims in quantity, not necessarily individual Muslims themselves, are seen as problematic. This stems from the assumption and fear that Muslims in quantity have the power to shift norms and can eventually impose unwanted changes on non-Muslims. In other words, the public opinion data demonstrate that a distinction exists between internal and external, whereby Muslims can be tolerated as external elements, but become objects of fear when they are seen to be permanent internal elements.

Convergence of Political Discourses across the Atlantic

The overall perception of Islam and Muslims as a threat has recently shifted away from the extreme right to mainstream political discourse. Islamophobic language is now utilized by a wide spectrum of European politicians and public figures. Although this type of discourse has been present in the European public sphere for several decades, it has emerged in the United States more explicitly after 9/11. At the center of most of these arguments is the conviction that Islam is incompatible with Western political and cultural values, which illustrates the Schmittian Liberalism described above. These discourses do not necessarily reflect the opinions of the majority of the population nor their behaviors vis-a-vis Islam and Muslims, but nonetheless, political actors are critical in framing the national narrative of their country regarding Islam and Muslims, as well as initiating polices that affect Muslims. As such, public discourse primarily focuses on, and feeds into, two perceptions: Islam as incompatible with Western values and Islam as the external enemy.

Incompatibility with Western Values

The public discourse stating that Islam is incompatible with Western values is phrased in different ways. First, discussions tend to point out the intrinsic differences between Christian and Enlightenment values of the West and the obscurantist creeds of Islam. In these particular circumstances, Christian values and Enlightenment ideas are conveniently combined (which is far from the historical and political experience of Europe). For example, the chairman of the Protestant Church in Germany, Nikolaus Schneider, has declared that Islam appeared "in our society unimpressed by Enlightenment and criticism of religion."[29] In the Netherlands, Geert Wilders, the controversial anti-Islam leader of the Freedom Party (PVV), tweeted his season's greetings in Arabic with a message reading, "Merry Christmas and less Islam in 2011."[30] Wilders also gave a speech for the Magna Carta Foundation in

March 2011 in which he called for a "Leave Islam Day" and formed one of several strategies to "turn the tide of Islamization" in Europe.[31] Additionally, Bjarte Ystebo, editor of the Christian paper *IDAG*, has spoken out against Muslims joining the Norwegian Christian Democratic Party (KrF), because Islam stands in opposition to Christian values of freedom, human rights, and pluralism. According to him, this is obvious from studying all the countries in the world where Islam is the main religion and has control over the state apparatus.[32]

Another way of phrasing the Islam-West incompatibility is through discussions on Muslims' inability to assimilate, which is closely related to the fear that such assimilation will degrade the national identities of Western countries. For instance, Chancellor Angela Merkel has expressed concern on several occasions that Germany has failed to integrate its immigrant communities. She argues that because Muslim immigrants, particularly Turks and Arabs, have kept their own languages, religion, and cultural habits, subworlds have been created within the larger German context.[33]

David Cameron, the prime minister of the United Kingdom, in a speech on February 5, 2011, also voiced the dangers of integration when he blamed "state multiculturalism" for a "weakening of our collective identity" and said it encouraged different cultures to live "separate lives, apart from each other and apart from the mainstream."[34] Additionally, a member of Parliament (Labour Party), Peter Hain, stated that Britain's Muslims, in particular, are "isolationist." The underlying assumption of such viewpoints is a categorization of culture and identity as fixed, therefore, ignoring the various national and global trends, known or unknown, that continuously shape local and international identities. These assumptions also do not take into account, or are unaware of, the deep acculturation that Muslims are experiencing in the European and American contexts, as our data in chapters 2, 3, and 4 will show.

Public discourse further creates the perception that integration of Muslims into European society would change the status quo. Such an outlook presumes that Western and Muslim cultures are two separate identities, independent of one another, and that the former is superior to the latter. Former Italian prime minister Silvio Berlusconi articulated this vision on September 27, 2002, when he publicly claimed that Western civilization was superior to the civilization of Islam: "We must be aware of the superiority of our civilization, a system that has guaranteed well-being, respect for human rights and—in contrast with Islamic countries—respect for religious and political rights."[35]

In the same vein, former president Sarkozy (2007–2010), on April 27, 2006, stressed on primetime news that immigrants will have to learn French and "learn to respect the country [and accept] French laws, even if they don't understand them," because "it is up to them to adapt, not France." Thus, he implicitly assumed that Muslim immigrants are not integrating because they maintain loyalty to their ethnic culture, which is incidentally not validated by sociological or anthropological evidence. In 2006, at the time of the Danish cartoons controversy, Sarkozy also argued that immigrants must accept the publication of religious cartoons in newspapers and women must provide uncovered photographs for identity cards as well as accept treatment by male doctors.[36] In this context, Sarkozy depicted Islamic norms, such as the nonrepresentational nature of the Prophet Muhammad and a conservative standard of female Muslim dress, as an impediment to Muslims' ability to integrate within French society. In the same vein, following the riots in the *banlieues* (poor suburbs) in October and November 2005, Sarkozy, then Minister of Interior, blamed "immigration," "culture," "polygamy," and "social origins" for the social unrest.[37]

More generally, public conversation across Western European countries centers on the threatening alteration that these immigrants' cultures and religion bring to Western laws and values. For example, Dutch municipalities began registering children of at least one Moroccan parent as Moroccan citizens because of a 2009 Moroccan law that grants automatic Moroccan citizenship to children born of at least one Moroccan parent. Several Dutch politicians criticized this level of cooperation, including conservative member of Parliament Paul de Krom, who said of this politics that it was "bizarre and shocking that the Dutch government is pro-actively cooperating with the territorial inclinations of another country, even when parents have not requested it themselves."[38] Here, the level of cooperation between two states is seen as a superimposition of Moroccan jurisdiction onto Dutch soil, and since Morocco is a predominately Muslim country, the analogy is taken further as an Islamic threat on Dutch governance.

Similarly, in 2000, a battle erupted in Germany over the use of the term *Leitkultur* (leading culture), which was promoted by leaders of the center-Right Christian party as connoting romantic German Christian nationalism. The term emerged at the same time that Chancellor Angela Merkel described German culture as one "in which we celebrate Christian holidays, not Muslim holidays."[39] Such a debate does not necessarily prove that Islam is viewed as a threat to German culture, but it does shed light on concerns about an Islamic cultural encroachment into German society, leading some public figures to reassert a German Christian identity of some sort.

Demographics are an additional recurrent topic that is representative of the fear that Islam is altering Europe. One example is the interview with Pierre Cattenoz, the archbishop of Avignon, when he told the French Christian magazine *Famille Chrétienne*, "We're at a turning point in the religious history of our country. 'Gallic' families, traditionally Christian, have on average two children. Muslims families living in France, have most often four, five, six children. From this, we can see that France will have a Muslim majority in twenty, thirty years."[40] In the same vein, a YouTube video titled "Muslim Demographics" presents demographic numbers and trends to argue that Muslim population will outnumber "indigenous" Europeans. Though this video has been criticized for its biased use of statistics, several million viewers have watched it.[41]

The threat to European material security and the large numbers of Muslim immigrants competing for jobs with European residents is a further important component of the anti-Islamic discourse. Muslims are often construed as a threat and a danger to the job market, and their ability to stimulate a successful economy is strongly questioned.

These recurrent positions voiced by European political leaders have ultimately led to increased opposition or rejection of Islamic signs and symbols, from mosque-building to prayer in public space and dress code. For instance, President Sarkozy said on New Year's Eve 2009 that Muslim prayers in the streets were "unacceptable."[42] Likewise, in December 2010, Marine Le Pen, leader of the French Front National party and daughter of Jean-Marie Le Pen (the founder of the party), compared the overflow of Muslims from mosques into the streets before and after prayer to Nazi occupation during World War II.[43] Additionally, she also told an audience of about 300 party members in Lyon that neighborhoods where Islamic law is applied is equivalent to an "occupation."[44]

Political resistance goes beyond prayer or dress codes and also targets gender relations. Former British home secretary Jack Straw told BBC's *Newsnight* in January 2011 that Pakistani young men were groomed to sexually abuse white girls since "they're fizzing and popping with testosterone, [and] they want some outlet for that. But Pakistani-heritage girls are off-limits and they are expected to marry a girl from Pakistan, typically. So they seek other avenues and they see these young women, white girls who are vulnerable...who they think are easy meat."[45] These declarations reveal the common perception that Islamic values and its social and public expressions pose a danger to the wider community, which will be discussed further in the chapter on Islam and secularity (chapter 6).

Feminist groups and left-wing intellectuals are key actors in conveying these positions. Western feminists across countries are almost unanimous in their denunciation of the hijab "as a symbol of the subordination and inferiority of women in Islam." German feminist Necla Kelek supports burqa bans and claims that they "have nothing to do with religion and religious freedoms" but rather symbolize that "women in public don't have the right to be human."[46] Polly Toynbee, a British feminist newspaper columnist, has written that "the ideology of the veil" is "covering and controlling women."[47] In December 2003, *Elle* magazine published a petition addressed to President Jacques Chirac, signed by a large number of left-wing intellectuals, artists, and leaders of Ni Putes Ni Soumises,[48] that stated, "To accept the Muslim headscarf in schools and public administration is to legitimize a symbol of the submission of women in places where the State should guarantee a strict equality of the sexes."[49]

Moreover, Fadela Amara, the leader of Ni Putes Ni Soumises, went on to say, "The hijab has become 'like a protective shield against male aggression' for many women and girls. I, who place great value on fundamental freedoms, think that the religious practice [of veiling] is legitimate when it is freely chosen, without pressure or constraint, but above all when it is done in accordance with respect for the communal rule, which is laïcité (French version of Secularism)."[50] Amara later stated that she "identifies the hijab as first and foremost a symbol of female oppression," and "the burqa represents not a piece of fabric but the political manipulation of a religion that enslaves women and disputes the principle of equality between men and women, one of the founding principles of our republic."[51] Overall, Amara calls the burqa "a kind of tomb, a horror for those trapped within it."[52]

External Enemy

When it comes to the perception of Islam as the external enemy, the main focus concerns national security, terrorism, and cultural threats. For example, in Germany, not just extreme right-wing but also mainstream parties, such as the German Social Democrat Party (SPD), invoke the security issue to attract voters. By using the image of the "foreign criminal" and "Muslim terrorist," German politicians regularly attempt to stoke public fears and promote demands for more restrictive policies on foreigners and asylum seekers. This is especially true with efforts attempting to deal with the problem of Turkish integration or to exclude Muslim organizations from the policy-making process.[53] The German media further exacerbates this image of the other by commonly referring to a criminal's foreign nationality or background if the person is an immigrant (even if he or she has German citizenship), but if the offender is German, his or her nationality normally will not be mentioned. Thus, the public message is that Muslims are a threat to society.[54]

Muslims are also often portrayed as a social threat, because Islam is associated with crime, terrorism, honor killings, backwardness, intolerance, and the oppression of women. Terms such as "Islamic Terror," "Muslim extremist," and "cancer/ulcer of Islamism" regularly appear in European newspapers.[55] For example, a member of Parliament for the Danish People's Party, Jesper Langballe, was convicted of libel after making controversial statements about Muslim fathers and rape in a heated debate in January 2010. Langballe stated, "Of course Lars Hedegaard shouldn't say that Muslim fathers rape their daughters when the truth is that they kill them (the so called honor killings)—and in addition don't pay notice to uncles' rape of their daughters."[56] Similarly, in early 2009, while still in the position of Danish Social Welfare minister, Karen Jespersen said Zubair Butt Hussain, spokesman for the Muslim Council of Denmark, advocated the stoning of women. The comments were made in connection with the government's cooperation with the association on preparing teaching materials about Islamic extremism.[57]

One of the most vivid examples that involved cultural values as an external threat was the Dutch film *Submission* (2004), which depicts Muslim women as oppressed and abused. For this reason, the filmmaker Theo Van Gogh was assassinated by Mohammed Bouyeri, a Dutch citizen of Moroccan background, in the name of Jihad. Hirsi Ali, a Somali-born Dutch politician, who wrote the scenario, had to go in hiding for a while and gained international attention for her virulent critique of Islam as a misogynistic and backward religion.[58]

In convergence with European discourses, the same concerns over the visibility of Islamic signs have been voiced in the United States in the recent years, the turning point being the election of President Barack Obama in 2008. However, unlike Europe, the themes of immigration and socioeconomic integration are not systematically connected with anti-Islamic rhetoric for already mentioned reasons that Muslims are neither the major immigrant population nor the most disenfranchised group. Instead, Islam is perceived as an external threat, and since 9/11, most of the concerns have been about Muslims endangering American security.

For example, Terry Jones, the Florida pastor who announced that he was going to burn Qur'ans on the 2010 anniversary of the 9/11 attacks, has said that Islam and the Qur'an only serve "violence, death, and terrorism."[59] Similarly, Representative Peter T. King, chairman of the House Committee on Homeland Security, created a special committee in 2011 to investigate radicalization of American Muslims and advocated that these hearings were "necessary."[60] Brigitte Gabriel, a Lebanese American journalist and activist, warned that "America has been infiltrated on all levels by radicals who wish to harm America," since "they have infiltrated us at the CIA, at the FBI, at the Pentagon, at the State Department. They are being radicalized at radical [*sic*] mosques in our cities and communities within the United States."[61] Additionally, Juan Williams, an American journalist, stirred up controversy in October 2010 when he commented, "When I get on the plane, I got to tell you, if I see people who are in Muslim garb and I think, you know, they are identifying themselves first and foremost as Muslims, I get worried. I get nervous."[62]

More specifically, the opposition to the "ground zero mosque" in New York City and several anti-shari'a law campaigns are evidence of a general movement across the United States against the Islamization of the country, which is seen as a threat not only to national security but also to core American political values. In response to the announcement that a mosque was to be built two blocks away from the site of the 9/11 terrorist attacks, a heated political debate erupted in 2010. Although various political figures and religious leaders in Manhattan had demonstrated support for the mosque (more correctly described as an Islamic center), several politicians, as well as bloggers, voiced staunch opposition to the project while fueling Islamophobic discourse. Representative King stated that the project was "particularly offensive" since "so many Muslim leaders have failed to speak out against radical Islam" and ultimately "against the attacks" of 9/11.[63] Furthermore, Rock Lazio, at the time the Republican candidate for New York governor, supported statements made by Debra Burlingame, the cofounder of a group called "9/11 Families for a Safe and Strong America," when she expressed her fear that the mosque would "bring people to Islam," and create "a Muslim-dominant America," which would serve as propaganda for "people who want to hurt this country."[64] Overall, most of these statements were about the "insensitivity" of a mosque project on ground zero and illustrated the growing social and cultural vulnerability of Americans ten years after 9/11.

The sentiment that Islam encompasses a political and legal system that seeks to destroy existing US laws and government has been reflected in a growing number of anti-shari'a campaigns within several states, which started in Oklahoma where a bill banning shari'a was passed by a margin of 70 to 30 percent on a special ballot in November 2010 (see chapter 5).[65]

The perceived threat of Islam has even led to suspicion toward public officials, as well as calls for constitutional changes to abolish the rights of Muslims under the First Amendment. President Obama has been the major public figure under scrutiny because of his father's origin. To the point that a poll from Pew shows that 17 percent of voters think he is a Muslim.[66] In the same vein, a *Newsweek* poll in August 2010 found that 52 percent of Republicans agreed with the statement, "Barack Obama sympathizes with the goals of Islamic fundamentalists who want to impose Islamic law around the world."[67] According to a Gallup poll conducted in June 2012, 34 percent of Americans identify Obama as Christian (Protestant), 11 percent believe him to be Muslim, and 44 percent are unsure.[68] In the same vein, a July 2012 Pew polling indicates that 30 percent of Republicans still think that Obama is a Muslim, which is an increase from an earlier, October 2008 poll when only 16 percent of Republican voters believed so.[69]

Another trend in the American public discourse is to put Muslims outside the protection of the First Amendment. For example, General William G. Boykin, former US general, argues:

> We tend to assume Islam deserves unquestioned First Amendment protection. But it is a totalitarian way of life with aggressive political goals, not just a religion. What is to be done? As we will see, shari'a law is totalitarian in nature, providing no individual freedoms while virtually enslaving those who live under its authority. This is absolutely not what the Founders intended in creating the Bill of Rights. Islam does have a religious component but it has many other components, which should not be entitled to the same level of constitutional protection. Our First Amendment was never meant to protect sedition or insurgency. It is time to stop applying it in this suicidal fashion. Even as you read this, law and policy in the United States are continuing to allow seditious insurgents hiding behind a naive misinterpretation of "religious freedom" to erode our values, undermine our liberties, and threaten our future. We must stop it now before we are incapable of stopping it at all.[70]

A More Ambiguous Public Opinion

A review of the most significant public opinion polls and surveys among European and American citizens conducted in the past decade confirms the widespread negative feelings toward Muslims and Islam as expressed by politicians.[71] These surveys, which stemmed from a plethora of sources ranging from the media to national research organizations, expressed a generally negative sentiment toward Muslims and Islam. They were conducted at both the city and national levels, and two surveys, Institut Français d'Opinion Publique (IFOP) and Pew, compared data collected across European countries and America. For instance, according to a Pew (2008) survey, "52 percent of Spanish people expressed a negative opinion of Muslims, a view shared by 50 percent of Germans, 46 percent of Poles, 38 percent of French, and 23 percent of British."[72]

In the United States, 48 percent of respondents to a *Washington Post*-ABC poll conducted in 2010 reported that they hold "an unfavorable view of Islam."[73] In a Gallup poll conducted the same year, nearly a third of Americans said their opinions about Islam were "not favorable at all."[74]

In Great Britain, France, Poland, Germany, and Spain, attitudes toward Muslims were notably more negative in 2008 than in 2005.[75]

Additionally, in a Gallup (2009) survey, 35 percent of French respondents did not think French Muslims were loyal to France and 21 percent said they did not know or refused to answer. Among the German and British publics, the percentages that did not think Muslim residents in their respective countries were loyal were even higher—49 percent of British respondents and 45 percent of German, and roughly one in six respondents said they did not know or refused to answer.[76]

In the same survey, when it came to the expression of one's religion and its effect on integration, 42 percent of British non-Muslim respondents, as against 13 percent of British Muslim respondents, thought that being less expressive about one's religion was necessary for integration. In France, 40 percent of the general public and 20 percent of French Muslims stated the same, while in Germany, 30 percent of the general public and 18 percent of Muslims thought toning down one's level of religious observance was necessary for integration.[77]

On the whole, important differences existed in these surveys concerning the negative perceptions of Muslims across countries. As seen above, the Spaniards had the most negative view toward Muslims, although this was part of a broader pattern, in which the favorability ratings for Muslims, Jews, Arabs, as well as Americans were lower in Spain than in any other Western country. In addition, the belief that a large number of Muslims support extremist groups (41 percent) was especially widespread in Spain, where terrorist attacks on commuter trains in Madrid killed 191 people in March 2004. However, the United States and Germany occupied a middle ground on the religious-cultural negativity index. In the former, views differed by age and party identification, with younger Americans holding somewhat less negative opinions and independents voicing fewer negative perceptions than Democrats or Republicans. Meanwhile, the British and French held the least negative views, despite high-profile tensions between Muslims and non-Muslims in both countries over the last few years, including the 2005 London bombings and the 2005 riots in France.

It is important to underline that one of the most significant surveys included here, the European Values Survey (EVS), did not ask specific questions about Muslims, Islam, or religion; rather, it asked questions about immigrants. As mentioned in the previous section, the relationship between immigrant and Muslim is complex. While in the European context, immigrant is often taken as a rough proxy for Muslim, the term "immigrant" inevitably comes loaded with meanings that are idiosyncratic to individual countries and, in turn, cannot be assumed to have the same meaning in each case. Indeed, there seems to be at least some indication that the public actively distinguished between immigrants and Muslims, which was evident in the Pew polling that showed broad support for continued immigration from North Africa and the Middle East, without making a connection between these immigrants and the primary religion to which they belong.[78]

A significant point to keep in mind about these surveys concerns questions about "feelings," or questions that explicitly ask about associating Islam with certain topics. A qualitative difference exists between questions that ask respondents whether or not they "associate" Islam with terrorism or fanaticism and questions that ask how significant one considers the issue of Muslims grouped in certain neighborhoods or schools, as well as Muslim integration.[79] For example, Islam was reported by many polls to be linked with terrorism, violence, and extremism, though overall, the data suggested that this link was most solid when the respondent was explicitly asked to draw such an association. When direct "yes" or "no" questions were asked, this link was more tenuous. In general, a more negative picture of Islam stemmed from the "association" question rather than from directed questions, and as such, questions about Islam and Muslims garnered different responses.

Perhaps in part because of these nuances, a clear majority opinion about Muslims, Islam, or the place of Muslims in Europe is difficult to extract. However, the sentiment that clearly comes across is a broadly felt discomfort with Islam and a widespread association of Islam and Muslims as a force of unwanted, and potentially irreversible, change. The primary trends identified from these surveys are as follows:

1) Muslims have not and will not integrate.
2) Muslims are a threat to national identity now and in the future.
3) Public practices, such as mosque-building, prayer, and clothing, should be kept to a minimum.
4) Islam and Muslims are incompatible with national and Western values.

A common point across surveys is that non-Muslims mostly fear that the presence of Muslims will affect their way of life or alter the norms of an assumed mainstream. In other words, while non-Muslims may not have a direct problem with Muslims or individual Muslims, they fear that Muslims—particularly growing numbers of them—will impose unwanted changes in their countries. In each of the analyzed countries, the expression and intensity of this fear varies, perhaps due to the nature of the survey questions, and ranges from France's muted concerns that Muslims have an impact on "national identity" to Dutch fears of a future of "imposed shari'a."

The opinions presented below are specifically in regard to the European context and follow the same trends of the internal/external enemy concept identified earlier in the political discourses.

Islam Is Incompatible with Western and National Values

Across the board, surveys indicate that Europeans consider Islam to be incompatible with Western values. This concern is expressed in some surveys as a direct threat or an essential incompatibility, but in other ones, it is phrased as a difference rather than an incompatibility of values. For example, in 2006, the EU Monitoring Centre for Racism and Xenophobia reported that 70 percent of non-Muslim Germans thought that there was a conflict between being a devout Muslim and living in modern society,[80] and a survey conducted in December 2003 found that 65 percent of Germans claimed that Islam could not fit with the West.[81] Additionally, one of the *"German Conditions"* (Deutsche Zustände) reports (2006) on anti-Semitism, Islamophobia, and xenophobia stated that 39 percent of Germans (up from 35 percent in 2004) had at least a partial feeling of strangeness in their own country due to the presence of Muslim co-citizens.[82] The newspaper *Der Spiegel* also reported in June 2006 that one out of three Germans felt that there was a need for a general ban on Muslim immigration. This matched a 2004 survey conducted by the Institute for Interdisciplinary Research on Conflict and Violence at the University of Bielefeld (Institut für interdisziplinäre Konflikt- und Gewaltforschung), which stated that around 30 percent of Germans living in the new federal states and 23 percent of those in the old states shared the opinion that "Muslims should be refused permission to migrate to Germany."[83]

When a Pew (2006) survey asked, "Is there a conflict between being a devout Muslim and living in a modern society?," with the exception of France, a majority of non-Muslims in surveyed countries answered "yes" to the question. As seen elsewhere, Germany was the most strident with 70 percent of the "mainstream population" stating "yes." Spain followed with 58 percent and then Great Britain with 54 percent. In contrast, the French mainstream population overwhelmingly (74 percent) said that there was no conflict. Correspondingly, in the Friedrich-Ebert-Stiftung survey, 49.8 percent of French agreed that "the Muslim culture fits well into [country/

Europe]," which was a significant number compared to the 16.6 percent of German, 38.7 percent of Dutch, and 39 percent of British who agreed to the same statement.[84] However, this data do not mean that the French do not perceive Muslims negatively according to other measures. Indeed, an opinion poll conducted by IFOP 2011 found that 42 percent of the interviewees agreed when asked, "Would you consider the presence of a Muslim community in France...mostly a threat to the nation's identity."[85]

According to a study by the Institute for Social and Political Opinion Research (2007–2008), close to half of Flemish voters had a negative image of Islam and Muslims; 46 percent believed that Islam had nothing to contribute to European culture, and 47 percent thought that Islamic values were a threat to Europe. Additionally, 37 percent believed that most Muslims had no respect for European culture and its way of life.[86] Yet, even as a tendency existed for the Flemish to view Islam as incompatible with their values, the numbers were not convincing everywhere. In all, much of the data gathered was inconclusive, showing near equivalent numbers for those who agreed and disagreed on Islam's incompatibility.

In Great Britain, a survey conducted by Omnibus/ICM in 2008 found that 33 percent of Brits "agreed" to the statement, "Islamic values are not compatible with British values," while 36 percent disagreed. In a more nuanced portion of the same survey, 37 percent of Christians (and 65 percent of Muslims) disagreed and 31 percent agreed that "Islamic faith is not compatible with occidental values."[87] In contrast, an overwhelming 84 percent of respondents agreed that "in general, Muslims play a valuable role in British society."[88] However, the annual British Social Attitudes Survey (2010) revealed a much deeper suspicion of British people toward their Muslim fellow citizens. A majority claimed that multiculturalism had failed, with 52 percent claiming that Britain was deeply divided along religious lines and 45 percent saying that religious diversity had a negative impact. Only a quarter felt positive about Muslims.[89] Moreover, the findings showed far greater opposition to Islam than to any other faith, and respondents revealed that they would be willing to limit freedom of speech in an attempt to silence religious extremists.[90]

Similar ambiguous results were present in IFOP's comparative analysis of France and Germany, where 31 percent and 34 percent, respectively, associated Islam with "a rejection of occidental values."[91] Moreover, while the same poll showed that 31 percent was in fact an increase in France (from 17 percent in 2001 and 12 percent in 1994), it also indicated that fewer French were associating Islam with "fanaticism" and "submission" compared to previous polls (37 percent in 2001 and 24 percent in 1994). While these were substantial minority opinions, it nevertheless denotes that a majority of respondents were either unclear, disagreed, or were reluctant to make such strident associations.

The obvious question raised by the data is what specifically about Islam and Muslims is incompatible with European and national values? Though

Muslims as immigrants are clearly seen as a problem, Muslims as holders of specific values—as opposed to more general notion of difference—do not seem to have a clear or precise profile. That being said, a very clear and overwhelming sense can be extracted from these studies that the status of Muslim women is incompatible with Western values. In the Open Society Institute (OSI) study mentioned above, 81 percent of respondents thought that Muslim men dominated their wives too much, and 53 percent believed that Muslim women should not wear a headscarf during public functions.[92] According to a YouGov poll conducted in the United Kingdom in 2010, 69 percent of respondents believed that Islam encouraged the repression of women.[93]

Another reason Islam and Muslims may be viewed as incompatible with Western values is because Islam is often linked to violence, terrorism, or intolerance. Among non-Muslims in Western Europe, an average of 58 percent labeled Muslims as fanatical and an average of 50 percent believed Muslims were violent. Additionally, a Pew (2011) survey found that more than two-thirds in Russia, Germany, Britain, the United States, and France "are worried about Islamic extremists in their country."[94] A 2003 survey by the Interdisciplinary Research on Conflict and Violence at the University of Bielefeld found that 83 percent of Germans associated Islam with terrorism.[95] According to the same survey, 46 percent of respondents agreed that "Islam is a backward religion," 34 percent said that they were "distrustful of people of Islamic religion," and 27 percent believed that "immigration to Germany should be forbidden for Muslims." In 2006, only 30 percent of Germans reported a "favorable opinion of Islam."[96] In the Netherlands, a June 2004 opinion poll revealed that 68 percent of respondents felt threatened by "immigrant or Muslim young people," and that 53 percent feared a terrorist attack by Muslims in the Netherlands.[97] In the United Kingdom, an online YouGov poll found that 58 percent of those questioned linked Islam with extremism.[98]

Similar trends can be seen in the United States. While most Americans reported between 2001 and 2010 that Arab Americans, Muslims, and immigrants were likely singled out "unfairly" following the 9/11 attacks (between 69 percent and 85 percent), a third of respondents have continuously declared that Muslim Americans "are more sympathetic to terrorists."[99] Pew (2009) data also showed that 45 percent of Americans viewed Islam as no more likely than other faiths to encourage violence among its believers, while 38 percent took the opposite view that Islam does encourage violence more than other faiths. This figure has declined since 2007, during which 45 percent of Americans reported at that time that Islam encourages violence more than other religions.[100]

Indeed, the possible differences between questions asked about association and those that are direct are worth underscoring again, as well as possible semantic differences. Thus, in Britain, while a large percentage of respondents "associated" Islam with terrorism and extremism, a larger percentage claimed that Islam poses no threat to national security when asked directly.[101] A 2007 questionnaire found that 67 percent of Brits said "no" to the question, "Does the presence of Muslims in this country pose a threat to national security or not?"[102] Furthermore, 68 percent disagreed that "the Muslim community in Britain bears any responsibility for the emergence of extremists willing to attack UK targets." Likewise, an ICM (2008) survey found that 59 percent (33 percent "strongly") disagreed with the statement, "I feel more uncomfortable in the presence of British Muslims since the London Bombing." Therefore, the British data may be a result of this semantic difference or may indicate differences in the country.

Above all other countries, Germany seems to feel most threatened by Muslims and immigrants. The *Local* newspaper reported that 40 percent of Germans in the former west of the country and 50 percent in the former east felt threatened by foreign cultures.[103] The Netherlands shows similar trends. According to a June 2004 opposition poll, 47 percent of Dutch reported that they feared that eventually the Netherlands would be ruled by Islamic law.[104] Additionally, a Pew (2011) report conveyed that 68 percent of those surveyed in France were worried about Islamic extremists in their country, and in Spain, 61 percent reported the same.[105]

Non-Muslims Do Not Support Mosques

Respondents in all of the surveys did not support the building of mosques. This result relates to a trend underlined earlier whereby non-Muslims are accepting of Muslims as long as they do not alter the norms and lifestyles associated with the mainstream, which in this case is an aesthetic, even aural, norm. As evidence, several polls in France and Britain indicate that Muslims are thought to be culturally enriching to the country (Britain) and are believed to be integrate-able (France).

In France, IFOP surveys conducted in 1989, 1994, 2001, 2009, and 2011 showed a consistent lack of support for mosque-building. In 2011, only 20 percent were favorable, while 39 and 34 percent were opposed or indifferent, respectively. Interestingly, the numbers over time have demonstrated a decrease in support for mosques (33 percent, 30 percent, 31 percent, 19 percent, and 20 percent) but a dip and rebound in opposition. In 1989, 38 percent of French opposed the building of mosques, which dropped to 22 percent in 2001 before bouncing up to 41 percent in 2009, probably a consequence of the minaret controversy in Switzerland.[106]

An IFOP survey in Germany demonstrated more clear opposition, with 50 percent opposed and only 18 percent in favor of mosque-building. Opinions in Switzerland were such that in 2009, the Swiss population voted by referendum to ban the construction of minarets, with 58 percent voting for the ban.[107] Within the United States, a *New York Times* poll in 2010 asked, "Do you favor or oppose the building of a mosque and Islamic community center two blocks from ground zero," to which 50 percent (37 percent "strongly") opposed. At the same time, 72 percent agreed that "people have the right to build a house of worship near ground zero," suggesting that the problem lay in the building of a *Muslim* house of worship.[108]

Muslims Do Not, Cannot, or Will Not Integrate

The issue of integration is a central one in Europe where, as already mentioned, the questions of immigration and Islam are intricately bound. Across the board, Europeans report that Muslims are not integrated, with nuances varying from statements indicating that Muslims are un-integratable to those that say Muslims could, but do not want to, integrate. According to a Pew (2006) multination report, a significant majority of the respondents declared that "Muslims in your country mostly want to...be distinct from society" rather than "adopt national customs."[109] French respondents to the IFOP (2011) report mirrored the same trend. When asked if "Muslims and those of Muslim origin are well integrated into French society," a large majority of 68 percent said they were not.[110] The same survey, this time with comparative data from Germany, indicated that most French (61 percent) and Germans (67 percent) believed that this failure to integrate was largely a result of Muslims refusal to do so. These numbers were much higher than those who attributed it to "strong cultural differences" (40 and 34 percent, respectively).[111]

Similar results existed in a Spanish survey, where 70 percent of respondents in 2010 reported that Muslim foreigners were integrating with difficulty in Spanish society. Only 21 percent stated that Muslims "coexist normally" with Spaniards. More specifically, when respondents compared Muslim immigrant children and adolescents to non-Muslims, 78 percent considered the non-Muslims to be integrated, while only 42 percent stated that Muslims were well-integrated.[112] These are telling figures, because once again, it highlights the fact that respondents make distinctions between immigration and the presence of Muslims.

This distinction between immigration and Islam was evident in a somewhat contradictory way in a Pew (2007) survey, when the majority of respondents in all countries reported that "immigration from the Middle East and North Africa is a...good thing." The report further demonstrated that support for immigration remains relatively stable. In Great Britain, figures of support ranged from 53 percent in 2002 to 61 percent in 2005, and 57 percent in 2006. In France, which witnessed the most significant change, support for immigration jumped from 44 percent in 2002 to 58 percent in 2006. Germany alone showed that the majority consistently were not in favor of immigration, with only 33 percent in favor in 2002, and 34 percent in 2005 and 2006.

In sum, from the public opinion surveys, different justifications are raised to portray Islam and Muslims as the internal and external enemy. Within countries, Muslims are viewed as unwilling to integrate into mainstream society, and Islamic beliefs and practices are not perceived as compatible with Western liberal values, such as women's rights and political and civic engagement. From an external standpoint, Islam and Muslims are commonly associated with terrorism and violence and, as such, are viewed as national security threats. Additionally, citizens across European countries and the United States tend to think that Muslim immigrants have external allegiances and are not loyal to their host countries.

Intriguingly, there is no empirical evidence from Muslim behaviors in European and American countries that supports this fear. Actually, Muslim political practices are not very different from those of their average fellow citizens. However, Muslim religious identity stands in stark contrast to European average forms of religiosity, as it will be discussed in the next chapter.

PART I

IN THEIR OWN VOICES: WHAT IT IS TO BE A MUSLIM AND A CITIZEN IN THE WEST

Methodological Introduction to Chapters Two, Three, and Four

In order to contextualize the analyses provided in chapters 2, 3, and 4, it is important to note that they build on three different sources: original research from the IIW program including 60 focus groups discussions, a structured survey conducted in Berlin, and an analytical review of preexisting quantitative data on Muslim religiosity and political participation.

Focus Group Data

From 2007 to 2010, nine to twelve focus groups were organized in Paris, London, Berlin, Amsterdam, and Boston under the auspices of the IIW program. These cities were selected to reflect the socioeconomic and cultural situation of most Western Muslims—from converts to second or third generations of immigrants.

From the existing literature, we know that most Muslims live in urban centers or their peripheries; they are engaged in a broad spectrum of professions and jobs, and represent a wide range of ages, ethnicities, and educational levels.[1]

In order to recruit the participants, our strategy was to deliberately avoid Muslim leaders and members of religious or social organizations. We wanted to reach out to people who are part of the "silent majority"—the anonymous Muslims who do not speak on a regular basis to media, politicians, or researchers. For this reason, we adopted an immersion strategy in different places where Muslims usually socialized, such as malls and coffee shops. We also distributed leaflets in different places in an attempt to be as random as possible in the selection of focus group participants (for focus group composition, see appendix 1).

This method, albeit more time consuming, facilitated the participation of a wide range of Muslims, including Somalis, Iraqis, Pakistanis, Moroccans,

Turks, Kurds, Lebanese, and Bangladeshis. Their age range and gender were equitably distributed, as well as the different generations of migrants. However, in London, due to the makeup of Muslims in the city, a significant representation of refugees was present. Moreover, as a rule, we tended to privilege second or third generations, as they are the groups at the center of the externalization process described in chapter 1.

For each city, we also targeted the most significant ethnic groups in their respective countries. For example:

- Algerians, Moroccans, Turks, and Senegalese in Paris;
- Turks and Moroccans in Amsterdam;
- Turks, Moroccans, and Bosnians in Berlin;
- Pakistani and Bangladeshi in London; and
- Pakistani, Turks, Lebanese, and African Americans in Boston.

In each city, we convened groups based on ethnicity and gender, as well as mixed groups in terms of each. The reason for such an arrangement was to capture the ethnic/cultural and gender variations. For instance, in Paris, groups were divided as follows:

- Male—North African/Turks/Senegalese and Women—North African/Turks/Senegalese (six groups),
- Coed based on ethnicity (three groups),
- Coed ethnically mixed (two groups), and
- Control group of immigrants from non-Muslim backgrounds (West African migrants).

Each group was led by two researchers, one male and one female for coed groups, and of same gender for gender-divided groups. One researcher was the main moderator while the other individual acted more like a rapporteur, although he or she could also ask questions or steer the discussion. All sessions were recorded and transcribed. Each session lasted an average of two to three hours.

In each group, discussions were generated to explore the following issues:

- attitudes toward participation in national politics
- political participation at the neighborhood, city, and national level
- feelings about important issues facing contemporary French, German, American, British, or Dutch society
- involvement in community activities
- assessment of non-Muslim perceptions of Muslims and changes in these perceptions since 9/11
- attitudes toward Islamic religious organizations at the local and national level
- involvement in religious organizations or mosques

(See focus group discussion guidelines in appendix 2.)

The focus groups had three goals. The first was to collect materials to explore the religiosity of Muslims across different cultural and political contexts. The second was to see how religiosity influences political participation, whether positively or negatively. And, based on this new research, the third was to produce specific questions that could more adequately measure Islamic religiosity.

With regard to the first goal, the group discussions produced a very rich, diverse, and, often times, contradictory approach to Islamic religiosity and political engagement. Concerning the second goal, we could identify interesting connections between attachment to Islam (belonging) and a sense of civic engagement and community, especially at the local level. Finally, regarding the third goal, the focus group results helped us create a new questionnaire on Islamic religious and political participation that was tested in Berlin.

Berlin Survey (2010)

The focus groups across European and American cities allowed us to identify some links between Muslim religiosity, civic and political participation, and local context. Building on the materials from the focus groups, our next step was to create a new questionnaire to better understand the interactions between Islam and political participation.

We utilize questions from standard surveys concerning voting pattern, partisan identification, and trust in political institutions (see questionnaire in appendix 3).

In standard surveys, however, questions regarding religious observance are either very rare or not adapted to Muslims. They tend to conflate mosque attendance with praying and pay insufficient attention to the fact that mosque attendance may be more ethnic or social than religious. As shown by a few surveys, mosques provide the opportunity to socialize in a preferred cultural network, especially after 9/11.[2]

We realized that we needed finer-grained questions than mosque attendance in order to understand various forms of Muslim religiosity and their relationship to societal engagement. Thus, we created a new battery of questions to examine the relationship between forms of Islam and levels of civic and political participation. Our goal was to respond to the following questions: is Islamic faith or a particular Islamic worldview associated with social or political engagement or with withdrawal from a hopelessly problematic society? Is civic and political participation seen as a vehicle for assimilation into the insider's world, a way to remake what counts from the "inside," or a way to maintain a cherished outsider's community? To narrow responses, we also added specific questions on social and cultural practices related to Islamic beliefs such as gender interactions or relationship with sexual minorities.

We tested the questionnaire in Berlin, conducted in face-to-face situation, from February to March 2010. Representative of the Muslim population in Berlin, the basic demographics of the group surveyed are as follows:

- 52 percent male (82 respondents)
- 48 percent female (75 respondents)
- 56 percent Turkish
- 20 percent Bosnian
- 25 percent Lebanese and Palestinian
- 5 percent other
- 33 percent 18–34 years old (53)
- 40 percent 36–50 years old (63)
- 22 percent over 50 years old (35)

The results of this experimental survey are presented in the following chapters in order to nuance the focus group findings regarding the influence of religion on political participation.

Content Analysis of the Focus Group Discussions

The transcripts from the focus groups were analyzed with the NVivo 9 program. It uses automated classification techniques to sort electronic transcripts of data and interviews into themes and groups.

We were interested in establishing both religious and political profiles for Muslims in each of the cities. We looked for the significant terms that define what it is to be a Muslim in Paris, London, Berlin, Amsterdam, and Boston; the idea being that the most relevant terms will garner number of references in the matrices. The religious terms of interest included:

- beliefs (system of morals and values associated with the individual or Islam),
- struggle of being a Muslim (difficulty and negativity associated with identity as a Muslim),
- hijab (head covering for Muslim women),
- identity (association of one's personality with certain values or beliefs),
- praying (religious act demonstrating faith to Islam), and
- social or cultural behaviors influenced by Islamic beliefs.

The political terms of interest included:

- citizenship (associated with civic duty to a country),
- government (local or national levels),
- participation (engagement in politically associated events and activities),

- politics (holding office or playing an active role in campaigns), and
- voting (act of voting or urging others to vote for public officials).

Other terms included community (the integration of an individual into the surrounding society) and family (one's blood relatives).

A portion of matrix dealing specifically with highly and minimally mentioned political terms of interest were compiled as well. The highly mentioned political topics included:

- 9/11 (refers to terrorist attacks perpetrated on the United States on September 11, 2001),
- country (one's nation),
- involvement (in community and political life),
- organizations (groups united under a certain commonality),
- politics,
- rules (binding guidelines regarding religious practices),
- true-truth (the integrity of Islam as a valid religion),
- vote.

Political terms of low interest compiled into the matrix included:

- animal rights,
- bad publicity,
- democratic structure,
- domestic politics,
- extremism,
- local politics,
- NGO (nongovernmental organization),
- social system.

NVivo 9 produced several key sources. First, it created a series of matrices that were essentially three-dimensional histograms, crossing topics of interest against a number of focus group interviews, with each bar measured by its respective focus group and topic's individual frequency (number of references in a focus group). The matrices were formed according to city, gender, ethnicity, and level of interest (high or low political interests). Each matrix combined political and religious terms of significance in order to better allow for comparisons of the relative importance of the various priorities in the Muslim community.

Second, we created a comprehensive topic-of-interest list that tabulated the number of references respondents made to certain topics of interest. That process also took into account the context in which a topic of interest was referenced (positive, negative, or neutral). Each topic of interest was broken down into these three contexts, thus, allowing for the possibility of investigating correlations. Positive correlations were observed by a low negative frequency and a high positive frequency. Negative correlations were the exact opposite, with high negative frequency and low positive frequency. The list of topics were the same as those of the matrices: beliefs, citizenship, community, country, family, government, being a Muslim, identity, participation, politics, praying, secularism, and vote. Another master word list was compiled of all of the political and religious terms and bodies of significance (for a complete list of these words, see appendix 6).

Third, the master word list was further filtered so as to tabulate only responses provided by the focus groups specific to each city. This separate list filtered out the following terms: associations with 9/11, the meaning of citizenship, civic involvement in the community, civil rights mobilization, Europe, identity of the respondents, institutionalized politics, important elements of Islam, the media.

Finally, a series of individual interviews was extracted from the focus group transcripts. From these transcripts, quotes of interest were compiled into a final report. The topics of interest were: what is Islam, identity, worship, morals, the importance of Islam, voting, trust in institutions and society, other religions and ethnicities, citizenship and community, loyalty, and the importance of country of origin in political perception.

The results of this content analysis were interpreted in the broader context of existing data on Muslim political participation and religiosity from surveys conducted in Western Europe and the United States.

Focus Group Results in Context

How do the focus group results fit into the broader context of existing data on Muslims in Europe and the United States?

First, existing surveys vary widely in terms of source, time period covered, question content, and nature. In terms of source, they come primarily from think tanks and research organizations (Open Society Foundation, the Pew Global Attitudes Surveys, and the Gallup Coexist Surveys), non-profit advocacy organizations (Bertelsmann Stiftung Foundation), and government-sponsored surveys, especially in the Netherlands and Germany.

Second, especially in regard to the European surveys conducted in recent years, the most serious bias concerns the control group to which the surveyed Muslims were compared. In almost all instances, Muslims were compared to the "general population" (presumably including a percentage of Muslims), referenced as "non Muslim". Only the French INED data separated non-Muslim respondents by confession (Protestant, Catholic, Other) and further separated those who have no religion.

Contrasting "Muslims" to undifferentiated "non-Muslims" or the "general public" is a misleading way to capture the specificity of Muslim religiosity. The relevant comparison would be between self-declared Muslims and other self-declared religious or nonreligious groups. In this regard, the surveys conducted in the United States by Pew and Gallup did differentiate the surveyed population according to religious affiliation and were therefore more relevant to our purpose (see appendix 5 for all surveys used for analytical review).

Overview of Part One

The following chapters explore the religious (chapter 2), social and political identities (chapters 3 and 4) of Muslims as revealed by the focus groups discussions and their comparison with preexisting quantitative data. This analysis shows that Islam is far from being "the independent variable" explaining their social and political behaviors. Most strikingly, the narrative of Muslims that implicitly emerges from the focus group discussions is at the antipodes of the Western narrative described in chapter 1. Specifically our results show that Muslims resist any collective identification to Islam, do not see incompatibility between their personal religious identity and their national community of residence, and even envision Islam as an asset to their civic engagement.

CHAPTER 2

ISLAM: BETWEEN PERSONAL AND SOCIAL IDENTITY MARKERS

Headline-breaking controversies over the Danish cartoons or the French headscarf ban might lead to a perception that Muslims in the West are more religious than European or American citizens of other faiths. Yet, as we will see, a complex interplay of identity issues and social expectations pushes Muslims toward and away from Islam—leaving conflicting opinions and no clear answers.

This chapter analyzes religious identities and practices in order to discuss issues that arise when attempting to evaluate Muslim religiosity. It weaves two sets of data. The first one comes from preexisting surveys conducted in different European countries and the United States. The second comes from our focus group exchanges that enrich and nuance the quantitative measurement of Islamic religiosity. More specifically, they reveal tensions between social and personal identification with Islam as well as dissonance between values and praxis in the definition of the "good Muslim."

In all of the quantitative surveys reviewed in this chapter, three types of questions are usually asked to measure Islamic religiosity. The first type of question addresses religious self-identification by measuring how important Islam is in a person's life. The second type explores interviewees' self-identification as religious or not religious. The third type assesses an individual's frequency of prayer and mosque attendance. Following is a look at each question.

The Challenge of Measuring Islamic Religiosity

Islam as an Identity Marker

Surveys by both Gallup (2009) and Pew (2006) ranked and compared religious affiliation to other affiliations, such as country or ethnic group. More specifically, Pew asked respondents whether they identified themselves as "national identity" or "Muslim" first, while Gallup asked how strongly respondents identified with "their religion" and "their country."

In the Gallup survey (figure 2.1), one interesting result is that Muslim respondents almost equally identified with their religion and country (of residence), religion scoring slightly higher. In contrast, "non-Muslims" did not display the same level of identification to religion but showed a similar or sometimes lower level of identification to their country.[1]

Particularly in Europe, striking differences emerged in the ranking of religion as an identity marker between Muslims and non-Muslims. In this regard, data from Germany are particularly significant. (For more charts related to France, the Netherlands, and the UK, see appendix 13.)

The Pew survey also shows that non-Muslims across European countries perceived Islamic identity to be on the rise, while Muslims believed the opposite. The United Kingdom was the sole exception to this trend, as more Muslims than non-Muslims said that Islamic identity was increasing (appendix 5).

Similar trends were identifiable in the Gallup (2011) surveys on American Muslims (figure 2.2). When asked how strongly they identified with certain groups (i.e., the United States, ethnic background, religion, or religious community), Muslims most identified with the United States followed by their

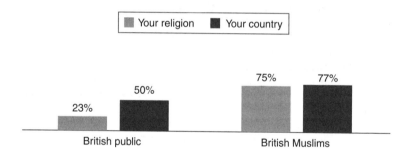

Figure 2.1 "How strongly do you identify with your country and your religion?," United Kingdom

Source: Gallup (2009)

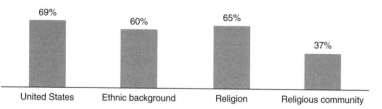

Figure 2.2 "How strongly do you identify with each of the following?," US Muslims

Source: Gallup (2011)

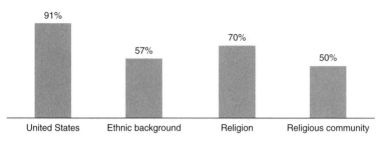

Figure 2.3   **"How strongly do you identify with each of the
following?," US Protestants**

Source: Gallup (2011)

religion. Interestingly, though, Muslims' self-identification with Islam was
much lower compared to other religious groups, such as Protestants and
Mormons (figure 2.3).

Self-declaration as Religious

When European respondents were asked to self-identify as religious or not
religious, a gap existed across surveys between Muslims and non-Muslims.
In other words, religion was significantly more important to the former than
the latter. For instance, the Gallup Coexist Survey (2009) establishes that in
Britain, France, and Germany, Muslims tended to report that religion was
far more important in their daily lives than non-Muslims (see figure 2.4).
However, as already mentioned, the major bias in these surveys was the
Muslim to non-Muslim dichotomy, which cannot fully measure whether
Muslims are more religious than other religious groups in their respective
countries.

In the United States, the trend is the opposite (figure 2.5). Muslims did
not display the highest rate of religiosity compared to other faiths. When
asked if religion was important to them, Muslims reported at levels either
equivalent to or sometimes lower than other religions.

Three important issues are raised by these results. First, it is not possible
to draw the conclusion that Muslims are more religious than any other group
because data from different European countries is not available for comparison. The second issue is that such declarations cannot be the decisive
measure of religiosity because they are not automatically connected to significant levels of religious practice. At best, these declarations measure the
social desirability of religion for Muslims, which is a point that will appear
strongly in the focus group findings below. The third issue is the multiple
and sometimes conflicting meanings of such self-declarations. These three
points will be discussed at length in our focus group analyses that follow.

Figure 2.4   "Is religion important in your daily life?," France
Source: Gallup (2009)

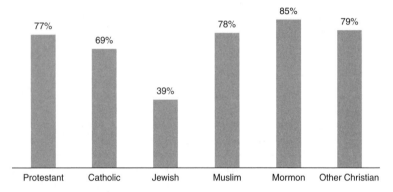

Figure 2.5   "Is religion important?," United States
Source: Gallup (2009)

Islam between Embracing and Distancing

Quantitative surveys cannot reflect the fluidity of identifications or, more importantly, highlight the tensions between personal and social identity, that were revealed in our focus groups' discussions. Though an abundance of literature exists on the compatibility between personal and social identity, the tensions between the two have been studied far less frequently.[2] Usually, identity is framed as the outcome of two ongoing, interrelated processes: identity embracement and identity distancing. The former defines congruence between personal and social identity. The latter refers to divergences between individual and social identity.[3]

The discussions in our focus groups reveal tensions between a person's identification to Islam and social identities based on ethnic, national, or social communities. The sections that follow take a closer look at how Muslims establish Islam as a personal identity marker while simultaneously expressing resistance and ambivalence toward Islam as a social identity, which is often imposed on them by the dominant, non-Muslim environment.

Muslim Self versus Muslim Group

In many of the focus group discussions, Islam appeared as a strong personal identity marker rather than a sign of communal or group identity. Oftentimes, identification with Islam was embedded in other labels, such as ethnicity or country of origin, and was rarely discussed as someone's unique or exclusive social identification. The exchange below expresses the importance of Islam in self-identification:

> *Moderator:* What does Islam mean to you?
> S: It is what I practice. So it is a part of my identity as well. Identity in the way that you start thinking about everything you do, to what extent it is acceptable in Islam...it's not as if you do exactly what Islam tells you to but it does make you stop and think...it does play a role in many of the things you do. And also in how you think and what you say.
> *Moderator:* Is it a way of life for you?
> O: Among other things. It determines my way of life to an important extent.
> (Amsterdam, Moroccan Coed)

Some participants expressed reluctance or resistance toward embracing Islam as their social identity and discussed instead other social markers, including the categories with which the majority population identifies them. For instance, respondents with immigrant backgrounds often identified with their country of origin in addition to Islam. In Boston, most people saw themselves as Americans but emphasis was placed on heritage, which resulted in identity markers such as "Lebanese American" or "Arab American." For Londoners and Parisians, whether or not one identified as Muslim first depended on the circumstances—social interactions, personal relationships, or employment. In Berlin, identification with ethnicity was more prevalent than with Islam because many respondents did not "feel" German.

> J: I do say I'm Lebanese and, yeah, I like the music. I like the food...Being Muslim is not eating falafel sandwiches. Being Lebanese, that's eating a falafel sandwich. (Boston, Lebanese)
> M: I do see myself as a foreigner here. My being a Muslim does not restrain me at all. Actually, I do not feel very German. (Berlin, Bosnian)
> A: I would agree with her that religion is a part of my identity. Precisely to your question how I introduce myself: Most of the time I say I am from Germany because I was born here. But then they say, "No, your parents."

> Then I reply, "My father is from Afghanistan and my mother is from Turkey." Then for most people the religion results automatically...When people then go on asking further, then I explain. (Berlin, International Coed)

Other interviewees discussed how their Muslim identity interacted with their national identity.

> *Moderator:* Do you feel mainly Dutch, Surinamese, or Muslim? In what order?
> *S:* All three of them.
> *H:* If I put it in order, I would say Muslim-Surinamese-Dutch. (Amsterdam Focus Group 6, Mixed Group of Surinamese Muslims)
> *J:* I would see my identity as Arab or Syrian. For me, religion is something between man and God. I do not have to mention it to others. (Berlin, International Coed)

In some cases—particularly when participants were talking about how they were perceived by non-Muslims or by political authorities—many used Muslim as a clear marker of group identity. They used Islam either to express their self-identity or to describe how the wider population perceived them as part of the Muslim group. In these cases, they embraced Islam as a social identity under "pressure" from their environment.

> *A:* I am presenting myself as Muslim. This simply belongs to my identity. I am not religious but I avow myself to be a Muslim. I do not care whether the others reject or accept it. I am a Muslim and I stand for it. (Berlin, International Coed)
> *B:* If you belong to a group you automatically become their representative. It does not stand out that much in my case, and I do not put it in the foreground. So when I then introduce myself (explicitly as a Muslim), often there is a big surprise. (Berlin, Bosnian Men)

The tensions between embracement and distancing highlighted above entail double or, sometimes, multiple frames of reference. This duality does not result in conflicting identities, even though it is often mistaken as such, but rather simultaneously influences a person's attachment to Islam and his or her identification to the national community. For example, when participants presented Islam as compatible with the other monotheistic religions, they apprehended Islamic values as universal. The distinctiveness of Islam, when participants expressed it, was not in its values but in cultural or social specifics, such as diet and dress code.

> *Moderator:* What does it mean to be a Muslim? If it's not an identity, what is it? What does it mean?
> *M:* It's a set of beliefs...
> *F:* Belief.

M: ... about what constitutes good and what constitutes bad, and things about how the world works.

F: You're trying to see the difference between religions? There is no difference.

M: There is no difference, I think. Good people are good, bad people are bad, wherever you are ...

F: There is the symbolism ... There is difference. That is all. It's All the difference is in the symbolism. The fact that the Christians go to church, that we go to the mosque, and the fact that they are allowed to do it. This is all the symbol stuff. We pray five times a day. We go to Mecca, and we do the fasting, and ...

M: We don't drink. We don't eat pork.

...

F: The only differences are in the little symbols, but in terms of what the religion is all about, and the conduct, the expectation of the way you conduct your life, it's all the same. (Boston, Lebanese Coed)

Just as focus group participants construed Islam as contributing to the universal values of other religions and cultures that surrounded them, they also interpreted their national community as shaping their Islamic identity. Moreover, this national dimension to Muslims' religious identification was understood as a positive contribution because, far from subverting it, some presented it as a way to improve their Muslim self. It was discussed across cities when participants wanted to express their communality with the wider population, particularly between Muslims and non-Muslims in Great Britain, France, and Germany. Undoubtedly, such an expression on communality is in striking opposition to the dominant political argument that Islam is the major divider between Muslims and the rest of the population.

In some accounts, respondents stated that the synergies between national and religious identities helped them to better realize their Muslim identity. For instance, a number of participants insisted on rediscovering their Islamic spirituality in the minority context and became more spiritual than they were in their country of origin. In all cities, a majority of respondents stated that their current residence was a good place to be Muslim compared to Muslim countries or countries of origin. An example is seen below where several Moroccan women in Amsterdam discussed their religious practices in Dutch society versus their practices in their country of origin.

Moderator: Have you ever thought about going to Morocco?

K: For me Morocco is a country for holidays.

B: Here you will never become Dutch. You look different. There you will never be a Moroccan. You're different. So you don't belong anywhere. What would be the alternative? Real Islamic countries do not exist. No country acts 100 percent according to Islam. And this (the Netherlands) is the country where I grew up; this is the country that I know. I would be interested in going to an Arabic country, for a few months, a year ... but just because of ... the atmosphere ...

K: Not even from an Islamic perspective?

B: Not necessarily. I would like to learn the language. I would like to get to know the culture and see more of the world. More from that perspective. But really living there . . . I think it would be very difficult for me to break all connections with the Netherlands because my family, at least my nuclear family, is here.

K: That way of living doesn't suit us. In that manner we are actually purely Dutch.

W: No, not purely Dutch. Moroccan Dutch. Actually, a culture of its own arose.

B: A subculture.

Moderator: Yes, what is it that you are the most: Dutch, Moroccan, Muslim?

W: I'm thinking about that now. I don't know yet.

K: Dutch Moroccan is not the same as Muslim. Being Muslim is above that.

B: In the first place you are a Muslim.

Moderator: So it's possible to feel more Dutch but you are Muslim in the first place.

B: I can also start living in the U.S. but then I'm still Muslim.

K: Then I'll become a Dutch Moroccan American Muslim.

W: Yes, there are of course also Dutch Muslims, being Muslim is above that, but whether I feel more Moroccan or Dutch, I really don't know.

K: But what determines the way you are? Not the country where I was born.

W: If I have to make a decision on something, I don't think "What would my Moroccan forefathers do? What would my Dutch neighbors do?" I will ask God what to do, but only purely ethical questions, not like "What am I going to eat tonight?" But ethical questions, then my frame of reference would be Islamic.

Moderator: So you also don't think that Morocco would be a better place to practice your religion?

B: No, I think worse.

W: I don't agree. When I was there for a week last January, I felt so comfortable there in terms of religion.

B: There are different aspects, if you look at societal politics, how you profile yourself . . . like here, I can work everywhere I would like with my headscarf. But there it would be difficult. I am from the capital, Rabat. I entered a couple of banks, just at the counters, none of the girls that work there wear headscarves.

Moderator: That's Rabat.

G: That doesn't matter.

B: Whole Morocco is like that. In Tunisia it is even forbidden to work in the public sector if you're wearing a headscarf. So in that sense you're constrained to practice your religion.

Moderator: This is not forbidden in Morocco, is it?

K: Not officially but in practice it is.

W: With regard to that, life is difficult, yes, but in terms of religion I would feel more . . .

B: Of course, everybody is Muslim. (Amsterdam, Moroccan Highly Educated Women)

A striking feature that emerges from these discussions is the construction of positive-sum relationships between minority and majority identities, and the contributions Muslims are willing to make to Britain, France, the Netherlands, and Germany. Some literature hypothesize that intergroup harmony (e.g., between two subgroups) may be promoted if the groups involved can be represented as contributing to a common team (i.e., a superordinate group).[4] The image of a team is potent because it implies *both* a sense of superordinate commonality *and* a sense of subgroup distinctiveness. This data suggests that minority group members are aware of the significance of such constructions and are active agents in their production and dissemination.

Believing, Behaving, and Belonging

In an attempt to overcome the limits of measuring Islamic religiosity discussed above, some quantitative surveys combine self-declarations with other indicators in order to create a scale of religious intensity. For example, Pew (2007) defined "highly religious" as attending a mosque at least once a week, praying all five *salat* (prayer) daily, and reporting that religion is "very important" in daily life. However, an argument can be made that ritual and worship are not sufficient to measure religiosity, as abundantly discussed by scholars of religions.[5] The main reason being that for all religious groups today, personalized expressions of faith tend to be more significant than ritualized and institutionalized practices.

The Religion Monitor (2008) data from Germany illustrates this point. According to this data, if mosque attendance and formal prayer solely define high devotion, only a small percentage of the respondents could be identified as such. However, if other indicators, such as private prayer, intellectual engagement, and feelings of devotion, were included along with self-identification, the number of highly religious persons significantly increased.

The Religious Monitor survey stands apart in European and American contexts because of its use of "six core dimensions" to gauge the religiosity of its respondents. These "dimensions" are as follows:

- intellect (interest and engagement in religious topics)
- ideology (belief in God or something divine, belief in life after death)
- public practice (church service)
- private practice (prayer, meditation)
- experience (personal experiences or feelings of religiousness)
- consequences (feelings of being at one, general relevance of religion in everyday life)

Each category has its own index comprising the classifications "highly religious," "religious," and "non-religious" in order to measure each dimension individually.

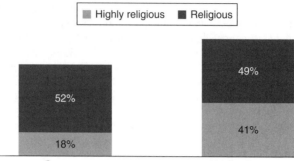

Figure 2.6   Religious levels, Germany
Source: Religion Monitor (2008)

Overall, the data (2008) showed that Muslim Germans were more religious than the general German public(figure 2.6). In some cases, age and gender did have an effect on levels of religiosity. Younger Muslims (18–29 years
old) believed in life after death and prayed more than older Muslims over 60
years. Furthermore, 53 percent of Muslim seniors (60+ years old) reported
that they had been raised to be religious whereas 58 percent of Muslim youth
(18–29 years old) reported the same. In almost every dimension used to measure religiosity, youth were found to be more religious than seniors.[6] Such a
trend can also be found in surveys of Muslims in other European countries[7]
as well as in the United States. It goes against the dominant expectation that
social integration or age are automatically connected to a decline of religious
practices. (See chapter 6 for an in-depth discussion of this topic.)

More generally, recent empirical work has highlighted an increasing
disjunction between believing, behaving, and belonging among followers
of all denominations, which makes evaluating religiosity on a few indicators of praxis even more challenging. Believing, behaving, and belonging
have historically been systematically linked or associated in the definition of a person's religiosity. They respectively refer to beliefs, religious
practices, and collective identity and have been for a long time defined as
simultaneously part and parcel of a person's religiosity. However, recent
sociological analyses have shed light on the increasing disjunction of these
three dimensions and apprehended this disjunction as modern forms of
religiosity.[8] Thus, a person can believe without automatically behaving and
belonging, can belong without believing or behaving, or can behave without believing or belonging. For example, surveys have shown that many
Christians maintain private, individual religious beliefs but do not practice on a regular basis (i.e., believing without behaving), or in some cases,

Christian identity has taken on more cultural than spiritual meaning to the point that Christianity becomes a marker of the national group as it will be discussed in chapter 6.

Within our focus groups, the conversations on Islam highlighted similar disjunctions but with some specificities. Muslims generally did not question their beliefs. They believed in God and, as discussed above, this belief was a strong component of their personal identity. The participants associated belief with faith and personal connection to the Creator or Allah. Interestingly, very few discussions arose on the truthfulness or the content of the Islamic creed itself. Debates over beliefs were not frequent or intense and were often sidestepped in favor of other aspects of religious life. This is a notable difference with current Christian expressions of religiosity, which are often focused on the content of faith and the true nature of the beliefs.[9] This is not to say that Muslims believe more or less but that believing is less subject to doubt among Muslims than it is among some Western Christians today.

In particular, participants tended to stress issues of behavior, that is, what Muslims *do*. In fact, in almost no instance was "belief"—in God, the Prophet, and so on—mentioned without also referring to practices (prayer, social relations).

> H: Islam, it's first of all a connection with my Creator. Allah *subhānahu wa-ta`āla* (May He be glorified and exalted). It's also the first issue the Prophet was attacked about. Islam is not that he came up with a new God; they already believed in Allah. But the thing was that they didn't want to identify in worship. So that you worship Allah, to me that is the most important thing in Islam.
>
> H: The *shahāda* (Attestation of Faith) is more than just believing in Allah. Because Christians and Jews also believe in Allah. But the *shahādatayn* (Attestation of Faith) or at least the first *Lā ilāha illa Allāh* [there is no God but God/Allah], means that you worship only Allah. So no graves, no dead people, no...
>
> H: Statues.
>
> H: That you worship only Allah, that is the most important. And else...else you fall into the opposite and that is *shirk* [polytheism]. And that cannot be forgiven. At least, it's not forgiven after death. And after this, it's my connection to my fellow man: How do I treat my fellow man? Muslim or non-Muslim. How do I treat my father? How do I treat my mother? Respect, and things like that. That is Islam to me."(Amsterdam, Moroccan Coed)

Belonging was also strongly asserted even in the case of weakness or of beliefs. When doubt or questioning of faith was brought up, it rarely impacted someone's identification as Muslim. Many of those who declared themselves as "nonbelievers" still identified as Muslim, and being Muslim was often viewed as "a way of life." Most, if not all, of the respondents drew a line between being a "practicing Muslim" and just "being Muslim." This difference indicates that being Muslim is an identity with no clear relation to a set of practices or even beliefs.

A widespread notion of "Muslim culture" with no fixed content seemed to override the more circumscribed definition of being Muslim that is usually measured in polls. More often than not, belief was assumed, and participants focused on the complexities of belonging and behaving. These complexities were evaluated against a set of practices considered to be Islamic, like the five pillars.[10] Thus, a sense of belonging and of being Muslim regardless of belief or practice became apparent.

> Ö: Sometimes we talk about these things to our German friends. Because I pay attention to some rules of Islam and a German friend sees that but then he talks to another Turkish friend in my class who is doing exactly the opposite. And then he comes to me and asks "How can this happen?" I mean, what should I say? Because you cannot say they are not Muslim or that they are bad Muslims because we do not have the right to say such things. So I say he does a bad deed by drinking alcohol. So on account of these contradictions, we discuss these things very often. (Berlin, Turkish Coed)

For those reasons, unlike belief, behaving as a Muslim was a more debated topic. Widespread agreement was present on the basic practices of a Muslim, including eating halal, prayer, and fasting, and on the core beliefs of Islam, such as belief in God and the Prophet. However, when the discussions turned to the relative merits of practicing, participants made clear that these practices, which were often produced in response to questions that defined Muslims, did not exclusively identify a Muslim, let alone a good Muslim. Instead the category Muslim increasingly was associated with more general categories such as "being a good person" or "being tolerant."

Most respondents tended to agree that abstract values like tolerance, respect, and honesty made a good Muslim rather than specific practices.

> B: That is difficult to say about someone else. You can never say what someone else has in his heart. Maybe someone is actually really religious.
> K: Also about smoking you can say, "Is it actually in the Qur'an?"
> W: Some girls do not know that much about Islam but they do fear God and really love God but maybe they accidentally do not know that it is sinful to smoke.
> K: It is not like they are doomed forever or something. It's possible to show repentance and start your life over.
> B: I do think that you're obliged to advise them, that you tell them, "Okay, what you're doing is not right because it's not good for your health." So not just from a religious perspective but also because of health. I know girls

who smoke and I try to make them all quit. On the basis of religion and
health.

W+K: Also, on the basis of faith, how do you do that?

B: It is possible to continue the analogy that it is forbidden. You can tell
them that smoking is the same as committing suicide. (Amsterdam, Highly
Educated Moroccan Young Women)

M: In the Prophet's hadith when the person came to the Prophet *sallallahu
alayhi wa sallam* (Peace be upon Him) and he said to him give me good
advice on how to be a Muslim or a good Muslim and he said to him just say
la ilaha ill-Allah (There is no other God than God) and be straight ... It's not
about praying ... just be straight, be the best human being you can be."

Moderator: Straight as in upright?

M: Straight as an arrow. Straight as in upright. (Boston, Mixed Ethnicity
Men)

K: You try to follow those five pillars. But if you only do three or you do none,
then that doesn't mean that you're not a good Muslim. You strive to do it.

A1: Look, it is more than that. It also has to do with behavior that is not included
in the five pillars. How you deal with your neighbors, your family, and so on.
That makes the picture more complete than just those five pillars.

Moderator: So your neighbors ...

A1: It's not just neighbors, it's about your fellow creatures, nature. It's more
like you know your place in society and that you have a positive attitude
towards that society and that you don't do any damage to that society.

K: It's not like a checklist: "If I do this I'm a good Muslim." It is about the
whole package. (Amsterdam, Moroccan Women, highly educated)

However, some participants emphasized practice, hence presenting behaving as a way to belong:

I think that as Muslims most of us we do take our religion for granted, but
Islam is built upon things that you have to do in order to be a Muslim. We
are all good Muslims but there are certain actions we do which affirm you
are a Muslim ... If you practice, you define yourself as a Muslim. (London,
Iraqi)

What makes Islam different from other religions is the fact that it emphasizes action, that it's just not ideological. That it's we have five pillars and
most of them are based on actions, like give *zakat* (Almsgiving) and fast and
do this ... You have to have the core belief but it's also based on your action,
which I think adds to the ethics and the character of Islam. (Boston, Pakistan
Coed)

Some went further by presenting practice or behavior as the condition not
only to belong but also to believe. In fact, belief was sometimes described as
the outcome of practicing.

F: What does it mean to be religious to me? ... A lot of other people would
just associate being religious as having faith and belief in spirituality but,

in Islam, a lot of people only consider being religious if you pray, and if you pay *zakat*, and if you fast. These are like symbols of your religiosity. That is why I think, in the world, Islam is considered a bit different because there is more practice to their religion that others adhere to…So, I consider myself religious because sometimes I [would?] say I am not that religious, but then my friends will be like, "Well, wait. You don't eat pork, and you don't drink, and you fast, and so how are you not?" They say, you are religious, and I'm like I guess I am, but I feel like I could be a lot more religious because I see people like my mother…In that sense, I think that other people see Muslims as being more religious than they might themselves see themselves. (Boston, Lebanese Coed)

Our Berlin survey confirmed the focus groups' trend that being Muslim was more of an *orthopraxis* rather than a belief-based *orthodoxy*. For example, when asked, "If being Muslim is a set of beliefs," 73 percent disagreed with the statement. However, when asked, "If being a Muslim is a relationship with God," a vast majority of respondents agreed.

The Berlin survey also demonstrated that gender was a significant variable in terms of adherence to normative Islamic practices. Except for mosque attendance, women tended to practice, adhere to dietary restrictions, and think and read about religion more than their male counterparts. Women also were generally more conservative on social issues, such as marriage and homosexuality.

Furthermore, 69.8 percent of the surveyed women talked about religion once a week or more and only 41.6 percent of men did the same. Similarly, in the case of the United States, age, ethnicity, and gender were all salient factors on the level of religious observance. The Pew (2007) and Gallup (2011) surveys also showed that younger Muslim Americans were more religiously observant than older Muslim Americans.[11]

The discussion above demonstrates that personal identifications to Islam reflect several, sometimes conflicting, meanings. The distancing and embracing process is also at work in the identification of different components of Islam, which is explored in the next section.

Being a Better Muslim: Positive Evaluation of Orthopraxis

Despite the consensus that universal values make a good Muslim, the focus group discussions also centered strongly around religious practice for personal improvement. Specifically, prayer was often referenced as both the most important and most distinctive practice (i.e., perceived by the participants as the ritual that sets Muslims apart from other religions). Additionally, the fast of the month of Ramadan was often cited as a nonnegotiable practice and donning the hijab for females was frequently mentioned as a way for personal development.

Moderator: Are the [five pillars] all equally important or are there also things that are not as important?

T: I think texts predominantly speak about prayer...[fasting during Ramadan, prayer] are obligations...That's also the case with giving alms. It's not compulsory if you have no money to do that...I don't think it's about means...the intention is really important. (Amsterdam, Predominantly Highly Educated Turkish Young Women)

K: I'll be honest, I don't always pray. Sometimes it takes a few days before I start praying again, sometimes even weeks. But I always strive for it. I believe that if I remain doing my best, I will eventually do it continuously without all those breaks. I also believe that if I remain trying, God will hopefully eventually forgive me. Then you are afraid of God, you don't feel good, on the moment that you're so tired in the evening that you're just too lazy [to pray]. If I fall asleep then, I don't sleep well. (Amsterdam, Moroccan Highly Educated Women)

Although a strong emphasis was placed on prayer, many of the participants did not pray regularly. Paradoxically, nearly all of the participants adhered to dietary rules to a certain degree, such as prohibition of alcohol and pork, but did not define these practices as religious. As justification for following such rules, respondents frequently said that these practices were engrained in their social and cultural behaviors, and rarely was a theological justification mentioned.

N: For example I do not eat pork, I do not let my children eat pork and I do not cook pork in my household.

E: And alcohol?

N: I do not drink. If my husband desires to drink then he can do that. And I will not offer my children alcohol until they are grown ups. Nor will I give them the opportunity. (Berlin, Turkish Highly Educated Women)

Our Berlin survey also demonstrates the importance of prayer in Muslims' practices: 56 percent of respondents stated that they "engage" in communal prayer and a majority of respondents reported that they participated in individual prayer, with many praying more than once a day. In contrast to the focus group results, a relative parity between genders emerged in terms of praying.

The Berlin data similarly exemplified the importance of Ramadan as a measure of correct "behavior" for Muslims. For example, when asked about their fasting habits during the month of Ramadan, 57 percent of respondents replied that they fasted all month while 34 percent did not fast at all. Moreover, within genders, women seemed to fast for a lengthier period of time than their male counterparts. Regarding alcohol, 67.3 percent of those surveyed in Berlin did not drink. Once more, gender played an important role in this practice as 87.4 percent of women reported as never having had alcohol and only 51.3 percent of men reported the same.

Mosque Attendance and Prayer

When it comes to religious services, the quantitative surveys show that Muslims across Europe tend to report higher levels of attendance than non-Muslims (figure 2.7), while this is not the case in the United States. As such, this difference between Europe and the United States is more significant than the level of mosque attendance *per se*.

In fact, Muslims in the United States did not show higher levels of religious service attendance compared to other faiths (figure 2.8).

Mosque attendance among US Muslims also tends to vary by ethnicity. The Pew (2007) survey portrayed that native-born Muslims, especially African Americans, were more likely to attend mosque weekly than were foreign-born Muslims. Furthermore, Muslims of Pakistani descent were more likely to be frequent attendees compared to other South Asians, and Muslims of first- or second-generation Iranian descent stood out for their

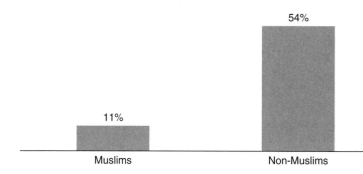

Figure 2.7 "Never attended a religious service," Germany
Source: Tausch (2006)

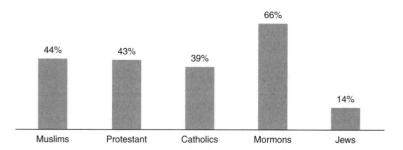

Figure 2.8 "Attend a religious service at least once a week," United States
Source: Gallup (2011)

very low levels of weekly mosque attendance (see appendix 13 for the details of the Pew survey).

Hijab

The discussions on the hijab once again highlighted the tensions between personal and social identity. Though the hijab was positively connoted in all of the focus group discussions, it did not mean that respondents felt women who did not wear the hijab were "bad" Muslims. In fact, the majority of women in the focus groups did not wear the hijab, and only a handful of respondents across all of the countries believed that the hijab was compulsory. Perhaps the most interesting point raised was the dual and somewhat contradictory nature of the hijab as both a marker of collective identity and a way to be a better Muslim.

Moderator: What do you mean by the stereotypical Muslim?

F: Right after 9/11, wherever I went…they'd say, "Oh, you're a Muslim, but you don't wear the hijab," or "You don't look like a Muslim." I don't know what a Muslim is supposed to look like. (Boston, Lebanese Coed)

Moderator: Do you think it's important for Muslims to dress in a particular way then?

No. 3: Yes.

Moderator: What would you say is important for a Muslim to do then?

No. 3: It is important to wear a certain dress code. That is a vital thing.

Moderator: Do you think that you could define what a Muslim should wear or is that different depending on your culture and background? Or do you think there should be one way of dressing for Muslims?

No. 8: You have to dress modestly whether you are a man or a woman. And that differs according to where you come from. For example, Muslims from the Indian subcontinent might wear *shalwar kameez* (loose pants and tunic worn by men and women) and hijab. And if you are from another country, you will wear different clothes but the main rule of modesty still applies. (London, Bangladeshi women)

J: Are you a good Muslim when you wear a headscarf or doesn't it matter? How does that work?

S: Actually it is…

R: …an obligation.

S: Actually, it is, but it doesn't mean that you're not a good Muslim if you don't wear a headscarf.

R: Yes.

Moderator: But you're saying it's an obligation.

R: Yes, it's an obligation.

S: Actually, it is.

R: I can give a very good example. My daughter's best friend came to our place last week. At that moment I was going to practice *salat* (prayer), but I don't wear a hijab. So she says to my daughter "Oh. that's funny. My mother wears a hijab but she doesn't practice *salat* and your mother wears no hijab but she does practice *salat*." So, well…what makes you a good Muslim?

J: Yes. So actually the headscarf is not a criterion for that.

R: Not for me. I don't know about others but not for me.

S: Yes, it's [not] true that somebody automatically becomes a good Muslim, when she wears a headscarf.

R: No.

S: …when she starts talking behind people's backs…

M: No, that's not necessarily the case. But it remains an obligation.

M/R: It's up to you.

H: You cannot escape it. It's just an obligation. If you don't do it, then that's up to you.

S: Yes, it's not about your *opinion*, it *is* like that.

Moderator: Ok, so it is an obligation. Do you share that opinion?

R: Eh…I know it's an obligation but I feel like…I make my own decision when I will start doing it. When I start doing hijab.

Moderator: But it's the intention that you start doing it at a certain moment?

R: That I will do that. Yes, that's true.

J: Ok. And what does it depend on?

R: The way I feel, I think.

R: You will have a turning point in your life at some point, that you're thinking like "Now I´m going to…"

R: Yes. Now I´m ready and now I totally want to go for it and now I'm going to do it. Of course, my husband would prefer that I started yesterday instead of today. (Amsterdam, Surinamese Mixed Gender)

As a group marker, some respondents said that wearing the hijab caused them to become more isolated from non-Muslims.

Moderator: Do you have friends from other religions?

N: I do. I have friends as well as neighbors. But when I was a child, it was easier for me to communicate with Germans. They were closer to me. But I do not think this changed because of me; I mean, I am the same. I did not change…But once I started to practice my religion and wearing headscarf, they ran away from me as if I were a monster. (Berlin, Turkish Women)

Women also stated that wearing the hijab was their own choice and independent of their husband's feelings toward it.

When I decided to wear a headscarf, my husband was not praying. He used to drink alcohol…My husband became a practicing Muslim on my account. But people ask me if I covered my head because of my husband. They could not believe that I was wearing my headscarf because of my own decision. Even my family could not believe this when they came over from Izmir to visit me. (Berlin, Turkish Women)

In the Berlin survey, more women (60.3 percent) than men (38.9 percent) gave their support for the hijab. This statistic actually contradicts the dominant discourse in Europe that women are forced by men to wear the hijab. At the same time, the emphasis on dress code as an identity marker for orthodox Muslims within the survey and focus groups reveals the salafization of Islamic identities, which will be explored in chapter 7.

CHAPTER 3

MULTIPLE COMMUNITIES OF ALLEGIANCE: HOW DO MUSLIMS SAY "WE"?

A key topic of participants' discussions was the groups or communities to which they identify and the effects of those identifications on their civic, political, and religious behaviors. As noted in the previous chapter, many respondents identified themselves as Muslims at a personal level but insisted on other identifications, such as nationality or ethnicity, to define themselves socially. In general, there was resistance to being exclusively identified as Muslim.

In the discussions, community identification appeared to be multiform and could refer to any of the following:

- local community (neighborhood, city)
- local ethnic community (i.e., Kurds in London)
- local Muslim community
- national community of residence
- national or European ethnic community
- national Muslim community
- the wider community of immigrants (ranging from other immigrants in the neighborhood to national or even European demographic immigrants)
- community consisting of members inside and outside a particular country of origin
- Muslims in general

Defining what "community" consisted of, also varied by city and country. For example, in London, community almost always referred to an ethnic community, usually connected to a particular location, and in Berlin, immigrant Muslim identity took precedence in dealings over non-Muslims. At odds with the dominant political discourse as well as with the Salafi interpretation of Islam (which will be discussed in chapter 7), the *Ummah* as the global community of believers was never invoked. As a whole, the main meanings and identifications to community were:

- the local community and Muslims' ability to bond with non-Muslims within it,
- the religious community as delineated by interreligious marriage,
- the community defined by the "discrimination experience,"
- the community of the country of origin,
- the community of the country of residence.

Following is a closer exploration of how Muslims identify to these different communities.

Local Community and Muslims' Ability to Bond with Non-Muslims within It

Participants often claimed they felt like "foreigners" in the cities in which they lived. Some of the participants also described feelings of isolation and alienation from their neighbors, and several people remarked that they had only Muslim friends.

> *M:* We are foreigners. This is their city.
> (Someone swears in Arabic.)
> *Moderator:* I understood that!
> *K:* They are ok when you talk to them but if there is an incident or something like that they are not always the best people to sort it out. One time, my dad had a problem. He was organizing parking at a Muslim function and he pushed a dog out of the way. He annoyed the person whose dog it was and the police came. It took weeks to sort it out. It is not a Muslim problem, though. It doesn't matter if you are black or white. They need to learn to be more community friendly. (London, Somali Men)
> *P:* I had a colleague at work, she is very religious. When she heard that I am a Muslim, she distanced herself from me. Somehow she had a feeling of fear. (Berlin, International Coed)
> *T:* I only have Muslim friends. "There are friends and there are friends" [Dutch expression meaning that there are real friends and friends that are less important].
> *T:* You have friends whom you discuss everything with and you have friends that you only say "hello" to.
> *Moderator:* Acquaintances.
> *T:* Yes, but my friends are really Muslim. (Amsterdam, Moroccan Men, highly educated)

At the same time, many participants described themselves as having and trusting non-Muslim friends too.

> *P:* I have many friends with different religions, Jews, Christians. We have a lot in common. The basis is the same: first you have to be human. (Berlin, International Coed)

Q: Do you have personal relationships with people from other faiths? Do you have personal relationships with people who do not have any faith?

No. 4: I do trust people personally rather than trust their religion.

No. 2: I do trust and believe Buddhism as a religion and I trust people who believe in Buddhism. I do not really believe in Muslim people.

No. 1: I trust. It is not important what they believe.

No. 6: Religion does not affect my trust.

No. 5: I would not question people's belief.

Q: Do you have any relation with people from other belief?

No. 1: I have Christian, Buddhist, Hindu friends.

No. 4: I have many friends from different backgrounds…[General agreement.]

Q: Do you feel that non-Muslims are respectful and kind towards British Muslims?

No. 3: I think they are much more respectful to Muslims than Muslims respect them…Muslim people judge but Christian people accept and try to find what his or her religion is about. Muslim people are not tolerant to non-Muslims. (London, Turkish Speaking Mixed Gender)

Numerous individuals said that they felt estranged from their co-citizens for a multiplicity of reasons, including their religion, ethnic background, immigrant status, and foreignness. Others insisted that, despite their religious, ethnic, or national differences, they were able to form friendships with non-Muslims.

Overall, the focus groups illustrated that Muslims' relations with non-Muslims were mixed. As we've seen above, while some viewed non-Muslims in a positive manner and engaged in friendships with them, others emphatically noted a feeling of seclusion from the local community. Two dimensions are particularly relevant to explain these differences. First, some of our participants were refugees (in London) or first generation immigrants (in some Dutch and German focus groups)and, therefore, were more limited in their interactions with main stream societies than the second or third generations (see section below on the meaning of citizenship). Second, residential distribution is also a key differentiator in Muslims' positions vis-à-vis non-Muslims. A higher concentration of one ethnic group in one territory often correlates to a higher sense of seclusion from the neighborhood or local community (see chapter 4 for a more in-depth analysis of this point). Moreover, many conflated isolation with ethnicity, religion, and immigrant status, which highlights the tension between the different identities that Muslims harbor.

The Religious Community as Delineated by Interreligious Marriage

In all countries, participants stressed the likelihood of a more successful marriage when Muslims marry Muslims or more generally when spouses share ethnicity, culture, and the like.

> *F:* I think that marriage is not just about you and him. You have to think about the children... Are they going to be Muslims? What are they going to be? So I don't know. It's a big question. And a lot of people have these problems. Either if a man is not a Muslim, it's a problem. If the woman is not a Muslim, it's a problem, too. There is a case that a Moroccan man is married to an American woman and they have kids. They have two girls. And he wants them to learn Arabic. Well, he brought them to Arabic school. They start but, I don't know, maybe their mom is not interested... and he works I think a lot of hours, so he doesn't have time to bring them to school... and he has really a lot of problems. So they stay at home like for a while, and then they come back... and you can see that they're not Moroccan, they're not Muslims. (Boston, Moroccan Women)
>
> *Moderator:* How would you react [if] your children would marry non-Muslims?
> *T (m):* Well, that's very unpleasant...
> *M (f):* It's always unpleasant. (Amsterdam, Surinamese Coed)

The main argument for such a choice was articulated in vague terms, such as "to have more in common."

> *Moderator:* It was stated that Bosnians have only few contacts to Christians. I would be interested in the subject of marriage. Some mentioned earlier that they would have problems with their kids marrying someone from another religion. Does this apply to all of you?
> *P:* Our families were very much mixed, in earlier times. I myself do not approve of that but I shall try to explain when I talk about it.
> *Moderator:* Does this have to do with experience or with religion?
> *P:* Rather with experience. I am wishing for a Muslim son-in-law and for a Muslim daughter-in-law.
> *P:* So do I. I wish them to be Muslims as well. We are a different culture.
> *P:* Less complicated.
> *P:* Less reason for dissent.
> *P:* My wife is not only my wife: She also has brothers. She also has parents.
> *O:* Your ex-wife was Muslim. Can you imagine to marry a non-Muslim in the future?
> *P:* No. We had such a case in my family. Judging from this experience, also from the children's point of view: One does not have any identity. You would have three identities: the identity of the mainstream culture, the Muslim identity, and the Jewish or Christian identity. That's just too complex. (Berlin, Bosnian Men)

Participants who felt that interreligious marriage was not a problem still articulated that such marriages were not allowed according to Islamic values or beliefs. In addition, a large portion of parents said that they might allow their sons to marry outside of the religion, but not their daughters. Although such resistance was grounded in theological prohibition,[1] respondents did not bring religious arguments forward for the latter case. Instead, they justified their opinions on a sociological basis. The restriction placed on Muslim females to marry only Muslim males was grounded in the continuity of identity. This attachment to religious marriage is confirmed by numerous quantitative surveys. For example, in a BVA report published in May 2009, 62 percent of Moroccans interviewed said that it was very important for their children to marry a Muslim, as did 82 percent of Dutch Muslims. In another report (IFOP, January 2011), 53 percent of French Muslims said that they were unwilling to marry a non-Muslim.

In this case, religion is defined as a trait that is passed from the father and inherited by his children. When a Muslim female marries a non-Muslim, her children are considered a member of their father's faith. For the focus group participants, such a situation was viewed as problematic because it automatically disconnected the children from their Muslim heritage.

Moderator: What about intermarriages? Marrying someone from another religion or marrying someone who does not have a religion at all.

Female 5: My son married a Lithuanian woman. She belongs to another religion. What it is the problem?

Moderator: But don't you think that it is less accepted for a woman to marry a man of another religion?

Men (together): Yes, a Muslim woman cannot marry someone who is not a Muslim.

Male 12: Technically, yes. But there are cases where women have married men of other faiths but it is more severe.

Male 8: Islam would not accept such a marriage so they cannot have a religious marriage. They cannot have a certificate of a religious marriage.

Male 10: A sheikh would not come and bless the wedding.

Moderator: So the girl would be rejected?

Male 8: From the point of view of the Muslims, she would be committing adultery. That is from the religious point of view.

Female 5: In my opinion, that is right that Muslims do not accept women marrying a person from another religion but, in my opinion, some of the people who are not of our religion, their behavior and ethics are very good…Some religious people, they are thieves, they are liars, cheating. I prefer the man who has values.

Female 1: This is important.

Female 5: There are some sheikhs who have given the fatwa that a woman can marry someone from another religion—a woman can.

Female 2: But that is not right. In Islam, a woman cannot marry a man from another religion. That man would have to convert.

Male 8: He would have to convert.

Female 2: And there are many cases where the man has accepted Islam to get married. Sometimes this is good. He becomes a good Muslim. (London, Iraq Coed)

Even though interreligious marriages were often frowned upon, mixed-ethnicity marriage was never seen as forbidden or as somehow dangerous to religion.

Moderator: Although other Muslim communities are living alongside you, have you started to marry with them yet?

No. 6: We are all already married so this not an issue. I think that according to Islam it is not a problem. We can marriage a Chinese, an English, but you have to understand that in the communities someone will feel like a Somalian and will want to marry a Somalian. In this respect, throughout the Muslim world, people's nation is emphasised.

No. 7: Nowadays it is beginning to happen. Our boys are marrying girls from other communities.

No. 10: That cultural divide is beginning to disappear now. It is more that Muslims are beginning to get married because of religious similarities. Maybe in the older generation it is still that you should get married to the person of the same religion and the same culture as well...It is being helped by the Internet. There are all these marriage sites for Muslims. You can specify religious belief and commitment but you do not have to specify what cultural background that you have. (London, Bangladeshi Men)

Several focus group participants related examples of interreligious or inter-ethnic marriages. These stories were particularly interesting because they often were framed in relation to the possibility of the relationship or the difficulty of it.

B: It is very difficult in my case. My wife is German. We do not have any pork nor alcohol. We made this agreement before the marriage. I only speak Arabic with [my son] so his mother would also learn something. Evening stories and Qur'an in the evening. I also try to make him join the morning prayer and the evening prayer. This is still a bit difficult. I hope that, next year, I can send him to Morocco for a couple of months so he speaks better Arabic. Later I am going to send him to school here. (Berlin, Arab Men)

Moderator: Regarding mixed marriage or to be married with a person from different ethnic or religious background, will it cause any problems within your family?

No. 5: Yes. I have a personal experience I can share. My girlfriend, she is coming from a Turkish background and raised in Holland. She is European Turkish. She has got European mentality. I am coming from Kurdish and Alawi background.[2] In the future, we will get married and, when I share my future plan with my mother, she does not care she is coming from a Turkish background. She does not care where she is coming from; she is a human being. But her first reaction was, "Are you sure? It can be serious problem, because you are coming from Alawi background and she is coming from a Sunni background. Maybe she was born in Holland and she does not have Islamic mentality or whatever but she is still coming from Sunni background. Maybe it is a problem for her family." I said I do not care...I will not marry with her family; I will get married with her. But there is still, you can see the problem is coming from her family and my family...I can see this is problem for the majority of people. It is not important where they live, maybe in Turkey or in Europe, but they still keep their originality and make it problem. (London, Turkish Speaking Men)

The Community Defined by the "Discrimination Experience"

Experiences of discrimination were often discussed in relation to community, especially in the European groups. Additionally, participants in the United States and London were the most vocal about the changes they have experienced since September 11, 2001, and the July 7, 2005, bombings in London.

> *Male 4:* A lot of change has happened since the bombings and a lot of rules and regulations have been put onto the Muslim community which has made us more aware of pressure. Before we just practiced our religion but now we have to practice it within rules and regulations about what [we] can and can't do. So a lot of change.
>
> *Male 6:* There is not much difference that I can see. There are rules and regulations that governments must make to impose peace. I practice and understand the religion the way I can under normal circumstances. There are rules and regulations to do with the police and government but, so long as this government is in charge, it uses rules against Muslims who are against peace. And if you are against peace, those rules will affect you. And if you are wrongly held, you can hire lawyers and address your grievances that way. (London, Somali)
>
> *Male 5:* The situation has changed after 7/7.
>
> *Moderator:* Because 9/11 happened in America, that's more general, but because we are in London and we had the 7/7 bombing, do you feel that that is what has made a difference?
>
> *Males:* Yes. [General agreement.]
>
> *Male 3:* When you are in an airplane with white people, they look at you and if you have a beard, it makes a difference. They are even more scared of you.
>
> *Male 5:* At 9/11, the guys who did it never wore a beard or anything. They wore suits and everything but just a couple of years after the bombings, people who look Muslim and who have beards—people say "I'm not flying with this guy. I don't trust him." which is kind of funny because when they were dressed like you and looked like you, you weren't scared but they were the bad guys.
>
> *Male 7:* It's the media.
>
> *Male 5:* Two months after the 7/7 bombings I heard a story of a man who came onto a London bus in Islamic dress and the passengers who were on the bus got off once he got on. (London, Somali Men)

As alluded to above, many participants commented that discrimination was likely determined by the way Muslims acted and looked. With no surprise, the focus groups comprised of women often described instances of discrimination related to wearing the hijab.

> *W:* You're working and you feel all those gazes…and when you look back, they look away and when you look away they're looking at you again. And

on that moment I felt like...well...I prefer that things would not go this way. (Amsterdam, Moroccan women)

B: I remember a friend of mine, she's Algerian, she wears hijab, and she has two girls, and we were in the Government Center Station and one woman...just hit her baby without saying anything. So what my friend did, she just followed her and started talking to her. That woman, she felt like, "Ok, I cannot intimidate these two women. They know their right, and they know how to act." So we followed her. She didn't ride with us. We were in Park Street. The woman, she was riding, she was going to get onto the T. The minute she saw us, she just ran away. So we were like, this is a victory for Muslim women. So in America I don't feel like I'm intimidated that I'm wearing hijab. But honestly and sadly, when I travel back to Morocco, that's [where] sometimes you get the bad treatment. (Boston, Moroccan Women)

London was an exception, because some women felt that Muslims and non-Muslims alike perceived the hijab positively. The reason is that Muslims tend to live in segregated areas of London so do not experience encounters with other non-Muslims as often.

Moderator: Do you think you are treated differently because of the way you dress?

No. 2: Maybe. Sometimes. If you are on a bus, they see you are a Muslim woman and they give you more respect. They let you pass and give up their seat.

Moderator: Is that respect from the Bangladeshi community?

No. 2: No. Anybody [in the wider community]. (London, Bangladeshi Women)

Participants also discussed a recent shift in the way non-Muslims perceived them. Most notably, they stated that they were primarily seen as Muslims rather than labeled by ethnicity.

No. 1: I think if a woman is wearing a scarf or a man has a beard that is obviously Muslim, I think that's when people notice them more. But I think if you wear a hijab or a man has a beard, people will see you as Muslim and not as an Asian. And I think that has really changed. Because when I was growing up I used to be called a "Paki" but now I'm called "Taliban." (London, Bangladeshi Women)

Moderator: You mentioned people who came here after the coup d'état.[3] Firstly, they were the "foreigners."

N: No, firstly they were "Turks" and then "foreigners" and now they are "Muslims." (Berlin, Turkish Coed)

D: This society pushes the religion from public area to private area. Because if you show your identity in a public institution you can be discriminated [against]. So a Muslim is usually faced with the question "Should I show my Islamic identity or not?" Because as soon as you say, people look differently at you. For example, when I apply to a juvenile bureau or another important public institution and they ask me how religious I am, then I would ask myself if I really should tell because as soon as you tell you become "the other." (Berlin, Turkish Coed)

Focus group participants further acknowledged that levels of discrimination varied by region. They often suggested that they experienced less discrimination in the more cosmopolitan areas, where residents were "used" to seeing Muslims.

> *A:* If you go out of London, people are more English, they are more white-orientated. They are not used to the headscarf. They are not used to even see colored people, so…when they see it, it does attract attention. They do not understand it and it is probably ignorance in that sense but I have faced this before when people look at me because of the color of my skin. (London, Iraqi)
> *K:* If you go in the South or in the Midwest, it's hard. You can live there 20 years without even having any incident but the risk is higher so some people can get killed.
> *Moderator:* What do you base that on, [that] the risk is higher?
> *K:* The risk of being hurt. The risk of being hurt as a Muslim. Or being singled out. You cannot find a job. You'll be rejected for a job application; you will be rejected for any services. Here [in Massachusetts] this is a liberal state, they accept you. They are used to diversity. (Boston, Moroccan Coed)
> *M:* I had a friend who has got difficulty to be accepted by [the] Turkish community of outside London. They need to talk to somebody in your language but they do not accept you, because you are Alawi. They do not see you as a Muslim. Even being Kurd is a problem in outside London. They do not give you job because you are Kurd. (London, Turkish Speaking Coed)

Unsurprisingly, due to the heated debate on Islam in French public arenas, the participants in the Paris groups were very concerned with the meanings of assimilation and integration. One of the idiosyncrasies of the discussion was the rejection by many of the participants of the automatic linkage that media and politicians make between Muslims in France and Muslims from foreign countries. In this regard, a lot of participants felt that foreign experts on Islam were more influential in politics affecting Muslims than they should be.

> *No. 7:* Beyond the topic of citizenship, what bothers me the most is the fact that each time there is an issue, like the headscarf, we turn to external Muslim countries, as if Muslims were subordinated to some external powers. [This refers to the French state asking Egyptian ulemas for a religious opinion regarding the ban of the headscarf in public schools.][4]

Though these sentiments were expressed mostly in France, they reflect broader trends identified previously. Indeed, many Muslims felt that they were excluded from the national identity or community, whether as Muslims or as foreigners. An exception to this trend was found in the Amsterdam group discussions, which rarely raised the topic of discrimination. In fact, only three of the groups even mentioned it. When it came up, participants generally felt that it was more an issue of ethnicity and immigration than religious motivation.

> *Moderator:* Have you ever felt discriminated against or felt "different," or is it not that bad?
>
> *N:* Well, I do feel like that sometimes but not necessarily because I'm Muslim, but rather because I'm foreign...So, not because I'm Muslim.
>
> *Moderator:* Ok, because you look different...
>
> *N:* Well, you are and remain a foreigner. (Amsterdam, Turkish Women)
>
> *H:* I noticed when a Dutch person came, they see the name, you know. If somebody is Dutch, they greet the person and shake his hand and talk, you know. But if a foreign person comes, they just mention the name and then say "You can enter now." (Amsterdam, Turkish women)
>
> *C:* My vermiform appendix was ruined. I had never been ill, but it happened to me once. I lived in Amsterdam-North then. I went to the police station there. I asked them to bring me to the doctor. I asked them where the hospital was. But they said to me, "Where are you from? Where are you from?" I said, "From Turkey." They said, "Leave. Go away." Why did they do this? Because I am a guest worker [a term commonly used to refer to immigrant laborers]. (Amsterdam, Turkish Speaking Men)

Amsterdam participants did not reference drastic changes stemming from 9/11 or the 7/7 bombings. Nor did they express greater discrimination vis-à-vis their religious practices, such as wearing the hijab. This was interesting, especially given the multiple opinion surveys confirming that the Dutch are among the most vehemently anti-Muslim nation in Europe. The perceived lack of discrimination on *religious ground* can be related to the fact that Dutch Muslims see themselves primarily defined by their national origin (Moroccan or Turkish) *in which* Islam is embedded. In other words, as discussed in chapter 2, group identification can impact communal feelings of alienation.

The Community of the Country of Origin

As already noted, participants tended to identify with—or felt others identified them with—their country of origin or immigrant status. They also continuously expressed that this group identification intermingled with and frequently overtook their identification as Muslim. Additionally, there were often comparisons between the country of origin and the current residence. Such comparisons were rarely related to politics but rather to questions of identity and religious practice. In all cities, overwhelming majorities mentioned the freedoms that allowed them to practice their religion (as discussed in chapter 1), and indicated that they preferred being Muslim in their current residence compared to Muslim countries or their countries of origin. For example, several Moroccan women in Amsterdam discussed their religious practices in Dutch society versus their practices in their country of origin (see chapter 2).

When discussions centered on civic participation and politics, the country of origin only occasionally came up contrary to expectations. In fact, when political involvement in one's country of origin did arise, it was almost always a response to a direct question from the interviewer.

> *Moderator:* Do you also vote in Turkey?
> *B:* Yes.
> *A:* The last two years I didn't.
> *C:* No.
> *D:* I didn't vote for 20 years in Turkey.
> *Moderator:* So, hardly any of them votes for Turkish politics. But I do see Turkish newspapers here.
> *D:* Yes, we have subscriptions.
> *Moderator:* So, they are occupied with Turkish news and politics. Why do they not vote?
> *A:* If you want to vote, you have to go to Turkey, you know. That costs money.
> *Moderator:* Do you go to Turkey often?
> *A:* Every year, or every two years, every three years… if I have money and my children are going…
> *D:* I go every year.
> *C:* I didn't go for three years. (Amsterdam, Turkish Elderly Men)

Because of the Internet and social media, it is easier for participants to stay abreast of news in their countries of origin. A few also have gotten involved in causes that impact their ethnic group or country of origin.

> *Moderator:* Are there any political or social causes you are fighting for or would you like to fight for in Britain?
> *No. 1:* I generally do human rights work. For now I am working for Kurdish human rights.
> *Moderator:* Are you a member of political or civic organizations? Why?
> *No. 1:* No.
> *No. 2:* Before the war in Iraq, I was kind of active in the "stop the war" coalition. I am not a member of any organisation.
> *Moderator:* Do you keep informed on the social and political situation of Britain?
> *No. 1:* Yes, I usually check BBC.
> *No. 2:* I try to keep myself updated on what is going on in Britain, because I am living here. I cannot isolate from the news in England. I mainly follow it from BBC.
> *No. 3:* I follow it through newspapers and television.
> *Moderator:* Do you read Milli gazette, Zaman or Vakit or Yeni Safak?[25]

No. 1: I usually check Yeni Safak on internet.

No. 4: I read Vakit.

No. 5: I read Zaman sometimes.

Moderator: Why do you read Vakit?

No. 4: Because they went crazy in the last debates in Turkey. I really like to follow it.

Moderator: So, you do not read it regarding to religion?

No. 4: No. It is just to keep myself updated on political issues in Turkey.

Moderator: How closely do you follow national politics? Do you feel that Muslims can make a difference in the outcome of, say, the next elections?

No. 2: I try to follow. I read some Turkish and Kurdish newspapers, try to keep updated about what is going on.

No. 1: Regarding Turkey I follow politics, but regarding here I do not concentrate.

No. 4: I am here very new and do not follow closely on what is going on in Britain. My knowledge is more about Turkey. I do not know what is happening here.

No. 5: What is happening in Britain is important but I cannot follow it often. (London, Turkish and Kurdish Women Participants)

Membership to any international group of Muslims was seldom mentioned, and the *Ummah* as the global community of Muslims was not referenced at all. This finding was one of the most surprising due to the systematic framing of Muslim identities in relation to the *Ummah* not only by media and politicians but also by some transnational Islamic actors (see chapter 7).

The Community of the Country of Residence

Nearly all focus group participants were asked about their feelings toward their host country. This yielded a wide spectrum of responses, ranging from those who felt that one could not really be Muslim in a non-Muslim country to those who felt that one could only be Muslim in the West.

As mentioned above, there were often comparisons between the country of origin and current residence. Although a majority of respondents stated that their current residence was a good place to be Muslim, a clear trend was difficult to identify. However, as discussed in chapter 2, some of the quantitative surveys we have reviewed provide clear statistics about Muslims' identification to their countries of residence in contrast to other affiliations such as religion, ethnicity, and local communities.

When confronted with an exclusive choice between religious identity and national identity by the question "Do you consider yourself a Muslim (Christian) or a citizen first?" 81 percent of Muslims in the United Kingdom said Muslim while only 24 percent of Christians said Christian. In Germany, the numbers were similar, as 66 percent of Muslims identified first with religion as opposed to 33 percent of Christians. Muslim religious identifications were lower in France as 46 percent of Muslims said they were Muslims first and 14 percent of Christians saw themselves as Christians first.[6] Interestingly, American Christians are more likely than their Western European counterparts to think of themselves first in terms of their religion rather than their nationality; 46 percent of Christians in the United States see themselves primarily as Christians and the same number consider themselves Americans first. In contrast, majorities of Christians in France (90%), Germany (70%), Britain (63%), and Spain (53%) identify primarily with their nationality rather than their religion.[7]

The Pew (2007) and Gallup (2011) surveys ask the same questions to American Muslims. Overall, according to the Pew data, 47 percent of Muslims saw themselves as Muslims first, which put them at the same level as Christian Americans.[8]

Our focus group discussions reveal that ethnicity is a significant factor that influences one's identification to the country of residence, especially for Moroccans and Turks in Europe (see chapter 2). More than any other ethnic group, Moroccans tended to identify first to their country of origin and second to their country of residence. This was true across all cities in Europe and in the United States (see appendix 13).

Meanings of Citizenship

Focus group participants also discussed their views on citizenship within their country of residence. Their positions can be divided into two main strains: citizenship as a practical good or resource for travel, work, and social mobility; and citizenship as a set of values. Another surprise was to discover that our respondents often associated civic and Islamic values but rarely put them in tension or contradiction, which is also very much at odds with the dominant political discourse.

It is important to note that the composition of our focus groups across the countries may have influenced the findings on citizenship. For instance, in certain London transcripts, participants were largely refugees, which is not conducive to an active civic engagement. In France, a majority of participants were citizens, which also explain their strong emphasis on values. In Germany, most participants were not citizens, which influences their attraction to more informal forms of political participation.[9]

Within the first trend, several nuances appeared. Some respondents described detachment from their country of residence while others expressed disappointment in the lack of "real" citizenship. In other words, they felt excluded as immigrants and/or Muslims even when they had the formal status of citizen. Additionally, participants expressed a variety of opinions on whether exclusion was due to their immigrant or Muslim status, although as seen in the section above, these identifications were not clearly demarcated.

C: You are a German citizen.

S: Yes, I am.

C: How much is this of importance to you?

S: There is no use of that. It is just a formality.

C: Can I say something about the German passport? There was a flat free for rent in Kreuzberg and the neighbors did not want foreigners to rent that flat. But when a German citizen with Turkish origins goes to rent that flat, the landlord says that he cannot rent the house to him because he is a foreigner. But the man says, "I'm not a foreigner. Look at my ID. It is a German one," and the landlord says, "Well, you are really not a foreigner but you look like one." (Berlin, Turkish Men)

Observer: No one of you has the German citizenship, so you can't vote, right?

I: Yes, I am German.

A: Me not yet.

Observer: But you're applying for it?

A: Yes, I do.

AI: I have two passports.

H: I'm also German. I have two passports, too.

Observer: And does this incites you to vote and influence politics to get the citizenship?

H: Well, I have the feeling, no matter what you vote, it's... only the name... and then as soon as they are voted for, it continues like before.

A: You could vote for the bike party. Yes, that's true. It is really nonsense.

Moderator: Would you like to get the German citizenship to be able to vote here and to influence politics here?

A: Of course, referring to me, yes. Not only because of voting but because things are easier.

AM: I would like to have the German citizenship just for the vacation, when I want to travel so that I don't have to go and apply for a visa when I want to go the Spain or Turkey. (Berlin, Arab Coed)

Regarding the second type of responses—those from citizens—the emphasis on values was sometimes linked to Islam. The examples below demonstrate how Islam was experienced as a set of values comparable to the civic values of the national community of residence.

K: The animal party [Dutch political party that stands up for the rights of animals].

A1: Even they say you're not allowed to slaughter halal.

A2: Maybe there should be a halal animal party.

Moderator: But do you vote at all?

K: Politics in the Netherlands has become a show. It's like GTST [Dutch soap opera], watching every evening, who said what... If you really want to know and do something in society, then it's better to go to a foundation. Then you actually do something good.

A2: Yes.

M: But I also don't want Geert Wilders [extreme right wing politician who has very controversial ideas about Muslims, such as that the Qur'an should be forbidden] to come into power or something.

A1: I don't vote to support a party, but I vote so that my vote doesn't go to somebody else, that's how I see it. (Amsterdam, Moroccan highly educated men focus group)

The positive connotation of dual citizenship was another important point that came out of the discussions. Being a citizen of two countries was never depicted as a conflict of allegiance, in clear contrast with the dominant public discourse described in chapter 1. In Amsterdam, participants in all focus groups expressed interest in maintaining their native citizenship and, if not, obtaining dual citizenship. As a participant in the Berlin Coed focus group mentioned above, those who did have citizenship indicated that it made international travel easier. Notably, obtaining dual citizenship or maintaining native citizenship was not discussed in the other cities.

A 2008–2009 survey from the Institut National des Etudes Demographiques (INED) (National Institute of Demographic Studies) confirms the same trend in France. Nearly half of the French immigrants surveyed retain their foreign citizenship. This is consistent with previous reports indicating that an increasing number of naturalized citizens choose to keep their former nationalities. For example, in 1992, only 7 percent of Algerian immigrants kept their Algerian citizenship, while the rate has skyrocketed to 67 percent in 2008. Moreover, two-thirds of North African immigrants, 55 percent of Turkish immigrants and 43 percent of Portuguese immigrants, declare dual citizenship. As the report notes, "For ethnic minorities, having multiple nationalities is seen as compatible with a full commitment to their Frenchness, indeed even as an enhancement to their Frenchness. They clearly do not see any contradiction in terms of loyalty."[10]

As discussed in the previous chapter on identity, most participants express a strong desire to be regarded as citizens of their country of residence. For example, in one group in Amsterdam, a participant expressed his wish to be a regular citizen rather than getting special treatment.

> *J:* We are seen as Dutch, why should we get a special treatment? That's not necessary at all. We are Dutch people of Moroccan descent who have Islam as their faith, that's why…[But] that's not necessary. I can take care of myself. (Amsterdam, Moroccan Mixed Gender)

For both citizens and non-citizens alike, citizenship was presented as a desirable status. Although citizenship was widely recognized as an important tool, most agreed that it did not guarantee inclusion in society. Such a mitigated attitude also explains some specific trends in political and civic participation.

Political and Civic Participation

Political involvement was perceived positively across all cities. In fact, a consensus emerged that Muslims should become more involved, especially if they want to have an impact in politics. Many pointed to the gap between the significant number of Muslim citizens and their absence in almost all domains of the political sphere. This was particularly apparent in the Paris group since the Muslim population in this city, and in France in general, is relatively large.

Across the board, voting was usually connoted positively, though doubts were expressed concerning its usefulness and efficiency. It is important to note that discussions on voting and political participation varied by country. This was mostly due to focus group composition as well as the different circumstances in each country, such as laws on immigrant, voter eligibility and the presence of anti-Islamic political groups. For example, in London, many participants viewed the far right British National Party (BNP) as a "dangerous" political group for both Muslims and immigrants. Therefore, participants saw it as their duty to be politically active in order to counterbalance the efforts of the BNP.

> *K:* As an immigrant, my interest is to stop the British National Party from taking over because they have shown to the world that they have are racist and the most dangerous group and they can affect the lifestyles of many people from other parts of the world into Britain. I have been involved in the anti-war movement. I am a very left-wing humanist/human rights activist and I am campaigning for human rights for anyone who needs me anywhere in the world. And I think that fighting the BNP is a major issue for me. (London, Iraqi)

Overall, there was a diversity of stances concerning the legitimacy or even existence of a Muslim vote. Participants clearly emphasized that they would not support just any political party, because they were concerned with the public image of Islam.

> *No. 12:* The majority of the people have no problem with us. There is a small minority like the BNP (British National Party) who hate us because we are migrants and Muslim.
>
> *No. 5:* We are living in the most democratic nation in the world and we have Bangladeshis who are in the House of Lords. That goes to show that the British people have accepted us and there are successful Bangladeshis out there. The British state and the British public have played their part in it. There is a small minority out there who do not like us but we live in a democratic state and that is a part of life.
>
> *No. 10:* I think there are capable leaders out there who represent the community. Like my dad who is a media person and represents the community. But I do not think that there is enough representation [for the younger generation]. There is so much bad publicity that goes round for young Bangladeshis and young Muslims in general, but there is no one representing them and no one to speak out. There is no leadership for us. (London, Bangladeshi Men)

In Berlin, Muslims stressed a need to be politically represented by a Muslim organization.

> *A:* We need a representation on the national level. It has to do with financial aspects. Same as on [the] local level. We do not have church tax. So we have

to consider whether the state can give financial aid, as it is done in Sweden, I think. (Berlin, Bosnian men)

B: An umbrella organization makes sense and would be desirable. I don't see that Muslims are adequately represented in the Berlin House of Representatives [*Abgeordneten Haus,* the parliament of Berlin]. Otherwise, one is governed by others, who just don't have an idea of who we are and what we want. (Berlin, International Coed)

C: I am wishing for a multi-ethnic Muslim representation here in Germany, like the *Islamrat* [Islamic Council] and the *Zentralrat der Muslime* [Central Muslim Council] are trying to establish. So that we can put forward our affairs as citizens of this society. And so that we can make a contribution to this society with our representation. (Berlin, Bosnian Men)

In the Boston focus groups, participants did feel a Muslim vote was present, but effective Muslim political participation did not rely solely on voting. Participants noted that Muslims should also be involved with civil society, community groups, and associations in order to assert their political sway.

Moderator: So Muslims you think are strong enough [that] if they are involved they could make the difference in this next election?

F: Yes.

M: I think the involvement—it's not only to cast your ballot—it should be more than that. If we are just taking that to be involved, just to go and vote, it's not going to be enough. [You need to be]...concerned and be motivated to participate in all levels of the civic life and be involved with associations, with groups, with anywhere you can. (Boston, Moroccan Coed)

Despite voting, participants were also involved in more informal political activities like volunteer work, or mobilization for social causes. However, this aspect of the discussion was rarely spontaneous. Instead, participants only described their involvement when specifically asked. In our Berlin survey, the majority of interviewees did not engage in formal political participation, which seems to contradict the positive perception of political participation that came from the focus groups. In accordance with our Berlin data, a significant portion, though not a majority, of Muslims (44.7 percent) voted in the past local elections. However, in the same survey, a majority of Muslims (53.7 percent) asserted that they did not participate.

This low level of formal political participation also was visible through other indicators, such as lack of support for political parties and engagement in political representation.

Quantitative surveys validate our analysis and highlight the following three trends (details can be found in appendix 7):

1. Muslims have lower formal and informal political participation than people of other faiths.

2. Age does not uniformly influence voting across Europe in a negative way, but it does in the United States.
3. European Muslims have left-leaning political identification.

Civic Engagement and Islam

Two interesting positions emerged when civic engagement was discussed. The first position concerned people involved within their own ethnic, religious, or local community organizations, such as youth soccer leagues, community cleanups, and mosque boards. The second one involved people who were civically engaged in the greater local or even national community organizations, including nonprofits, political parties, university organizations, and citywide student associations.

> *Moderator:* Are you in an Islamic organization? In a political party? In an association? What are you doing voluntarily/honorary? Where are you engaged?
>
> *P:* I am politically active though not in relation to religion but in relation to migrational background [Migrationshintergrund]. I am working with refugees. I am trying to work more on the problems of Muslim in the future. I am working in the Council of Refugees Berlin [Flüchtlingsrat Berlin] and in Juveniles without Borders [Jugendliche ohne Grenzen]. I am a member in the Muslim Youth Germany [Muslimische Jugend Deuschland] and, every now and then, in the German-Speaking Circle of Muslims [Deutschsprachiger Muslimkreis]. As an association I am engaged in Inssan and the German-speaking circle of Muslims. And I am active in interreligious dialogue. I am active in the community of the Ahmadis, and I am organizing events. Also I am doing youth work ... Where I come from, it is dangerous to be engaged politically. However, I am trying to use the freedom here and become active. Not in a religious way, but in a social or human context. (Berlin, International Coed)

A clear difference emerged between those who saw their civic participation as part of their behaviors as Muslims and those who did not. Thus, a community organizer for Muslim youth may not have seen his behavior as part of being Muslim, while a Greenpeace volunteer may have viewed his involvement as part of his Muslim obligation to be engaged positively in his community.

> *B:* It plays a role but I think that it is so unified with the person you are, that you automatically find it important, besides the fact that it is obligatory. That you don't see it as an obligation in religion but an obligation as a being human.
>
> *Moderator:* Why did you start doing volunteer work?
>
> *K:* I just wanted to contribute, help, and play a role of significance in someone's life. Maybe I'm really naive, but I really believe that the youth has the future. And I can keep on complaining "What are those youngsters

doing there? Why are they not going home? Why are they not going to school?" But to what extent is it possible to keep on saying that when you don't do anything yourself? It was not out of religion, but out of my personality, and my personality and religion are unified. (Amsterdam, Moroccan Women)

Interestingly, participants tended to discuss motivations for political and civic engagement separately during discussions of "being a good Muslim" rather than during the political discussions. The vast majority of participants did not explicitly explain their civic engagement or political involvement in terms of being Muslim. However, many of these same participants would later make clear that they envisioned participation in general as an obligation, or at least a cornerstone, of being a good Muslim.

M: I always thought it was a shame that the boys next door ended up badly or tended to end up badly. I always thought that was a shame. They are your friends after all. You got into a lot of mischief with them, fought with them, but made friends with them as well. I tried to stimulate them and send them on the right path. I've always been their spokesperson for example. They wanted me to. Why? Cause, er, yeah, you're studying so you know the right words. Imagine, for example, we stormed the city district office with 25 Moroccan street ruffians. Like a protest, hey, not like terrorism or like that. (Laughter)

M: It was always like this. Like, "M, what are we going to do because we don't have a community center, whereas that neighborhood does and we don't?" Then I said, "You know what we're going to do? It's our political right. We'll storm the city precinct. And that'll be our community center. But behave yourselves. Don't act like you're on the streets that you can spit or whatever."

H: Haha, you were a recruiter.

M: Yeah, something like that. Behave yourself and things will work out. And indeed, they were talking with us and listening to us. And we managed to get a youth center, a community center in that way. And [this] community center is still there and [this] community center has created employment. And I think that ten out of those 25 guys got a job because of that. As a youth worker, is perhaps not much and doesn't sound all that interesting, but they're grateful because they did manage to create a family with kids because of it.

G: Did you also do it inspired by your religion?

M: You mean with *al-ajar* [(in view of divine) compensation]?

G: Yes, in the back of your mind that it good because of [your] religion.

M: No, I didn't think of that specifically. I've always been raised in *khayr* [goodness], *Alhamdulilaah* [praise be to God]. So I've always been taught to do *khayr* (good). Even though they do the bad thing to you, do *khayr*. And then you always try to do your best. (Amsterdam, Moroccan Mixed Gender)

Some participants did express their responsibility to the political community as a religious duty.

> *M:* Community does not just mean the Islamic community, because Islam is not just for the Islamic community but for the whole community. That you are a good example, so to say. If you are good to fellow Muslims but not to other people, then you are also not a good Muslim.
>
> *A2:* Exactly. But providing a good definition of a good Muslim is just very difficult. I think there are different meanings for everybody. One person is satisfied with the rules or just a little bit more, the other person is not satisfied with that. That person will do volunteer work on the weekend to feel like a better Muslim, because it stimulates you to be good for your environment. Personally, I think just sticking to the rules is not enough. (Amsterdam, Moroccan Highly Educated Men Focus Group)

Trust in Government Institutions

Closely related to the issue of political participation is whether people have trust in their national and local government institutions. According to a Gallup (2009) survey, Muslims in France were (slightly) less likely to trust national government institutions than the general French population, while in Germany and the United Kingdom, Muslims trust slightly more than the average population (see detailed figures in appendix 13).

In the United States, the Gallup (2011) survey show that Muslims trusted the national government more than all other religious groups, except when it came to law enforcement. In particular, Muslim respondents expressed strong trust in American legal and civic institutions, showed relatively strong trust in the American media and courts, and had more confidence in the fairness of elections than any other religious group. However, Muslim Americans' trust was significantly lower than other religious groups when asked about the military, FBI, and local police organizations.

When looking at data on trust in local institutions, different results appeared. The graph below (figure 3.1) summarizes the responses to questions

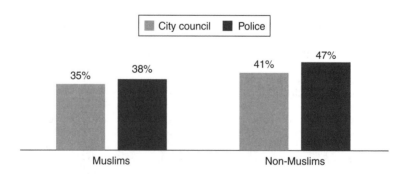

Figure 3.1   Trust "a fair amount," across 11 European cities
Source: OSI (2009)

on local government and police for both Muslims and non-Muslims across Europe. A slight difference was noticeable between the two groups for trust in the city council, but a more substantial distinction appeared when it came to trust in the police.

CHAPTER 4

RELIGIOSITY, POLITICAL PARTICIPATION, AND CIVIC ENGAGEMENT

As discussed in chapter 2, being Muslim has multiple meanings that are entangled in a complex web of ethnic, regional, and national identities, and cannot be reduced to a set of beliefs, practices, or, even, cultural norms. For this reason, predefined attributes of religiosity, such as mosque attendance or prayer, are not the best predictors of religiosity.

One major point that stands out from our investigation is that Muslims across European countries consider themselves to be more religious than their non-Muslim and Christian counterparts. In this condition, to what extent, if any, does being Muslim and religiosity among Muslims impact their political participation in their societies?

The Debated Question of Mosque Attendance and Political Participation

Mosque attendance is often used as a strong indicator of religiosity in most European and American surveys. Yet measuring mosque attendance in the same way as church attendance is problematic for several reasons. First, Muslims may go to mosques for reasons that are not directly related to praying and worship because social and cultural events are often held in a mosque. This contrasts with church attendance, which has a more religious connotation rather than social or communal meaning, especially in Europe. Second, according to existing surveys, Muslim women tend to go to the mosque less than men in both Europe and the United States (see appendix 13); therefore, if religiosity is measured only by mosque attendance, women would be considered less religious than men. However, according to all other indicators of religiosity, such as adherence to prayer, fasting, and dietary restrictions, Muslim women appear to be more religious than men. Such a gender gap undermines any strong correlation between religiosity defined as mosque attendance and political participation. However, some surveys, such as the 2011 Gallup polling, support such correlation (see appendix 13).

According to this polling, American Muslim respondents who reported high levels of political participation were more likely to attend mosque services on a frequent (45 percent at least weekly) or regular basis (68 percent at least monthly). Muslim respondents who declared low levels of political participation were more likely to never or seldom attend mosque services (49 percent). Additionally, those who reported elevated (high or moderate) levels of political participation were more likely to believe that religion is important (35 percent), while political participation was high only among 25 percent of those who did not perceive religion to be important.

By contrast, young people in the United States, as in Europe, tended to identify more strongly with their religion and appeared more religious in many survey indicators. However, as a group, they were also the least likely to participate politically as discussed in the second trend in chapter 3.

The focus group discussions and our Berlin survey shed light on a few unknown facts concerning Muslim political and religious participation that can cast a different light on the political influence of Islamic religiosity. First, they illustrate that Islam is an important element of self-identification but *not* necessarily the most significant element for group identity. Instead, participants often presented it as an imposition on Muslims' social interactions with mainstream society. Second, multiple and conflicting meanings are associated with Islam. Conformity to "orthodox" practices, such as dress code and rituals, often were framed in opposition to "universal" Islamic values. However, in a somewhat contradictory fashion, when participants discussed how to become a "better Muslim," they emphasized the importance of orthodox behavior to achieve this goal. This emphasis was particularly striking when the topic of hijab came up, as women, in particular, explained how adopting the hijab was a way to become a better Muslim.

A third contradiction emerged between participants' positive view of political participation and the fact that Muslims actually do not often participate (see chapter 3 for discussion on this pattern and its meanings). In the same vein, most participants expressed a positive appreciation for their country of residence, especially when it came to the political and religious freedoms they experienced there. This is a particularly noteworthy point to highlight at a time when Muslims are under suspicion for their supposed lack of loyalty and acceptance of Western values.

Finally, the focus group discussions hinted at a positive correlation between being Muslim and being a good citizen. This seems to converge with a broader trend abundantly documented among other religious groups in the United States, which is the positive influence of religion on political participation.

Numerous surveys in the United States have shown that religious identification increases political and civic participation. In this context, religious participation refers to social networking or inclusion in a group connected to a place of worship that provides "social support to their members and social services to the wider community…by nurturing civic-skilled church people."[1]

For example, the Economic Values Survey found that "Evangelicals who attended frequently were six times more likely and Protestants were twice as likely to do volunteer work for their churches as opposed to co-religionists who attended less frequently."[2] Therefore, church attendance is critical for civic and political participation, not simply membership. In this sense, religious institutions function as an incubator for civic skills, which then overflow into other areas of collective life.[3]

When it comes to Muslims in the United States, Amaney Jamal raises important questions as she underscores the unclear causal relationship between religious attendance and civic/political participation.[4] She distinguishes the following possibilities: direct mobilization where institutions or elites recruit individuals into the political process, the "overflow" of civic skills developed through the religious institutions, and the increase in "group consciousness" that may come about among congregations.[5] In her 2005 study, mosques were "directly linked to political activity, civic participation, and group consciousness" for Arab Muslims. Whereas for African and Arab Americans, the mosque served more "as a collectivizing forum that highlights Muslim common struggles in mainstream American society."[6] When looking at South Asian Muslims, the results were very different in that "mosque participation enhances South Asian civic participation but not political engagement or group consciousness"[7] (see appendix 13).

Other findings from Jen'nan Reid make an important distinction that is very much in line with our empirical results. In her 2007 study of Arab Americans, she concluded that subjective dimensions of religiosity—prayer and salience of religion in daily life—did not have an influence on political participation, but mosque attendance did. In this regard, the mosque appears as a place for expressing belonging or one's identification to the Muslim group. Thus, it is important to distinguish personal markers of Islamic religiosity, such as praying or fasting, and collective markers, such as mosque attendance, since the latter is the one that seems to have some influence on political participation.

Reid also noticed an important difference between genders, as mosque attendance for women was not correlated to an increase in political participation. This is similar to our findings, as well as to the Gallup (2011) data. According to the Gallup survey, 38 percent of women and 35 percent of men attended a mosque at least once a week, and 9 percent of women and 7 percent of men attended a mosque every week. However, as an indicator of political participation, 61 percent of Muslim women were registered to vote compared to 66 percent of Muslim men.

Both Amaney Jamal and Jen'nan Reid implicitly point out the importance of context in shaping Islamic group identity. In other words, a direct connection is not present between the fact that someone can identify to an Islamic group and the fact that this person is born in a certain ethnic or cultural

Muslim group. Demographic characteristics, national origin, duration of US residency, and age are important elements that influence the probability for a Muslim to endorse such a group identity. For instance, more recent immigrant arrivals typically have stronger ties to their ethnic identities and may live in ethnic enclaves for social and economic support on arrival to the United States. They also may experience greater levels of discrimination, which in turn strengthens their group consciousness and affects their decisions to participate politically. In other words, group identity based on culture and interaction with the dominant environment probably has as much influence as Islam per se on the level of political participation of Muslims.

Regarding Muslims in Europe, the challenge of identifying a positive correlation between religious and political participation is even higher. First, as addressed in chapter 2, Muslim religiosity is still largely unknown and not properly analyzed beyond self-identification and mosque attendance. Second, the recent increase of surveys on Muslims in Europe is not very useful, because the results cannot be compared to a control group of other faiths discussed within the surveys. Instead, these surveys compare Muslims with a fictitious non-Muslim population. Third, religion is studied in connection with values, whereas in American surveys, religion is studied in connection with practices.[8]

Due to this lack of cumulative data, some studies support the thesis that Muslims' religious attendance influences civic and political participation while others do not. For example, in the 2011 study titled "Social Capital, Political Participation and Migration in Europe: Making Multicultural Democracy Work,"[9] the impact of religion on political participation is investigated to analyze protest activities among Muslim migrant populations in Barcelona, London, Milan, and Zurich. This study concludes that religious membership is positively related to social capital. In this regard, it is consistent with other surveys on church membership indicating that "civic skills or group consciousness necessary to political involvement are provided by membership in associations rather than by attendance at religious services."[10]

In this perspective, political influence of religion is not defined by personal religiosity, that is beliefs or religious practices. But belonging or identification to a religious group seems to be influential on political participation.

From an opposite perspective, Imène Ajala describes Muslims' religiosity as negatively correlated with political participation in France. Though French Muslims can be considered more religious than their non-Muslim French co-citizens, they are mostly distinguished by their *lack* of formal political participation, which is indicated by their relatively low voter-registration numbers.[11] Furthermore, Ajala writes that "religious preferences do not seem relevant to understand Muslims' political positions," and she claims economic and social exclusion are far more influential in relation to French Muslims' choices for candidates and voting trends. Thus, Ajala believes that, in the French case, Muslims' religiosity is *not* a significant variable in relation to political participation.

Convergent with our analysis, Ajala addresses the problematic issue of church and mosque attendance as inefficient tools to measure religiosity. With about five million Muslims, France counts the largest Muslim population of any Western European country. Ajala's study found that 78 percent of French Muslims considered themselves to be "religiously" Muslim. However, if religiosity is defined as mosque attendance, the number of religious Muslims drastically decreased.[12] Only 36 percent of Muslims declared themselves as practicing and merely 15 percent regularly attended the mosque.

As in the United States, ethnic and cultural differences among Muslims in Europe influence Islamic group identities. A study from the Netherlands (2010) analyzed the different Islamic identities of Moroccan Dutch and Turkish Dutch Muslims as well as their influence on political mobilization. Participants were asked if they would be willing to act together politically as Muslims citizens, thus, asserting their religious identity in opposition to the dominant non-Muslim majority if conflicts arose. Moroccan Dutch Muslims, more than Turkish Dutch Muslims, responded that they would be willing to act as Muslim citizens on political issues. According to the authors of the survey, Moroccan Dutch Muslims overall had a stronger Islamic identity, because they were less socially and economically integrated in Dutch society than the Turkish Dutch.

The results of our Berlin survey also highlight the necessity to contextualize and adopt a more nuanced approach to Muslims' religiosity. The majority of the interviewees declared that they were not members of a mosque, but when asked "Do you regularly attend the same mosque community? Are you engaged in a mosque community?" nearly 30 percent claimed that they did. In terms of personal worship outside the mosque, a majority of respondents indicated that they conducted individual prayer. Additionally, 56 percent stated that they talked about religion once a week or more, and 57 percent fasted the entire month of Ramadan. When asked to define what it meant to be a Muslim, 77 percent of the respondents said that being Muslim was a relationship with God. In the same vein, a majority of respondents defined being a Muslim in terms of Islamic values and qualities, which included a relationship with God or a way of life. These alternative definitions of being a Muslim do not require mosque attendance at its core. In other words, measuring religiosity primarily through mosque attendance is not adapted to understand the political influence (or lack) of more personal forms of religious practices.

For example, in our Berlin survey, indicators of personal faith outside of mosque attendance did not correlate positively with greater political engagement. More specifically, our results show the following:

- Interviewees who more frequently participated in individual prayer were less likely to engage in a union, support a political party, or contact public officials.

- Interviewees who talked about religion more frequently were slightly less likely to support a political party.
- Interviewees who did not drink alcohol were also slightly less likely to support a political party or work for a campaign.

However, other indicators did correlate with greater political engagement:[13]

In brief, according to our investigation, it is not possible to assert that religiosity increases Muslims' political participation, because data differs greatly from one country to another—as well as from one Muslim group to another—according to ethnic origin, location, and the type of question asked. At the same time, it is not possible to assert that Muslims' religiosity has a negative effect on civic participation. Other dimensions, such as ethnicity and class, also influence Muslim's religiosity and, alternatively, civic and political participation. Therefore, it is crucial to produce more data that explicitly takes into account these specific factors in order to contextualize religiosity. Ethnicity is one of these factors.

Ethnicity and Its Correlation to Political Participation and Trust

Our focus group participants indirectly raised the question of whether or not ethnic diversity engenders or inhibits social cohesion. Several participants expressed feelings of confinement in a specific ethnic or sociocultural group along with isolation from mainstream society. This did not foster strong solidarity or trust for the majority group. In this sense, focus group discussions validated the "conflict theory" that states that isolation fosters out-group distrust. However, two factors seem to change this conflict situation: the density of the minority group (for example, the percentage of the locality that is composed of members of that minority) and the cultural and social diversity of the whole population in the locality. For example, a 2008 British study showed that the density of ethno-religious minorities within a culturally diverse environment always leads to higher voter turnout among those minorities.[14] Therefore, density was far more significant than diversity per se in terms of minority political and civic participation. Interestingly, the same survey shows that the density of the Muslim population has a negative effect on the non-Muslim majority turnout in a given area.[15] In other words, diversity and density did not decrease political participation among Muslims but did negatively affect political engagement of members of the majority population.

Other surveys, however, have illustrated the opposite trend and assert that, in fact, ethnic diversity has a negative effect on trust and social cohesion. This theory, known as the "constrict theory," has become prominent in the United States.[16] In the European context, however, it is not systematically validated by the existing data. Some surveys have shown that ethnic diversity limits social trust. For example, a Dutch study (2007) focusing on the neighborhood level concluded that diversity has a negative impact on individual trust among neighbors. But, diversity has also a positive impact on intra-ethnic trust, which means individuals tend to trust the other groups less and trust their own ethnic groups more.[17]

Similarly, a 2010 study conducted across 19 different countries with various types of immigrants concludes that "diversity is detrimental to a vibrant civil society."[18] However, the authors nuanced their conclusions by emphasizing the role of "institutional arrangements" in how diversity affects a society. In a country of "greater economic insecurity, residents might feel more threatened by immigration and, therefore, withdraw more from collective life." The study ultimately concedes that any relationship between immigration and collective mindedness is mediated by institutional structures and state policies. If immigration is threatening—economically or culturally— it leads to "hunkering down." Although this survey confirmed that social cohesion can be hindered by ethnic diversity, it also emphasized that institutional arrangements can potentially work to counter such a hindrance. For example, in the 1970s, Sweden and the Netherlands began implementing multicultural policies, such as funding for ethnic or immigrant organizations and non-majority language learning, along with public recognition of immigrants. These policies have promoted social cohesion and have provided immigrants with support and symbolic legitimacy that have increased their "overall 'stocks' of social capital as immigrant populations grow."[19] The authors also made clear that the hunkering down concerns *the majority* groups, not so much the Muslim or immigrant groups.[20]

Overall, no clear trend emerges from these different surveys to confirm either the conflict or the constrict (hunkering down) theories. Altogether, though, these studies do shed light on a few factors that influence the positive or negative effects of ethnic diversity on social cohesion. First, it seems that, in European contexts, the *majority groups* more than the minorities tend to hunker down in an ethnically diverse environment. Such results indirectly confirm our analysis of chapter 1 that majority groups tend to externalize and exclude Muslim minorities as the internal and external enemy. Second, institutional arrangements and existing policies also affect social trust in the context of an ethnically diverse community. Finally, for minority groups, other elements, such as ethnic density cumulated with class and socioeconomic levels, facilitate or prevent social cohesion.

Due to these complex layers of factors, scholarly work has political weight. Specifically, it is very important to develop analyses that take into account *context-level variables,* such as policy making, institutions, and majority/ minority divides, in order to avoid sweeping generalizations on the positive or negative influence of ethnic diversity that can be politically instrumentalized. For this reason, scholars should be aware of the political use of their generalizations, such as the often blanket assertion that "ethnic diversity leads to hunkering down."[21]

As we will discuss in chapter 5, critique of ethnic diversity as eroding social cohesion in Europe has become a staple of the anti-immigration discourse along with the critique of multiculturalism. The underlying assumption of this discourse is that immigrants are the ones who show insufficient trust or eagerness to participate in mainstream society, especially if they have a Muslim background. The more general the argument concerning the negative effects of ethnic diversity, the more public traction it gains for politicians and pundits who want to make a case against immigration and welfare politics, even if the premise of such an argument is not validated by empirical data.

Conclusion: Social and Cultural Contexts Impact the Influence of Religion on Political Participation

Three major conclusions can be drawn from the analysis above. First, the gap is not between religious Muslims and "secular" Europeans or Americans but rather between the European and American contexts in which Muslims are living. Across European countries, the level of self-declared religiosity in the general population is systematically much lower than among Muslim groups, while in the United States, this is not the case. In other words, the general context of religiosity and social legitimacy of religions in each country is the real discriminatory factor that must be understood to grasp the situation of Islam and Muslims.

Second, Muslims—who by all indicators attend religious services more frequently than any other group in Europe and declare themselves to be more religious—should be more politically and civically engaged. However, this does not correspond to the data presented in chapters 2 and 3. Instead, Muslims participate in the formal political process less than the average non-Muslim in Europe. At the same time, they show an equivalent level of trust and political loyalty to mainstream institutions. This also is true in the United States, as Muslims demonstrate levels of religiosity comparable to other faiths but simultaneously appear politically less engaged than other religious groups. Again, these differences may be due to other factors—including race, ethnicity, class, and immigrant status—that may weigh more heavily than Islam on political participation. Undeniably, more data is needed to evaluate accurately which forms of religiosity influence the various forms of political participation.

Finally, the ethnic density of Muslims and their isolation in certain urban areas seem to negatively influence their trust vis-à-vis the community at large. However, on the opposite side, ethnic density appears to facilitate political participation among Muslim immigrants. That is to say, when Muslims are a significant ethnic or religious group among several other cultural or ethnic groups, they seem to show more trust in relation to the whole local community. At the same time, non-Muslims in Europe demonstrate a lower level of trust for the majority group when a part of a more ethnically diverse community.

In sum, this research cannot definitively conclude that the more religious an individual Muslim is, the more politically active he or she becomes. Other dimensions, such as ethnic affiliation, immigrant status, and residential distribution, seem to affect the level and intensity of political participation. Unfortunately, none of these dimensions have been systematically and comparatively examined for Muslims in Europe and in the United States. Three take aways from our research could serve as a starting place for future investigation:

1. Further research is needed to distinguish Islam as a marker of identity group from Islam as personal faith. The former more positively influences political participation. This is counterintuitive at a time when Islam is defined as a collective ideology opposed to the West.

2. *Context-level* variables, such as local and/or regional ethnicity, religious makeup, and institutional arrangements should be taken into account in order to establish relevant correlation between Islam and political participation.

3. The political culture and existing norms of the region and nations in which Muslims live need to be identified, due to their importance on the shaping of Muslim identities.

For now, our findings indicate that religious assertiveness or practice cannot be proven as an impediment to Muslim political participation. Why, then, is this assumption largely unchallenged in Europe and even gaining ground in the United States? We will respond to this question in the next chapters.

PART II

STRUCTURAL CONDITIONS OF THE EXTERNALIZATION OF ISLAM

Overview

Several factors influence the externalization of Islam. For Western Europe, where a vast majority of Muslims have an immigrant background and low socioeconomic status, the crisis of the welfare state and pauperization of the middle classes contribute to the demonization of Islam. For these reasons, a substantial body of literature on labor, immigration, and welfare policies argues that immigration can be a disadvantage for recipient states while at the same time an advantage for immigrants themselves.[1] In other words, immigrants are able to get employment in these countries, but existing labor markets are then strained due to the influx of additional workers, which overall adds to the pressure of welfare budgets in these States.

Our position is that these structural conditions indeed influence the externalization process. However, they cannot explain why integration policies are increasingly evaluated on cultural terms and, therefore, are perceived as a failure, even when they have not failed.

Integration and incorporation of immigrants have several dimensions and different meanings. The socio economic dimension has been the object of numerous studies that provide a more positive picture of Muslim immigrants.[2] For example, in contrast with the pessimistic political discourse, employment and education integration policies have been quite good in some European countries (the United Kingdom) and not so much in others (France).[3]

Another significant dimension that is at the core of our research is political integration that includes access to institutions, political representation, and political participation. Concerning political representation, the United Kingdom is also scoring better than France and Germany, both at the local and national level.[4] As noted by the authors of a 2013 report on Muslim political participation in the UK, there has been, since the 1990s, a steady increase of Muslim councillors at the local level, as well as of engagements between Muslim groups and local and national governemental agencies.

During the same time, however, the authors point at the paradox which is at the core of our own investigation, by noting that the public discourse on Muslims and Islam has worsened.[5] The paradox turns into irony, when as discussed in chapters 2 and 3, even when their political integration is very low, Muslims do not show decreased levels of trust or positive evaluation of national customs and institutions of the country in which they live.

As Martin Schain rightly points out, "The integration problem confronting now French and other European governments resembles the class crisis of the twentieth century, which posed a constant challenge to the democratic order."[6] At the time, the solution for the class crisis came from a gradual integration of the working class into the political system. So why is the current situation of Muslim immigrants framed in cultural rather than political terms?

We consider that the international conditions of war on terror (chapter 5), the specificities of European secular cultures (chapter 6), and the global competition of ideas illustrated by Salafism (chapter 7) are cumulative factors that contribute to the culturalization of integration politics and, therefore, the demonization of Islam.

SECURITIZATION OF ISLAM IN EUROPE: THE EMBODIMENT OF ISLAM AS AN EXCEPTION*

Europaean nations face a paradox: even though they seek to facilitate the socioeconomic integration of Muslims, antiterrorism and security concerns fuel a desire to compromise liberties and restrict Islam from the public space. The securitization paradigm encompasses the multifaceted process through which the normal rule of law is suspended in favor of exceptional measures justified by extraordinary situations that threaten the survival of the political community. As noted by Weaver and Buzan, the initial authors of this paradigm, securitization operates outside the domain of "normal politics," because it aims to respond to an existential threat.[1] In the case of Islam, it involves political actors who apprehend Islam as an existential threat to European and American political and secular order and thereby argue for extraordinary measures to contain it. A successful securitization rests on the capacity of a securitizing actor (primarily state officials and politicians) to "speak security," namely, to present a certain problem as a significant menace that challenges the survival of a referent group or community, in a way that resonates with a "significant audience." In this regard, Islamic extremism, especially since 9/11 and 7/7, has become a key security issue across the Atlantic.

The dominant paradigm within securitization studies pays attention to the securitization of Islam through extraordinary speech acts, such as the justification for the War on Terror and the persistent conflation of Islam with political violence.[2] In our first chapter, we provided an overview of the political discourse that pictures Islam and Muslims as the Enemy. In this chapter, we will highlight the intellectual dimension of this public discourse. Arguments from intellectuals or artists grant the securitization of Islam a greater legitimacy that transcends partisan politics, especially when, as we shall see, some of these intellectuals are Muslim themselves. Our analysis however, departs from the dominant securitization approach by analyzing, not only discourses but also political measures indirectly related to terrorism, such as immigration policies and administrative measures limiting Islamic practices. In other words, we focus on political

actions targeting Muslims within the bounds of regular political procedures. In this regard, ordinary legal or political work can be used to reinforce the perception of Islam and Muslims as the typical "others within
the West." Consequently, Muslims are under increased political scrutiny
and control, especially those who assert their religious affiliation through
dress code and engagement in public religious activities. Furthermore,
the signs of these activities, such as mosques and minarets, have become
highly suspect.

This chapter examines these matters for the countries where we conducted our focus groups—France, the United Kingdom, the Netherlands,
Germany, and the United States. We deliberately did not include antiterrorism policies that have been studied at length since 9/11.[3] By exploring the
culturalization of policies like immigration or citizenship, we broaden up
the apprehension of Islamophobia, usually defined as anti Islamic speech or
acts of discrimination or abuse against Muslims.

The embodiment of the securitization or exceptionalism of Islam in daily
political practices is reinforced by what Mahmood Mamdani refers to as
"cultural talk" in *Good Muslim, Bad Muslim*.[4]

The Rise of Anti-Islamic Discourse

The cultural talk essentializes Islam as a unified ideology spreading from
Europe all the way to Iraq and Afghanistan. In this perspective, Muslims
are determined by history and fit a mold from which they cannot escape,
defined by their so-called conformity to the past and incapacity to address
the current challenges of political development and liberal religious thinking. Such an approach justifies the imaginary creation of an insurmount-
able boundary between modern and premodern times, between secularism
and Islam, and, therefore, supports exceptional political measures to
fight against ensuing anti-modern and anti-Western forces.[5] The cultural talk operates under the assumption that Islam is a radical ideology
and, therefore, cannot be treated like all other religions. As mentioned
in chapter 1, this position is expressed by politicians. It is also conveyed
by prominent intellectual and public figures. Most notably, political
commentator Oriana Fallaci's book *The Rage and the Pride*, published in
2002, depicts Muslims as members of a warlike religion bent on destroying Italy's Christian society. The book sold at least 1.5 million copies and
was adopted by various right-wing political movements. In Spain, political
science professor Antonio Elorza argued that Islam is a "religion of com-
bat" that defends terrorism as a "legitimate defense,"[6] a position shared
by Professor Fernando Reinares, who opposes Muslim migration since it
may allow entrance to Islamist terrorists.[7] In the Netherlands, philosophy professor Herman Philipse has claimed that Islam is a violent tribal
culture incompatible with modernity and democracy; law professor Paul
Cliteur claims that religion causes violence and sees secularization as the

only solution; and political scientist Paul Scheffer stirred public debate by seriously questioning the viability of multicultural societies by critically looking at Muslim immigrants.[8]

Furthermore, the intellectuals garnering attention are being praised rather than disputed. In France, a pamphlet by Caroline Fourest, "La Sensation obscurantiste," which is a warning for the fascination of the Left with radical Islam, won an award from the French Assembly in 2006. This kind of speech is presented as courageous truth-telling in the face of moral relativists and dangerous Muslims. In the same vein, a trend of anti-Islamic literature has emerged in Europe. Some titles in French include *Les islamistes sont déjà là: Enquête sur une guerre secrete* (Deloire, 2004) and *La France malade de l'islamisme: Menaces terroristes sur l'Hexagone* (Sifaoui, 2002).

In the United Kingdom, Richard Dwakins, Christopher Hitchens, and Sam Harris, also known as the "Unholy Trinity," are recognized academics who use science to denigrate religion in general and Islam in particular. They are at the forefront of the movement of New Atheism for which Islam represents all the evil aspects of religion, in contrast with past atheists who were targeting Christianity.[9]

The evolutionary biologist, Richard Dawkins, declared on March 21 2013: "Of course you can have an opinion about Islam without having read Qur'an. You don't have to read Mein Kampf to have an opinion about Nazism."[10]

Neuroscientist turned into leading atheist figure, Sam Harris is also very active in the anti Islam campaign. In one of his publication *Letter to a Christian Nation* (2006), he wrote that to think that Islam is a 'peaceful religion hijacked by extremists' is a particularly dangerous fantasy. In the same vein, Christopher Hitchens, journalist and essayist who passed away in 2011, wrote a book called God is not Great: How Religion Poisons Everything (2007) seen as the foundational act of this new atheism movement, in which he vigorously attacked all monotheisms, including Islam.

Bernard Lewis, renown historian of the Middle East and emeritus professor at Princeton University, wrote a book titled What Went Wrong?: The Clash Between Islam and Modernity in the Middle East (2002) in which he considers the decline of the Islamic civilization the main reason for the 9/11 attacks. In the same vein, Daniel Pipes, American historian and political commentator who has held a number of faculty positions at American Universities and is currently director of the Middle East Forum think tank, has been supportive of the extreme-right Dutch parliamentarian, Geert Wilders.[11] In response to the 2012 film "The Innocence of Muslims" mocking the prophet Mohammed, he stated that over time and being "exposed to our way [western norms], which is freedom to blasphemy and to mock" Muslims would become accustomed to western norms.[12]

Thomas Friedman, essayist and journalist at The New York Times, has been criticized by several Middle East and Islamic scholars, for his anti-Islamic language and reasoning that suggest Muslims have not been outspoken enough against terrorism, and thus must in some way be supportive of it.[13]

We could also mention German public intellectual, Thilo Sarrazin, author in 2010 of the controversial book titled Deutschland schafft sich ab (*Germany Does Away With Itself* or *Germany Abolishes Itself*) in which he warns that Germans could become "strangers in their own country" because of the unknown effects that integration of immigrant Muslims could have on society, as he argues that Muslims are not compatible with German society.[14]

What is at stake in the emergence of these intellectual figures in the public debate, is not the critique of Islam or religion but the use of polemicist and populist arguments by scholars or academics, otherwise respected for their intellectual rigor.

Two other trends in current political discourse are worth mentioning. First, the distinction between radical, "bad" Islam and law-abiding, "good" Islam has become a common political frame. The fact that Muslims must be named as good or law-abiding shed light on the underlying assumption that there is such a thing as "bad" Islam and that it can be a menace to society.[15] The second trend is the rise of Muslim spokespeople, who criticize Islam. As members of the minority, these spokespeople can voice criticism that would seem unduly harsh if made by the majority population. It is interesting to note that most of these mediatized critics are women. Probably the most celebrated is Ayaan Hirsi Ali, a former Dutch legislator born in Somalia. She particularly gained media attention as the script author of the film that cost Theo Van Gogh his life. For several years, she was regarded as an expert on Islam and, thus, a plausible critic of it in Dutch public life. She switched her political allegiance from left to right as her prominence in this debate increased, and her message found more resonance with right wing parties. She has declared that even moderate forms of Islam are fundamentally incompatible with liberal democracy and called the Prophet Muhammad "a pedophile" and "a perverse tyrant." Her Muslim origin lends her opinions a form of legitimacy denied to non-Muslim critics of Islam even though she has publicly stated that she does not consider herself a Muslim. She is the author of two international bestsellers, *Infidel* (2007) and *Nomad: From Islam to America; A Personal Journey through the Clash of Civilizations* (2010), which extended her reputation as a fervent critic of Islam in the United States and even granted her in 2013 an affiliation with the Harvard Kennedy School of Government.

Similarly, Irshad Manji, a Canadian author and journalist, strongly advocates for reform within Islam and is a well-known critic of traditional Islamic practices. Her book *The Trouble with Islam Today* (2005) was both hailed and denounced for its critique on Muslims' apparent inability to adapt to modern ideas. In the same vein, Necla Kelek, a prominent German feminist and social scientist, is best known for opposing the "oppression" of women in Islam and strongly believes that Islamic ideals are inherently incompatible with Western society. Her vocal activism against arranged marriages made her a popular writer for conservative forums and outlets in German society.

Securitization of Islam and Its Consequences on Policy Making

As we have discussed, concerns for transnational Islamic terrorism have led to increased security measures that affect *national* populations, therefore, blurring the line between international and domestic policies. In other words, aspects of sociopolitical integration—including education, urban development, and economic integration—are increasingly interpreted through the lens of culture and Islam, while concerns about socioeconomic development or social mobility are increasingly conflated with the War on Terror and with Islam. Consequently, policies concerning immigration, citizenship, and the regulation of religion in the public sphere have become culturalized. Similar culturalization processes can be observed in American policies too.

Culturalization of Immigration and Citizenship

Since 9/11, measures have been taken by all European countries to restrict immigration flows by raising the requirements that the newcomers must meet. We should be careful, however, not to simply assume that these various measures are solely directed toward Muslim immigrants, but since Muslims constitute a significant part of the immigration flows to Europe, they do face new cultural barriers when applying for a residence permit, a visa, or for citizenship. This section elucidates these culturalized barriers in more detail and carefully situates them within their national contexts. Although 9/11 has justified the greater criminalization of immigrants and reinforced control measures, we have chosen not to include US immigration policy in this section, as its culturalization was less strong than the European examples discussed below.

In the Netherlands, the culturalization of immigration policies is part of the government's overall goal since the 1970s to reduce the flows of immigrants and asylum seekers.[16] Another factor that influences the culturalization of immigration is the national debate on integration and the effectiveness of multiculturalism. These two factors combined, resulted in a series of restrictions, which are described below.

The introduction of civic integration courses in 1998 greatly changed the immigration landscape in the Netherlands. The controversial Integration of Newcomers Act (WIN) stipulated that civic integration courses become mandatory and influenced all ensuing legislation.[17] It was complemented by a Dutch language examination as of March 5, 2006.[18] Migrants who wanted to join their spouses henceforth had to pass a "civic integration test abroad" (*inburgeringsexamen buitenland*) at the Dutch embassy in their country of residence. As part of the study material, applicants had to buy a video titled "Coming to the Netherlands," which included images of gay men kissing and topless women lying on the beach. This video was very controversial at the time of its introduction because it seemed to be designed to provoke Muslim migrants.

Minister R. Verdonk sarcastically commented at the time, "If they can't stomach it, they need not apply."[19] A spokeswoman of the ministry, Maud Bredero, explained in a televised interview broadcasted on Channel 4: "We are still open but we want people to be like us. We don't want differences in Holland. We just want the same rights and the same opportunities."[20] The voices of immigrants themselves also are used, and an immigrant named "Akim" was interviewed in the film. His life was said to be "different from how Akim had imagined it to be," after which he declared: "If someone from abroad is planning to come here, I would tell them 'think hard about what you are doing.'" In essence, it is obvious that the film used a variety of techniques to communicate to its viewers that the Netherlands was among the least attractive destinations for Muslims planning to come to Western Europe.

Since 2007, new immigrants no longer have to attend a civic integration course but they still have to pass a civic integration exam to be eligible for a permanent residence permit. In a further development, civic integration duty (*inburgeringsplicht*) became mandatory to immigrants who arrived in the Netherlands before 1998 (*oudkomers*), which mostly involves people on welfare and spiritual leaders like imams.[21] The civic integration exam must be passed within five years after an *oudkomer* has been summoned by the municipality. If the person fails the test, he or she can be fined. Furthermore, immigrants are now required to pay for the integration courses, although loans are available from the municipality.[22]

In the same vein, since 2004, the conditions for family reunification and formation are stricter. The age at which a person can bring over a partner has been raised from 18 to 21, and the partner residing in the Netherlands should earn 120 percent of the legal minimum wage. An exception is made for spouses from the United States, Japan, Switzerland, Australia, and European Union member states. These exceptions are based on bilateral treaties, but they also reflect the fear that people from other countries are more likely to be economic immigrants who use marriage as a way to enter the country. Since 2006, a significant drop in family applications has been recorded.[23]

The success of these increasing restrictions on immigration is mixed. Between 2001 and 2005, there was more emigration than immigration, which may be attributed to the new, strict anti-immigration policies put into place by the 2002 government and the 1998 requirements. However, in 2010, the Netherlands received 150,000 immigrants, which was the highest number of annual newcomers ever.[24] Interestingly, only 24 percent of these immigrants were of non-Western origin, while the remainder consisted of European citizens (40 percent) and Dutchmen returning from abroad (30 percent, among whom were a substantial number of Dutch citizens with a non-Western background who had moved back to their homelands but decided to return to the Netherlands).

The securitization of Islam also has significantly influenced Dutch integration policies. In the 1980s, the Dutch government pursued an explicitly multicultural policy to integrate newcomers through which cultural diversity was institutionalized in areas such as education and public broadcasting. In the 1990s, the focus of integration policies shifted from cultural preservation to labor market integration by providing equal opportunities to the four main immigrant groups in the Netherlands (Turks, Surinamese, Moroccans, and Antilleans). Their socioeconomic status remained greatly disadvantaged, and minority youth were overrepresented in crime statistics. Education in immigrants' native languages was limited and the importance of learning Dutch was stressed.[25]

The turning point in the growing conflation of immigration and Islam in the Netherlands was 9/11. The political trajectory of Pim Fortuyn illustrates this major shift. As the leader of the Leefbaar Nederland (Liveable Holland) party, he expressed himself boldly, calling Islam a "backward religion" and saying that the "leftwing church" has pampered immigrants at the expense of native Dutch citizens. He also argued that the Netherlands should close its borders to all immigrants, including refugees, until those already present are fully integrated. The years of political correctness regarding immigrant issues seemed to be over. It was—and is—often remarked that Fortuyn "said what people had been thinking all along."[26] Fortuyn dearly paid for breaking these taboos as the Leefbaar Nederland party leader fired him for having argued in an interview with *De Volkskrant*, a major newspaper, that the equality section of the constitution should be revoked. Fortuyn moved on to establish his own party, the Lijst Pim Fortuyn or LPF.

Fortuyn's political career came to an abrupt end when he was killed on May 6, 2002, one week prior to the general elections.[27] It was the first political assassination in the Netherlands in centuries. However, even without its leader, LPF came in second position with 26 seats, representing 17.6 percent of all votes. It entered into a coalition with the Christen Democrats (CDA), which pushed toward a hardening of immigration policies. In a symbolic gesture, the Ministry of Integration and Metropolitan Issues was reformed into a ministerial position for Integration and Immigration and was placed within the Justice Department, thus, linking immigration and immigrants to crime.

Despite LPF's major loss of seats in the 2003 elections, the discourse against immigrants in general—and Muslim immigrants in particular—has maintained its focus on the defense of Western norms and values. Consequently, the Integration Policy New Style was introduced to foster emotions of shared citizenship based on common norms and values.[28] Two years later, the minister of Integration and Alien Affairs, Rita Verdonk, argued that the time when public authorities merely engaged with Muslim association by "cozy tea drinking" was over, and that it was crucial that autochthonous populations and newcomers not be afraid to mutually criticize one another.[29] The suggestion that there should be more room for "mutual critique" in practice, however, has resulted in more room for Dutch politicians and "native" Dutch citizens to critique Muslims and Islam.

In the 2006 elections, the LPF lost political momentum but the debate on integration and immigration has continued to be as polemical as ever. Geert Wilders, who has made a name for himself with extremist statements about Muslims, warned about a "tsunami of Islamization" hitting the Netherlands and has emerged as the contender for Fortuyn's heritage. More controversial actions, such as suggesting a complete ban on the Qur'an and calling it a "fascist book" contributed to his fame. After the 2007 elections, his Partij voor de Vrijheid (Freedom Party, PVV) was given 9 seats in parliament, which increased to 24 seats in the 2010 elections.[30]

In accordance with the stricter approach toward immigrant integration in general, citizenship requirements, too, have been tightened.[31] Granting citizenship is no longer seen as a means for facilitating integration but more as a reward that should only be given to people who have proven that they have integrated successfully. To test the integration level of citizenship applicants, the naturalization exam was reformed in 2003. Unlike the previous exam, which was oral, the new one is a written test that assesses both the applicant's language proficiency and his or her knowledge of Dutch culture and society. The introduction of the new test has led to a further decrease in the naturalization rate, which since 2005 has been around 3 percent. Furthermore, proposals to revoke citizenship rights within certain circumstances and plans for the expulsion of criminal nonnationals from the Netherlands gained followers.[32]

As a consequence of the increased culturalization of citizenship, the government introduced at the end of the 1990s a terminology that distinguished between "autochthon" and "allochthon" Dutchmen. Autochthones are defined as people whose parents are both born in the Netherlands and "allochthones" are persons of whom at least one parent is born outside the Netherlands.[33] Further official distinctions are made between so-called Western and non-Western allochthones, whereby Western allochthones include not only Europeans and North Americans but also Japanese and Indonesian nationals.[34] In 2010, more than half of the total number of three million allochthones (around 15 percent of the population) was deemed non-Western and half of this group was Muslim. The largest national-ethnic communities among Muslims were Turks, Moroccans, and Surinamese.[35]

These changes in immigration and integration policies illustrate how Islam and Muslim populations in the Netherlands have become mired by the popular tune of the "need for civic integration" and are increasingly perceived as posing specific cultural challenges to integration. Moreover, all kinds of societal issues—from domestic violence to youth delinquency—are lumped together related to Islam. Consequently, religious diversity and Islam are represented not as parts of a developing Dutch society but as a result of immigration and extraneous to some sort of "pure" version of it.

In Germany, although the 2001 immigration policy shifted toward inclusiveness by automatically granting German citizenship to all children of foreigners up to age 23 after eight years of legal residence, newer policies have created barriers for immigrants.[36] In 2004, the then-coalition of the SPD and the Greens introduced Germany's first Immigration Law (Zuwanderungsgesetz). It initiated an active integration policy with a focus on restricting new immigration. According to this law, only temporary immigration of qualified individuals and immigration based on family reunification premises are legal. In addition, since January 2005, new immigrants are obliged to attend integration courses taught by the new Federal Bureau for Migration and Refugees (BAMF). The courses convey general knowledge on Germany, the state system, and the German language, and a final test must be passed successfully.

The naturalization of Muslims continues to be a topic of heated debate in Germany. For instance, in 2005, the German commissioner for Integration, Migration, and Refugees wrote in her report *Beauftragten der Bundesregierung für Migration, Flüchtlinge und Integration* (Federal Commission on Immigration, Integration, and Refugees) that naturalization has been denied to members of the IGMG (Islamische Gemeinschaft Mili Görüsch)[37] and members of similar organizations on the grounds of their "strife against the constitution." Furthermore, the German Interior Intelligence Service has provided information on membership to these discredited organizations. This practice has been justified by German laws against international terrorism (Gesetz zur Bekämpfung des internationalen Terrorismus) since January 2002.

In the case of IGMG membership, courts have made different decisions in various German states. Whereas a number of courts decided that mere membership is an indicator of hostility toward the German Constitution, others argued that the individual has to be found guilty of supporting actual actions against the constitution. Thus, membership of the IGMG alone has not been found sufficient to prove such an action. Due to this ambivalence, some courts have ruled that members are not to be denied citizenship on these grounds.[38] Contradicting decisions on similar cases have led to different standards in the German naturalization process.

Another discussion focuses on the guidelines for investigations concerning applications for naturalization in the state of Baden-Württemberg in January 2006. The investigations were meant to expose dishonest applicants when pledging the oath of allegiance to the German Constitution as required by the new citizenship law of 2000. It soon became obvious that only applicants from the 57 member states of the Islamic Charta had to be interviewed with a special questionnaire on "democratic and moral attitudes." Other candidates were subjected to the procedure only in exceptional cases, when their honesty was doubted by a state official. The test asked applicants about their opinions on religious freedom, equality of the sexes, homosexuality, freedom of expression, the concept of honor, and forced marriage. Questions included: "Do you think a wife should obey her husband and that he can beat her if she is disobedient?" "Would you allow your daughter to participate in sports and swimming classes at school?" "What do you think of the fact that parents forcibly marry off their children?" and "Do you think such marriages are compatible with human dignity?"

The practice was heavily criticized, especially by representatives of the Green Party, the social democrats, and the liberals. They demanded that the citizenship tests be employed based on the principles of equality, with no special reference to the religion of the applicant. After a long and controversial discussion among the secretaries for Interior Affairs of the German Länder (states), a final compromise was found on May 6, 2006. The questions about opinions and attitudes toward the so-called Western values were abolished, and all German states now hold the same criteria for naturalization. Knowledge about Germany, its constitution, the democratic structure of the state, and proficiency in the German language remain obligatory. This knowledge can be obtained in special citizenship courses.[39]

In France, too, immigration and civic integration have become increasingly linked to Islamic concerns. The influence of Islam on the integration process lies at the heart of the debate. The events of 9/11 exacerbated already existing anti-immigration policies and increased legitimacy of strong nationalist discourses exemplified by the results of Jean-Marie Le Pen and the National Front at the 2002 presidential elections.

The right-wing government elected in 2003 issued stricter immigration laws in November and December of the same year. More rigorous family reunification conditions were adopted, and the creation of an electronic database of visa statistics was initiated. Deporting individuals who "have committed acts justifying a criminal trial" or whose behavior "threatens public order" became substantially easier as well. Earlier versions of this law empowered police forces to deport foreigners for participating in political demonstrations. France also drew up a list of "safe countries" from which asylum seekers would henceforth be denied.[40]

Police repression was one of the key themes under the leadership of former interior minister Nicolas Sarkozy. However, in 2005, events spiraled out of control when riots erupted and youth mobs wreaked havoc in a number of French *banlieues*. The incident was a turning point in the hardening of immigration laws. The second anti-immigration law presented to the National Assembly in May 2006 greatly restricted the conditions for immigration, the duration of the stay of foreigners in France, and the possibility to obtain French nationality. The law also increased the period after which immigrants could legally file a request for family reunion from 12 months to 19 months. Perhaps most stigmatizing was the emphasis on an "integration contract"—first discussed by the Stasi Commission and already included in the 2003 law—that became mandatory. It entailed "civic trainings" and, if necessary, language courses for all immigrants.

Left-wing politicians in France also share responsibility for the increased culturalization of immigration issues. Malek Boutih, former president of the antiracist organization SOS-Racisme and national secretary of the Social Party in charge of social affairs from 2003 to 2008, defended a sort of "moral criterion" as a precondition to the immigration policy that would selectively limit immigrant numbers not only based on desired professional skills but also on respect for cultural norms such as laicite (French secularism) and gender equality.[41] This poorly disguised reference to the "Muslim problem" emanating from the left is symptomatic of the rise of "Schmittian liberalism" shared by all sides of the political spectrum.

Cultural justifications of socioeconomic issues have lead to the conflation of social unrest with problems related to Islam and immigration. For example, the 2005 riots in the *banlieues* were attributed by politicans to the influence of Islamic groups, even invoking polygamy as a cause, and promising to expel foreigners involved in the uprisings. The long-term effect of this discourse was investigated by the National Commission for Human Rights (Commission Nationale Consultative des Droits de l'Homme) which explained these extreme statements by the growing hostility toward Muslims as shown in its quantitative surveys.[42]

This cultural talk has contributed to the increased legitimacy of the Far Right's discourse on the cultural incompatibility between Islam and French values. To the point that it is now a shared theme across the ideological landscape. This continuous association of security and culture became clear during the 2012 presidential campaign, when candidate François Hollande said he would firmly support France's ban on the niqab (face veil). He was also very emphatic that there would be no Turkish accession to the European Union during his upcoming five-year presidential term.

In the United Kingdom, little has changed in immigration policies impacting Muslim communities since 9/11 with the exception of the Nationality Immigration, and Asylum Bill, which proposed to repeal certain provisions of the 1999 Immigration and Asylum Act and was adopted in November 2002. The former home secretary David Blunkett announced that the automatic right of asylum seekers to appeal a bail hearing was amended to make sure future "wholly unfounded" claimants could be sent home without appeal. In addition, the bill included proposals for the children of some asylum seekers to be forced to enroll into separate schools instead of the mainstream schools that they were previously allowed to attend.[43]

Generally, asylum seekers who in common parlance include also immigrants, have become more vulnerable than ever.[44] Even before 9/11, a sensational and, often, vitriolic campaign was waged by national tabloid newspapers against them. The *Daily Express* and the *Daily Mail* focused on their perceived negative traits and on their allegedly detrimental effect on British society, in particular on the welfare state. Asylum seekers were depicted as a "threat" and, more importantly, as an unwanted and unnecessary obstacle to societal harmony. Such discourse was given even greater impetus following the acknowledgement that some of the 9/11 perpetrators had resided in European Union countries as asylum seekers.

The 7/7 attacks and the failed London train bombing attempts two weeks later fed into this trend. The *Daily Mail* was particularly active in associating terrorism with Islam. Its headline, "Bombers Came to United Kingdom as Sons of Asylum Seekers," was supplemented with information on the defendant's social benefits over the last five years.[45] The situation of asylum seekers was exacerbated by the disproportionately large share of Muslim voices on the fringes of mainstream opinion granted by the tabloid press. After their establishment as spokespeople for the Muslim community, many of these individuals made for easy victims by exploiting their past as asylum seekers in the United Kingdom. For instance, Omar Bakri Mohammad, the leader of al-Muhajiroun, the European branch of the transnational Islamist group *Hizb ut-Tahrir*,[46] fled the United Kingdom in the aftermath of 7/7 because of a newspaper campaign against him, whilst Abu Hamza al-Masri, the leader of the "Supporters of Shari'a", has since been imprisoned on a number of charges. Much of the media coverage of both men in this period focused on their legal status within Britain and on the fact that they had originally come to Britain as asylum seekers.

In other words, the status of asylum seekers became a target of the securitization process fueled by 9/11 and other events. The large percentage of recent asylum seekers from Muslim countries—in part from the wars in Afghanistan and Iraq—has complicated the situation even further because of Britain's involvement in these ongoing conflicts. In sum, the term "asylum seeker" has become derogatory and operates as a proxy for Muslims, with the rise of very crude and often dehumanizing portrayals in the media.

Restrictions on Islamic Practices and Activities

Besides the culturalization of immigration laws and redefinitions of citizenship, the perception of Muslims as the enemy also has affected the practice of Islam—from the circulation of imams to religious education in schools and use of shari'a.

Chasing the Imams

The expulsion of imams has become a common practice across Europe. Often based on antiterrorist invocations, these actions highlight the precarious status of the profession. From 2001 to 2012, France expelled more than 125 imams.[47] The case of Abdelkader Bouziane perfectly illustrates the situation. After the publication of several statements in a controversial interview that seemed to condone violence against women, a Salafi imam in Vénissieux (Greater Lyon) was hastily expelled from France on April 21, 2004, on the grounds of being a major threat to the state and public security ("nécessité impérieuse pour la sûreté de l'Etat et la sécurité publique"). After Bouziane appealed the court's decision, he was granted the right to return to France. His good fortune did not last long as he would soon be expelled again. This time, a note by the French Intelligence Service accusing Bouziane of having issued a fatwa against American interests in Iraq was invoked in court, but no further evidence was presented to substantiate the accusation.[48] The case raised complicated questions of legal hermeneutics, as the Correctional Court eventually decided that Bouziane's controversial declarations were made in the context of a reference to the Qur'an and could not constitute an incitement to violate a person's physical integrity. Judge Fernand Schir concluded that "the Jurisdiction has no right...to intrude in a domain which belongs to religious conscience."[49]

In the Netherlands, the concern of controlling imams was channeled into providing mandatory civic training sessions for clergy personnel. At the time of this writing, there is still no state-sponsored imam program despite efforts to establish such a facility. While the admission of foreign imams to the Netherlands cannot be prevented due to principles of religious freedom and equal treatment, a mandatory civic integration program for immigrant "clergy" was adopted in 2002. This training program is officially destined for all kinds of immigrant religious personnel, although it is first and foremost intended for new imams and, to a lesser extent, Hindu teachers.[50]

In the United Kingdom, the education and training of imams has been institutionalized and managed professionally since 1981.[51] There are two institutions dedicated to this effect: the Muslim College in London, established in 1981, and the Markfield Institute of Higher Education in Leicestershire, where an ambitious set of courses was created in 2000.[52] Instead of using the term "imam", preference is given to the term "Muslim faith leader" in order to avoid working with different interpretations of the profession within Sunni and Shia Islam. Thus, other roles—chaplain, teacher, youth worker, and the like—often make up part of an imam's responsibilities.

In 2010, the Muslim Faith Leadership Training Review, which evaluates current training provisions for imams and examines how to build the capacity of Islamic seminaries, identified crucial areas of improvement needed in the training and education of Muslim faith leaders. For example, the review pointed out that greater efforts were needed with regard to the roles and perspectives of women, the integration of theological insights with practical experience in initial training, professional development, and better facilitation of relations with the government.[53]

In Germany, top security and law officials agreed to enact in 2008 new computer surveillance regulations to pay more attention to imams. The framework, designed by Interior Minister Wolfgang Schüble of the center-Right Christian Democrats (CDU) and Justice Minister Brigitte Zypries of the center-Left Social Democrats (SPD), has allowed federal security officials to monitor computers in cases related to terrorism or other serious crimes. The new framework complies with a legal ruling made by the country's highest court in February 2009.[54]

The establishment of Islamic studies at universities in Germany has also been a political concern, particularly since 9/11. In 2004, the Turkish Islamic Union for Religious Affairs (DTB, an extension of the Turkish Ministry of Religious Affairs) financed two chairs at Frankfurt's Goethe University. In 2005, the University of Munster established the first study course for Islamic religious teaching (Islamkunde) while the University of Osnabruck followed suit in 2007. In 2009, a new Islamic school was established to train Muslim clergymen in Berlin. The first of its kind in the German capital, the school has the capacity for 68 students and offers six-year training courses to future imams.[55]

Most of Germany's imams grew up and received religious training outside of the country, often in Turkey. Turkey's religious affairs office regularly sends theologians to over 800 German mosques but few come with German language skills. As such, the government established the "Imams for Integration," program which is a joint initiative organized by the Goethe Institute, the Federal Office for Migration and Refugees (BAMF), and the German association of Turkish Muslim congregations (DITIB) that also complements the efforts of the Islamic studies programs at the aforementioned universities and schools. The program consists of 500 hours of German language classes and 12 days of lessons on intercultural and German topics, such as the powers of the state, life in a pluralistic society, religious diversity, the educational system, migration, and community work. Overall, the four-month study program aims to develop imams' potential to be a force for integration and is designed to make them fluent in German culture and language.[56]

The desire to establish a German Islamic theology appears to have become a common cause for all the major political parties in Germany. Islamic theology and the education of Islamic religious teachers and imams are viewed by many as the magic formula for the integration of Muslims. In this context, special attention must be paid to the promotion of young academics in the field of Islamic theology, because at present, there are virtually no eligible German-speaking Islamic theologians available to take up such a cause.[57]

Restraints on Islamic Practices

Convergent with our research, Jonathan Fox and Yasemin Akbaba documented the actual restriction of religious practices across 86 religious minorities in 27 Western democracies from 1990 to 2008.[58] They identified a significant increase in discrimination against Islam in particular, especially post-9/11, which wasn't reflected in the level of intolerance against majority religions, nor against other minority religions. According to our own investigation, the restrictions primarily affect the building of mosques, the mode of Islamic education and women's dress code.

Mosques

It is important to note that extreme political proposals such as banning mosques cannot be legally implemented as they would violate constitutional rights of freedom of religion and equal treatment of all citizens, which is one of the distinctive feature of Western democracies.

In Germany, right-wing radicals established the country's first anti-Islamic Party that launched a vehement national campaign against the building of mosques in 2005. The movement started off as Pro Cologne, to protest the establishment of a mosque in Cologne and has since gained significant followership. Several other groups such as the Pro NRW (Pro North Rhine-Westphalia) initiated campaigns for similar purposes.[59] This group, which holds five city council seats but currently does not hold any seats in the House of Representatives, aims to create alliances with other Far Right groups in Europe, such as Austria's Freedom Party (FPO), to generate larger national and international support for its cause. This initiative directly influenced the campaign of the two Swiss right-wing parties (SVP and EDU) that led to the much mediatized ban of minarets in Switzerland after the Egerkingen Committee, a group composed of leaders of both right-wing political parties, launched a referendum to ban the construction of minarets that was approved by 57.6 percent of voters in 2009. The ban reflected a fear of Islamic fundamentalism, yet "the Federal Council [took] the view that a ban on the construction of new minarets [was] not a feasible means of countering extremists tendencies"[60] and ultimately declared it illegal.

In the same vein, there have been several attempts to stop the building of mosques throughout the United States since the ground zero mosque controversy in 2010. In response to the announcement that a mosque was going to be built two blocks away from the site of the 9/11 terrorist attacks, strong political and social objections were aired. Various politicians and religious leaders in Manhattan demonstrated support for the mosque, more correctly described as an Islamic center, while others, both politicians and bloggers, voiced staunch opposition to the project as well as fueling Islamophobic discourse. Republican representative for New York, Peter King, stated that the project was "particularly offensive" since "so many Muslim leaders have failed to speak out against radical Islam" and, ultimately, "against the attacks" of 9/11. Furthermore, Rock Lazio, a former republican candidate for New York governor, supported statements made by Debra Burlingame, the cofounder of a group called 9/11 Families for a Safe and Strong America, as she voiced her fears that the mosque would "bring people to Islam" and create "a Muslim-dominant America" that would serve as propaganda for "people who want to hurt this country." Most of these statements expressed concerns about the "insensitivity" of a mosque project in ground zero. They illustrate the growing social and cultural vulnerability of Americans ten years after 9/11.

Similarly, in Tennessee, Wisconsin, and California, communities have fiercely protested against mosque projects at various moments during their conception.[61] In 2012, Muslims in St. Anthony, Minnesota, experienced troubles as well. Supporters of the Islamic Center claimed that the city discriminated against Muslims and questioned the city's real motivation behind putting the project on hold while it studied whether the area's industrial zoning would be appropriate for the center's activities.[62] Their justification is the same as in Europe: mosques attract extremists and Islam threatens Western civilization. Opposition to mosque-building is part of a larger movement against the Islamization of America that is illustrated by groups such as Stop Islamization of America (SIOA), Virginia Anti-Shari'a Task Force (VAST), and American Freedom Defense Initiative (AFDI). All collaborate with one another to fight what they consider to be the "infringing nature and presence of Islam in America."[63]

In the United Kingdom, the construction of mosques is not a political issue anymore.[64] Similarly, in France, the project of devising a "French Islam" has ironically provided impetus to a greater legitimacy of Islamic practices, including the construction of "transparent" mosques approved by local political authorities as counterpoints to an informal "Islam of the caves." The construction of minarets, however legal, is usually discouraged to meet neighborhood demands.

Additionally, resistance has not completely disappeared. For example, when the mayor of Strasbourg agreed in 2009 to the building of a mosque in the city, he demanded more vigorous actions of Muslim organization against youth delinquency as a condition for moving along. In Nice, local authorities in 2005 opposed the building of a mosque in the city center, where most Muslims live, on the grounds of potentially furthering "ghettoïsation." A 2004 study commissioned by the Fonds d'Action et de Soutien pour l'Intégration et la Lutte contre les Discriminations (FASILD) (Funds for Integration and Anti Discrimination) established a typology of mayoral attitudes to the construction of visible Muslim places of worship,[65] which reveals a remarkable diversity of attitudes.

Religious Education

Islamic Schools and Islamic Education A second major restriction on the practice of Islam across Western Europe concerns the development of Muslim schools as well as the status of Islamic education in public schools when allowed. This restriction is not grounded in any empirical evidence that Islamic schools are obstructive to integration. In the Netherlands, for instance, reports have concluded that, on the whole, Islamic schools do not obstruct immigrant integration.[66] Investigations by the Inspectorate of Education in 2005 concluded that almost all Islamic schools have an open attitude toward Dutch society and play a positive role in creating the necessary conditions for social cohesion.[67] Michael Merry and Geert Driessen, leading experts on Islamic schools in the Netherlands, write that there is a broader attempt to openly discuss the Dutch school system but Muslims are commonly seen as a threatening political presence in a way that the other groups generally are not. Equality on paper, therefore, has not translated into equality in practice. Notwithstanding the positive reports issued by the Dutch Inspectorate of Education, Islamic schools continue to be viewed with distrust, and elections make Islamic schools easy targets for vilification as unemployment and crime turn popular opinion against the presence of a visible minority groups. Case in point: in the wake of the Van Gogh murder, (2004) some mosques and Islamic schools became targets of vandalism or arson.[68]

Nevertheless, Minister of Education van der Hoeven decided in the spring of 2004 that any new Islamic school must have a school board that only comprises members of Dutch nationality. A general ban on Islamic schools would demand a change of the Dutch Constitution, however, and would imply that other denominational schools would also be closed down. Consequently, a ferocious debate took hold of the public agenda, initiated by Ayaan Hirsi Ali and others. As of 2006, there were 46 Islamic primary schools in the Netherlands with a potential stipulated need of 120 such schools.[69]

In most of the German states, religious education is part of public schools' standard curriculum. Teachers of religion need permission from both the state and their church to practice. Islamic instructors have, however, very often been denied permission to teach Islam by regional governments due to the lack of a clear hierarchy within Muslim organizations, unlike the Protestant Church (see chapter 6 for more details.). The practice of teaching Islam in German schools, thus, becomes very controversial.[70] While Muslim migrant organizations regard themselves as the voice of Muslims in Germany, officials state that only about 20 percent of Muslims[71] are actual members of these organizations. In their opinion, clearly identified Muslims representatives, are therefore, lacking.

Religious education for Muslims in Germany is, thus, practiced very differently from other classes on religion and is often incorporated in native language courses.[72] These classes serve as a proxy for teaching Islam even if they are lawfully open to all students. Since 2000, various test projects have been launched to experiment with new possibilities for teaching religion to Muslims in German. While in North Rhine-Westphalia and Bavaria these initiatives were led by the state, in Berlin[73] and Baden-Württemberg, Islamic organizations are closely involved in their development and realization. In Berlin, the Islamic Federation was authorized to teach Islam, in 2006, although the decision was heavily criticized by the media due to the "Islamist" background of the Federation.[74] In 2003, Bremen established religious courses in German (Islamkunde) for Muslims under state control without the participation of Islamic organizations, mainly to counter the conservative and sometimes Islamist orientation of some of those organizations. Such initiative clearly oversteps the legitimacy of the state in religious matters even though the German concept of secularism is not based on a radical separation of church and state. But, according to the legal status of religion (Staatskirchenrecht), the state's right to regulate religious communities is limited, while religious organizations are encouraged to maintain a strong public presence and to partake in various social and cultural tasks of the state. As a result, the Christian churches and the Jewish community have their own official representatives; they are entitled to membership in various bodies to which the state has delegated certain tasks such as the provision of social services. Such liberties are still not granted to Muslim organizations, as they often operate in a specific political context characterized by a tight cooperation between the state and religious communities.[75] The controversial discussions concerning the state's role in teaching religion to Muslims in German continue to this day.

In the United Kingdom, both schools that receive state funding and private Islamic schools without accreditation from the government, provide religious education. There are 140 private Islamic schools, 11 of which are state funded.[76] Research by the Muslim Council of Britain found that Muslims identified access to quality education as the issue most important to them.[77] But the majority of Muslims continue to be educated in non-Muslim state schools, and many Muslim communities have expressed concern about the ability of these schools to meet their pupils' (language) needs. Many Muslim children will learn to read Arabic in order to read the Qur'an, irrespective of its availability as a curriculum option. Such classes take place in mosques but the quality of the language tuition is unregulated. Since 1997, the Labour government has extended state funding opportunities to include minority faiths. At present, seven Muslim schools receive state funding, including Al Furqan School in Birmingham, Islamia School in London, and Feversham College in Bradford, while an additional quarter of England's independent Muslim schools would be interested in receiving monetary aid. Controversy exists over the expansion of state-funded religious schools as they could potentially hurt multiculturalism and limit integration.

As of 2012, there were 29 Islamic private schools in France, most of which emerged as a consequence of the 2004 law prohibiting religious signs in public schools.[78] A growing number of Muslim parents are seeking to educate their children in confessional schools. In the 2000s, Islamic schools were opened in Aubervilliers (2001), Lille (2003, Lycée Averroes), and Lyon (2007, Lycée Al Kindi), joining the first school established in La Réunion several decades ago. The Lycée Averroes is under contract with the French state and in 2013 was ranked first high school based on its 100% success at the Baccalaureat (the final exam marking the end of high school). In addition to state-mandated courses, the schools offer classes on Arabic and Islam.

Dress Code (Hijab and Niqab ban)

Hijab Ban for Students A third field of restriction on Islamic practices concerns hijab and niqab. In 2004, a law was adopted that prohibited the use of religious signs in French public schools based on the need to defend the principle of *laïcité*.(French secularism)[79] Although the measure did not affect

Muslims alone, its main motivation was to ban the hijab. We will discuss in chapter 6 the meaning of such a ban or similar limitations across Europe in relation to the ongoing redefinition of secularism, even though they were with no doubt precipitated by the post-9/11 securitization context.

The recent increase of burqa bans however is directly related to the perception of assertive Muslims as "the enemy." On April 26, 2006, a proposal to ban the niqab in France from all "Republican territories" was discussed at the National Assembly under the title of "Law proposal seeking to fight against infringements to women's dignity resulting from certain religious practices" by Jacques Myard from the center-right UMP.[80] The proposal recommends criminalizing both the practice of wearing and encouragement to wear the niqab, as well as to expel foreigners found guilty of the offense, again based on the need to defend *laïcité*. The initiative eventually led to a complete ban of the burqa in France in 2010.

The law took effect in April 2011, and there have been varied responses to the ban, with supporters stating that "the face is a person's dignity. The face is your passport…so when you refuse me to see you, I am a victim," and covered women responding that "under no circumstances [will I] stop wearing my veil."[81] The ban received worldwide media coverage, since it was the first measure of its sort in Europe. The international public outside of Europe mostly reacted with astonishment at the apparent infringement of human rights in (formerly) liberal Europe and openly questioned the effectiveness—as not the aggressors but the presumed victims are punished—and proportionality—very small number of women actually wear the burqa in Europe—of the ban.[82] Feminist national organizations fiercely protested against the measure but failed to attract popular support for a "misogynistic symbol of oppression."

Other countries experienced similar restrictive actions. In 2010, the Belgian lower house of parliament passed a ban on the burqa as the first country in Europe, which couldn't be enforced until 2011 for lack of a legitimate government. This is remarkable due to the country's non-explicit secular character, which stands in stark contrast to France's clear stance on *laïcité*. The law was authored by Daniel Bacquelaine, who said that the "burqa is incompatible with basic security as everyone in public must be recognizable and clashes with the principles of an emancipated society that respects the rights of all."[83] The lower house of parliament overwhelmingly voted in favor of the law; not a single MP voted against the measure and two people abstained.[84] Both Amnesty International and Human Rights Watch called upon members to vote against the law.

In the Netherlands, when the Far Right MP Geert Wilders suggested in 2005 that a ban on the burqa was necessary for "security reasons," Minister Verdonk happily took up the suggestion and promised to investigate the matter.[85] The investigation eventually led to the approval of the ban by the Dutch cabinet in all public spaces in January 2012, which has not been put into effect at the time of this writing. Critics have argued that the number of Muslim women actually wearing the burqa in the Netherlands is so small (ranging from a handful to around 100) that a special "legal ban on the burqa" mainly serves political interests of politicians who want to show that they are "tough on Islam." In several Dutch cities, such as Amsterdam and Utrecht, policy proposals have been introduced to reduce the unemployment benefits for women wearing a burqa. Local authorities argue that by wearing it, women seriously reduce their chances of finding a job in the Netherlands.

In anticipation of the controversy that will rise if the ban takes effect, Deputy Prime Minister Verhagen stated that it was not explicitly a ban on religious clothing and emphasized "that uncovered faces are an important part of 'open' communication in Dutch society."[86] Verhagen further explained that "the ban was intended to ensure that a tradition of open communication cherished in Dutch society was upheld and to prevent people from concealing their identity in order to do harm."[87] Maurits Berger, professor of Islam at Leiden University, has opposed the ban and stated that it would apply only to "a few hundred women" in the Netherlands. Furthermore, he emphasized that the ban is "highly symbolic, it is part of the deal made with the PVV [Party for Freedom or Partij voor de Vrijheid]...we are in the middle of a crisis [*sic*]. There are worse things to tackle."[88]

In Germany, the Christian Democrats (CDU) of the German state of Hesse have also launched a debated on the burqa ban in January 2012. Politician Alexander Bauer led the discussion on behalf of his party, "People have to be willing to 'show their face' if they live in Germany," he is alleged to have said.[89] As in France, it has become a major political issue.

In contrast to these continental situations, Britain has declared that it would not follow France in banning Muslim women from wearing in public as such a move would run contrary to the conventions of a "tolerant and respectful society." Immigration Minister Damian Green said that the move to ban women from wearing face veils would be "rather un-British" in an interview with the *Sunday Telegraph*, despite in July 2010 opinion poll showing widespread public support for such an action.[90] Claiming it would be "undesirable" for Parliament to vote on a burqa ban in Britain similar to that approved in France, he said:

> We're a tolerant and mutually respectful society...Very few women in France actually wear the burqa. They (the French parliament) are doing it for demonstration effects. The French political culture is very different. They are an aggressively secular state. They can ban the burqa, they ban crucifixes in schools, and things like that. We have schools run explicitly by religions. I think there's absolutely no read-across to immigration policy from what the French are doing about the burqa.[91]

The minister's comments could have dismayed the growing number of British supporters of such a ban—a YouGov survey found in April 2011 that

67 percent of respondents wanted the wearing of full-face veils to be made illegal. His comments also came after the new head of the Muslim Council of Britain (MCB) said that the United Kingdom was the most welcoming country in Europe for Muslims.[92]

Anti-Shari'a Law in the United States The securitization of Islam reached a new peak in American politics with a wave of anti-shari'a legislation in several states. Womick, a Republican politician in Tennessee, described shari'a as not just an expression of faith but as a political and legal system that seeks world domination. This sentiment is reflected in a growing anti-shari'a campaign,[93] which started in Oklahoma where a bill banning shari'a law was passed by a margin of 70 to 30 percent in a special ballot in November 2010. The Supreme Court of Oklahoma, however, struck down the move stating that it was inappropriate to reference religion in a state law.[94] Three reasons underpinned their ruling. First, the law violated the First Amendment's "Establishment Clause," which says that "Congress shall make no law respecting an establishment of religion." Second, they stated that "the First Amendment mandates governmental neutrality between religion and religion…The State may not adopt programs or practices which aid or oppose any religion."[95] Third, the judges said that "they did not know of even a single instance where an Oklahoma court had applied *shari'a* law or used the legal precepts of other nations or cultures, let alone that such applications or uses had resulted in concrete problems in Oklahoma," and, as such, the amendment didn't seek to solve any problem but rather sought to intimidate and discriminate against Muslim Americans needlessly.[96]

Nevertheless, between 2011 and 2013, 29 states[97] introduced some kind of legislation aiming to ban foreign law, although not specifically shari'a, in the state legislature. Three states—Alabama, Iowa, and New Mexico—called for an amendment to their state constitution to prohibit any further "contamination" from happening. Nine states—Alaska, Florida, Kansas, Oklahoma, South Dakota, Missouri, Indiana, Tennessee, and Virginia—actually had their proposed antiforeign legislation approved at the state level.[98]

Examples of such anti-shari'a laws include Alaska's prohibition to apply foreign laws if they would violate the constitution. "A court, arbitrator, mediator, administrative agency, or enforcement authority" is prohibited "from applying a foreign law if application of the foreign law would violate an individual's right guaranteed by the Constitution of the State of Alaska or the United States Constitution."[99] Missouri also explicitly hails its own and the nation's constitution over potential foreign sources. "Mandates that any court, arbitration, tribunal, or administrative agency ruling shall be unenforceable if based on a foreign law that does not grant the parties the same rights as the parties have under the United States and Missouri constitutions."[100] Indiana, finally, does not waste any more words than strictly necessary: "A court may not apply, enforce, or grant comity, res judicata, claim preclusion, or issue preclusion to a foreign law, ruling, or judgment."[101]

Conclusion: The Paradox of Accommodating Islam

The securitization of Islam does not consist solely of emotionally powerful and politically symbolic speech acts. As described above, it also alters immigration policies by culturalizing their goals and proceedings, which are aiming to limit Muslim presence in accord with European societies' liberal values. The same logic of "civilizing the alien" has led to question the merits of multiculturalism. Prevailing sentiment in European societies favors the rejection of cultural differences. Although an increase in religious diversity is a key issue, the status of cultural diversity is also at stake: as Muslim immigration to Europe increased, a specific integration process was designed, distinct from the older systems such as regionalism in the United Kingdom or pillars in the Netherlands. Initially, the concept of multiculturalism "connoted compromise, interdependence, [and] a relativizing universalism" expected to lead to an "intercultural community." Over time, however, it seemed that multiculturalism meant an institutionalization of difference with "autonomous cultural discourses and separated interactional communities."[102]

In the United Kingdom, the shock of the 7/7 subway attacks by "homegrown bombers" led to increased questioning of the entire possibility of cultural difference. The consensus was that Muslims must become more like some abstractly defined, ideal British citizen. However, this debate began earlier: the Rushdie Affair of 1988 in particular created the conditions for a critique of public culture (see chapter 6). As a counterpoint to its new laws on terrorism and political radicalism, the Blair government pushed for the criminalization of incitement to religious hatred, but the House of Lords restricted the application of the law, limiting it to threatening language rather than the broader rules on insults and abuse desired by the government. Despite the continuing efforts of the Blair government, Parliament maintained the weaker provisions, specifically prohibiting only intentionally threatening words.

In the Netherlands, multiculturalism was the explicit policy of the government since its inception in the mid-1980s.[103] However, since the 1990s, immigrant and minority incorporation policies have placed much greater emphasis on cultural assimilation. "Good citizenship" and "civic integration" became important new policy goals. Minorities were expected to assimilate into the dominant public culture and to maintain any divergent practices in the private sphere. The 1998 Law on the Civic Integration of Newcomers made integration courses compulsory. As part of the continuing debate, there was a parliamentary commission on Dutch Integration policies in 2004.[104] Although the report had some optimistic conclusions, multiculturalism is viewed as a failure in the eyes of the general public. The late Pim Fortuyn made this argument best when he claimed that Muslims were undermining the traditional liberalism of Dutch culture.

A fundamental tenet of French political society is the republican ideal that downplays ethnic and cultural differences. However, faced with the difficulties of integrating its sizable minority population, France has moved toward a pluralist conception that advocates positive discrimination. In 2001, the Constitutional Council recognized that sometimes difference must be recognized in the pursuit of true equality. One solution has been to make nominal distinctions on a territorial, rather than ethnic, basis so the ideal of individual equality can be maintained; priority zones for education are a manifestation of this policy. The creation of the state organization, the Muslim Council, in 2003, can be seen as an attempt to integrate immigrant populations as can the creation of the Ministry for Equal Opportunities, in 2006.

The same boundary between liberal and alien values can be observed in the management of Islamic religious practices, as discussed in this chapter. Such a perspective sheds light on the ambiguity and contradictions of integrating Islam within European societies.

CHAPTER 6

HOW ISLAM QUESTIONS THE UNIVERSALISM OF WESTERN SECULARISM

In March 2000, an atheist association claimed the right to broadcast a message on the nonexistence of God, for several minutes each week in reaction to the call to prayer granted to the grand mosque of Oslo by the municipality.[1] This is one of many examples of the rejection of Islamic signs perceived as a violation of secular principles in Europe that, unlike in the United States, predates 9/11. Since then, more acute crises have occurred across European countries, including the September 2005 Danish cartoon incident; the November 2009 minaret ban in Switzerland; and the 2010 to 2011 wave of niqab bans in France, Belgium, and Spain.

All of these controversies reveal the increasing disjunction between secularism and secularity. I define secularism as the multiple ideological and cultural narratives that Western countries have built to justify separation of religion and politics. Secularity by contrast refers to two major principles—political neutrality of the state vis-à-vis all religions and equality of all religion in public spaces.[2] They can be implemented in multiple legal ways according to the specific political culture and history of each country as the differences among European countries and the United States attest. Ultimately, these specific cultures frame social expectations about the status of religion in public space. Two common denominators of these expectations are separation of religion and politics and the disjunction between private and public behaviors. The requirement of state neutrality vis-à-vis religion is implemented across Europe and in the United States through different forms of differentiation of religion and politics. The private/public separation refers to the split between personal and social behaviors that is expected from citizens acting in public spaces.

Islam presents a challenge to both of those requirements. First, European states have launched initiatives to create representative bodies of Islam that incidentally lead not only to a reshaping of the religion but also to its politicization. Second, Islamic practices from dress code to minaret are seen as a major challenge to the private/public dichotomy.

In Search of the Good Muslims:
How European States Are Reshaping Islam

The principle of political neutrality, does not equate to separation of church and state. If this were the case, France would be the only secular country in Europe. Rather, it refers to differentiation *and* cooperation between church and state.

The differentiation takes three main forms across Europe and the United States. The first form includes the existence of a state religion as well as the extension of rights to other religious groups, as is the case in the United Kingdom and the Scandinavian countries. The second form entails formal agreements of cooperation between state and religious institutions, as is the case in Belgium, Germany, Spain, Italy, and the Netherlands. The third form is the separation between state and religious institutions, as is the case in France and the United States.

Cooperation between state and religious institutions is also implemented in different ways: either the state provides for the teaching of religion in public schools, grants religious organizations free access to public-owned media, or gives direct/indirect funding to religious institutions.[3] Usually, religious organizations must comply with specific state requirements in order to receive this conditional support. For example, religious groups must organize local and national representative bodies to serve as counterparts to state institutions. In countries where a denominational teaching of religion is offered in public schools, as is the case in Germany and Spain, the religious community is required to design a central religious authority that serves as an interlocutor with the state. This authority gives credentials to teachers of religion in public schools, cooperates with state agencies to train the teachers, and approves curricula. For groups with strong religious infrastructure, like the Catholic Church, such requirements are easy to fulfill. But for others, like the Muslims, such institutions have often been built from scratch. The situation is very different in the case of American secularism, which does not necessitate the same level of cooperation between the state and religious organizations. That is why, there is no need for a grand mufti or centralized religious institution to serve as interlocutors with state or national government.

Due to these particular circumstances, facilitating the cooperation between the state and Muslim groups has been a common concern of European governments and has led to the creation of Muslim representative bodies in Belgium, Spain, and France. For state agents, these bodies are aimed at reducing the gap between the political and legal status enjoyed by other religious groups and Muslims. They also are seen as a way to assuage feelings of discrimination that could potentially fuel Islamic radicalism and, ultimately, ensure that the leadership of Muslim organizations falls into the hands of "moderates."[4]

As noted by many scholars from Fetzer and Sope to Laurence,[5] these representative bodies are the outcome of successive state actions to create umbrella organizations by gathering the most "representative" Islamic organizations and facilitating elections from the Muslim population to create institutions (assembly and executive committee). Even in the United Kingdom, in the 1990s, the Muslim Council of Britain gained status as a representative body, at least until the 7/7 attacks. After that, at the different levels of the British governement, the strategy has been to move away from "(...) the demand for a vertically integrated Muslim body that speaks for all Muslims" toward a diversification of representatives.[6] (See appendix 8 for a list of these councils across Europe.)

Interestingly, this institutional integration of Islam within the dominant framework of European secularisms shows the willingness—even the eagerness in some cases—of major Muslim organizations to cooperate with the state. However, such cooperation is rarely presented in the public discourse as a positive sign of Muslim integration, and the dominant rhetoric continues to describe Islam in opposition to secularism.

At a deeper and even less explored level, the state has become an active agent in reshaping Islam by creating new Islamic institutions and leaders. Those leaders are state-appointed or bureaucratic leaders who often compete or conflict with religious leaders who derive their authority from other sources, primarily scholarly expertise or transnational networks (see chapter 7).

The heads of the new representative bodies are increasingly supplanting the bureaucratic leaders of the countries of origin,[7] revealing a profile of leadership tailored to the specifics of European secular states. First, most of them have secular background with some Islamic knowledge. For example, Mohammed Moussaoui, the current head of the Conseil Français du Culte Musulman (CFCM) (French Council of Muslims Faith), born in East Morocco, became a French citizen in 2008. He obtained his diploma in mathematics and physics in 1984 in Morocco and his doctorate in Mathematics in 1990 from the University of Montpellier. In Morocco, he received training in theology and delivered *khotba*s (Friday sermons) for 20 years. He was elected president of the CFCM in 2008 and still holds this position at the time of this writing.[8]

Şemsettin Uğurlu, president of the Executives of Belgian Muslims, is a Turkish Belgium-born Muslim with training in Islamic studies. Before becoming president he was an imam and professor of Islamic religion in Belgium. Additionally, Isabelle Praile, vice president of the organization, is a Belgian-born convert to Shi'ism with a secular background.

The main role of these bodies is to support state actions toward Islam, especially when they are seen as hostile to some Islamic practices. For example, Dalil Boubakeur, who in 2003 was the head of the CFCM, initially expressed disagreement with the project of a bill to ban religious signs in French public schools. However, after President Jacques Chirac's speech on December 17, 2003, supporting the bill, Boubakeur changed his position and made an announcement asking Muslims to respect the law if it was passed and urging them not to protest. Other members of the CFCM, however, such as Vice President Fouad Alaoui leader of Union des Organizations

Islamiques de France (UOIF) (Union of Islamic Organizations of France), one of the major Islamic organization in France), criticized the proposed law. In the end, the CFCM's decision not to contest the 2004 headscarf ban has been cited as one reason for its relatively "seamless-execution."[9] Dalil Boubakeur was willing to concede that the ban might be in the best interests of the common good when he stated "we believe Muslims must embrace a modern form of Islam in the name of the Republic."[10]

The CFCM leadership provided the same support to the French state at the time of the debate on the niqab ban in 2010. Mohammad Moussaoui declared that he was "opposed to the full veil and would try to convince the tiny minority of veiled women that it was not a religious obligation and was out of place in France."[11] He also declared, "Nobody accepts it...A veiled woman cannot have a normal social life."[12] At the same time, the leaders of the CFCM warned the government that they would not impose the ban on their mosque goers, be instructed to force the women to unveil or "act as agents of the state" in helping enforce the ban.[13]

In sum, these new bureaucratic leaders act as mediators between state administrations and Muslim populations. This role was particularly visible at the time of the cartoons crisis when the CFCM leaders were able to call for moderation while expressing their disapproval of the caricatures. Initially, Dalil Boubakeur was extremely critical of the newspaper *Le Soir*'s publication of the 12 caricatures of the Prophet Muhammad (first made notorious by the Danish daily *Jyllands-Posten*). The CFCM threatened to sue [*Le Soir*] but decided against litigation after the newspaper's owner fired the editor. In his condemnation of the publication, Dalil Boubakeur rejected the idea that Muslim objection to the publication was a sign of radicalism. "We attach enormous importance to this image," he said, "and we will not allow it to be distorted. I myself oppose the extremist forms of Islam; we reject this parallel." As a result, the reactions of French Muslims were more muted than in other European countries, including the United Kingdom.[14]

At a less explicit level, these representative bodies work as political tools to "civilize" Islam by shaping the image of the good Muslim. This "ideal" good Muslim is loyal to state institutions and values, subordinates shari'a to state law, refuses transnational allegiances such as the Muslim Brotherhood or salafi groups, distances himself from ethnic-national allegiances, and supports gender equality and freedom of speech. In brief, he or she is the dream of a Muslim coming true. Consequentially, through state active strategy, "Muslim" becomes a political category palatable to the specificity of the country public culture. Case in point, some individual members of the German Islamic Conference present themselves by referring to categories such as secular, liberal, or conservative to address public or social issues pertaining to Islam.

According to this nomenclature approved by the German Islamic conference, a secular Muslim advocates the limitation of Islamic practices to private space and rejects Islamism. Turgut Yüksel, a sociologist and founder of the Initiative for secular Muslims in Hessen, is emblematic of this secular good Muslim of Germany. Similarly, Gönül Halat-Mec, a lawyer who specializes in family law with a focus on migrants, promotes the idea that religion should be a personal and private matter and critiques religious doctrines that discriminate against women and conflict with the plural democratic societal order.[15] The "liberal" is different from the secular Muslim, in the sense that he or she expresses attachment to the social visibility of Islam as long as it does not conflict with liberal principles of human rights. Bernd Ridwan Bauknech, a teacher of Islamic studies at a public school, is one of those "liberal Muslims" whose goal is to assist Muslim students and youngsters in their integration without losing their Islamic identity. Sineb el Masrar, chief editor of the women and migrant magazine *Gazelle*, stands for the recognition of Muslims and their contribution to German society. Another example is Bülent Ucar, professor of Islamic religious education, who promotes mutual participation and recognition between Muslims and non-Muslims as fundamental parts of the integration process. He also advocates state support for the education of imams in Germany.[16]

The conservative Muslim category includes traditional religious leaders. Abdelmalik Hibaoui, an imam and preacher, expects the Islam Conference to support the creation of Islamic theology centers at universities. Tuba Isik-Yigit, affiliated with the Center for Theology and Cultural Sciences at the University of Paderborn, also supports the establishment of centers for theology training and provides support to veiled women.[17]

Strikingly, state involvement in the redefinition of the good Muslim persona constitutes an unprecedented breach of the rule of noninterference of political institutions on the internal function of a religious group, which is one of the foundational principles of secular legal tradition. Such intrusions have consequences for the internal organization of Islam in Europe by producing new leaders. At the same time, the influence of these new leaders is undermined by international and transnational religious authorities who have a more decisive appeal on Muslim groups. Interestingly, the consequences of these state initiatives have never really been discussed in public space. In fact, there is very little probability that they will be. More heated discussions have taken center stage in European public discourse about the ability of Muslims to disconnect religious convictions from public behaviors.

The Private/Public Disjunction and Its Multiple Manifestations

The disjunction between private convictions and public behaviors is the result of what Charles Taylor calls the second mutation of the Western secularization process. The first mutation happened during the Renaissance period when states started to assert their political sovereignty over the church, with the consequence of altering the social status of the latter. It means that the roles of the church were increasingly understood exclusively in terms of "worldly" goals and values—peace, prosperity, growth, flourishing, and the like.[18]

This shift led to two major changes: first, the concept of good political order and social virtues was disconnected from Christian ethics; second, the world became divided between the immanent and the transcendent. This divide was the invention of Latin Christendom and, incidentally, Christendom's contribution to the secularization process.[19] The Western understanding of the secular builds on this separation. It affirms, in effect, that the "lower" immanent or secular order is all that there is and that the "higher," or transcendent, order is not to regulate the lower. A believer in the transcendent is, therefore, expected to keep it to himself and not let belief influence the political or social practices in which he engages. This is the foundational principle of the difference between private convictions and public behaviors.[20]

Most of the controversies surrounding the presence of Muslims in secular societies relate to three major manifestations of this principle: secular justification, primacy of individual rights over collective rights, effacement of the religious self in public space. On all accounts, Muslims are at fault because they are noncompliant to the principle of secular justification, as they privilege collective rights over individual rights and bring the religious self in public space.

Islam and the Principle of Secular Justification

According to the principle of secular justification, only arguments based on secular reasoning are legitimate in political or public debates outcomes are binding decisions or laws.[21] Interestingly, most of the recent crises related to Islam in public space can be interpreted as the critique that Muslims are unable or unwilling to conform to this principle of secular justification.

For example, the Rushdie affair, which is usually seen as a multicultural conflict of minority rights versus individual rights,[22] can also be read as Muslims' difficulty to comply with the principle of secular justification. In this sense, the condemnation of the Satanic Verses and the push by some Muslims to have the book banned, highlight their incapacity or unwillingness to accept the disjunction between private convictions and public behaviors that characterize the "immanent frame" described by Charles Taylor. Additionally, some Muslims have not built a strong "buffered self"[23] and, therefore, are unable to accept that individual rights and freedom of religion can operate independent of religious convictions.

It is worth pointing out that the liberal definition of secular public space poses a special burden on the shoulders of *all* religious citizens.[24] The main reason is that many believers are not always able to undertake an artificial division between their private convictions and public behavior without destabilizing their existence as pious persons. However, according to our survey discussed in chapter 2, it seems that the vast majority of Muslims are already living their religion within the immanent framework. The problem is that some, specifically religious leaders, do not systematically communicate or express their opinions within this framework. This was evident when a Moroccan imam condemned homosexuality during a Dutch TV program in 2001 and defined it as a "sin."[25] His comment ignited public outcry against Muslims, who since then have been described as homophobic and unable to live in a liberal society. In other words, tensions between Islamic claims and secular norms emerge when the convictions of believers or their spokespeople are not seen as compatible with the immanent frame.

If the Rushdie affair instigated public debate about freedom of speech, the cartoon crisis highlighted tensions between freedom of speech and religious freedom—two concepts that do not exactly line up in European public spheres. When the Danish newspaper *Jyllands-Posten* printed on September 30, 2005, 12 editorial cartoons depicting the Prophet Mohammed, many Muslims across Europe found the images distasteful and offensive[26] and demanded respect for the convictions of minority religions.

Some religious leaders argued that the cartoons constituted a blasphemous act. For example, Danish imams Raed Hlayhel, Ahmed Akkari, and Ahmed Abu Laban organized the Committee for the Defense of the Honor of the Prophet, which consisted of 27 other mosque leaders and Muslims groups.[27] At the bequest of Abu Laban, the leader of the Islamic Society in Denmark, Muslim diplomats in Denmark wrote a letter to the Danish prime minister, Rasmussen, in October 2005. They declared that the "Danish press and public representatives should not be allowed to abuse Islam in the name of democracy, freedom of expression, and human rights."[28] Rasmussen responded later, saying that "freedom of expression is the very foundation of Danish democracy" and that describing the cartoons as blasphemous and consequently liable under the law was a process for the courts, not the Danish government.[29] Raed Hlayhel commented that "this type of democracy is worthless for Muslims. Muslims will never accept this kind of humiliation."[30]

Interestingly, because blasphemy laws exist in Scandinavian countries, Muslim groups were able to make (unsuccessful) claims against the cartoons. In fact, the appeal by some Muslims to these laws, led in some cases to their abolition.[31] The only exception was Norway, where Parliament amended their Penal Code to criminalize blasphemy, which since February 2006 is punishable by fine or imprisonment.[32]

However, even when Muslim leaders respected the principle of secular justification, their claim was not heard. That is why the cartoon crisis shed light on the hierarchy among group demands in public space: some being more acceptable than others.

Some Claims Are More Equal than Others, or the False Universalism of Secularism

For this reason, the cartoon crisis directly challenges John Rawls' conception of public space. In his view, people with conflicting but reasonable metaphysical and/or religious views can agree to regulate the basic structure of society. Rawls' account is an attempt to secure the possibility of a liberal consensus regardless of the "deep" religious or metaphysical values that the parties endorse, so long as people remain open to compromise that is "reasonable." The ideal result is conceived as an overlapping consensus because different and often conflicting accounts of morality and nature are intended to overlap with each other on the question of governance. However, Rawls is clear that such political agreement is narrow and focused on justice. This consensus is reached, in part, by avoiding the deepest arguments in religion and philosophy in favor of sharing core values of human rights, freedom, democracy, and the rule of law. In this sense, Muslims' call for censoring the cartoons from newspapers because they considered printing them an act of blasphemy could be seen as a breach in the overlapping consensus concerning the right of freedom of speech.

The Western legacy of open critique undeniably plays into this controversy, as some Muslims are unable to accept any critique of their faith, instead labeling criticism as an insult as discussed above. Yet, in the name of freedom of speech, some opinions that insult a specific faith, group, or culture can also be considered a breach of the overlapping consensus. This is particularly true regarding legislation throughout Europe that creates legal limits on speeches that might contain offensive language to a specific religious or ethnic group. In this context, the cartoons debate highlights the fact that Islam and Muslims are not necessarily protected by such laws. Muslim claims to be protected by this type of legislation was actually not taken into consideration, even when some leaders utilized arguments about hate speech and political acts that can incite violence and are, therefore, punishable by these laws.[33] For example, the Union of European Turkish Democrats in Cologne filed in March 2006 a criminal complaint against the newspaper *Die Welt* for printing the cartoons by referencing the German law that forbids public insults against "religious societies, beliefs, and groups that support specific world views." However, no legal action was ultimately taken against *Die Welt*.[34] Similarly, several Muslim organizations in Denmark, instead of referring to the blasphemy law as discussed above, placed a complaint with the police on the basis that the cartoons were racist under Criminal Code Article 266b.[35]

In the United States, there is no equivalent to these European laws on blasphemy and hate speech. Interestingly, almost no newspapers reprinted the cartoons at the time of the controversy. However, since 2008, the rise of anti-Islamic rhetoric has led to greater concern about the effect of hate speech, and some media have responded by restraining their coverage of such speech. For example, when Pastor Jones decided to publicly burn the Qur'an on the tenth anniversary of the 9/11 attacks, the American media decided not to cover the event. Even more significantly, the restriction on hate speech also has started to influence legal decisions. During a 2011

Halloween parade, a man dressed as a zombie Muhammad was assaulted by a Muslim and decided to press harassment charges. In his February 2012 decision, the judge dismissed the claim of the defendant on the ground that his behavior was inciting racial hatred. Such a decision was very much criticized by lawyers as they saw it as a violation of the First Amendment.[36]

In brief, the cartoon crisis reveals the arbitrary limits of the secular public space, which is not an open space *for all* even when they conform to the principle of secular justification. In other words, despite liberal claims, secular spaces are not "equally" shared by different groups that accept and abide by the same principles or ethics of citizenship. Instead, they appear as heterogeneous landscapes, divided by competition of different social groups to access it. As pointed out by Talal Asad, the "liberal public sphere" since its inception has excluded certain types of people: women throughout the nineteenth and twentieth centuries, poor classes, immigrants, religious groups, and others.[37] Therefore, the advancement of rights in Western democracies can be read as the struggle for outsider groups (poor, women, sexual minorities, and the like) to get "in" the public space. Muslims are now the outsider group that challenges the dominant civil order, especially in Europe.

Individual Rights versus Collective Recognition: The Shari'a Debate

The recognition of Islamic law within existing legal systems, and the concern that specific subcultures can stifle individual rights, is another example of the tension between political order and Muslim communities. The debate was set in motion in February 2008 by the declaration of the archbishop of Canterbury approving the inclusion of shari'a principles within European legislations.[38]

Shari'a as a Political Construction

Like the term Muslim, shari'a has become a construct used in political debates to oppose Islam to Western democratic principles. The construct operates on the historical and political decontextualization of shari'a as a fixed medieval set of laws. It also projects into Europe the situation of some Muslim-majority countries.

In most Muslim-majority countries, shari'a is confined to family law, although there has recently been an expansion of shari'a to areas of criminal law (*hudud*) —including stoning to death and harsh corporeal punishments— in countries like Mauritania or Afghanistan.[39]

The concern about the intolerant use of shari'a in some Muslim states is transferred to Europe without taking into account the completely different context in which references to shari'a operate. Where there is democratic constitutionalism, the debate does not stem from constitutional issues.

Contrary to the widespread belief that Muslims in the West seek the inclusion of shari'a in the constitutions of European countries, as analyzed in our previous chapters, most surveys show that they are quite satisfied with the secular nature of European political regimes. When Muslims agitate for change, they engage in politics and the democratic process, utilizing mainstream parties and institutions.[40] Yet as our survey results have shown, this does not mean that they renounce Islamic principles and legal rules to guide or structure their daily lives.[41]

The shari'a ban in the United States, discussed in chapter 5, is a similar reaction to what is perceived as a fixed medieval code of laws applied across the Muslim world. However, it has not been addressed within the parameters of American secular principles because, as described in chapter 5, the shari'a ban was declared unconstitutional. This prohibition obliged anti-shari'a political actors to orient the prohibition against foreign laws and, therefore, grounded the debate even more into security issues.

Although the fear of *hudud* or constitutional Islamic law is not founded, questions remain regarding the compatibility of shari'a with legal pluralism.

Shari'a and Legal Pluralism

Legal pluralism is historically related to the inclusion of customary laws into legal systems of postcolonial countries. Later, it was embraced by postmodernist scholars and lawyers to describe the fragmentation and competition between multiple legal systems in modern societies. As noted by Andrea Buchler, the consideration of Islamic prescriptions within secular law is part of a broader trend of the pluralization of family law that has been developing in Europe since the end of the nineteenth century. Due to cultural and demographic changes, such as increased divorce, sexual cohabitation outside of marriage, the rise of single parent families, and declining birth rates, family values per se have transformed and pluralized to include a variety of definitions.[42] Therefore, European family law has become less "institutionalized and more contractual in its nature."[43] It is within this changing framework of pluralization of family law, and the growing importance of contract and arbitration, that Islamic norms may find a place within European legal references. Additionally, the right to cultural identity, which is a part of European legislation,[44] can be used to justify and promulgate the recognition of Islamic legal norms in Europe. There is, however, a restrictive condition to the possible recognition of shari'a within legal pluralism, which is that Islamic norms should not contradict the basic principles of equality between individuals. In this regard, possible tensions between law and norm can emerge. The latter is the set of rules and conventions accepted by a specific social group, while the former is the set of permissions and prohibitions enforced by state institutions. In other words, shari'a as a set of norms recognized by some Muslims can potentially clash with state laws. These clashes have surfaced in countries where arbitration procedures are permitted. It is, therefore, not surprising that these procedures have become the focus of political concern about shari'a misuse.

Arbitration can be carried out by two adults if, prior to the procedure, they sign an agreement (the Arbitration Agreement) that defines rules they will both accept in order to solve their disagreement. The arbitration can be conducted in accordance with any rules or legal system that is specified in the arbitration agreement, including shari'a. The final judgment or decision is registered with a civil court and enforced as if the trial had taken place in a civil court. Arbitration agreements are allowed in some countries like the United Kingdom and Canada and do not concern shari'a *per se*. However, the use of Islamic prescriptions through this procedure has raised objections because of the potential conflict between some Islamic norms and respect of human rights.[45] For example, the opponents to Shari'a courts in the state of Ontario saw such courts as a threat to gender equality. When the Islamic Council of Canada announced by the end of 2003 that it would seek arbitration courts based on shari'a, a heated debate broke out about the legitimacy of using Islamic principles within the arbitration framework. Particularly active in this debate were feminists groups, especially the Canadian Council of Muslim Women and the International Campaign against Shari'a Courts, led by Iranian refugee turned citizen Homa Arjomand. The controversy came to a close when in 2005 the governor of Ontario declared that he would not allow his province to become the first Western government to legitimize the use of Islamic law to settle family disputes and that the boundaries between church and state would be clearer if religious arbitration was banned completely.[46] The political result of this heated controversy was the rejection of all forms of religious arbitration from Ontario courts.[47]

Interestingly, such a fear of human rights abuse was not supported by the behaviors of most of Muslims in Canada. For example, Christopher Cutting shows that Muslim families in Canada turn for guidance to imams but do not request official arbitration.[48] In the same vein, other surveys on shari'a courts in the United Kingdom describe how imams can be very active in defending female rights against abusive husbands, especially in the case of "limping marriages."[49]

Thus, religiosity and use of law is a complex negotiation. Research suggests different and sometimes contradictory attitudes among Muslims toward European and North American secular laws; complete rejection of secular law is rare while complete acceptance of civil law is also rare. This nuance is further complicated by the heightened securitization context on both continents following the 9/11 and 7/7 attacks that we discussed in the previous chapter. Nevertheless, the general trend across Europe is accommodation of some Islamic requirements within national laws. This accommodation has often been conducted in an indirect way through European judges rather than Islamic legal experts or Muslim theologians.[50] Consequently, a slow and "invisible" form of personal Islamic law is being constructed and adapted to Western secular laws.[51] Of course, European judges do not claim Islamic authority, but the fact that most clerics do not contest their decisions—or sometimes even endorse them—illustrates the law's adaptation. It is as well reflective of the malleability of shari'a itself.

We examined the literature and jurisprudence of several key European countries in order to ascertain the arguments used by the courts and by Muslims when conflicts arise between the two.[52] The plethora of national laws in Europe and the diversity among Muslim groups makes comparison difficult, but we found a general trend of recognizing foreign law. It means that legal systems distinguish between national and foreign jurisprudence, therefore, giving the possibility to residents to utilize their national laws. In these situations, the country of residence applies foreign law even if it is discriminatory. It is worth noting that Islamic laws on marriage, divorce, and custody greatly differ[53] according to the family law of each country of origin. Some countries (such as Pakistan or Algeria) have more restrictions than others, such as Tunisia, Turkey, and Morocco, where family law has been progressively amended to comply to equality between men and women.

However, some abusive practices justified by Islamic law do persist. For this reason, in 2011, British activists ran the campaign called One Law For All, which led Baroness Caroline Cox to introduce the Arbitration and Mediation Services (Equality) Bill in the House of Lords on June 7, 2011.[54] Similarly, it is difficult to abate the persistence of customs that can be discriminatory toward women and presented as "Islamic" by some Muslims. For example, in the 1990s, honor killings became a topic of public debate in the United Kingdom and led several Muslim clerics to publicly condemn such killings as non-Islamic. Similarly in Canada, a father and his son of Pakistani origin were sentenced in June 2010 for the murder of their daughter/sister because she was rebelling against the honor rules and had demanded more freedom. The father argued that he was acting in accordance to what his community dictated since her behavior was an insult to him.[55]

Such cultural claims can sometimes influence the judge's interpretation in ways detrimental to the principle of equality. For example, in 2007, a Muslim woman was denied a fast-track divorce in Germany on the basis of domestic violence because the judge reasoned that the Qur'an allows physical abuse against one's wife. Several politicians, legal experts, and Muslim leaders noted that they "were confounded that a German judge would put seventh century Islamic religious teaching ahead of modern German law in deciding about a situation involving domestic violence."[56] Because of the ensuing outcry, the court removed the judge from the case and several legal experts further explained that this was a judicial misstep rather than a trend.[57]

Sometimes, the political context can affect the judge's decision. One example is a 2008 divorce case in French court. The husband, of Moroccan origin, wanted a divorce because his wife was not a virgin at the time of the marriage. The judge annulled the marriage because "the woman had lied over what is called in French law an 'essential quality,' in this case her virginity."[58]

According to the contract logic, the annulment was correct.[59] However, because of the politically sensitive nature of the case, the initial ruling was overturned in October 2008 by the French Court of Appeals, which found that virginity "is not an essential quality in that its absence has no repercussion on the matrimonial life."[60] The recognition of such a discriminatory cultural practice by the French judge was at the time highly criticized as a breach of the principle of equality and seen as an implicit acceptance of the discriminatory status of shari'a—although this is not found in Islamic law and is a cultural practice—even if the wife had initially accepted the annulment of the marriage.

These extreme cases remain atypical, especially when it comes to nationals of European countries with a Muslim background. In this situation, negotiation is still the strategy of choice for most families. The recognition of individual freedom and the consideration of each party's best interests lead to compromises that change not only the letter but also the spirit of Islamic laws, stripping them of the official meanings they have in Muslim-majority societies. One example of this transformation, in which Islamic regulations are "acclimatized" to Western legal norms, concerns the acceptable period of time one's widowhood should last. Traditional Islamic law specifying the time that must elapse before one is allowed to remarry cannot be strictly enforced in European societies.

Laws governing inheritance offer another example of the flexibility involved in translating old practices into new contexts. Most of Islamic laws on inheritance specify that for every part given to the daughter, two parts must be given to the son. This ruling cannot always be strictly adhered to in practice, especially in legal systems influenced by Roman law, which ensures that each descendant be provided for equally. In 1975, Sheikh Zaki Badawi (1922–2006), president of the Muslim College in London, established a ready-made Islamic will to solve the contradiction between European and Islamic norms. For years, according to his own admission, no one used it,[61] perhaps indicating that Muslims in Europe are generally quite comfortable with Western norms of inheritance.

Changes in Islamic law in matters of divorce have been not only the most significant but also the most difficult to identify. Even though a divorce can still officially be carried out within religious law, unofficially it may have been already initiated by the wife herself in the civil court system. In addition, divorce is increasingly a topic of discussion for both members of the married couple. The fact that husband and wife both abide by Islamic law does not necessarily determine the degree of oppression or inequality within a marriage. Negotiation in divorce proceedings and polygamous marriages are two main categories in which Islamic laws are transformed within the context of Western democratic societies.[62]

There is no doubt, however, that some interpretations of Islamic norms are at the antipodes of secular legislations.[63] Most of these interpretations are increasingly transnational and easily accessible everywhere due to electronic *fatwas* of all kinds, as it will be addressed in the next chapter. Even though the silent majority of European Muslims accept Islam's compatibility with the basic precepts of human rights, some fringes or marginal groups reject this paradigm and can act in ways that strongly prejudice Europe's perception of Islam and Muslims.[64] For example, the group Shari'a for the UK emerged in 2009 with the sole agenda of promoting shari'a in the United Kingdom. This group's leaders declared,

> We hereby request all Muslims in the United Kingdom to join us and collectively declare that as submitters to Almighty Allah, we have had enough of democracy and man-made law and the depravity of the British culture. On this day [October 31, 2009] we will call for a complete upheaval of the British ruling system its members and legislature, and demand the full implementation of *shari'a* in Britain.[65]

The same claim has spread to the Netherlands and Belgium with the emergence of Shari'a4Holland and Shari'a4Belgium groups.[66] One reason for the appeal to illiberal forms of Islamic law is the globalization of Salafi interpretations of Islam that have gained influence among all Muslim countries and the West. As we shall discuss in the next chapter, salafis promote shari'a as the opposite of secular law, which reinforces the dominant opinion that Islam is incompatible with the West.

In sum, the ongoing search for a balance between individual rights and collective identity reveals the complexities of political interactions between disparate stakeholder communities. As noted above, this complexity comes from the involvement of not only lay Muslims and clerics but also lawyers and judicial systems in a highly politicized context. For this reason, we see again the gap between the daily interactions of Muslims with public institutions and the construction of shari'a as a political problem.

Religious Self and Secular Space

The increased resistance against Islamic signs of piety illustrates the third level of disjunction between private convictions and public behaviors: the legitimate manifestations of the religious person in public life.

Since the eighteenth century, the general tendency across Europe has been to push religious customs and rituals outside the area of civil legality. In most countries, such an evolution has affected the presence of religious voices in the broader public space and has contributed to the decline of religious identification among citizens. A majority of Europeans assert that they are not religious, that they do not belong to religious groups, and that God is not important in their lives.[67] Even when they identify themselves as believers, citizens participate less and less in the broader public space in the name of religious beliefs. The debate on crucifixes in public spaces in Italy provides a good example of this seemingly inexorable trend. In March 2011, the European Court of Human Rights ruled that crucifixes are acceptable in Italian public school classrooms since they are seen as an "'essentially passive symbol' with no obvious religious influence."[68] Interestingly, this ruling directly contradicts the one issued by the same court in 2009 that stated that the use of crucifixes in Italian classrooms violated "the right of parents to educate their children as they saw fit and ran counter to the child's right to freedom of religion."[69] This shift in interpretation illustrates the emerging political consensus across Europe that tends to legitimize the visibility of the religious signs of the dominant religion, interpreted as elements of the public culture, while the religious signs of other religions are seen as inappropriate in the public space.

That is why controversies irrupt when Muslims exhibit social markers based on religious convictions in societies where the engrained perception of religion is that it is part of individual intimacy and should not be visible in the makeup of one's social self. This disjunction is the outcome of several centuries of socialization that has associated modernization, progress, and individual empowerment with the decline of religious practices. Of course, it does not manifest itself uniformly across countries and historical periods. For example, there is a greater tolerance for dress codes or other religious signs in British and American society in contrast to the French rejection of such signs in some, if not all, parts of the public space and social interactions.

Nevertheless, most European citizens tend to consider expressions of faith misplaced and illegitimate within civil context. The idea that religion cannot play a role in the general well-being of societies—a mark of the secularized mind—is, in fact, common throughout all of Europe, despite differences among the national contracts between states and organized religions addressed in the previous section of this chapter. It is important to note that religious groups other than Muslims also can be challenged by this core principle of mainstream secularism. For example, in 1995, a Bavarian school ordinance allowed the display of crucifix in every elementary classroom. In stark contrast with the ulterior decision of the European Court of Human Rights of 2011, the Federal Constitutional Court held at the time that because the crucifix is a core symbol of Christian faith, such a gesture by the school was seen as proselytizing and was unconstitutional.[70] Nevertheless, main strands of public culture in the political and intellectual spheres and media are highly secularized, and, therefore, tend to ignore or reject religious dimensions and references that are still meaningful to some segments of society. The implication of such secularism is that the various manifestations of Islam in Europe have become troublesome or even unacceptable, especially, when they act as body markers or discriminate between genders.

Body Markers, Religious Beliefs, and Sexual Equality

In secularized public cultures, the cognitive dimension of religion, defined primarily as beliefs and values relegated to the intimacy of the private self, has become preeminent with the outcome that religious beliefs and body markers do not match anymore. In these conditions, what Talal Asad calls "embodied practices of religion," such as dress code or circumcision, seem to violate the neutrality of European public spaces.[71]

In other words, at the core of Western secular discourse is the rejection of what Michael Connolly calls the "visceral" dimension of religious expressions. Secularism suffers, in his view, from its failure to thematize how the "infrasensible register" shapes social and cultural dispositions operating below the threshold of consciousness. Kant's marginalization of Christian theology in favor of a "rational religion" grounded in moral reasoning is a key moment, in Connolly's account, of the philosophical development of this moral repulsion for the visceral. As he notes, Kant degrades ritual and arts of the self by subordinating them to the supersensible realm, or domain of the moral obligations drawn by the power of the intellect. Secularists later carry this Kantian project of diminishment a step or two further.[72] With Enlightenment and its central critique of Christianity, reason and intellect were prioritized over emotions and ecstasy, especially in the Protestant forms of religiosity. Eventually, almost all other religions (present in the West) were influenced by this more intellectual worldview and gave priority to reason and logic over the ecstatic. In this sense, the Enlightenment period engendered a fundamental shift in the relationship between the body and the mind. As new theories of agency, responsibility, and individuality emerged, the body became an object controlled by the mind of the individual.

As summarized by Hirshkind,[73] the secular subject—the Kantian dinner host—is one whose speech and comportment incorporates recognition of the distinctions authorized by the twin categories of religious and secular. Put differently, a secular person is someone whose affective-gestural repertoires express a negative relation to forms of embodiment historically associated with, but not limited to, theistic religion. In this regard, the genealogy of the secular includes, from the sixteenth to the eighteenth century, a variety of social transformations that are key to our understanding of the modern subject. Among them are the desensualization of knowledge as described by Walter Ong, the stilling of passionate expression within courtly society examined by Norbert Elias, the increasing internalization of psychic and emotional life within bourgeois society, and the transfer of vast realms of experience from the surface of public life into the invisible depths of the lonely individual.[74] It is then not surprising that Muslim embodied practices appear as shockingly "uncivic."

The other cause of suspicion vis-à-vis embodied practices of Islam is related to gender equality. The Islamic headscarf worn by women is often interpreted as a sign of rejection of individual female emancipation. This interpretation has provoked the wrath of those groups spearheading the defense of secular ideology: teachers, intellectuals, feminists, civil servants, and so forth. The French law prohibiting religious signs in public schools, adopted in March 2004, is a case in point. It also illustrates the importance of a specific political sensitivity regarding gender issues. Since 1989, the legitimacy of headscarves in public schools has been debated with great passion, showing conflicting interpretations of *laïcité*.[75] However, the specific political conditions of 2004 rendered the change in law possible. At this time, young women in the disfranchised suburbs were continuously harassed and sometimes killed by young men unless they adopted the Islamic dress code. The movement called Neither Whores nor Submitted led by young women from these suburbs encapsulates the false dilemma of the public discourse where the headscarf comes to symbolize the submission of young women who have to veil in order to protect themselves. The fight against the headscarf could hence be justified as a fight against female oppression and a way to liberate them against male domination and religious obscurantism. The fact that some of these young women have made the choice to wear the headscarf was not even discussed in the months leading to the vote of the law. If it was mentioned, it was typically discarded as insignificant or irrelevant to the greater "cause" of liberating women, which was much more in tune with the sexual politics and culture of the country. In this sense, the 2004 law is quite specific as it modifies the secular principle to render social expression of religious beliefs illegal. In other countries, like Germany, only some groups of civil servants have been prohibited of wearing the hijab, like public school teachers.[76] Social pressures however are exerted on students to dissuade them to wear the hijab. A lot of German educators see it as their "moral duty" to try to reduce the number of headscarves at their schools, as they think this will support the girls' enhanced integration in society. A Protestant secondary school in Gelsenkirchen, for instance, only allows female Muslim students to wear a headscarf on two conditions. They have to be 14 or older (the official age of religious maturity in Germany) and are obliged to pass a test from the school council about their reasons for wearing the scarf. This way, the school's headmaster declared, he wanted to find out whether the girls decided to wear the headscarf for their own reasons or whether they were forced by their families or the surrounding Muslim community. In other schools, psychological pressure is exerted on parents not to "force" their daughters to wear this "sign of disintegration" by suggesting they would otherwise face significant problems at school and in society.

Niqab versus Hijab

As discussed in chapter 5, the ban of the niqab is justified by security issues more than by secularism for two reasons. First, while the hijab ban is a French "specificity", the niqab ban can be found in countries that have been accommodating to the headscarf like Spain or the Netherlands. Second, the security argument in support of the niqab ban is the same everywhere. Europeans view Muslims as threats, so their states respond with measures purporting to rid their lands of terrorism.

It should be said, however, that the niqab, unlike the hijab, does present a challenge for secular democratic spaces. There is no doubt that, sociologically and culturally speaking, such a dress code reveals an attempt to separate from mainstream society. It is, as such, incompatible with the kind of face-to-face encounters that are constitutive of the citizenship status: when you vote, when you take part in a public debate or mobilization, or when you take an exam. Therefore, it can indeed be questioned and its use rightly restricted when such civic encounters occur. It is regrettable that, by linking together Islam and security, the real issues of integration of Islamic practices within secular democratic spaces are not really addressed. In this sense, a complete prohibition may not be the most efficient response to the few Muslim women who choose to adopt an illiberal lifestyle in the midst of liberal democracies.

Conclusion: Modern Individualism and Religious Individualism Are Not Synonymous

Islam is disturbing because Muslims claim—or demonstrate by embodied practices—that modern and religious individualism are not synonymous. By covering, distinguishing, and separating, they inconveniently remind us that the individual, especially his or her body, is not absolutely powerful. In the current phase of modernity, the body has become the primary vehicle for individual expression in the public sphere. Individuality is expressed not only through ownership of the body (including upholding legal rights) but also through choices regarding gender and sexuality. In other words, in a modern and consumer-driven capitalist world, individuals choose to change their physical bodies—from makeup and beauty salons to plastic surgery and gender reconstruction.

Interestingly, this greater emphasis on corporality has resulted in a recovered sense of sensuality that challenges the dominant intellectualization of western religion highlighted above. The tensions between these two perceptions of the body—the sensuous-oriented and the cognitive-oriented—can be seen throughout contemporary societies. The cognitive realm is manifested in popular obsessions with diet, health, and medical discourses that were already central to the Protestant Reformation. The sensuous-oriented self claims its rights to sexuality and empowerment over the biological restrictions of the body. In other words, the modern individual exercises personal body rights with the new tools of advanced science and medicine, including procedures such as cloning, gender changes, and fertility treatments. In contrast to the premodern perspective, consumerist culture emphasizes the right to body control and the right to pleasure. Hedonistic images dominate mainstream culture, most clearly in advertising and popular entertainment. Predictably, these new corporeal-focused forms of individualization seep into contemporary forms of religiosity.

More specifically, religiosity has been affected to the point that modern individualism is often equated with religious individualism. Very much influenced by Protestantism, this conflation is reflected in the way in which religion has largely been understood by Western scholarship. Scholarly literature on religion emphasizes ideas and beliefs—values that are central to the Protestant Reformation—over behavior and functions of the body. As Talal Asad argues, such a focus leads in turn to the construction of religion as a transhistorical/ideational object of study, removed from social contexts or groups.[77] This perspective has contributed to the dominant consensus that religious modernity is synonymous with religious individualism. Concretely, it means that the modern individual has (almost) unlimited capacity of religious choice.

The consequence is that most Westerners have forgotten that in all religious traditions, including Islam, there is a concept of the individual—personal responsibility of the believer vis-à-vis God, obligations of the believers—but it is far from being similar to the modern individual. The religious individual is restricted by discipline, control and asceticism, and thus cannot follow through all personal motives or desires. However, the modern individual is defined by the absence of limits in the pursuit of his or her desires. Therefore, the so-called irresistible progression of the individualization of beliefs is a staple of the Western narrative but does not reflect the historical tension between the autonomy of the subject as a believer and the modern individual. In this sense, the current discourses and concerns of Muslim believers vis-à-vis the body reflect these tensions but are not specific to Islam.

For example, with the shift from religious obligation to consumption in Europe, religion, which was at one time imposed or inherited, has become a personal choice.[78] As noted by Grace Davies, a decrease in teenage confirmations in the Church of England suggests teens are less obligated to perform this religious ritual and an increase in adult confirmations reveals that more people are choosing to be religious in their adult life. Similarly, Daniele Hervieu-Leger argues that the breakdown of the clergy in France represents the change from the church as the representative of society and cultural memory to religion constituted by individual choice.[79] Furthermore, traditional religious authorities have been increasingly challenged and sometimes replaced by mutual validation of small groups of believers that do not need or seek the priest or cleric confirmation.[80] For example, in modern-day Catholicism, smaller groups of believers recognize homosexuality whereas the clerical establishment continues to reject it.

It can be argued that, as part of their integration process, Muslims may in the long term experience a similar conflation of the modern and religious individualism. Our focus group discussions, however, tell another story and highlight acute tensions between modern and religious individualism, especially among the second and third generations of immigrants.

The first reason for such tensions is that Islam in the West is part and parcel of global Islam and, therefore, still connected to Muslim-majority countries that have not experienced a reformation of the body similar to the Protestant one. More generally, in the Islamic tradition, the body is a vital aspect of religiosity. Far from the Protestant Reformation, corporality in Islam is intrinsically part of the religious experience as an aspect of spirituality. In the classical Islamic view, custodianship of the body is fundamental to a meaningful spiritual life. This is a viewpoint that even Muslim scientists have held in both medieval and modern times. The scholar Majed A. Ashy observes, "Praying five times a day helps to reduce psychological stress and to keep structure and discipline in the life of the individual."[81] From the more mundane perspective, the body is integral and intertwined into both the mental and spiritual realms. Contrary to the contemporary Western perspective, Ashy continues, "it offers both individual and group strength in times of hardships through belief in a powerful God."[82]

The second reason is related to the modernization experiences of Muslim countries. In this regard, it would be very misleading to think that Islamic societies did not undergo a process of modernization. In fact, since the eighteenth century onward, their modernization process has created renewed tensions between the modern and the religious individual—triggering persistent discussion on the monitoring of the body as a part of religious life. This attentiveness to the body has included prescriptions that range from diet to sexual rules to regulation of modesty, such as the hijab, which vary according to the cultural setting.

In the postcolonial era, these tensions have been exacerbated by the role of the nation-state. More precisely, debates in the Islamic tradition have contended with state-centered modernization and its participation in identity-formation and influence on religious practice. As a result, institutions and communities within the Muslim world have universally experienced an increasing amount of state-controlled and state-redefined religion.[83]

This redefinition of Islamic norms has created cognitive dissonance for Muslim believers between civic obligation and personal piety. There is an internal struggle between the empowerment of individuals as citizens and the significance of Islamic religious norms. This personal struggle is also a global one, amplified by competing interpretations of Islamic orthodoxy from multiple transnational actors. The anxiety of the Muslim individual, then, is not only felt in a national context but also in a global one.

It would be misleading, however, to interpret body-centered religiosity of Islam as an exceptional resistance to postmodernity. As mentioned above, Muslim communities are not unique in their struggle with the modern sense of corporality. Everywhere, believers are grappling with the "tyranny of the body."

It is, therefore, not surprising that the body is the topic through which many Islamic religious authorities are redefining the "true" Islam.

The female body particularly is the major site of these cultural and political tensions, which take the form of binary oppositions in stark conflict to Western values: Islam versus the West, past versus present, and communal integrity versus individual freedom, as we will see in the next chapter.

CHAPTER 7

SALAFIZATION OF ISLAMIC NORMS AND ITS INFLUENCE ON THE EXTERNALIZATION OF ISLAM

Debates concerning Islam and Muslims in the West are inscribed in several transnational spaces. As described in chapter 3, identifications and connections to countries of origin are still a significant part of Muslim religious identities. Despite the fact that transnational identifications to Islam were not discussed in our focus groups, they nevertheless influence the definition of what is true Islam not only for Muslims but also for political agencies and media in the West. These transnational trends are part of a broad space defined by multiple and contradictory religious authoritative voices.

The proliferation of religious authorities and the shrinking realm of their authority is by no means a new phenomenon and has been the subject of many studies.[1] Both mass education and new forms of communication have contributed to the increase of actors who claim the right to talk on behalf of Islam in both authoritative and normative ways. Therefore, established religious figures, such as the sheikhs of Al-Azhar or Medina, are increasingly challenged by the engineer, the student, the businessman, and the autodidact, who mobilize the masses and speak for Islam in sports stadiums, on the blogosphere, and over airwaves worldwide. This trend predates the Internet and is related to public education programs and the increased availability of new technological communicative mediums, such as magazines, cassette tapes, and CDs.[2]

However, the Internet has added a new element to this proliferation of religious voices: the greater influence of globalized authority figures who have an audience beyond their particular cultural background. This trans-nationalization of religious voices can be defined as neo–pan-Islamism. Although there are multiple forms of this contemporary pan-Islam, contemporary Salafism has become the most widespread, and in the context of our investigation is influential because it contributes to the binary opposition between the West and Islam.

Renewed Forms of Pan-Islamism

We have seen in chapter 4 that national versions of Islam from Turkey to Morocco and Pakistan are still relevant for Muslims in Europe and in the United States. At the same time, transnational movements have gained significant influence as contenders of religious legitimacy, giving a new meaning to pan-Islamism.

Historically, pan-Islamism refers to religio-political transnational movements that emphasized the unity of the Community of Believers (*Ummah*) over specific cultural, national, or ethnic loyalties. These movements were particularly active in the defense of the caliphate at the end of the Ottoman Empire. Today, as stated above, the conditions for communication and the circulation of people and ideas make the *Ummah* all the more effective as a concept, especially, considering the fact that nationalist ideologies have been waning. The imagined *Ummah* has a variety of forms, the most influential of which emphasizes direct access to the Qur'an and Muslim unity that transcends national and cultural diversity. In this sense, those extolling this modern trend can be called pan-Islamists even though the restoration of the caliphate is no longer their priority.[3] It is worth noting that not all these movements are reactionary or defensive. For this reason, a distinction must be drawn between the Wahhabi/Salafi and Tablighi movements on one hand and the Muslim Brotherhood on the other. Both trends dominate global interpretations of Islam but have very different positions vis-à-vis modernity.

Wahhabism as a specific interpretation of the Islamic tradition emerged in the eighteenth century in the Arabian Peninsula with the teachings of Muhammad Ibn Abdel Wahab (1703–1792), whose literalist interpretations of the Qur'an became the official doctrine of the Saudi Kingdom upon its creation in 1932. Wahhabism is characterized by a rejection of critical approaches to the Islamic tradition. Mystical approaches and historical interpretations alike are held in contempt. Orthodox practice can be defined as a direct relation to the revealed Text, with no recourse to the historical contributions of the various juridical schools (*madhab*). In this literalist interpretation of Islam, nothing must come between the believer and the Text: customs, culture, and Sufism must all be done away with.

The heirs of this rigorist and puritanical line of thought are the clerics of the Saudi religious establishment, also known as Salafi. However, compared with Wahhabism, Salafism's orientation—at least at its inception—was significantly broader and more diverse.[4] Adherents of Wahhabism have rejected all ideas and concepts that are deemed Western, maintaining a strictly revivalist agenda. They contend that the Qur'an and Hadith, when interpreted according to the precedents of the Pious Forefathers (*al-salaf al-salih*), offer the most superior form of guidance to Muslims. As a stringently revivalist movement, Wahhabism seeks the "Islamization of societies"[5] that entails formulating contemporary ways of life in relation to the conditions of seventh century Arabia by "returning to the sources" whose "true meaning," Wahhabis argue, was lost over the centuries following Prophet Muhammad's death.[6] In their resistance to Western expansionism and globalization, Wahhabis have remained true to their literalist, antihistorical, and anti-traditionalist origins and continue to uphold the Qur'an and Sunna as literal instruction manuals.[7]

In sum, the Wahhabi interpretation can be defined as a revivalist movement premised upon the return to the "unadulterated" Islam of the "Pious Forefathers."

The only significant difference between the global Salafi Islam of today and the original Wahhabi period is its audience: in other words, Salafi decisions and interpretations are no longer limited to the Saudi Kingdom but are now followed by Muslims around the world. The fatwas of Sheikh Abdul Aziz Ibn Baaz (d. 1999), Grand Mufti of the Saudi Kingdom, and of Sheikh Al-Albani (d. 1999) are the shared points of reference for their followers in Europe and the United States, and, more generally, throughout the Muslim world. The movement has succeeded in imposing its beliefs not as one interpretation among many but as the global orthodox doctrine of Sunni Islam.

The considerable financial resources of the Saudi state have certainly helped create this situation of religious monopoly. In the 1970s, Saudi Arabia began investing internationally in a number of organizations that "widely distributed Wahhabi literature in all the major languages of the world, gave out awards and grants, and provided funding for a massive network of publishers, schools, mosques, organizations, and individuals."[8] In the West, this *dawa* (proselytization) resulted in the building of new Islamic centers in Malaga, Madrid, Milan, Mantes-la-Jolie, Edinburgh, Brussels, Lisbon, Zagreb, Washington, Chicago, and Toronto, to name just a few; the financing of Islamic Studies chairs in American universities; and the multiplication of multilingual Internet sites. In March 2002, the official Saudi magazine *Ain al-Yaqin* estimated that the Saudi royal family has "wholly or partly financed" approximately 210 Islamic centers; 1,500 mosques; 202 colleges; and 2,000 Islamic schools in Muslim-minority countries.[9] It is important to note that these estimates do not include the number of institutions funded by the Saudi Government in its entirety or other sources within Saudi Arabia that finance Wahhabi proselytizing.[10] According to some estimates, the Saudi Kingdom spent over $80 billion on various Islam-related causes in Muslim-minority countries between 1973 and 2002.[11] King Fahd alone invested over $75 billion dollars in the construction of schools, mosques, and Islamic institutions outside of the kingdom in the 1970s and 1980s.[12] This massive effort of propagation has contributed to the promotion of Wahhabism as the sole legitimate guardian of Islamic thought.[13]

The construction of mosques, schools, and other Islamic institutions is only one strategy of the Saudis to circulate the Wahhabi doctrine. They also rely heavily on media to promote and spread their message, through the circulation of handouts, the creation of websites, or the airing of satellite television shows. For example, in 1984, the Kingdom of Saudi Arabia opened the King Fahd Complex for printing the Holy Qur'an in Medina. According to the website of the now-deceased king Fahd bin 'Abdul 'Aziz, the complex produces between 10 and 30 million copies of the Qur'an each year. Copies of the Qur'an is also available in Braille, as are video and audio recordings of Qur'anic recitations. By 2000, the complex had produced 138 million copies of the Qur'an translated into 20 languages.[14]

It is extremely difficult to gauge the precise influence exerted by Wahhabism on Muslim religious practice. In the case of European and American Muslims, the influence cannot simply be measured by statistics. In a minority culture, lacking both institutions for religious education and the means by which to produce new forms of knowledge, the easy access to theology that Salafism offers is one of the main reasons for its popularity. The widespread diffusion of Salafi teachings means that even non-Salafi Muslims evaluate their Islamic practice by Wahhabite standards. In other words, even if most Muslims do not follow Wahhabite dress codes—white tunic, head-covering, beard for men, niqab[15] for women—the Salafi norm often becomes the standard image of what a good Muslim ought to be.[16]

Despite the strong presence of many different interpretations at the grassroots level,[17] the Salafi revivalist interpretation of Islam dominates the Internet *dawa*.

The Salafi Voice Dominates the Internet: Forging "Homo Occidentalis"

Our systematic review of online religious sites by a team of multilingual researchers has confirmed that the Salafi interpretation of Islam has come to dominate other forms of religious guidance on the Internet. The review of Islam-centered websites was the basis for an online research project called Islamopedia[18]—a collection of religious forums, fatwas, and other resources from a variety of international websites (see appendix 9). The religious opinions collected on Islamopedia Online provide evidence of the Salafization of Islamic thought and discourse in regions well beyond Saudi Arabia such as Europe, Africa, and Urdu-speaking countries. Across the Muslim world, religious authorities tend to adopt aspects of Salafi doctrine in their Islamic practice and activism, either implicitly or explicitly. (See appendix 7 for a description of the building of Islamopedia fatwa database.) This does not imply that more liberal trends do not exist in what may be categorized as Islamic websites, but Salafi sites have been more expressive and successful in laying claim to what they argue is the true and "authentic" Islam. Of course, the majority of Muslims do not follow these instructions (as we have shown in chapters 2 and 3). However, the Salafi interpretation is significant because, as discussed previously, it has come to be perceived as the true or "correct" form of Islam, or at least a significant interpretation that must be addressed by religious authorities who compete for the definition of orthodoxy. Thus, even Muslims who criticize the stringency of the Salafi interpretation must take this opinion into account. Many Muslims use this interpretation as delineation of what a good Muslim is and judge themselves against this norm.

The Salafis' success on the Internet can be explained by what anthropologist Michael Wesch calls "context collapse." This refers to the unique features of digital places where individuals can ask and discuss intimate questions, with no fear of exposing themselves, that they would not feel comfortable broaching in person because the Internet annihilates the context and the identity of the user.

Most interestingly, it makes the traditional dichotomies between "devotional" and "non-devotional" less acute. This means that users of fatwas online consume orthodoxy without automatically implementing it. Consequently, Islam is not any longer only a set of rituals, beliefs, and doctrines, but also a symbolic commodity relevant to social demands for multiple lifestyles, and enjoyment. This use of Islamic websites is, therefore, a way to express the religious self. It also globalizes a vision of Islam pitched against the West.

The Binary World of the Salafis

With the diffusion of the Salafi doctrine worldwide, fundamentalism has become global. This global fundamentalism is defined, above all, by an exclusive and hierarchical vision of the world as well as by a taxonomy of religions that places Islam at the top. The expanded use of the term *kafir* (infidel, heretic), for example, is very common among Wahhabis. In the classical Islamic tradition, this term was used only for polytheists, not for members of competing monotheistic faiths. In globalized fundamentalist groups, however, it has been extended to include Jews, Christians, and sometimes even non-practicing Muslims.

Thus, the world is divided into Muslims and infidels. The image of the West, automatically associated with moral depravity, is always a negative one. It contributes to the building of Homo Occidentalis: sexually promiscuous, materially greedy, and impure. This topos mirrors the Western imaginary of Homo Islamicus presented in chapter 1.

Also common to these movements is a worldview that separates the various aspects of life—family, work, leisure—and classifies everything according to the opposition between *haram* (forbidden) and *halal* (permitted). Everything that did not already exist or happen during the time of the Prophet is an innovation, thus *haram*. Khaled Abou El Fadl has called this particular interpretation, the culture of "*Mamnu*" (what is forbidden).[19] Islam as it existed during the time of the Prophet, especially during his stay in Medina, is idealized and essentialized, functioning as an "epic past" and gold standard for life in the present. The smallest aspect of this period serves as the basis for the present day, for "in this era, everything is good, and all the good things have already come to pass."[20]

Another characteristic common to both Tablighis and Salafis is their extreme inflexibility regarding the status of women. The rules determining proper dress for women—namely niqab and a long loose garment covering the entire body—are presented as absolute and may never be questioned. Salafis are more extreme than Tablighis in their imposition of dress code; for Salafis, a woman must cover not only her hair but also her face and hands. The niqab, gloves, and long tunic fashionable in Saudi Arabia are what distinguish the Salafi woman from the Tablighi woman. The latter also wears a long tunic, but in a neutral color (not necessarily black) and covers her hair with the hijab only.

This puritanical interpretation of women's behavior regulates not only their dress but also their role as wife, as mother and daughter, and as a participant (or nonparticipant) in the community. Mixed-gender interaction is forbidden in both public spaces and schools, and male superiority is constantly reaffirmed, along with the Qur'anic legitimacy of corporal punishment for women (Qur'an, 4:34). This question of women's status—both within the family and in society—functions as a kind of litmus test, according to which the various interpretations of Islam may be classified from the most reactionary to the most liberal.[21] As mentioned in the previous chapter, the politicization of the female body is a general feature of Muslim societies from the colonial to the postcolonial periods. A consistent theme throughout this development on which the Salafi movement has capitalized is that women are the symbolic embodiment of morality and, therefore, are key to securing familial, national, and religious values in the uncertain maelstrom of social change.

In this light, Islam serves as a countercultural voice that simultaneously rebukes Western cultural hegemony and serves the respective political interests of Islamic religious authorities. In other words, Islam is conveniently used by both politicians and religious authorities in Middle Eastern countries to critique Western and secular values.

The female body has become the major site of this cultural and political tension that pitches Islam against the West, the past against the present, and community rights against individual rights.

The Subordination of the Religious Self to the Community

Similarly, the religious self is often defined by ritual action and public behaviors. Whereas in the West equality refers to uniform sets of individual rights, in the Salafi version, equality is the shared obligation of individuals to promote communal welfare. Hence, the moral obligation of the family allows no room for the "promotion of self" above the interests of the community. Globalization and consumerism challenge the adepts of this puritan and reactive vision of the world, which, in return, regards consumerism as the pinnacle of Western moral depravity.

In the same vein, these fundamentalist movements reject political participation, holding that the believer must maintain a separatist stance in relation to public institutions. A concrete example of this position is the fatwa, issued in 1996 by an American Salafi group, approving the actions of Abdul Rauf, a black Muslim basketball player who refused to rise for the singing of the national anthem.[22]

It is, therefore, no surprise that the themes on the most popular Salafi sites in the West concern primarily women's rights, sexuality, and relationships with non-Muslims.

Women Rights and Status
Most of the responses provided to questions on women reassert the Salafi orthodoxy:

- Women need to pick careers that allow them to observe Islamic legal boundaries, that is, a teacher for female students or a doctor for female patients ("women's work outside the home is permissible as long as it is not in conflict with modesty").[23]
- Women are weak and need the companionship of a male family member while traveling ("a woman traveling without a *mahram* (a chaperon) is a way to adultery").[24]
- The full-face veil (the niqab) is the correct dress code for women (not wearing the full-face veil could trigger "lust or even incest").[25]
- It is not justified for a woman to remove her hijab because the law forbids her from wearing it.[26]
- The marriage age for women is whenever she reaches puberty ("the issue of marriage is linked with the age of menstruation").[27]
- Although women are allowed to drive, they should beware of the consequences of driving (i.e., if the car breaks down, a woman might be put in a bad situation).[28]
- Women should not be alone with men in an elevator ("Allah has forbidden a man to be alone with a woman who is not her *mahram*...This meaning applies when a woman travels in an elevator with a man.").[29]
- Women and men should not shake hands ("Verily, I do not shake hands with women."—Bin Baz).[30]

Sexuality
The review of European Salafi sites shows that one of the great concerns of Muslims living in Western countries is about birth control and fornication.

The most common responses to questions regarding these topics are as follows:

- Sex education in school is "religiously forbidden for it contains description of male and female genitalia; exposing young children to this form of education can be indecent and immoral."[31]
- Birth control should not be used ("It is not allowed to take birth control pills. Allah has sanctioned the means that lead to procreation and a larger Muslim nation."—Bin Baz).[32]
- A couple that fornicates together is advised to get married.
- Homosexuality is unequivocally forbidden.

Relations with Non-Salafis and Non-Muslims

Most responses regarding relations with non-Muslims are summarized in the following points:

- Westernization is a great threat facing Muslim youth and is "one of the great threats facing the Muslim *Ummah*." Therefore, Muslims should try their best to avoid the influences of it.[33]
- Muslims should treat non-Muslims with respect but should not become friends or loyal to non-Muslims ("Be true in your sayings with your brothers and with those non-Muslims whom you live along with.").[34]
- Salafi Muslims should treat Shiites with respect and advise them on the right path, but should not pray with them ("Advise them to the right path and on what's wrong and what's right; show them that is a duty to like Ali bin Abi talib, but not to overpay reverence to him and his family.").[35]
- Avoid eating meat slaughtered by Shiites ("To be on the safe side avoid eating their meat" unless they are proven not to be *kaafir*.).[36]
- "A Muslim is not to shake hands with Jews or Christians."[37]
- A Muslim can only swear allegiance to a Muslim ruler ("Allegiance... means: a pledge to obey; it is as if the one who swears allegiance is promising his ruler that he will accept his authority with regard to his own affairs and the affairs of the Muslims.").[38]
- It is permissible for a Muslim to obtain the nationality of a non-Muslim state only after he has sought the nationality of a Muslim state, and only if he can practice his religion ("If a person is compelled to seek the nationality of a *kaafir* state because he has been forced to leave his own country and he can find no [Muslim] country to give him refuge, then this is permissible on the condition that he is able to practise his religion openly... But with regard to obtaining *kaafir* nationality for purely worldly purposes, I do not think that this is permissible.").[39]

There are a few instances when original opinion comes into some of the clerics' responses. When asked if it is permissible to speak at a community center that has a bar, Shaykh Jneid said that this is allowed as long as alcohol is not being served during the event.

Regarding politics and whether or not it is permissible to take part in elections there are varying views, depending on the political or apolitical orientation of the site. The latter reject political participation because they see it as giving power to an authority other than God. However, the former, particularly those in the Netherlands, encourage political participation. Shaykh Fawaz Jneid states that it is permissible to vote in elections if one does so in an effort to build justice within society. [40]

Conclusion: The Performance of Authenticity

The globalization of Salafism is somewhat at odds with the commodification of religious goods observed across all religious groups today. To be clear, Muslims like all other believers do consume their religion.[41] But it is not clear that this commodification leads to free-floating signifiers as described by Miller.[42] According to this author, commodification of religion has reduced religious beliefs, symbols, and values into free-floating signifiers to be consumed like anything else. As such, it takes them from their original contexts and throws them into a cultural marketplace where they can be embraced in a shallow fashion but not put into practice. In the case of the Muslims we have surveyed, their relation to Islam is not completely defined by this level of consumerism. What is at stake instead is a tension between Islam as the main communal marker and Islam as the marker of the religious self. In this context, the Salafi interpretation is only *one* way to draw boundary between religious community and religious self. But it is certainly the most accessible to Western political actors and media, on which they build their understanding of Islam.

To conclude, this visibility of Salafism leads to the confrontation of two opposite tropes. One comes from the dominant Western society, which seeks to posit Islam as its enemy, backward and incompatible with Western values of modernity, equality, and freedom. The other is the Salafi trope, in which the West is regarded as the enemy of Islam, Western developments as corruption of the Muslim faith, and Western influences as a threat to Islamic purity. Thus, these exclusivist tropes operate on a reversed but parallel process of, on one hand, putting Western culture outside the realm of the true Islam and, on the other, reinforcing the image perpetrated in many Western circles that Islam is incompatible with the values of the West. These two ideologies work simultaneously within each European society discussed above and tend to solidify the divide between Muslims and non-Muslims. These two mindsets leave no room for compromise or negotiation and convey intolerant and exclusive visions of the public space that feed into and reinforce each other, widening the gap between Islam and the West.

CONCLUSION

NAKED PUBLIC SPHERES:
ISLAM WITHIN LIBERAL AND
SECULAR DEMOCRACIES

In the previous chapters, we have shown that Muslims are politically constructed as the other of Western democracies. As synthesized by David Theo Goldberg:

> The Muslim in Europe has come to represent the threat of death...The Muslim image in contemporary Europe is overwhelmingly one of fanaticism, fundamentalism, female (women and girls') suppression, subjugation and repression. The Muslim in this view foments conflict...*He* is a traditionalist, pre-modern, in the tradition of racial historicism difficult if not impossible to modernize, at least without ceasing to be "the Muslim."[1]

This book is an attempt to unveil the multiple mechanisms at work in the binary opposition that pitches Islam against the West. To do so, it has operated at two different levels.

The first level was to de-link the empirical political and religious behaviors of Muslims from the putative monolithic religion that supposedly is Islam. To shed light on the way Muslims "of flesh of blood" behave and interact within current political conditions, we produced original data on Muslim religiosity and political participation. Our inquiry draws a complex and rich web of meanings and behaviors both on what it is to be a Muslim *and* a citizen in a European country or the United States. It is not possible from the existing data to conclude that Islamic religiosity impinges on political participation. Most interestingly, the data reveals that Islam is not per se the main factor in the building of Muslims' social identities or in their political participation. Instead, other elements—ethnicity, class, and residential distribution among them—have an effect that requires further investigation.

Since the empirical behavior of Muslims in the West is not the major reason behind the reification of Islam as the enemy, the second level of investigation was an exploration of three political and cultural factors that influence it: the War on Terror, the religious integration of Islam in secular spaces, and the salafization of Islamic thinking. Introducing Salafism was important in order to show that the putative opposition of Islam to the West is not just a construct of the West. It is also the outcome of a specific theology in which Islam is cast into a narrative defined, point-by-point, in opposition to the Western narrative.

This dual opposition is at the core of the symbolic politics that externalizes Islam from Western national communities. Our goal was to reach beyond discourse analysis to contextualize how the projection of Islam versus the West influences policymaking as well as social and cultural practices. To do so, we took into account the multifaceted transnational environment that lends space to this oppositional narrative. This environment includes relations between European countries; Europe and the United States; the United States and Muslim-majority countries; Muslim-majority countries and Muslim minorities in the West.

Across the chapters of this book, liberalism and secularism have appeared as the two major idioms used in the West to make sense of the Muslim presence.

Contextualizing Liberalism

The "Islamic Problem" in Europe is a consequence of immigrant settlement that in the last two decades has been phrased in cultural and religious terms. Or, to say it differently, "the radicalized, 'non-Western' poors, held politically responsible for the systemic changes of neoliberal globalization to European labor markets in the 1990s, have been fused with suspect Muslim communities since September 2001. Culturally unassimilated, ideologically inassimilable, and transnationally implicated as disloyal, the 'racial politics of the War on Terror' has produced 'intolerable subjects.'"[2]

The rise of the Islamic Problem is with no doubt due to the fact that Muslims stand at the core of three major social "problems"—immigration, class and economic integration, ethnicity and multiculturalism—as we have shown in chapter 5. In the United States, as mentioned several times, this culturalization is more recent and primarily related to security concerns.

Therefore, categories of immigrant and Muslim overlap in Western Europe, unlike in the United States where immigration debates center on economic and social concerns such as wages, assimilation, and language.[3]

The outcome of these social shifts is visible in the apocalyptic turn of the public rhetoric on Islam in Europe. Extreme Right political figures like Geert Wilders speaks of "the lights going out over Europe" or of "the sheer survival of the West." He further suggests that the problem is not just a "particular strain of violent revolutionary Islam, but Islam itself: 'If you want to compare Islam to anything, compare it to communism or National Socialism—a totalitarian ideology.'"[4]

It would be misleading to think that this existential war is waged only on the margins of European societies. In fact, numerous opinion surveys as well as political discourses analyzed in chapter 1 show that the perception of Islam as a danger to Western core political values is shared across political allegiances and nations. This existential war manifests itself in the political distinction between good and bad Muslims as well as in the defense of West's universal liberal values.

Good Muslim versus Bad Muslim: The Clash of Essentialisms[5]

In Mamdani's terms, the "good" Muslims are secular and Westernized while the "bad" Muslims are doctrinal, antimodern, and virulent.[6] In other words, a distinction between radical, bad Islam and moderate, good Islam has become a common political framing across European and American democracies.[7]

We have shown in chapter 7 that the same distinction, used in the opposite way, is at the core of global Salafi thinking. Good Muslims are religiously conservative, wear hijab, follow a strict gender separation, avoid promiscuity, and limit their relations with non-Muslims or Muslims who do not behave like them. In contrast, bad Muslims have been contaminated by the Western lifestyle and values and, therefore, are in need of purification. As already explained, this discourse fails to reflect the malleability and flexibility of Muslim religious practices. Nevertheless, it still operates as an authoritative interpretation of Islamic orthodoxy and influences Muslims' identification to their religious tradition. Thus, the good Muslim becomes an ontological category based on total acceptance without critique of divine law, which is defined as immutable. In the mirror, the good Muslim of the West also operates on the same essentialization of liberal values at the core of Western political civilization.

In this sense, the clash is not between civilizations but between essentialized and inverted perceptions of Islam and Muslims that reinforce each other.

The Alliance of Liberalism and Feminism

The other manifestation of this existential war is the rise of a values-centered liberalism that pitches itself against the recognition of religious and cultural diversity. For example, British prime minister David Cameron declared in February 2011 at the annual Munich Security Conference of world leaders: "Frankly, we need a lot less of the passive tolerance of recent years and much more active, muscular liberalism."[8]

It is important to emphasize that, historically, political liberalism at the foundation of Western democracies is not necessarily incompatible with the recognition of pluralism. Based on toleration, the liberal state is traditionally expected to grant equality to citizens of all religious and cultural backgrounds.[9]

In contrast, the new liberal discourse sees recognition of minority rights as a threat to freedom of expression and women's rights that are apprehended as the core values of national communities. Hence, it advocates a strong cultural integration of newcomers. As a consequence it has created very significant policy shifts in countries usually characterized by multiculturalism such as the United Kingdom or the Netherlands. For example, the multicultural project of recognition of "cultural diversity in a context of mutual tolerance" of Labour Home Secretary Roy Jenkins in 1966[10] is now strongly criticized. According to Arun Kundani:

> Looking back, many liberals feel that the formula should have been "cultural diversity in an atmosphere of British values." They argue that if Britain had asserted national values as the non-negotiable limit to any accommodation of cultural difference, then liberalism now would have less difficulty with diversity, and the process of producing appropriately liberal minority subjects would have begun much earlier.[11]

In brief, the new political consensus is to prioritize strong cultural assimilation to British values over minority rights. Interestingly, as we discussed in part 2, such a negative perception of multiculturalism is not grounded in an assessment of the outcomes of multicultural policies which have actually positively contributed to the political integration of Muslims.[12]

This "new integrationism" is widely shared across European countries and, interestingly, is promoted by former left-wing activists. Gender equality and rejection of religious authority, which were primary left-wing topics of struggle in the 1960s, have become in the present decade the legitimate markers of European identity.[13] As Kundnani points out: "Liberalism, nationalism, and civilization are intertwined, apparently seamlessly, into a unified discourse of identity. However, now this European legacy is regarded as under threat from alien identities—symbolized by the Muslim presence in Europe—which do not value this liberal legacy."[14]

In these conditions, all groups and individuals are required to demonstrate conformity to these liberal values in order to become legitimate members of national communities. The "moderate Muslims" label discussed in chapter 6 serves this purpose. It creates a distinction that is supposedly not based on Islam as such but on the adherence of Muslims to liberal values.

Strikingly, feminist groups have become key actors in shaping this discourse. Major feminist figures, including Susan Oskin, have been particularly vehement against group rights and especially against any Islamic principles that could undermine gender equality as we have seen in the Ontario controversy on shari'a courts. Their concern is justified by the following argument:

(1) Some group rights, if granted, would harm women more than they would harm men (that is they would harm women differentially).

(2) Liberal institutions typically will fail to distinguish harmful from innocuous rights.

(3) Liberal institutions should not grant rights that would harm women differentially.

(4) Therefore, liberal institutions should not grant group rights.[15]

As noted by Jasmine Zine,[16] this feminist discourse silences the Muslim women that it purports to defend. As a consequence, Muslim women are transformed into subalterns in a way that is similar to the colonial and postcolonial vision of the Muslim subject. As seen in the controversies analyzed throughout this book, state, Muslim leaders, intellectuals, and feminists all speak for Muslim women, thereby infantilizing them and reinscribing colonial binary oppositions—secular/religious, free/oppressed, liberal/illiberal, and the like—that further deprive them of agency.

This new integrationist discourse goes hand in hand with states' active policies to transform the behaviors and identities of their Muslim citizens. For example, state-led production of Muslim subjects with the correct moral identity is reflected in various policies: value tests and oaths of allegiance for would-be migrants and citizens, recruitment of moderate Muslims as state-sponsored role models and community leaders, and formal and informal restrictions on Islamic practices seen as extremist or illiberal.

All these policies can be summed up as an attempt to civilize the enemy. Such a project is not only a speech act but also translates into discreet or invisible regulations of Muslim cultural and social practices as we discussed in chapter 5. Interestingly, most Muslims we interviewed reveal that they are already "civilized" and are trying to find commonality with the dominant group. Most of the time, however, they are silenced or reduced to the reification of their bodies, dress, or minarets.

One of our most striking findings is the non-contentious nature of being a Muslim *and* a citizen, while it is this exact dichotomy that puts Muslims at odds with the social expectations of most Europeans.

At the core of the European shift is the blind spot of the social legitimacy of religion that has been completely eliminated from most of national discourse and values.

Contextualizing Secularism

The presence of Islam unveils (pun intended) the specifics of European secular cultures and demonstrates the limits of the universal claim of secularism. In this book, we have defined secularism as the specific political culture shaping secular principles of legal neutrality and equality of all religions. Such an approach is not new. Several historical studies have pointed out that, far from being explained by teleological arguments of natural progress and reason, European secularism is actually the result of particular historical and sociological conditions.[17] More specifically, separation of church and state, often presented as the universal principle of secularity, is in fact the result of the seventeenth-century political compromise designed to deal with the emergent religious pluralism and its devastating consequences for political stability. This compromise led to privatization of religion or bracketing religious differences off from the sphere of public regulation.

This historical compromise has been erected as the universal standard in which secularization means separation of state and religion, privatization of religious activities, and decline of religious practices. Therefore, when citizens with a religious background are contradicting this universalism by adopting dress code, dietary rules, or other religious obligations with social implications, the secular political cultures of the West are in crisis. Muslims are troublesome, because they express their individuality through religious postures that for most of Europeans are not compatible with the idealized secular civism.

Two major consequences ensue from this contextualization of secularism. First, it reveals that the institutional and conceptual forms of secularism are actually linked to Christianity. As shown by Talal Asad,[18] the definition of religion as a set of private beliefs is the result of the historical evolution of Christianity in Europe. It is more specifically linked to the Protestant Reformation that makes the personal, private, and cognitive relationship to God the key element of religiosity. In these circumstances, secularism is not simply a legal procedure to distinguish what is private and what is public for religions. It is also a way to discipline all religions other than Protestantism when they include prescriptions and commitments that do not conform to this neat private-public division.[19] According to Danielle Celermajer:

> Adherents of non-Protestant religions point to the implicit Protestant theology underpinning the apparent neutrality of a certain model of secularism. In these conditions, the popular idea of "Islamic exceptionalism" is questionable because the religious commitments intrinsic to various religions, including Catholicism and Judaism, also cross over into the public sphere and that accommodations have been made by playing at the boundaries, rather than through these religions' intrinsic compatibility with privatization.[20]

The second consequence of contextualizing secularism is to reveal how secularism can turn into an ideology or counter-religion aimed against any form of religion in public space.[21] The French version of secularism, or *laïcité*, is an illustration of this extreme ideological interpretation of secular principles.

To conclude, the symbolic integration of Muslims within national communities would require a dramatic change in the current liberal and secularist narratives. It is a daunting task, but it can be done.

On March 10, 2011, the hearings of the Congress Commission on Radicalization of American Muslims provided a platform for at least two individuals to weave Muslims into the American narrative. In his testimony,

Congressman Keith Ellison (D-MN), the first Muslim elected to Congress, tearfully etched into America's consciousness the story of Salman Ahmad, a Muslim paramedic and New York police cadet killed trying to help fellow New Yorkers on 9/11. Additionally, Congressman Brian Higgins, a Catholic, stated that America's tradition is "Christian-Judeo-Islamic," not simply "Christian-Judeo."[22]

This can be seen as empty feel-good talk, but it can also be the prefiguration of how historical references can be used to achieve symbolic integration and counter the dominant narrative that tends to present Islam as an alien religion.

APPENDIX 1

FOCUS GROUP DESCRIPTION

Amsterdam Focus Groups

No.	Category	Date
1	Moroccan highly educated women	July 25, 2008
2	Moroccan highly educated men	August 13, 2008
3	Turkish highly educated women	August 6, 2008
4	Turkish elderly women	September 3, 2008
5	Turkish Elderly Men	September 4, 2008
6	Surinamese mixed gender (Muslims)	September 14, 2008
7	Moroccan mixed gender	October 9, 2008
8	Interethnic male	October 10, 2008
9	Turkish mixed gender	October 14, 2008
10	Control group (Surinamese non-Muslim)	October 30, 2008
11	Interethnic female	November 10, 2008

Berlin Focus Groups

No.	Category	Date
1	Bosnian women	June 15, 2008
2	Turkish women	June 17, 2008
3	Turkish coed	June 17, 2008
4	Arab men	July 4, 2008
5	Turkish men	July 5, 2008
6	Bosnian men	July 4, 2008
7	All ethnicities coed	June 17, 2008
8	Arab women	July 10, 2008
9	Arab coed	July 10, 2008
10	Non-Muslim immigrants	August 15, 2008
11	Non-Muslim immigrants	October 3, 2008

Paris Focus Groups

No.	Category	Date
1	Coed	July 25, 2008
2	Moroccan highly educated men	August 13, 2008
3	Turkish highly educated women	August 6, 2008
4	Turkish elderly women	September 3, 2008
5	Turkish elderly men	September 4, 2008
6	Surinamese mixed gender (Muslims)	September 14, 2008
7	Moroccan mixed gender	October 9, 2008
8	Interethnic male	October 10, 2008
9	Turkish mixed gender	October 14, 2008
10	Control group (Surinamese non-Muslim)	October 30, 2008
11	Interethnic female	November 10, 2008

Boston Focus Groups

No.	Category	Date
1	African American	July 9, 2008
2	Lebanese coed	March 2, 2008
3	Mixed ethnicity men	May 18, 2008
4	Mixed ethnicity women	May 18, 2008
5	Moroccan coed	March 23, 2008
6	Moroccan females	March 11, 2008
7	Moroccan men	December 17, 2007
8	Muslim community leaders	June 24, 2008
9	Pakistani coed	February 10, 2008
10	Pakistani females	May 4, 2008
11	Pakistani men	May 4, 2008
12	Turkish coed	April 13, 2008

London Focus Groups

No.	Category	Date
1	Bangladeshi men	September 6, 2009
2	Bangladeshi women	September 6, 2009
3	Bangladeshi mix	September 6, 2009
4	Focus group 3—Turkish speaking men	September 7, 2009

5	Focus group 7—Turkish speaking mix gender	September 7, 2009
6	Focus group 8—London Turkish, Kurdish women participants	September 7, 2009
7	Iraqi men	September 8, 2009
8	Iraqi mixed 1	September 8, 2009
9	Iraqi women	September 8, 2009
10	Somali men	September 10, 2009

FOCUS GROUP: MODERATOR GUIDELINES

Introduction (10 minutes)

1. Moderator to introduce self and other staff members present.
2. Welcome the participants and verify if each subject's consent form has been signed and collected.
3. Ask participants to fill in a background survey (age/education/professional activity/ethnic and national background/address and contact) (do not sign)—place in large envelope and return to Gwen.
4. Briefly explain the nature and purpose of the focus group: to discuss Islam and citizenship to help create a questionnaire.

Today's focus group is meant to be an open and frank exchange of viewpoints. Naturally, opinions will differ, so a couple of things are worth mentioning. First, we're not looking for "right" or "wrong" answers; instead, the key thing is to hear a variety of perspectives and opinions. Second, it's OK to disagree; what's important though is to be considerate of each other's right to express a differing opinion.

My role is to moderate the discussion and keep it moving and "focused" on the main questions. I'm here to facilitate the discussion, not participate. Talk to each other and not just to me.

As you can see, we are recording today's focus group. This is important because it's very hard for us to take notes and still listen carefully to what you are saying. No one outside of our research team will ever (hear/see) this tape, nor will any of you be identified by name.

Moderator: Start the discussion by asking the subjects to briefly introduce themselves.

Questions

1. I'd like to begin by asking you to talk about how you see your identity. By "identity," I mean your personal sense of "who you are" as both an individual and in relation to other people. First, let me ask this:

Outside of family and relatives, how important is it for other people to know that you are Muslim?

Probe:

Feel connectedness to other Muslims?

- Does being Muslim figure into your social relationships—like friendships, socialization, workplace?
- More conscious of being Muslim in different situations or times?
- Racial or ethnic identity, for example "Arab," "Black," "Latino," "South Asian"—important for other people to know that you are (racial or ethnic group)?
- Other people see you as either Muslim or (racial or ethnic group)?
- Influence of family, relatives?

2. In America, you're pretty much free to follow any religion you want, including the freedom to have no religion at all. Generally speaking, do you think it's necessary for an American to have religious beliefs to be a good, moral person?

Probe:

- Is religion important to you in your daily life?
- What is to be religious for you—like doing prayers, fasting, reading/listening to the Qur'an, going to a mosque?
- Is dress code important?
- Moral values? Which ones?
- Do religious values influence your sexual life?
- Confidence in Muslim religious or spiritual leaders in America? Which ones?
- Confidence in Muslim spiritual leaders outside? Which ones?
- In case of stress or difficult times in your life, do you turn to religion for help—for example, praying or listening to the Qur'an?
- Even the most religious people can sometimes doubt or question their beliefs. Have you ever questioned your own religious beliefs? What made you feel that way? Thoughts of converting? Disbelief in God?
- Is American society a proper environment to be a Muslim? (Give reasons.)
- Do you find particular challenges to be Muslim in the United States (versus a Muslim in a Muslim country)?
- Do you trust in people from other religions—Christianity, Judaism, Hinduism, and Buddhism?
- Do you have personal relationships with people from other faiths?
- Do you have personal relationships with people who do not have any faith?

3. Now, let me ask you for your thoughts about some of the challenges facing Muslim Americans today. First, generally speaking, do you feel that non-Muslim Americans are respectful and kind toward Muslim Americans?

Probe:
   • Since 9/11, has discrimination against Muslim Americans increased, decreased, stayed about the same?
   • Have you personally faced any verbal or physical abuse because of your religion or ethnicity? In the workplace? In public places?
   • Has anyone (non-Muslim) showed you support or solidarity?
   • What has changed for you as a Muslim in America since 9/11?

4. Are there political or social causes you are fighting for or would like to fight for in the United States?

Probe:
   • Are you member of political or civic organizations? Why?
   • Do you keep yourself informed on the social and political situation of the United States?

Closure

5. At present, are you satisfied with the way things are going in American society?
6. Are there any important questions or issues that you feel we missed or should have raised?

[Moderator: Distribute gift cards/cash and have each person sign a receipt.]

APPENDIX 3

DRAFT SURVEY OF THE CIVIC AND POLITICAL PARTICIPATION OF GERMAN MUSLIMS

Demographic/Background/General Questions (Many But Not All Having to Do with Vertical Dimension of Status Or National/Ethnic Background)

v001. In what year were you born?
[VALID ENTRIES 1885 TO 1988]

> RECORD YEAR (4-DIGITS) _____
> -1=(DO NOT READ) Don't know / No opinion
> -2=(DO NOT READ) No answer / Refused
> -3=Not relevant

v002. Family status = Are you currently:

> 1=Married
> 2=Separated
> 3=Divorced
> 4=Widowed
> 5=Never married
> 6=Living with a partner
> -1=(DO NOT READ) Don't know / No opinion
> -2=(DO NOT READ) No answer / Refused
> -3=Not relevant

v003. Employment status = Next, I would like to ask a few questions about work. We'd like to know if you are working now full-time, working now part-time, temporarily laid off, or if you are unemployed, retired, incapacitated, looking after the home, a student, or what?

> 1=Working now full-time
> 2=Working now part-time
> 3=Temporarily laid off
> 4=Unemployed
> 5=Retired

6="Disabled"
7=Looking after the home
8=Student
9=No work permit/labor permit
10=Other (SPECIFY)
-1=(DO NOT READ) Don't know / No opinion
-2=(DO NOT READ) No answer / Refused
-3=Not relevant

v004. What is your job or occupation? Note job description and ask categories:

1=Worker
2=Clerk
3=Public official
4=Unemployed
5=Self-employed person
-1=(DO NOT READ) Don't know / No opinion
-2=(DO NOT READ) No answer / Refused
-3=Not relevant

v005. What is your household income?

1=Under 1000€
2=1000–2000€
3=2000–3000€
4=3000–4000€
5=4000–5000€
6=Above 5000€
-1=(DO NOT READ) Don't know / No opinion
-2=(DO NOT READ) No answer / Refused
-3=Not relevant

v006. What is the highest grade of school or year of college you have completed?

1=None or grade 1–8
2=High school incomplete (grades 9–11)
3=High school grad
4=Business, technical, or vocational school after high school
5=Some college, no 4-year degree
6=College graduate
7=Postgraduate training or professional schooling
-1=(DO NOT READ) Don't know / No opinion
-2=(DO NOT READ) No answer / Refused
-3=Not relevant

v007. Do you aspire any further grade or education?

v008.   Are you a German citizen?

1=Yes
0=No
-1=(DO NOT READ) Don't know / No opinion
-2=(DO NOT READ) No answer / Refused
-3=Not relevant

v008a. If not, which residence status do you have?

1=Toleration (Duldung)
2=Temporary
3=Unlimited
-1=(DO NOT READ) Don't know / No opinion
-2=(DO NOT READ) No answer / Refused
-3=Not relevant

v009.   What country were you born in?_____

v009a. [If not born in Germany, ask:] What year did you come here?

v010.   Are you also a citizen of another country?

0=No
1=Yes
-1=(DO NOT READ) Don't know / No opinion
-2=(DO NOT READ) No answer / Refused
-3=Not relevant

v010a. If so, what country? _____

v010b. Do you possess an identity card from Lebanon?

0=No
1=Yes
-1=(DO NOT READ) Don't know / No opinion
-2=(DO NOT READ) No answer / Refused
-3=Not relevant

v011.   If you have not chosen to become a citizen of Germany, why not?

Because I don't think the German citizenship would give me any
    advantages.
I don't want to give up my current citizenship.
I do not meet all the preconditions (yet).
-1=(DO NOT READ) Don't know / No opinion
-2=(DO NOT READ) No answer / Refused
-3=Not relevant

v012.   Were your parents born in Germany?

1=Yes, both parents born in Germany.

2=One parent born in Germany.
3=No, neither parent born in Germany.
-1=(DO NOT READ) Don't know / No opinion
-2=(DO NOT READ) No answer / Refused
-3=Not relevant

vo13. If not Germany: What country was your mother born in?

_____

vo14. If not Germany: What country was your father born in?

_____

What country or countries do you identify with most? (Skip if R said "don't know" or did not answer previous question.)

vo15a. First mention (own country of birth)
vo15b. Second mention (country of birth of mother)
vo15c. Third mention (country of birth of father)
vo15d. Other
vo15e. None/can't choose (0=No, 1=Yes, -1=Don't know, -2=No answer, -3=Not relevant)

Why did you or your parents come to German?

vo16a. Political reasons (to seek asylum)
vo16b. Economic reasons (to work)
vo16c. Educational reasons (to study, get a degree)
vo16d. Family reunion (to live together as a family)
vo16e. My grandparents already came to Germany
vo16f. Other
vo16g. None of my parents or grandparents migrated to Germany
-1=(DO NOT READ) Don't know / No opinion
-2=(DO NOT READ) No answer / Refused
-3=Not relevant

vo17. Please choose the answer that applies best to your situation now. In your family: (Here there is no possibility for a third language: Turkish and Kurdish, Arabic and Turkish, Bosnian and Serb.)

1=You speak German but your parents/grandparents speak only another language.
2=Everybody speaks another language instead of German.
3=Everybody speaks German only.
4=Everybody speaks German and another language.
-1=(DO NOT READ) Don't know / No opinion
-2=(DO NOT READ) No answer / Refused
-3=Not relevant

Which of the following aspects is more important for who you are from your perspective: job, cultural background, ethnic background, religion, family? Can you weigh the aspects from 1=very important to 5=less important?

vo18a. Job
vo18b. Cultural background
vo18c. Ethnic background
vo18d. Religion
vo18e. Family

> -1=(DO NOT READ) Don't know / No opinion
> -2=(DO NOT READ) No answer / Refused
> -3=Not relevant

What do you identify with the most?

vo20a. To be a Berliner
vo20b. To be a German
vo20c. To be a European
vo20d. With my neighborhood, that means to be from Kreuzberg, Neukolln, Wedding, etc.
vo20e. With my country of origin/country of origin of my ancestors

> -1=(DO NOT READ) Don't know / No opinion
> -2=(DO NOT READ) No answer / Refused
> -3=Not relevant

vo21. What is the highest level of education of your spouse?

> 1=None or grade 1–8
> 2=High school incomplete (grades 9–11)
> 3=High school grad
> 4=Business, technical, or vocational school after high school
> 5=Some college, no 4-year degree
> 6=College graduate
> 7=Post-graduate training or professional schooling after college
> -1=(DO NOT READ) Don't know / No opinion
> -2=(DO NOT READ) No answer / Refused
> -3=Not relevant

vo22. If your spouse works for pay outside the home, what is his/her job?

> 1=Worker
> 2=Clerk
> 3=Public official
> 4=Unemployed
> 5=Self-employed person
> -1=(DO NOT READ) Don't know / No opinion
> -2=(DO NOT READ) No answer / refused
> -3=Not relevant

v023.   What is your spouse's country of origin?

v024.   What was your father's highest level of education?

1=None or grade 1–8
2=High school incomplete (grades 9–11)
3=High school grad
4=Business, technical, or vocational school after high school
5=Some college, no 4-year degree
6=College graduate
7=Post-graduate training or professional schooling after college
-1=(DO NOT READ) Don't know / No opinion
-2=(DO NOT READ) No answer / Refused
-3=Not relevant

v025.   What was your mother's highest level of education?

1=None or grade 1–8
2=High school incomplete (grades 9–11)
3=High school grad
4=Business, technical, or vocational school after high school
5=Some college, no 4-year degree
6=College graduate
7=Post-graduate training or professional schooling after college
-1=(DO NOT READ) Don't know / No opinion
-2=(DO NOT READ) No answer / Refused
-3=Not relevant

v026.   My country of origin / the country of my ancestors is:

v027.   I go to my country of origin / to the country of my ancestors for (Yes, No)

v027a.   Business purposes

v027aa. If yes, how often: 1=Once a year, 2=Several times a year, 3=Sporadically, -1=DK, -2=NA, -3=NR

v027b.   Leisure

v027bb. If yes, how often: 1=Once a year, 2=Several times a year, 3=Sporadically, -1=DK, -2=NA, -3=NR

v027c.   Religious education

v027cc. If yes, how often: 1=Once a year, 2=Several times a year, 3=Sporadically, -1=DK, -2=NA, -3=NR

v027d.   Visit family or friends

v027dd. If yes, how often: 1=Once a year, 2=Several times a year, 3=Sporadically, -1=DK, -2=NA, -3=NR

v027e.   Never, 1=Cannot, 2=Do not want to, -1=DK, -2=NA, -3=NR

v027f.   Why can't you?: _____

I go to Muslim countries outside my country of origin for:

v031a. Business purposes

v031aa. If yes, how often: 1=Once a year, 2=Several times a year, 3=Sporadically, -1=DK, -2=NA, -3=NR

v031b. Leisure

v031bb. If yes, how often: 1=Once a year, 2=Several times a year, 3=Sporadically, -1=DK, -2=NA, -3=NR

v031c. Religious education

v031cc. If yes, how often: 1=Once a year, 2=Several times a year, 3=Sporadically, -1=DK, -2=NA, -3=NR

v031d. Visit family or friends

v031dd. If yes, how often: 1=Once a year, 2=Several times a year, 3=Sporadically, -1=DK, -2=NA, -3=NR

v031e. Never

v031ee. 1=Cannot, 2=Do not want to, -1=DK, -2=NA, -3=NR

v031f. Why can't you?:

v036a-e. Which Muslim country(ies) do you visit? (#1–#5)

Questions about Religion, Religiosity - total?: 50

r001. Do you regard yourself as belonging to any particular religion? If yes, which?

1 Catholic
2 Protestant
3 Jewish
4 Muslim
5 Buddhist
6 Other
7 None
-1 Don't know
-2 Refuse or no answer
-3 Not relevant

r001a. Other, specify: _____

r002. When you were growing up, did you have the same religious preference as you do now or a different religious preference?

1 Yes, same
0 No, different
-1=DK, -2=NA, -3=NR

r003. If different, what was your religious preference growing up?

1 Catholic
2 Protestant

3 Jewish
4 Muslim
5 Buddhist
6 Other
7 None
-1=DK, -2=NA, -3=NR

r003a. Other, specify: _____

4. If married, divorced, or widowed: What is/was your husband's/wife's/ partner's religion?

1 Catholic
2 Protestant
3 Jewish
4 Muslim
5 Buddhist
6 Other
7 None
-1=DK, -2=NA, -3=NR

r004a. Other, specify: _____

r005. How often nowadays do you attend services or meetings connected with your religion? (READ STEM ONLY. DO NOT READ RESPONSE CATEGORIES INITIALLY. USE RESPONSE CATEGORIES AS PROBE ONLY IF NECESSARY)

1 One or more times per week
2 One or several times a month
3 Several times a year
4 About once or twice a year
5 Less than once a year
6 Only for festivities (Bayram, Eid al-Adha)
7 Only in Ramadan
8 Only on Fridays
9 Never
-1=DK, -2=NA, -3=NR

r006. Are you officially a member of a mosque association or other place of worship?
1 Yes
0 No
-1=DK, -2=NA, -3=NR

r007. Do you regularly attend the same mosque community? / Are you engaged in a mosque community?
1 Yes

        0 No
        -1=DK, -2=NA, -3=NR

r008.   Do you visit *several* mosques or other places of worship regularly?
        0 No
        1 No, only one
        2 Yes, two
        3 Yes, three or more
        4 I don't have a special place of worship
        -1=DK, -2=NA, -3=NR

Some Muslims don't go to mosques for prayer. Here is a list of reasons. Are there reasons among these that you find plausible?

        r00901 There is no place of worship in the area.
        r00902 The places of worship are dominated by extremists.
        r00903 The places of worship are under surveillance of German security.
        r00904 The person feels discriminated in the places of worship because of his/her ethnic, linguistic, religious background.
        r00905 A Muslim can do his/her prayers everywhere and not only in a mosque.
        r00906 No, it is a religious duty and no reasons can speak against this
           -1=DK, -2=NA, -3=NR
        r00907 Other reasons: _____

We'd like to ask about various ways in which some people practice religion, whether or not they belong to a particular congregation. The first/next item is (INSERT):

        r010. a. Participation in communal prayer (including Friday and daily prayers).
        r010. b. Individual prayers:
           1 Once or several times a day
           2 Once a day
           3 Once or several times a month
           4 Once or several times a year
           5 Never
           -1=DK, -2=NA, -3=NR
        r010. c. Read about religion and listen to programs on religion on the radio or TV.
        r010. d. Talk about religion with your family and friends:
           1 Once or several times a day
           2 Once a day
           3 Once or several times a week
           4 Once a week
           5 Once or several times a month

6 Several times a year
7 Less frequent
8 Never
-1=DK, -2=NA, -3=NR

ro15.   Did you fast this year during Ramadan?

1=I did not fast at all.
2=I fasted some of the days.
3=I fasted most days.
4=I fasted the whole month (without the exceptional days because of sickness, menstruation, breastfeeding).
5=Others.
-1=DK, -2=NA, -3=NR

ro15a.   Others:

ro16.   If you are invited to a non-Muslim household, what is your response?

1=I accept with no problem, and eat and drink everything offered.
2=I accept and avoid eating pork and drinking alcohol.
3=I accept and avoid eating pork.
4=I accept and eat strictly vegetarian food and don't drink alcohol.
5=I accept if the food is halal/tarbiyyah.
6=I accept if no alcohol is served and drunk.
7=I refuse.
8=Others.
-1=DK, -2=NA, -3=NR

ro16a.   Others, specify: _____

ro17.   Do you drink alcohol?

1=Yes
2=Sometimes (which occasion?)
3=Never
-1=DK, -2=NA, -3=NR

ro18a.   (For women): Are you wearing a headscarf outside the house? Yes / No /Occasionally

ro18b.   (For men with a partner): Is your wife or partner wearing a headscarf outside the house? Yes/No

ro18c.   (For widowed/separated/divorced men): Did your wife or partner wear a headscarf outside the house? Yes/No

ro18d.   (For single men): If you had a partner, would you want her to wear a headscarf outside the house? Yes/No

-1=DK, -2=NA, -3=NR

r01801. Should people who work with the general public be allowed to dress in a way that shows their religious faith, for example by wearing veils, turbans or crucifixes?

    1=Yes, 0=No, -1=DK, -2=NA, -3=NR

Muslim women who don't wear a headscarf give several reasons. Which do you find plausible?

r019a. The school teacher does not approve of it.
r019b. Friends, spouse, parents don't approve of it.
r019c. The woman herself doesn't approve of it.
r019d. If a woman doesn't find a job.
r019e. If a woman fears verbal and physical harassment in public.
r019f. Because it is not a religious duty.
    -1=DK, -2=NA, -3=NR

20.   If your son wanted to marry a non-Muslim woman, your reaction would be:

I would approve.
It would be his decision, and he doesn't need my approval.
I would be against it but approve.
I would disapprove.
-1=DK, -2=NA, -3=NR

r021. If your daughter wanted to marry a non-Muslim man, your reaction would be:

I would approve.
It would be her decision, and she doesn't need my approval.
I would be against it but approve.
I would disapprove.
-1=DK, -2=NA, -3=NR

Which thoughts are important when naming a child?

    r022a. The name should be easy to pronounce for Germans.
    r022b. That the religious/ethnic affiliation background becomes clear.
    r022c. Family traditions (name of father/mother, grandfather/grandmother etc.).
    r022d. That the name has a beautiful meaning.
    r022e. That the name was carried by famous persons, politicians, actors, stars.
    r022f. That children will not be mocked because of their name.
    r022g. Others: _____

r023. Which comes closer to your views? In matters of right and wrong, some people say it is important to faithfully follow the leaders and teachings of one's religion; others say it is more important to follow one's own conscience. (READ CHOICES; ENTER ONE ONLY)

1 Leaders and religious teachings
2 Own conscience
3 (VOLUNTEERED) Mixture of leaders/teaching and own conscience
-1=DK, -2=NA, -3=NR

Being Muslim is primarily (RANKED):

r024a. Having a set of beliefs
r024b. A relationship to God
r024c. Following the example of the Prophet
r024d. A way of life
r024e. Practicing a set of rituals (prayer, fasting, etc.)
r024f. Belonging to the *Ummah*
r024g. Adhering to certain moral standards
r024h. Doing good
r024i. Cultural background (being born into a Muslim family)
r024j. Being discriminated against as a Muslim
r024k. Others, specify: _____
-1=DK, -2=NA, -3=NR

r025a. About praying in a mosque, do you think that:

1=Women should not be allowed in mosques.
2=Women should be separate from men, in another area of the mosque or behind a curtain.
3=Women should pray behind men, with no curtain.
4=Women should pray in an area alongside men, with no curtain.
5=Others.
-1=DK, -2=NA, -3=NR

r025b. Can a woman lead the prayer?

1=In a communal prayer of women
2=In a mixed communal prayer of men and women together
3=In a mixed Friday prayer
-1=DK, -2=NA, -3=NR

r025c. Which of these statements comes closest to describing your feelings about the Qur'an:

r025c1 The Qur'an is the actual word of God and has to be taken literally, word for word.
r025c2 The Qur'an is the actual word of God and will always be filtered through the interpretation of human beings.
r025c3 The Qur'an is an ancient book of fables, legends, history, and moral precepts recorded by men.
-1=DK, -2=NA, -3=NR

r025d. Some people contribute money for a wide variety of causes while others don't.

During the past 12 months, did you or your household happen to give any money to any charitable or religious cause?

> 1=Yes
> 0=No
> -1=DK, -2=NA, -3=NR

How has your behavior as a Muslim changed in the past 10 years? Please mark 1 through 5, where 1 is a lot and 5 is not at all.

> r026a. Tried to become goodwill ambassador for Islam
> r026b. Tried to hide Islamic identity from strangers
> r026c. Tried to learn more about Islam
> r026d. Went (more often) to public debates on Islam and Muslims
> r026e. Got more involved (interested) in politics in U.S.
> r026f. Got more involved (interested) in politics of my home country or country of ancestors
> r026g. Got more involved (interested) in politics of another country.
> r026g1. If so, which? _____
> r026h. Changed my name or accent to sound less foreign
> -1=DK, -2=NA, -3=NR

r034. In the past two years, I:

> r034a. Started donating money to Muslim charities
> r034b. Stopped donating money to some Muslim charities
> r034c. Put on the hijab or changed appearance in Islamic way
> r034d. Took off hijab or changed appearance away from Islamic way
> r034e. Started going to the mosque
> r034f. Stopped going to the mosque
> 1-Exactly right... 4-Not right at all
> -1=DK, -2=NA, -3=NR

r037 Agree or disagree (Strongly agree, tend to agree, neither agree nor disagree, tend to disagree, strongly disagree):

> r037 a. I feel more free to practice Islam in Germany than in Muslim countries.
> r037 b. In Germany, Muslims have to reason their doing constantly; that is why they reflect more on religion.
> r037 c. Religious conviction should be better protected by the government.
> r037 d. Prayer in public school should be permitted.
> r037 e. Normal people don't have influence on decision making.
> r037 f. I have the feeling that my engagement/participation has positive effects on society.
> r037 g. Islam is not just good for the Islamic community but for the whole society.

r037 h. You don't do yourself any good if you don't participate in the community.

r037 i. Muslims should actively participate in society.

r037 j. It is better to get involved in Muslim organizations than in nondenominational groups.

r037 k. Church groups have more power than other religious groups in this country.

r037 l. Atheists have too much power in this country.

-1=DK, -2=NA, -3=NR

r050. How concerned, if at all, are you about the rise of Islamic extremism around the world these days? Are you very concerned, somewhat concerned, not too concerned or not at all concerned about the rise of Islamic extremism around the world these days?

1. =Very concerned
2. =Somewhat concerned
3. =Not too concerned
4. =Not at all concerned
-1=DK, -2=NA, -3=NR

r051. How concerned, if at all, are you about the possible rise of Islamic extremism in Germany? Are you very concerned, somewhat concerned, not too concerned, or not at all concerned about the possible rise of Islamic extremism in Germany?

1=Very concerned
2=Somewhat concerned
3=Not too concerned
4=Not at all concerned
-1=DK, -2=NA, -3=NR

Questions about Civic and Political Participation, Including Religious Participation

p001. How about volunteering? Some people volunteer, others don't. How many times, if any, did you volunteer in the past 12 months? By volunteering, we mean tasks and work that you did voluntarily and that was not paid or only with a small compensation. (This explanation is taken from a Germany-wide survey on voluntary work.)

0=Never
1=Once or a few times
2=Once every few months
3=About once or twice a month on average
4=About once a week or more on average
-1=DK, -2=NA, -3=NR

2. Are you engaged in one of these fields?

    p002a. Religious association / mosque association
    p002b. Inter-religious dialogue
    p002c. Union (representation of workers)
    p002d. Political representation (party, political organization, Amnesty
        International, migrant organization)
    p002e. Parent representation
    p002f. Environmental initiative
    p002g. Youth work, education (school, kindergarden)
    p002h. Justice, prevention of criminality
    p002i. Neighborhood initiative
    p002j. Help organizations (voluntary firemen, Red Cross, etc.)
    p002k. Voluntary social work
    p002l. Sports (trainer, team guide)
    p002m. Culture, theater, music
    p002n. Leisure
    p002o. Health sector
    -1=DK, -2=NA, -3=NR

p003. Do you feel you belong to a community? If yes, what kind of com-
    munity is that?

    p00301. Neighborhood community
    p00302. Religious association / mosque association
    p00303. Ethnic community
    p00304. Political party
    p00305. Political or environmental initiative
    p003a. Others: _____
    -1=DK, -2=NA, -3=NR

4. If you are engaged, would you agree with the following statements?
    I am involved in my community mostly because:

    p004a. Of my moral beliefs
    p004b. Of my religious beliefs
    p004c. It is part of being a citizen
    p004d. All people should get involved
    p004e. It enriches my life
    p004f. I want to better the society, my environment or the world
    p004g. Others: _____
    -1=DK, -2=NA, -3=NR

p005. If you are not engaged, can you say why?

    1=I would like to, but have no time.
    2=My engagement wouldn't change anything anyway.
    3=I am afraid to get into trouble.
    4=I don't have the feeling that my engagement would be welcomed.

    5=I have other priorities (i.e., family is more important for me).
    6=I am happy with my life and therefore I deem engagement not necessary.
    7=Others.
    -1=DK, -2=NA, -3=NR

p005a. Others, specify: _____

p006.   Do you remember occasions when you had the feeling your engagement was welcomed?

    1=Yes
    2=No
    -1=DK, -2=NA, -3=NR

p007.   If yes, can you give us an example?: _____

    -1=DK, -2=NA, -3=NR

p008.   Are you entitled to vote?

    1=Yes
    0=No
    -1=DK, -2=NA, -3=NR

p008a.   Others, specify: _____

p008b   Thinking back to the last parliamentary election—that is the one in 2009—do you remember which party you voted for then, or perhaps you didn't vote in that election? Please tick one box only.

    0=Did not vote
    Voted:
    1=No answer
    2=CDU
    3=SPD
    4=Greens
    5=FDP
    6=The Left
    7=NPD
    8=Other
    -1=DK, -2=NA, -3=NR

p008c.   PLEASE WRITE IN: _____

p009.   Some people vote in local elections, others don't. Thinking about recent local elections, have you voted in all of them, most of them, some of them, a few, or none?

    1 All of them
    2 Most of them
    3 Some of them
    4 A few

5 None
-1=DK, -2=NA, -3=NR

po10. Agree or not?

1=Strongly agree 2=Somewhat agree 3=Somewhat disagree 4=Strongly disagree

po10a. I feel well represented by the elected parliamentarians.

po10b. Politicians and parliamentarians show interest in my worries and problems.

po10c. Parliamentarians are well reachable for me when I have a concrete problem or suggestion.

po10d. Politicians from my country of origin or the country of my ancestors can

represent my interests better.

-1=DK, -2=NA, -3=NR

po11. Generally speaking, do you think of yourself as a supporter of any one political party?

1=Yes
0=No
-1=DK, -2=NA, -3=NR

po11a. If yes, which one? _____

po12. If no, do you think of yourself as a little closer to one political party than to the others?

1=Yes
2=No
3=I am not so well versed in landscape of parties
-1=DK, -2=NA, -3=NR

po12a. If so, which one? _____

po13. The Dutch Muslim Party (NMP) is going to run for the next parliamentary elections in the Netherlands. Would you like to be a member of a party in Germany that calls on Islamic basic values if one existed?

1=Yes
2=No
3=That would depend on how the parties understanding and representation of Islamic values
-1=DK, -2=NA, -3=NR

po14. Do you think that an Islamic political party would improve or worsen:

1 "The moral tone of politics in Germany..."
2 The image of Muslims in Germany

3 The situation of Muslims in Germany
4 The situation of Muslims in the world

po14a. Others, FILL IN: _____

po15. If many more of our elected officials were deeply religious, do you think that the laws and policy decisions they make would probably be better or would probably be worse?

1=Probably better
2=Probably worse
3=(VOLUNTEERED) Neither better nor worse
-1=DK, -2=NA, -3=NR

po16. Which do you think is more important: protecting your civil liberties and privacy from being invaded or protecting your safety and surroundings from terrorism?

1=Protecting your civil liberties
2=Protecting your safety and surroundings from terrorism
3=Both equally important
4=Both equally not important
-1=DK, -2=NA, -3=NR

po17. In the past two years, have you (Yes, No):

po17a. Contacted a public official about a problem
po17b. Worked with neighbors or friends to solve a community problem
po17c. Contributed money to a political campaign or candidate
po17d. Worked for a campaign or candidate, either for pay or as a volunteer
po17e. Signed a petition or participated in a boycott
po17f. Participated in a protest or march
po17g. Voted in any public election
0=No, 1=Yes, -1=DK, -2=NA, -3=NR

po24. Please choose the degree (Completely, Moderately, Not at all) to which you trust the following institutions:

po24a. German court system
po24b. Democratic institution in Germany
po24c. German economic system
po24d. German social system
po24e. Muslim organizations in Germany
po24f. Imams in Germany
po24g. German media, such as TV and newspapers
po24h. German police
po24i. The German public school system
po24j. The German Chancelor

po24k The German President
po24l. The German Bundestag
po24m. German banks
po24n. The German Bundeswehr
-1=DK, -2=NA, -3=NR

Questions about Belonging in Germany, "What It Means to Be German."

1. I'm going to read a list of things that some people say are important in making someone a true German. The first one is…

    zoo1a. Being born in Germany
    zoo1b. Being a Christian
    zoo1c. Having German ancestors
    zoo1d. having white skin, fair hair and blue eyes
    zoo1e. Pursuing economic success through hard work
    zoo1f. Respecting Germany's institutions and laws
    zoo1g. Having German citizenship zoo1h. Being punctual
    zoo1i. Being a member of an associationzoo1j. Thinking of oneself
        as German
    zoo1k. Being informed about communal and national politics
    zoo1l. Being engaged in communal and national politics
    zoo1m. To know the cultural traditions of one's ancestors, i.e., the
        language and food.
    zoo1n. Respecting other people's cultural differences
    zoo1o. Blending into the larger society
    zoo1p. Seeing people of all backgrounds as German
    zoo1q. Being able to speak German
    zoo1r. Feeling German
    -1=DK, -2=NA, -3=NR
    Rank
    1=Very important
    2=Somewhat important
    3=Somewhat unimportant
    4=Very unimportant

zo19. For the next set of questions, please tell me if you strongly agree, somewhat agree, somewhat disagree or strongly disagree. (Rotate randomly.)

    1=Strongly Agree 2=Somewhat Agree 3=Somewhat Disagree 4=Strongly
        Disagree
    zo19a. When I think of the German people, I think of people who
        are a lot like me.

z019b. Being a German is important to the way I think of myself as a person.

z019c. I would feel good if I were described as a typical German.

z019d. When someone criticizes Germany, it doesn't bother me at all.

z019e. I am proud to be a German.

z019f. In many respects, I am different from most Germans.

z019g. I agree when someone says "You are not a real German."

z023. Next I am going to read a list of possible obligations. For each one, please tell me if you think this is an obligation you owe to other Germans.

z023a. Serving in the military

z023b. Giving money to charities

z023c. Paying taxes

z023d. Helping when there is a crisis or disaster in the nation

z023e. Volunteering in your local community

z023f. Voting

1=Yes, an obligation 2=No, not an obligation 3=Depends (VOL)

-1=DK, -2=NA, -3=NR

Other, Including Discrimination and More on Religion

a001. I'm going to read a list of some statements that some people agree with and others don't. Please tell me how much you agree or disagree with each statement? (1=Strongly agree ... 4=Strongly disagree):

a001a. People have the right to give a speech defending organizations such as ETA, IRA or al-Qaeda.

a001b. Religious diversity has been good for Germany.

a001c. People have the right to give a speech defending far right political parties, such as the NPD.

-1=DK, -2=NA, -3=NR

a004. Which of these statements comes closest to your view about how same-sex couples should be treated in law? Please tick one box only (Yes, No):

1=Should be allowed legally to marry

2=Should be allowed legally to form civil unions, but not marry

3=Should not be allowed to obtain legal recognition of their relationships

-1=DK, -2=NA, -3=NR

a005. Have any of these things happened to you in Germany? (Yes, No):

a005a. I have been made to go through extra security at an airport.

a005b. I have been physically hurt by someone.
a005c. People have said hurtful comments to me.
a005d. People have treated me poorly at work or school.
a005e. People have treated me poorly when I was out in public.
a005f. The police have treated me roughly.
a005g. People supposed to be providing service or helping me have treated me poorly.
a005h. Public officials have treated me poorly.

  0=No, 1=Yes, -1=DK, -2=NA, -3=NR

a013. For each "yes," how many times in the past two years?

  1=Once or twice
  2=Few times a year
  3=Once a month
  4=Couple times a month
  5=Weekly
  6=More often that that
  7=Not in the last two last years
  -1=DK, -2=NA, -3=NR

14. For each "yes," was that because of your:

  a01401. Religious affiliation
  a01402. Race or ethnic background
  a01403. Gender or sex
  a01404. Economic situation
  -1=DK, -2=NA, -3=NR
  a01405. Other, specify: _____

15. In your own words, what do you think are the most important problems facing Muslims living in Germany today?

  [RECORD VERBATIM RESPONSE. PROBE FOR CLARITY; IF RESPONDENT SAYS "none" OR INDICATES THERE ARE NO PROBLEMS, SOFT PROBE ONCE WITH "nothing in particular?" OR "there are no right or wrong answers...does anything come to mind?"; PROBE ONCE FOR ADDITIONAL MENTIONS, "any other problems?"; IF MORE THAN ONE MENTION RECORD UP TO THREE RESPONSES IN ORDER OF MENTION.]

  a015a. Discrimination/racism/prejudice
  a015b. Viewed as terrorists
  a015c. Ignorance/misconceptions of Islam
  a015d. Stereotyping/generalizing about all Muslims
  a015e. Negative media portrayals
  a015f. Not treated fairly/harassment
  a015g. Religious/cultural problems

a015h. War/German foreign policy
a015i. Antiterrorism measures/racial profiling
a015j. Radical Islam/fundamentalism/religious extremism
a015k. Hatred/fear/distrust of Muslims
a015l. Unemployment/jobs/financial crisis
a015m. Lack of representation/community involvement
a015n. Mistreatment of Muslim women in society/in Muslim communities/in Muslim families
a015o. Racism/exclusivism among Muslims
a015p. Other
a015p. None
0=No, 1=Yes, -1=DK, -2=NA, -3=NR

16. I'd like to get your feelings toward a number of different groups. I'll read the name of a group and I'd like you to rate that group using something we call the feeling thermometer. Ratings between 50 degrees and 100 degrees mean that you feel favorable and warm toward the group. Ratings between 0 degrees and 50 degrees mean that you don't feel favorable and don't care too much for that group. You would rate the group at the 50-degree mark if you don't feel particularly warm or cold toward the group. Feel free to use the entire extent of the scale. The (first/next) group is…[ROTATE ITEMS]

_____ (RECORD NUMBER 1 TO 100)

NN   None
DD   (DO NOT READ) Don't know / No opinion
RR   (DO NOT READ) No answer / Refused

NOTE: SPLIT INTO 2 QUESTIONS WITH 2 CLUSTERS: RELIGION-ORIENTED GROUPS and OTHER

a016a. Conservatives
a016b. Poor people
a016c. Rich people
a016d. Liberals
a016e. Homeless people
a016f. Business owners
a016g. Manual workers
a016h. Manager
a016i. Legal immigrants
a016j. Illegal immigrants
a016k. Black people
a016l. White people
a016m. Vietnamese
a016n. Catholic people
a016o. Jewish people
a016p. Muslim people

a016q. People who are not religious
a016r. People who are deeply religious
a016s. People with the same ethnic or national background as you
a016t. Gay men and lesbians, that is, homosexuals
a016u. Russland-Germans
a016v. Mainline Protestants
-1=DK, -2=NA, -3=NR

BERLIN SURVEY DESCRIPTION (JANUARY 2010)

Demographic Profile of Respondents

According to the frequencies (the demographic profile for Muslims interviewed in this survey is predominately male, of low-middle income, with a high school degree, and of Turkish descent. In the study, more men were interviewed than women, however, the study displays near parity of gender (the difference is only seven respondents). Income, however, has a very skewed distribution with most interviewees being of low to middle income. There were very few interviewees who reported incomes of over 3,000 euros, making inferences for this group based on the survey population extremely difficult. In terms of education, the distribution of educational levels was relatively well balanced, however, a lack of respondents in the trade school and postgraduate level make inferences for these strata problematic. The median level of education is to have completed high school. Finally, in terms of nationality, the distribution of respondents in the various categories is extremely skewed. As is shown above the plurality of respondents was of Turkish (not including Kurds) descent. Unfortunately a dearth of respondents from Azerbaijan, Iraq, Turkish Kurdistan, and Palestine will make inferences about nationality based on the sample very difficult.

Responses to Questions on Religion

Question 1: Are you a member of a mosque?
As we can see from the survey responses, most Muslims surveyed are not members of any mosque. In terms of gender distributions, it appears that men and women have very similar rates of mosque attendance (roughly 20% of men and 26% of women) were reported as members of mosques. Regarding income, it appears that the highest rate of mosque membership was reported among the lower classes, particularly those with incomes of less than 1,000 euros. However, here I should caution that the low numbers of respondents sampled in the higher-income categories significantly bias comparisons

between lower- and higher-income respondents, making it impossible to truly measure the correlation between income and mosque attendance. Consistent with the findings for income, respondents with lower levels of education also appear to have a higher rate of mosque membership than those who are more highly educated. Here, inferences are more sound due to a greater number of respondents in each category; however, I would still recommend that a more representative sample should be taken for robust results. Furthermore, among age categories, it appears that respondents in the second quartile of age (31–40) appear to have lower rates of mosque attendance (14%) than their counterparts (roughly 30% on average). Finally, in terms of nationality, the highest rates of mosque membership are witnessed among those immigrating from Bosnia and Turkey (not Kurdistan). Yet again, the dearth of respondents from the Azerbaijani, Kurdish-Turk, and Iraqi populations makes inferences about those groups difficult.

This question is correlated with the following measures of informal political participation:

- belonging to a religious association (respondents who are members of a mosque are more likely to belong to a religious association)
- feeling part of a religious association (respondents who are members of a mosque are more likely to feel part of a religious association)

And the following measures of formal political participation:

- feeling part of a political or environmental initiative (respondents are members of a to mosque are less likely to feel part of environmental or political initiatives)
- voting for parties that promote Islamic values (respondents who are members of a mosque are more likely to vote for parties that promote Islamic values)
- believing that deeply religious leaders perform better (respondents who are members of a mosque are more likely to believe that religious leaders perform better)

And, finally, the following measures of trust:

- trust in the German economic system (respondents who are members of a mosque are more likely to trust the German economic system)
- trust in the German courts (respondents who are members of a mosque are more likely to trust the German courts)

Question 2: Do you regularly attend the same mosque community? Are you engaged in a mosque community?
Interestingly, the number of respondents claiming to attend the same mosque community outweighs that of those who claim to have membership in a

mosque. According to the statistics nearly one-third of respondents do claim to attend mosque regularly, though again the dominant response is to not attend mosque. In terms of gender, mosque attendance by men and women tend to be relatively on par with roughly one-fourth of men and women attending mosque regularly. Additionally, once again we see that those of lower income levels tend to attend mosque more regularly (though this time, attendance rates are relatively the same among all income levels below 3,000 euros). Lower levels of education too seem to be correlated with higher rates of mosque attendance, although as previously noted, inferences for the higher levels of income and education are significantly biased. Additionally, in terms of age, younger respondents (aged 22–30) seem more likely to regularly attend mosque, while the lowest attendance rates are among the 30–40 age group. Finally, results from the nationality cross tabulations seem to mirror those found for Question 1 above with the exception that Germans seem to report very high levels of mosque attendance relative to their membership.

This question is correlated with the following measures of informal political participation:

- belonging to a religious association (respondents who frequently attend a mosque are more likely to belong to a religious association)
- feeling part of a religious association (respondents who frequently attend a mosque are more likely to feel part of a religious association)

And the following measures of formal political participation:

- voting for parties that promote Islamic values (respondents who frequently attend a mosque are more likely to vote for parties that promote Islamic values)
- believing that deeply religious leaders perform better (respondents who frequently attend a mosque are more likely to believe that deeply religious leaders perform better)

And, finally, the following measures of trust:

- trust in the German banks (respondents who frequently attend a mosque are more likely to trust the German banks)

Question 3: Participation in communal prayer

Examining alternative religious behaviors, we see that consistent with previous findings, the plurality of Muslims interviewed do not participate in communal prayers. Although we see more participation in these informal religious practices, for example, 56 percent of respondents engage in communal prayer versus 27 percent who regularly attend mosque, the median level of participation in communal prayer is still infrequent (monthly). Once again the gender distribution demonstrates relative parity between genders in terms of participation in prayer, leading us to believe there are no significant gender differences with respect to this practice. In contrast, for income, lower levels of earning are again associated with higher levels of participation in prayer though there are not enough respondents at upper levels to make serious inferences. Consistent with findings on income, lower levels of education are also associated with increased participation in prayer, although college educated individuals appear to have relatively high levels of participation as well. In terms of age, older respondents (aged 50–90) are more likely to participate in communal prayer often, while those in their 30s are least likely to frequently participate in prayer. Finally, once again Bosnians, Germans, and Turks displayed the highest frequency of participation, though these are nearly the only categories with populations substantial enough to make inferences.

This question is correlated with the following measures of informal political participation:

- belonging to a religious association (respondents who participate in communal prayer more frequently are more likely to belong to a religious association)
- being engaged in interreligious dialogue (respondents who participate in communal prayer more frequently are more likely to be engaged in interreligious dialogue)
- feeling part of a religious association (respondents who participate in communal prayer more frequently are more likely to feel part of a religious association)

And the following measures of formal political participation:

- belonging to a political party (respondents who participate in communal prayer more frequently are less likely to belong to a political party)

Question 4: Participation in individual prayer

In contrast to communal prayer, a significant majority of respondents participate in individual prayer, with the majority participating in prayer more than once a day. Interestingly, for this behavior, men seem less inclined than women to participate in frequent prayer. Significantly more men than women report never participating in individual prayer (32 men vs. 9 women) and more women report participating in daily prayer than their male counterparts. Yet again, people in lower levels of income participate in individual prayer at a higher rate than those in higher tiers of socio economic status (SES). Similarly, regarding education, respondents who achieved higher levels of education tend to engage in individual prayers very rarely, however, persons who have completed college tend to engage in daily prayer at a substantial rate (44.8%). By contrast, regarding age groups, there is no significant difference in terms of participating in individual prayer. Finally, for nationality groups, Bosnians, Lebanese, and Turkish respondents appear to predominately engage in individual prayer more than once a day. Among German respondents, however, the response was somewhat dichotomized with nearly equal pluralities of interviewees responding that they never engage in individual prayer or engage in individual prayer more than once a day.

This question is correlated with the following measures of informal political participation:

- belonging to a religious association (respondents who participate in individual prayer more frequently are more likely to belong to a religious association)
- being engaged in interreligious dialogue (respondents who participate in individual prayer more frequently are more likely to be engaged in interreligious dialogue)
- being engaged in parental representation (respondents who participate in individual prayer more frequently are more likely to be engaged in parental representation)
- being engaged in youth work (respondents who participate in individual prayer more frequently are more likely to be engaged in youth work)
- being engaged in justice work (respondents who participate in individual prayer more frequently are more likely to be engaged in justice work)
- being engaged in a neighborhood initiative (respondents who participate in individual prayer more frequently are more likely to be engaged in a neighborhood initiative)
- being engaged in voluntary social work (respondents who participate in individual prayer more frequently are more likely to be engaged in voluntary social work)
- being engaged in sports (respondents who participate in individual prayer more frequently are less likely to be engaged in sports)
- being engaged in the health sector (respondents who participate in individual prayer more frequently are slightly less likely to be engaged in the health sector)
- feeling part of a religious association (respondents who participate in individual prayer more frequently are more likely to feel part of a religious association)

And the following measures of formal political participation:

- being engaged in a union (respondents who participate in individual prayer more frequently are less likely to be engaged in a union)
- feeling that parliamentarians show interest in worries (respondents who participate in individual prayer more frequently are less likely to believe that parliamentarians show interest in their worries)

- feeling that politicians from home country can represent interests better (respondents who participate in individual prayer more frequently are more likely to believe politicians from their home country can better represent them)
- supporting a political party (respondents who participate in individual prayer more frequently are less likely to support a political party)
- voting for parties that promote Islamic values (respondents who participate in individual prayer more frequently are more likely to vote for Islamic parties)
- believing that deeply religious leaders perform better (respondents who participate in individual prayer more frequently are more likely to believe that deeply religious leaders perform better)
- contacting public officials (respondents who participate in individual prayer more frequently are less likely to contact public officials)
- working for a campaign (respondents who participate in individual prayer more frequently are more likely to work for a campaign)

Question 5: Read about religion

Examining the distribution of responses, there appears to be no consistent pattern. Although more respondents seem to fall in the less-frequently, more-than-once-a-week, and once-a-day category. In this category, as with the other alternative religious practices, women more frequently read about religion than their male counterparts. However, in terms of income patterns, reading about religion is inconsistent with previous results. According to the information, people at mid-high and low levels of income read more frequently than those at middle and high levels of income. In terms of education, there is no consistent pattern, as those categories with high frequency of reading also have several respondents in the lowest frequencies of reading. Similarly regarding age groups, there is no significant difference among different generations. In terms of nationality, Germans appear to read about religion less frequently, while Turkish residents read once a week or more.

This question is correlated with the following measures of informal political participation:

- being engaged in parental representation (respondents who read about religion more frequently are more likely to be engaged in parental representation)
- being engaged in voluntary social work (respondents who read about religion more frequently are more likely to be engaged in voluntary social work)
- being engaged in sports (respondents who read about religion more frequently are less likely to be engaged in sports)

- being engaged in the health sector (respondents who read about religion more frequently are less likely to be engaged in the health sector)
- feeling part of a religious association (respondents who read about religion more frequently are more likely to feel part of a religious association)

And the following measures of formal political participation:

- supporting a political party (respondents who read about religion more frequently are slight less likely to support a political party)

Nearly equal amounts of Germans read more than once a week and less frequently.

Question 6: Talk about religion

Looking at the distribution of responses, people seem to talk about religion at consistent levels across the board. For example, nearly the same number of respondents speak about religion once a week or more, as well as less than once a week. Across gender, women seem to talk about religion more than men (69.8% of women talk about religion once a week or more and only 41.6% of men). In terms of income, it appears that people at the low-mid and highest levels of income talk about religion more often than other groups. However, estimates for the top tiers of income are biased due to small sampling sizes. Similarly, it is difficult to make inferences for education, however, it appears that those with grade school, partial college, and professional degrees talk about religion most frequently. Regarding age groups, there is no significant difference among different generations In terms of nationality, Bosnians tend to talk about religion relatively often (59% talk more than once a week about religion) as do Turks (68%).

This question is correlated with the following measures of informal political participation:

- being engaged in interreligious dialogue (respondents who talk about religion more frequently are more likely to belong to a religious association)
- being engaged in an environmental initiative (respondents who talk about religion more frequently are more likely to be engaged in an environmental initiative)
- being engaged in a neighborhood initiative (respondents who talk about religion more frequently are more likely to be engaged in a neighborhood initiative)

- being engaged in voluntary social work (respondents who talk about religion more frequently are more likely to be engaged in voluntary social work)

And the following measures of formal political participation:

- belonging to a political party (respondents who talk about religion more frequently are more likely to belong to a political party)
- belonging to a political or environmental initiative (respondents who talk about religion more frequently are more likely to belong to a political or environmental initiative)

Question 7: Fasting during Ramadan

A reasonable majority of respondents (57%) fast all month while a large plurality of respondents (34.4%) do not fast at all. Within genders, women seem to fast for a lengthier period than their male counterparts. Again in terms of income, inferences are difficult but people at the lowest (less than 200 euros) and highest (4,000 euros or more) levels of income tend to fast for longer than the middle-income categories. For education categories, inferences are similarly difficult, however, fasting seems to endure longest among those with low levels of education attainment (partial high school or less), business/technical school education, and professional schooling. Among age categories there appears to be no significant difference between ages in response. As previously mentioned, a reasonable majority of respondents (on an average 55%) from each category fast all month.

This question is correlated with the following measures of informal political participation:

- belonging to a religious association (respondents who fast during most of Ramadan are more likely to belong to a religious association)
- being engaged in interreligious dialogue (respondents who fast during most of Ramadan are more likely to be engaged in interreligious dialogue)
- feeling part of a religious association (respondents who fast during most of Ramadan are more likely to be part of a religious association)

And the following measures of formal political participation:

- feeling that parliamentarians show interest in worries (respondents who fast during most of Ramadan are less likely to feel that parliamentarians represent their interests)
- supporting a political party (respondents who fast during most of Ramadan are more likely to support a political party)

- voting for parties that promote Islamic values (respondents who fast during most of Ramadan are more likely to vote for parties that promote Islamic values)
- believing that deeply religious leaders perform better (respondents who fast during most of Ramadan are more likely to believe that religious leaders perform better)

Question 8: Drinking alcohol

According to the distribution of responses, most Muslims (67.3%) do not drink alcohol. However, separating the results by gender, women drink alcohol much less frequently than men (87.4% of women report never having alcohol, and only 51.3% of men report never having alcohol). There is no specific pattern across incomes, but the income categories with the lowest rates of alcohol consumption are the less than 2,000 euros and 4,000–5,000 euros categories. Again generalizing across education is difficult due to low sampling size, but people with grade school, business/vocational, and professional degrees seem to have the lowest rates of consumption. Although it should be noted that nearly all educational levels have over 60 percent of respondents who report never having drunk alcohol. Among age categories, there are no significant differences in response. Finally, Bosnians and Lebanese respondents seem to consume alcohol less frequently than respondents in more secular states such as Turkey and Germany.

This question is correlated with the following measures of informal political participation:

- belonging to a religious association (respondents who do not drink alcohol are more likely to belong to a religious association)
- being engaged in interreligious dialogue (respondents who do not drink alcohol are more likely to engage in religious dialogue)
- being engaged in neighborhood initiatives (respondents who do not drink alcohol are more likely to be engaged in neighborhood initiatives)
- being engaged in leisure activities (respondents who do not drink alcohol are less likely to be engaged in leisure activities)
- being engaged in the health sector (respondents who do not drink alcohol are less likely to be engaged in the health sector)
- feeling part of a religious association (respondents who do not drink alcohol are more likely to feel part of a religious association)

And the following measures of formal political participation:

- being engaged in a union (respondents who do not drink alcohol are slightly less likely to be engaged in a union)

- supporting a political party (respondents who do not drink alcohol are less likely to support a political party)
- voting for parties that promote Islamic values (respondents who do not drink alcohol are more likely to vote for parties that promote Islamic values)
- believing that deeply religious leaders perform better (respondents who do not drink alcohol are more likely to believe that deeply religious leaders can perform better)
- working for a campaign (respondents who do not drink alcohol are less likely to work for a campaign)

Question 9: Support for hijab

In terms of the distribution for support for the hijab, nearly the same number of respondents support the wearing of the hijab as do not. Regarding gender, women tend to support wearing the hijab more than men: 60.3 percent of women support the hijab as compared 38.9 percent of men. There is no particular pattern across incomes, and within each income category, nearly equal numbers of respondents support and do not support hijab. Similarly, there is not really a consistent pattern across educational levels, although respondents with grade school or business/vocational school education tend to support hijab more. For nationality, respondents from countries in the Middle East, for which inferences are possible (Lebanon and Palestine), tend to support hijab more than their Westernized counterparts.

This question is correlated with the following measures of informal political participation:

- belonging to a religious association (respondents who support wearing hijab are more likely to belong to a religious association)
- feeling part of a religious association (respondents who support wearing hijab are more likely to feel part of religious association)

And the following measures of formal political participation:

- voting for parties that promote Islamic values (respondents who support wearing hijab are more likely to vote for parties that promote Islamic values)
- believing that deeply religious leaders perform better (respondents who support wearing hijab are more likely to feel that deeply religious politicians can perform better)

And, finally, the following measures of trust:

- trust in the German social system (respondents who support wearing hijab are more likely to trust the German social system)

- trust in the German media (respondents who support wearing hijab are more likely to trust the German media)
- trust in the German chancellor (respondents who support wearing hijab are more likely to trust the German chancellor)
- trust in the German Bundeswehr (respondents who support wearing hijab are more likely to trust the German Bundeswehr)
- trust in the German Bundestag respondents who support wearing hijab are more likely to trust the German Bundestag)

Question 10: Being Muslim is…a set of beliefs

Most respondents (72.7%) disagree that being Muslim is a set of beliefs. Among gender categories, there is relative parity in the level of disagreement/agreement with this statement. Within income, high numbers of low-income respondents (less than 1,000 euros) and mid-upper–income respondents (4,000–5,000 euros) agree that being Muslim is a set of beliefs, however, given the small number of respondents in the high-income category, we cannot infer anything about this population. Amongst education levels, people with partial high school and business/vocational school education display the highest levels of agreement with this statement, as they are the only group to have more than 30 percent of respondents to agree. In terms of age, respondents in the third quartile (41–49 years of age) are more likely to disagree with this statement, although the difference is slight (10%) and is insignificant. Germans and Turks also seem to display relatively high levels of agreement with this statement as compared to their counterparts.

This question is correlated with the following measures of informal political participation:

- feeling part of a neighborhood community (people who answer yes to the above are more likely to feel like they belong to a neighborhood community)
- feeling part of a religious association (people who answer yes to the above are more likely to feel like they belong to a religious association)
- feeling part of an ethnic community (people who answer yes to the above are only slightly more likely to feel like they belong to an ethnic community)

And the following measures of formal political participation:

- voting in the past local elections (people who answer yes to the above are less likely to vote for the Greens and Linke)
- feeling able to reach parliamentarians when you have a problem (people who answer yes to the above are more likely to disagree that they can reach parliamentarians)

And, finally, the following measures of trust:

- trust in the German economic system (people who answer yes to the above are more likely to trust the German economic system)
- trust in the German media (people who answer yes to the above are more likely to trust the German media)
- trust in the German Bundestag (people who answer yes to the above are more likely to trust the German Bundestag)
- trust in the German Bundeswehr (people who answer yes to the above are more likely to trust the German Bundeswehr)

Question 11: Being a Muslim is … a relationship with God

The vast majority of respondents (77.6%) believe that being Muslim is a relationship with God. Slightly more women than men (83.3% vs. 71.8%) endorse this view within the sample. There appears to be no consistent pattern among income categories, although inferences for most income groups are not possible given small sample sizes. Similarly, there seems to be no significant difference between educational levels or age groups on this question. Finally, German, Lebanese, and Turkish respondents seem to agree with this statement more than other nationalities.

This question is not correlated with any measures of informal behavior but is correlated with the following measures of formal behavior:

- feeling able to reach parliamentarians when you have a problem (people who believe being Muslim is having a relationship with God are more likely to agree that they can reach parliamentarians)
- voting for Islamic parties (people who believe being Muslim is having a relationship with God are more likely to be for voting for a party that emphasizes Islamic values)
- believing that public officials should be more religious (people who believe being Muslim is having a relationship with God are more likely to agree with politicians being more religious)

And, finally, the following measures of trust:

- trust in the German economic system (people who believe being Muslim is having a relationship with God are more likely to trust the German economic system)
- trust in the German media (people who believe being Muslim is having a relationship with God are more likely to trust the German media)
- trust in the German police (people who believe being Muslim is having a relationship with God are more likely to trust the German police)
- trust in the German school system (people who believe being Muslim is having a relationship with God are more likely to trust the German school system)

Question 12: Being a Muslim is…following the example of the Prophet

The majority of respondents in the survey (61.5%) agree that being a Muslim means following the example of the Prophet. Among income categories for which we can make reasonable inferences, there seems to be no clear pattern of responses. Most income categories agree with this statement at similar rates. In terms of education, high school and college graduates seem to have low levels of agreement with the statement (almost equal numbers of respondents agree and disagree with the statement). Among age categories as well, there is no noticeable difference between generations in terms of response. For nationality, more German and Lebanese respondents seem to agree with this statement, while Bosnian and Turkish respondents have relatively equal numbers that agree and do not agree that being Muslim is following the example of the Prophet.

This question is correlated with the following measures of informal behavior:

- volunteering (people who believe being Muslim is following the example of the Prophet are more likely to volunteer often)
- feeling part of a religious association (people who believe being Muslim is following the example of the Prophet are more likely to feel as though they belong)

And the following measures of formal participation:

- voting for Islamic parties (people who believe being Muslim is following the example of the Prophet are more likely to vote for a party that emphasizes Islamic values)
- believing that public officials should be more religious (people who believe being Muslim is following the example of the Prophet are more likely to agree with politicians being more religious)

And, finally, the following measures of trust:

- trusting the German Court system (people who believe being Muslim is following the example of the Prophet are more likely to distrust the German Court system)
- trust in the German social system (people who believe being Muslim is following the example of the Prophet are more likely to trust the German social system)

Question 13: Being a Muslim is…a way of life

Nearly equal numbers of respondents agree and disagree with the statement, being Muslim is a way of life. Similarly, among gender categories there is relative parity among men and women in levels of agreement with this statement. For income categories for which inferences are possible, equal numbers of respondents agree and disagree with this statement across all categories. Similarly, education seems to have no effect on agreement with this statement as most educational levels display similar and relatively equivalent numbers of people who agree and disagree with this statement. In terms of age, it appears that respondents in the second and fourth quartiles of age (31–40 and 50+ respectively) have slightly lower levels of agreement with this question, although this difference is not significant. Finally, there appears to be no correlation between nationality and response to this question either.

This question is correlated with the following measures of informal behavior:

- volunteering (people who think that being a Muslim is a way of life are more likely to volunteer often)
- being engaged in a religious association (people who think that being a Muslim is a way of life are more likely to be engaged in a religious association)
- feeling like you belong to a religious association (people who think that being a Muslim is a way of life are more likely to feel like they belong to a religious association)

And the following measures of formal political behavior:

- voting in the last local election (people who think that being a Muslim is a way of life are more likely to not vote)
- politicians show interest in worries (people who think that being a Muslim is a way of life are only slightly more likely to agree with this statement)
- voting for Islamic parties (people who believe being Muslim is a way of life are more likely to be for voting for a party that emphasizes Islamic values)
- believing that public officials should be more religious (people who believe being Muslim is a way of life are more likely to agree with politicians being more religious)

And the following measures of trust:

- trust in the German social system (people who think that being a Muslim is a way of life are more likely to trust the German social system)
- trust in the German Bundestag (people who think that being a Muslim is a way of life are more likely to trust the German Bundestag)

And, finally, the following measures of religious behavior:

- belief that the Qur'an is the actual word of God and has to be taken literally, word for word (positive correlation)
- belief that the Qur'an is an ancient book of fables, legends, history and moral precepts recorded by men (negative correlation)

Question 14: Being a Muslim is…practicing a set of rituals

There was an even split between those who answered yes and no to the veracity of this statement. Among genders, there was a cleave; women in particular were more likely to say yes (58.3% of women to 39.4% of men). In terms of income, virtually all income levels had an equal split between yes and no. Similarly, among age groups, there is little to no difference. Those with a higher level of education were slightly more likely to respond no, particularly high school graduates and college graduates; low rates of response make it difficult to draw further conclusions. Those hailing from Bosnia-Herzegovina were more likely to say no in a 2:1 ratio, whereas those from Lebanon were twice as more likely to say yes.

This question is correlated with the following measures of informal behavior:

- volunteering (people who think that being a Muslim is a practicing a set of rituals are more likely to volunteer often)
- being engaged in youth work (people who think that being a Muslim is a practicing a set of rituals are more likely to be engaged in youth work)
- feeling like you belong to a religious association (people who think that being a Muslim is a practicing a set of rituals are more likely to feel like they belong to a religious association)

And the following measures of formal political behavior:

- politicians show interest in worries (people who think that being a Muslim is a practicing a set of rituals are only slightly more likely to agree with this statement)
- believing that public officials should be more religious (people who believe being Muslim is practicing a set of rituals are more likely to agree with politicians being more religious)

And, finally, the following measures of trust:

- trust in the German Court system (people who think that being a Muslim is a practicing a set of rituals are more likely to trust the German Court system)
- trust in the German Bundeswehr (people who think that being a Muslim is a practicing a set of rituals are more likely to trust the German Bundeswehr)

Question 15: Being a Muslim is…belonging to the Ummah
While many respondents did not seem to think being Muslim meant belonging to the *Ummah* by an almost 2:1 ratio, gender appears able to explain the entirety of this shift: 71.8 percent of men said no while 28.2 percent of men said yes. In women, the matchup was much closer: 54.2 percent saying no while 45.8 percent saying yes; thus, one can say with high likelihood that men are more likely not to believe belonging to the *Ummah* is related to being a Muslim. Across all levels of measurable income, there was a relatively equal likelihood of responding no, so there is no correlation between income and this question. In terms of education, though it is more difficult to conclude because of numbers, one can say with a degree of certainty that high school graduates, college students, and college graduates are very likely to say no, with as much as a 6:1 ratio of college graduates who responded no to yes. In terms of age, it appears that older respondents (aged 50+) are more likely to agree with this statement. Finally, in nationality, while Bosnians, Germans, Lebanese, Palestinians, and Turks all seemed more likely to say no, no group was particularly more likely than any other to say no.

This question is correlated with the following measures of informal behavior:

- volunteering (people who think that being a Muslim is belonging to the *Ummah* are more likely to volunteer often)
- feeling like you belong to a neighborhood community (people who think that being a Muslim is belonging to the *Ummah* are more likely to feel like they belong to a neighborhood community)
- feeling like you belong to a religious association (people who think that being a Muslim is belonging to the *Ummah* are more likely to feel like they belong to a religious association)

And the following measures of formal political behavior:

- I feel well represented by parliamentarians (people who think that being a Muslim is belonging to the *Ummah* are only slightly more likely to agree with this statement)
- voting for Islamic parties (people who believe being Muslim is belonging to the *Ummah* are more likely to be for voting for a party that emphasizes Islamic values)

And, finally, the following measures of trust:

- trust in the German social system (people who think that being a Muslim is belonging to the *Ummah* are more likely to trust the German social system)

Question 16: About prayer in the mosque, do you believe that (1) women shouldn't be allowed in mosques; (2) women should pray separately from men or behind a curtain; (3) women should pray behind men, without a curtain; or (4) women should pray alongside men with no curtain?

The total polling data shows that 42.7 percent of respondents prefer statement 2, with statement 3, statement 4, and statement 1 following in that order in terms of decreasing agreement. Men were slightly more likely to agree with statement 3 than women and less so with statement 4 than women, but it is not a very large discrepancy. Across income, there appears to be no correlation. By education, there is also no apparent correlation. In terms of age groups, it seems that younger groups (ages 22–40) have more egalitarian responses and are more likely to approve of women praying in the same room as men without separation—almost 70 percent of respondents in these categories responded favorably to women participation in the mosque as compared to 30–50 percent for older age groups. Regarding nationality, Bosnians and Turks appeared twice as likely as the rest of the population to respond affirmatively to statement 4.

This question is correlated with the following measures of informal behavior:

- being engaged in sports (people who are more likely to believe that women should pray with men are more likely to be engaged in sports)

And the following measures of formal behavior:

- belonging to a political party (people who are more likely to believe that women should pray with men are more likely to belong to a political party)
- belonging to a political or environmental initiative (people who are more likely to believe that women should pray with men are more likely to belong to a political or environmental initiative)
- believing that parliamentarians are well reachable (people who are more likely to believe that women should pray with men are more likely to agree that parliamentarians are well reachable)
- feeling close to a party (people who are more likely to believe that women should pray with men are more likely to feel close to a particular political party)
- voting for Islamic parties (people who are more likely to believe that women should pray with men are less likely to vote for parties that promote Islamic values)
- signing a petition or participating in a boycott (people who are more likely to believe that women should pray with men are more likely to have signed a petition or participated in a boycott)

Question 17: Can a woman be prayer leader ... in communal prayer of women?

Overall, respondents were responding 4:1 in favor of women being able to lead prayers in communal prayer of women. Gender did not appear to have any effect on this ratio. By income, those of middle income, from 2,000–3,000 euros per year, were extremely disposed to answering yes, with 92.3 percent saying yes compared to just 7.7 percent saying no. Neither education nor age appeared to be particularly correlated with any response. By nationality, Palestinians and Lebanese were extremely likely to say yes, with all of the Palestinian respondents, though there were only 5 of them, reporting 100 percent yes, and 85 percent of the Lebanese reporting no.

This question is correlated with the following measures of informal behavior:

- belonging to an ethnic community (people who believe women can lead women in prayer are less likely to feel like they belong to an ethnic community)

And the following measures of formal behavior:

- belonging to a political or environmental initiative (people who believe women can lead women in prayer are less likely to feel like they belong to a political or environmental initiative)
- feeling close to a particular political party (people who believe women can lead women in prayer are more likely to feel like they belong to a political party)
- voting for Islamic parties (people who believe women can lead women in prayer are more likely to vote for Islamic parties)
- believing that deeply religious politicians perform better (people who believe women can lead women in prayer are more likely to believe that deeply religious politicians perform better)

This question is correlated with the following measures of religious behavior:

- belief that the Qur'an is the actual word of God and has to be taken literally, word for word (negative correlation)
- belief that the Qur'an is an ancient book of fables, legends, history and moral precepts recorded by men (positive correlation)

Question 18: Can a woman be prayer leader ... in mixed communal prayer of men and women?

Respondents generally responded no to this question in a 2:1 ratio. Women were particularly more likely to say no to this question, with five-sixth of respondents saying no; men were somewhat closer to an equal response on this question, with only 56.4 percent of men saying no. By income, there did not appear to be much deviation from the population. By education, the least educated (from grades 1–8 or no education at all) were much more likely to respond no, but some of the most educated, college graduates, were much more likely to say no. College graduates came to an almost 50–50 parity. Interestingly, respondents aged 31–40 seem most likely to respond yes (55.6%) to the above question while even younger respondents aged 22–30 have lesser yes responses (roughly 30%). By nationality, Germans and Turks were actually slightly more likely to respond yes, reaching almost parity. Palestinians, however, were all very opposed to the idea; though with only 5 of them responding, 100 percent said no.

This question is correlated with the following measures of formal behavior:

- belonging to a political or environmental initiative (people who believe women can lead mixed groups in prayer are more likely to feel like they belong to a political or environmental initiative)
- believing that politicians from your home country can perform better (people who believe women can lead mixed groups in prayer are less likely to believe that politicians from their home country can perform better)
- voting for Islamic parties (people who believe women can lead mixed groups in prayer are less likely to vote for Islamic parties)
- believing that deeply religious politicians perform better (people who believe women can lead mixed groups in prayer are less likely to believe that deeply religious politicians perform better)

Question 19: Can a woman be prayer leader…in mixed Friday prayer?

A strong majority said no, with 81.2 percent to 18.8 percent, more than a 4:1 ratio. Gender reflected a similar rate, as did the income levels. By education level, however, those with least education—those with none or just grades 1–8, those who have not completed high school, and those who are high school graduates—responded in a ratio that comes to about 87 percent to 12 percent against the idea of women leading mixed Friday prayer, which is not a huge deviation, but shows a slight skew toward these levels of education. Again, respondents in their 30s appeared most egalitarian in their responses (50% agreed) while younger respondents (22–30) had responses similar to older age groups. By nationality, Bosnians were slightly more likely to say no while Palestinians were united in saying no (interestingly, they've been united on all the past 3 questions regarding female prayer).

Question 20: The Qur'an should be interpreted as…the actual word of God, to be taken literally

Responses to this question tended to split slightly in favor of yes, 57.7 percent to 42.3 percent. There is no discernible trend by gender or income for responses to this question. Those with educations that do not extend past grades 1–8 tend to be more likely to say yes to this question (85.2%), while high school graduates and college graduates are all somewhat more likely to say no, opposing the general population in an approximately 3:2 ratio. Those with some college degree appear to oppose this interpretation of the Qur'an very much, but they have an extremely small sample size as well. In terms of age, the frequency of yes responses appears to increase with age. Finally, by nationality, Bosnians and Germans appeared more likely to respond no, while Turks were markedly more likely to respond yes as well as the Lebanese, but to a lesser extent than the Turks.

This question is correlated with the following measures of informal political participation:

- feeling like you belong to a religious association (people who take the Qur'an literally are more likely to belong to a religious association)

And the measures of formal participation:

- believing that politicians from his/her country of origin can represent him/her better (people who take the Qur'an literally are more likely to agree with this statement)
- feeling closer to one political party (people who take the Qur'an literally tend to not feel close to one political party)
- voting for Islamic parties (people who take the Qur'an literally are more likely to vote for a party that emphasizes basic Islamic values)

And, finally, the following measures of trust:

- trusting the German Court system (people who take the Qur'an literally are more likely to either trust completely or not trust at all, i.e., take extreme positions)
- trusting German media (people who take the Qur'an literally are more likely to not trust the German media)

Question 21: The Qur'an should be interpreted as . . . the actual word of God, which will always be filtered through the interpretation of humans
There was parity in yes and no responses to this interpretation of the Qur'an. There appeared to be no correlation with gender. Those of middle income, technically, the highest measurable income, were much more likely to say no to this interpretation, with 61.9 percent, against 38.1 percent responding yes. In education, there is a slight trend in those with lower levels of education being more likely to say no compared to those of higher incomes appearing slightly more likely to say yes. Predictably, among age groups, younger respondents were more likely to give positive responses to this question. By nationality, Bosnians and Germans were more likely to say yes, while Turks and Lebanese were more likely to say no.

This question is not correlated with any measures of informal political participation but is correlated with the following measures of formal participation:

- feeling able to reach parliamentarians when you have a problem (people who agree with this are more likely to disagree that they can reach parliamentarians)
- feeling closer to a political party (people who agree with this are more likely to feel close to a political party)
- voting for Islamic parties (people who agree with this are more likely to be neutral or even opposed to voting for a party that emphasizes Islamic values)
- believing that public officials should be more religious (people who agree with this are more likely to feel neutral about politicians being more religious)

And the following measures of trust:

- trusting German media (people who agree with this are more likely to give mediated—partially trust, moderate, or partially distrust—responses to this question)
- trusting the German Bundeswehr (people who agree with this are more likely to partially distrust the German army)

Question 22: The Qur'an should be interpreted as . . . an ancient book of fables, legends, and history recorded by men

There is an overwhelming rejection of this interpretation of the Qur'an, with 85.9 percent saying no compared to 14.1 percent saying yes. By gender, females are particularly likely to reject this view of the Qur'an, with 95.6 percent saying no. However, there does not appear to be a correlation by income against responses for this question. By education, those with high school incomplete were very strongly against this interpretation, 92.5 percent to 7.5 percent, though this is only a moderate deviation, and it is not really seen in any other educational group. Among age groups, there seems to be no significant difference in rates of response between agreement and disagreement. By nationality, Bosnians, Lebanese, and Palestinians (small sample) all seemed to be particularly opposed to this interpretation of the Qur'an (100 percent responded no).

This question is not correlated with any measures of informal political participation but is correlated with the following measures of formal participation:

- voting for Islamic parties (people who believe the Qur'an is a book of fables are more likely to be opposed to voting for a party that emphasizes Islamic values)

- believing that public officials should be more religious (people who believe the Qur'an is a book of fables are more likely to disagree with politicians being more religious)

And the following measures of trust:

- trusting the German Court system (people who believe the Qur'an is a book of fables are more likely to moderately trust the German Court system)
- trusting the German economic system (people who believe the Qur'an is a book of fables are more likely to trust the German social system)
- trusting the German social system (people who believe the Qur'an is a book of fables are more likely to trust the German social system)
- trusting the German police (people who believe the Qur'an is a book of fables are more likely to moderately trust or distrust the German police)
- trusting the German school system (people who believe the Qur'an is a book of fables are more likely to moderately trust or distrust the German school system)
- trusting the German president (people who believe the Qur'an is a book of fables are more likely to moderately trust or distrust the German president)
- trusting the German banks (people who believe the Qur'an is a book of fables are more likely to moderately trust or distrust the German banks)
- trusting the German Bundeswehr (people who believe the Qur'an is a book of fables are more likely to moderately trust or distrust the German Bundeswehr)

Question 23: You don't do yourself any good if you don't participate in the community

There is a tendency to agree with this statement, with 61.7 percent strongly agreeing and a full quarter of the population agreeing with the statement. Of those that disagreed, 5.7 percent merely disagreed while 7.1 percent strongly disagreed. There was not a deviation from this original breakdown by gender or income. By education, college graduates tended not to agree as strongly as the population (44.4% strongly agree, 40.7% agree) and as vocational school graduates (40% strongly agree, 50% agree). However, those who have not completed high school tended to agree more strongly (76.9%). In terms of age, older respondents are more likely to strongly agree with the above statement as compared to younger respondents. Bosnians were not as likely to agree as strongly (47.6% strongly agreed, 28.6% agreed) as Germans (46.9% strongly agree, 31.3% agree). The Lebanese, however, tended to agree more strongly, with 80 percent saying they strongly agree and only 8 percent agreeing. In general, these kinds of conclusions are hard to draw, however, given how many categories there are in terms of level of agreement.

Question 24: Muslims should actively participate in society

Similar to the previous question, there is a tendency to agree with this statement, with 66.9 percent saying they strongly agree, 18.4 percent agreeing, 8.8 percent disagreeing, and 5.9 percent strongly disagreeing. Gender tends to follow these trends, though women are somewhat more likely to agree, with 72.7 percent strongly agreeing and 21.2 percent agreeing. By income, for those with measurable levels of responses, those of lower income tended to agree more strongly than those of higher income; the rates of those who strongly agree are 76.2 percent, 64.7 percent, and 52.4 percent for income levels of < 1,000 euros; 1,000–2,000 euros; and 2,000–3,000 euros respectively. By education, those with lowest education, that is, not past grade 8, tend to agree more strongly with the statement (85.2%); college graduates, however, do not tend to have such a strong level of agreement, with only 50 percent agreeing strongly and 32.1 percent agreeing. Again in age groups, younger respondents are more likely to disagree that Muslims should actively participate in society, especially among those aged 22–30. Bosnians, Lebanese, and Turks tend to agree with this statement slightly more than the population, whereas, Germans tend to agree less with this statement.

Question 25: It is better to get involved in Muslim organizations than in nondenominational groups

The numbers for this statement tend to be different than the previous questions, with a favor this time instead toward those who strongly disagree. There were 43.5 percent who strongly disagreed, 22.5 percent who disagreed, 13.8 percent who agreed, and 20.3 percent who strongly agreed. Of these, men were more likely to strongly disagree than women, though women tend to disagree slightly more. Women also tend to strongly agree more, giving an impression that men are more likely to have stronger opinions on the issue. By income, those with less than 1,000 euros of income are more likely to strongly agree (34.8% strongly agree, 26.1% strongly disagree) and oppose the population trend. There is a trend in this, as those with higher income, to disagree more with this statement (for 1,000–2,000 euros, 53.8% strongly disagree ; for 2,000–3,000 euros, 57.9% strongly disagree) and to agree less (for 1,000–2,000 euros, 19.2% strongly agree; for 2,000–3,000 euros, 10.5% strongly agree). By education, those of the lowest level of education tended to strongly agree much more than the other education levels (46.2%), while college graduates tend to strongly disagree more than the other education levels (59.3%). From income and education, we may want to draw a conclusion that those of lower socioeconomic status are more willing to accept aid from Muslim organizations than non-denominational groups while the more affluent tend not to discriminate between the groups they participate in. Regarding age, the only outstanding category appears to be respondents aged 50 and above, who appear more likely to agree with this statement than their younger counterparts. By nationality, Bosnians tend to strongly agree, whereas Lebanese tend to strongly disagree.

This question is correlated with the following measures of religious behavior:

- belief that the Qur'an is the actual word of God and has to be taken literally, word for word (negative correlation)
- belief that the Qur'an is an ancient book of fables, legends, history, and moral precepts recorded by men (positive correlation)

Question 26: Interreligious marriage

Interestingly there is a slight difference among respondents who would approve of an interreligious marriage for their sons versus their daughters. For sons, although the rates of approval and disapproval are relatively even, for daughters, more respondents (68.1%) would disapprove of an interreligious marriage. Although there are no noticeable patterns across income or education levels, one can note that in nationality categories those from less secular states (Bosnia and Lebanon) have higher rates of disapproval for interreligious marriages for their sons and daughters.

Question 27: How should same sex couples be treated in law?

A majority has responded that they do not believe same sex couples should be allowed legal recognition (62.1%), and about a quarter (26.6%) believe that they should be allowed to legally marry while 10.5 percent would prefer if they were allowed to have civil unions. Women were more likely than men to believe that same sex couples should not be allowed legal recognition (68.3% to 55.7%) while men were more likely to believe that they should be allowed legally to marry (37.7% to 15.9%). With respect to income, increase in income led to decrease in willingness to agree that same sex couples should be allowed to form civil unions, but not marry; as income increased, many gravitated to one of the more certain answers. With respect to education, there is no comprehensively whole correlation that holds true, but for those with education of a high school grad or lower, there appears to be a positive correlation for being allowed to legally marry and a negative one for not allowing legal recognition. By nationality, Lebanese and Bosnians were especially likely to oppose legal recognition, with rates of 76.5 percent and 72.2 percent respectively.

Responses to Questions on Political Behavior

Measures of Informal Participation

Question 28: How many times, if any, did you volunteer in the past 12 months? Of those who responded to this question, 44.1 percent never volunteered, 16.6 percent volunteered once or several times a year, 7.6 percent did once every few months, 11.7 percent did once a month, and 13.8 percent did once a week. When it comes to gender, it does not appear that there is a truly discernible difference in male and female rates of voluntary engagement, though men tend to be more likely to have no voluntary engagement (55.3% of men to 31.9% of women). With regard to income, though it may be a consequence of small sample size, the higher one's income is, the more likely that person is to engage in some kind of voluntary engagement; there's no real trend on who actually engages the most, however, though 31.6 percent of those with 2,000–3,000 euros per year participate at least once a month. There's a relatively consistent trend in education that those of higher education tend to be more likely to be involved in voluntary engagement of some sort (rate of no participation: 65.4% for those with no education past grade 8, 56.1% for those who did not complete high school, 45.2% for high school grads, 18.2% for business/technical/vocational school students, 16.7% for college students, and 23.1% for college graduates). However, it also appears that a fifth of high school grads and a full half of business/technical/vocational school students volunteered at least once a month. Although there is no significant trend among age groups, it appears that middle-aged respondents—41–49 years of age—volunteer more than other age groups. Though Turks were slightly more likely than Bosnians, Germans, and Lebanese to not volunteer, there was no other discernible trend among the other volunteering capacities.

Question 29: Are you engaged in a religious or mosque association? Of those that responded, only 22.4 percent said they were engaged in religious or mosque associations. Women were more likely to engage, with a rate of 29 percent to men's 16.2 percent rate. By income, those who tended to make more seemed to be more likely to engage in religious or mosque associations, while the data shows that all those who are making over 3,000 euros a year report that they do not engage in these kinds of associations; their low sample sizes makes it possible that these results are not reflective of the reality. There is also a trend in income that those of higher income are less likely to belong to these kinds of association groups (rate of no engagement in mosque or religious associations: none past grade 8, 75%; none past high school, 78.6%; high school graduates, 83.3%; business or vocation or technical school students, 54.5%; college graduates, 77.8%). Among age groups, there was no significant difference in responses. While most nationalities were not particularly inclined to participate in a religious or mosque association, the Lebanese were extremely likely to say no, with 100 percent of all the 21 respondents responding with no religious or mosque association.

Question 30: Are you engaged in interreligious dialogue?

Most respondents were surveyed to say no to this question, with 84.6 percent responding no. Women were twice as likely as men to engage in interreligious dialogue, 20.3 percent to 10.8 percent. There is no obvious trend along income; those of middle income—2,000–3,000 euros per year—tended to have a 25 percent reporting yes against about 14 percent for those with incomes lower than 2,000 euros. Those of higher income did not respond in a sufficient degree to make any conclusions about their populations. With regard to education, there is a definite trend with those of lesser education having fewer interreligious dialogue than their more educated counterparts (those with no education past grade 8 actually reported 100% no, with 24 responses, compared to the 90.5% of high school incomplete, 86.7% of high school grad, and 63.6% of business/technical/vocational school students who also reported no). In terms of age groupings, it appears that the older respondents are less likely to engage in interreligious dialogue. By nationality, Bosnians and were particularly more likely to say yes while Lebanese were particularly likely to say no.

Question 31: Are you engaged in parental representation?

A strong majority responded no to this question (84.6%). As to be expected, a very significantly higher rate of women reported on this than men, with 23.2 percent reporting a yes compared to 8.1 percent of men. With respect to income, those of higher income appeared to be more likely to report a higher rate of parent representation. With respect to education, a similar trend of higher education correlated with higher rates of parental representation existed, though not to as strong of a degree as in income (high school graduates tended to say no at a higher rate than expected). As would be expected, those of middling ages, 31–49, are more likely than their younger and older counterparts to be engaged in parental representation. By nationality, one outlier nationality was those who had a Bosnian background, reporting a 100 percent no response compared to the about 16 percent average for Turks, Lebanese, and Germans (Germans had a high rate of yes, 23.5%).

Question 32: Are you engaged in environmental initiatives?

Extremely few of those polled responded yes to this question (2.8%). Gender, income, nationality, level of education, and age all appear to not have an impact on engagement in environmental initiatives. There appears to be a generally low level of interest in engaging in environmental initiatives.

Question 33: Are you engaged in youth work or education?
A majority of those that responded tended to say no (72%). Women are almost 3 times as likely to be engaged in youth work and education, which is not altogether surprising (40.6% to 16.2% of men). Those of higher income levels have a consistent correlation with likelihood to work in youth work and education. There is also a consistent, though less strong, trend in education; those of higher education levels tended to engage more in youth work (48.1% of college graduates, 40% of those with some college, 54.5% of those with business/vocational/technical backgrounds, 20% of high school grads, 21.4% of high school students, and 8.3% of those who did not finish past grade 8). By age, it appears that middle-aged respondents are slightly more likely to engage in youth work than their counterparts while older respondents (50 years and above) are less likely to engage. Germans (41.2%) and Lebanese (38.1%) were much more likely to be engaged in youth work and education, especially compared to Bosnians (18.2%).

Question 34: Are you engaged in justice and the prevention of criminality?
Very few tended to say yes to this question, only 6.3 percent. Neither gender tended to be more or less engaged than the other in justice and the prevention of criminality. Income did not appear to terribly affect participation in this activity, though those of the lowest income of under 1,000 euros a year showed 100 percent response rate for no. Of education responses, only college graduates showed a higher propensity to say yes. In age categories, it appears that respondents from the second and third quartiles of age (31–49) are slightly more likely to engage in justice and criminality prevention, although rates are still very low (less than 10%). Of nationalities, only Turks seemed to have a significant percentage who said yes (12.3%); the other nationalities all virtually said no.

Question 35: Are you engaged in neighborhood initiatives?
A big majority of those who responded tended to say no to this question (86%). Women are more likely than men to be involved in neighborhood initiatives (23.2% to 5.4%). Income does not appear to be very strongly correlated with engagement in neighborhood initiatives; education, however, appears to have a relatively moderate correlation with level of engagement in neighborhood educations, with business/technical/vocational students and college graduates having the highest rates of neighborhood engagement. In terms of age, engagement in neighborhood initiatives tends to increase with age. However, the oldest respondents (aged 50 and above) report slightly lower rates of engagement than those who are middle aged. Turks and Germans also tended to have the highest rates of neighborhood engagement at 21.1 percent and 17.6 percent respectively; Lebanese and Bosnians had remarkably low rates, 4.8 percent and 0 percent respectively.

Question 36: Are you engaged in helping organizations, such as firemen or the Red Cross?
A majority responded no to this question (88.1%). Women are slightly more likely than men to be engaged in helping organizations like these. Income does not appear to have an impact on this participation; education also does not appear to have a strong correlation, though very faintly may be positively correlated. In terms of age, engagement in helping organizations increases as respondents get older. By nationality, while Turks and Lebanese appear to have a slightly elevated rate of engagement, there are no outstanding trends or groups.

Question 37: Are you engaged in voluntary social work?
Very few of those who were polled were engaged in voluntary social work (18.2%). Women are much more likely to be engaged in voluntary social work, 29 percent to men's 8.1 percent. Those making less than 1,000 euros a year replied with a 100 percent no, while those of higher levels of income and significant number of responses had rates of about 30 percent saying yes (those of 1,000–2,000 euros and 2,000–3,000 euros). With regard to education level, those with higher levels of education tended to be more likely to engage in voluntary social work. Again in age categories, there appears to be a significant increase in engagement with age; however, the oldest tier of respondents represents a significant anomaly. Turks had a significant level of participation in this question, registering 26.3 percent compared to the around 14 percent level of Bosnians, Germans, and Lebanese.

Question 38: Are you engaged in sports (as a trainer or team guide)?
Very few were engaged in sports at all (8.4%). Interestingly, there is no relation between gender and this type of engagement, though one usually expects men to be more engaged in sports. In fact, generally speaking, most Muslims did not appear engaged in sports; though a correlation exists in income level and engagement, the level of engagement only increases from 4.2 percent for those making less than 1,000 euros a year to 10 percent for those making 2,000–3,000 euros a year. A correlation exists between education level and level of engagement in sports, with those who have an education that does not surpass grade 8 all responding no and college graduates with 25.9 percent responding yes. An anomaly exists in business/technical/vocational students that all said no, but this does not altogether defeat the correlation. Surprisingly engagement in sports activities appears to engage with age, however, yet again particularly elderly respondents (50 years and above) do not display high rates of engagement. There does not appear to be any relationship between nationalities and rates of engagement.

Question 39: Are you engaged in culture, theater, or music?
A strong majority of respondents tended to say no (88.8%). Females are slightly more likely to be engaged in these activities than men (14.5% to 8.1%). Income, nationality, age, and educational degree do not appear to have much of a correlative effect on this type of engagement.

Question 40: Are you engaged in leisure?
A full 93 percent said that they were not engaged in leisure at all. There is no significant difference according to gender or income (though those who make 2,000–3,000 euros a year had a 20% rate of engagement in leisure compared to 8.3% of those making under 2,000 euros). Education also does not appear to have a consistent effect upon engagement in leisure; though it appears that those with higher educations are more likely to engage in leisure, this may be attributable to low response rates and sampling sizes. Again in age categories, there appears to be a significant increase in engagement with age; however, the oldest tier of respondents represents an anomaly in this trend. Germans are slightly more likely to have a higher engagement in leisure, at 14.7 percent compared to the lower Bosnian (4.5%), Lebanese (9.5%) and Turkish (3.5%) rates.

Question 41: Are you engaged in the health sector?
Only 5.6 percent of those who responded said that they were engaged in the health sector. Gender, income, and education do not have any consistent effect on the responses to engagement in the health sector. Nationality also appears not to have much of an effect, though Turks reported an 8.8 percent response rate for yes. In terms of age, older respondents are slightly more likely to engage in the health sector in all categories. All in all, it does not appear that those polled are interested in engaging with the health sector at all.

Question 42: Do you belong to a neighborhood community?
On the whole most respondents (85.2%) respond that they do not belong to a neighborhood community. Looking at responses by gender, a larger percentage of females (24.3% as compared to 4.2%) state that they do belong to a neighborhood community, indicating a possible gender bias. Among income categories for which inferences can be made (those with adequate sample sizes), there appears to be no significant difference in participation in a neighborhood community. Similarly among educational levels, the results appear very similar, with most respondents (roughly 80% in each education category) answering that they do not belong to a neighborhood community. With regard to age, it appears that middle-aged respondents (41–49 years of age) are more likely to feel as though they belong to a neighborhood community. Finally, in terms of nationality, for the categories for which there are

sufficient sample populations to draw inferences, it appears that Lebanese respondents are more likely to be engaged in a neighborhood community, while Bosnians are the least likely to be involved.

Question 43: Do you belong to a religious association?

Again most respondents (68.5%) claim to not be involved in a religious association. Concerning gender there is relative parity among men and females, although female respondents are slightly (insignificantly) more likely to be involved in religious associations. In terms of income, there is no noticeable difference among income categories, however, education displays a slight upward trend in the number of positive responses as education increases. Small sampling populations at the higher levels of education, however, bias this result. In terms of age, there is also no significant difference among respondents. Finally, in terms of nationality, it appears that Bosnians and Turks are more likely to be involved in religious associations than their counterparts.

Question 44: Do you belong to an ethnic community?

Interestingly the vast majority of respondents, roughly 87.4 percent, feel that they do not belong to an ethnic community. Although women feel this to a lesser extent than their male counterparts, there is no significant difference between genders in responses to this question. In terms of income and education, there is also no significant difference among categories, although respondents with high school degrees are slightly more likely than their counterparts to claim engagement in an ethnic community. Similarly, in terms of age, there is no significant difference among respondents. Additionally, across nationalities, there seems to be little difference in responses to this question, with most nationality categories claiming high levels of disengagement.

Question 45: Do you belong to an environmental organization?

Again the vast majority (91.6%) of respondents claim to not belong to environmental organizations. Despite slight differences between men and women, there is no significant difference between genders on belonging to environmental organizations. Similarly, there is no significant difference among the categories in income, education, or nationality. In terms of age, however, there is a significant split among the first, second, third, and fourth quartiles of age. The rate of belonging among respondents younger than 40 years of age is on an average 10.5 percent, while for older respondents, it is 3.1 percent.

Question 46: In the past two years, have you worked with neighbors to solve community problems?

The issue of working with neighbors to solve community problems is not very popular; 61.5 percent did not work with their neighbors over any community problem. Women were twice as likely as men to respond yes to this question (54.3% and 23.3%, respectively). People with higher levels of income were more likely to work with their neighbors (rates of yes responses: for those making under 1,000 euros a year, 29.2%; for those making 1,000–2,000 euros a year, 36%; for those making 2,000–3,000 euros a year, 52.4%). Those with higher levels of education tend to respond yes at a higher rate than those of lower levels of education. In age categories, there appears to be a significant increase in engagement with age; however, the oldest tier of respondents represents an anomaly in this trend. By nationality, those most likely to work with their neighbors to solve community problems were the Lebanese (57.1%). Germans, Bosnians, and Turks were, for the most part, hovering from 30 percent–40 percent in terms of responding yes to this question.

Measures of Formal Political Participation

Question 47: Do you think of yourself as a supporter of any political party?
There's a majority that do not support any political party (79.7%). Men were about 3 times more likely to think of themselves as supporters of a particular political party (30.1% to 10%). Income and educational degree both do not seem to have an effect on this response, as the percentage of yes responses were relatively random across the various income levels and educational degrees. In terms of age, middle-aged respondents (41–49 years of age) are less likely to support a political party than other groupings. By nationality, Germans and Turks were particularly likely to respond yes, with respective rates of 21.2 percent and 31 percent.

Question 48: If so, which?
The response is as follows: 16 percent support AKP, 16 percent support CDU (Christlich Demokratische Union Deutschlands), 12 percent support Green, 4 percent support SCU (Christlich-Soziale Union in Bayern), 32 percent support SPD (Sozialdemokratische Partei Deutschlands), and 20 percent support the Left. Though there were more responses for this identification question, there were also just as many, if not more, potential response variable answers (in this case, more possible parties to choose). The sample size is still too small to draw conclusions about gender, income, educational level, or nationality with regard to which political party respondents feel close to.

Question 49: Are you engaged in any union activities (representation of workers)?
A strong majority did not engage in any union activities (93.7%). Gender did not reflect any correlation with engagement in a union. There is a tendency to want to say that most of middle income are not engaged in unions, since 100 percent of those making 2,000–3,000 euros all replied no; however, lack of responses for those making more than 3,000 euros makes this a hard

conclusion to pin down. In education, however, those of higher levels of education tended to be more involved with unions, except for high school graduates. With regard to age groups, there is no significant difference among respondents of different ages. By nationality, while most nationalities were very likely to say no, Bosnians had a perfect 100 percent rate who said no, out of 22 responses, compared to the around 90 percent responses who said no among Germans, Lebanese, and Turks.

Question 50: Are you engaged in any political representation?

A strong majority responded no to this question (86.5%). Men were more likely to be engaged in political representation at a rate of 18.9 percent to women's 7.2 percent. Income did not appear to have any obvious correlation; though those of lowest income had the highest rate of political representation, this did not hold as true for those of next lowest income. However, education showed a significant correlation, with those of higher education levels having a higher rate of political representation, except for business/technical/vocational school students, 100 percent of whom, reported no(100 % of those with no education past grade 8 also reported no). In terms of age, there are no significant differences in responses among age groups. By nationality, while nothing was terribly significant, in order from lowest level of political representation to highest for those with enough sample responses, the order is Bosnians, Turks, Germans, and Lebanese.

Question 51: If more elected officials would be deeply religious, would the policy decisions be better, worse, or neither better nor worse?

The response is as follows: 40.8 percent thought that the policy decisions would probably be better; 25.6 percent thought it would probably be worse; and 33.6 percent thought it would probably be the same. Women were more likely to believe that deeply religious officials would produce better policy decisions (54.1% compared to 28.1% of men), while men were more likely to be ambivalent (42.2% said "neither better nor worse" compared to 24.6% of women). With respect to income, the more a person makes per year, the more likely was the response to be ambivalent about the election of deeply religious officials, with a trend of those making less than 1,000 euros per year reporting 27.3 percent, those making 1,000–2,000 euros per year reporting 35.4 percent, and those making 2,000–3,000 euros per year reporting 58.8 percent. There is a similar trend with education, that is, those with higher education tend to feel more ambivalent about the policy decisions of deeply religious elected officials. With regard to age, middle-aged respondents tend to agree that deeply religious politicians would perform better to a greater degree than other age groupings. Bosnians and Turks were likely to think that this would be better (55% and 45.3%, respectively); meanwhile, Germans and Lebanese were likely to be more ambivalent (42.9% and 61.1% respectively).

Question 52: In the past two years, have you contacted a public official about a problem?
A large percentage of those surveyed replied no to this question (66.9%). There is no correlation with gender on this issue, nor is there a correlation with income. For educational degrees, there is generally no correlation; however, those without educations that surpass grade 8 tend to have a significantly lower level of contact with public officials, responding yes at a 15.4 percent rate compared to the average 33–40 percent rate exhibited by other education levels. Although there are no significant differences among age groupings, the oldest tier of respondents appear least likely to contact public officials. Germans and Turks were slightly more likely than other races to contact public officials (39.4% and 38.3%, respectively).

Question 53: In the past two years, have you contributed money to a political party, campaign, or candidate?
Only 13.3 percent of the population has contributed money to a political party, campaign, or candidate. Neither gender nor campaign appears to have much of an effect on contributions to political causes. There was also no educational skew in terms of contributions to political causes, and no race was particularly interested in contributing money to political causes. Interestingly, older respondents (aged 50+) were most likely to contribute money to a political campaign while middle-aged respondents are least likely (0%). In general, part of this can be explained by the unwillingness to contribute money to political causes at all; the total percentage of people who answered yes to this question was 7.7 percent.

Question 54: In the past two years, have you worked for a campaign or candidate, either for pay or as a volunteer?
Only 13.5 percent of the population has worked for a campaign or candidate. Men were twice as likely as women to respond yes to this question (17.8% of men to 8.6% of women). Income did not appear to have any correlation with the responses to this question; however, education appears to have a positive correlation with those who respond yes. College graduates were most likely to work for campaigns or candidates (30.8%) while 7.7 percent of those with no education past grade 8 responded yes; the lowest was for those who had some college education, with all of them responding no, but since their sample size was only 6, there is a higher chance that this is an anomaly of sorts. In terms of age, there are no significant differences among respondents of different age categories. By nationality, all Bosnian respondents replied no, as did most Turks and Lebanese and Germans, though Turks had the highest rate of those who said yes (18.3%). Like the previous question, with only 13.5 percent responding yes, there are fewer trends for those who ended up responding yes due to a lack of responses.

Question 55: In the past two years, have you signed a petition or participated in a boycott?

A slight majority responded no to this question (55.2%). Women are slightly more likely than men to respond yes to this question by a thin margin. As income goes up, the number of respondents who reply yes tend to decrease; those making under 1,000 euros per year had a 58.3 percent response rate for yes, whereas those making 1,000–2,000 euros had a 48 percent yes response rate and those making 2,000–3,000 euros had a 38.1 percent yes response rate. However, those with a higher level education tended to have a positive correlation with signing a petition or participating in a boycott, with college graduates being especially active, exhibiting a 69.2 percent yes rate(compared to the 15.4% yes rate for those whose education does not surpass grade 8). Regarding age, older respondents were more likely than their younger counterparts in virtually every category to participate in boycotts or sign petitions. Germans and Turks were especially likely to participate in signing a petition or in a boycott, with rates of 50 percent and 51.7 percent respectively responding yes.

Question 56: In the past two years, have you participated in a protest or a march?

A slight majority responded no to this question (54.5%). In responding to this question, men and women were equally likely to respond yes. There was no consistent trend in terms of income's effect on this question; however, those who had a higher level of education had a very consistently higher level of participation in protests and marches, especially for college graduates for whom the rate of participation was 73.1 percent compared to 11.5 percent for those without education past grade 8. By nationality, Lebanese and Turks were the most likely to have participated in this kind of activity (57.1% and 46.7% respectively).

Question 57: In the past two years, have you voted in any public election?

A majority of respondents said no to this question (62%). Women were more likely than men to have voted in a public election (44.3% to 31.9%). There is also a relatively strong positive correlation between income as well as educational degree and those who did vote in a public election. Germans and Lebanese were most likely to have voted in public elections (47.1% and 65%, respectively), and Bosnians were extremely unlikely(9.1%).

Question 58: Do you belong to a political party?

Relatively none of the respondents questioned state that they belong to a political party. Only 2.8 percent of respondents claim involvement in political parties, suggesting a very low level of formal participation within the sampling population. Within gender, there are no significant differences in participation, and income and education show no specific pattern either. In terms of age, respondents from the second quartile (31–40 years of age) seem slightly less likely to belong to a political party, although this difference is insignificant. Similarly, among nationality categories, there appears to be no difference in the distribution of responses.

Question 59: Did you vote in the last Federal elections in 2009?
Looking at the distribution of responses, it appears that the majority of respondents did not vote (53.5%). Among those that did vote, however, most Muslims voted for SPD and the Left. In terms of gender, women vote slightly more than men; however, the distribution of respondents within each party is nearly equal among men and women. For those income categories for which we can draw inferences, there seems to be little difference among the parties selected within income groups. Similarly, there are not many noticeable patters among educational levels; however, it appears that high school educated individuals vote for SPD at higher rates than other groups. Additionally, among age groups, no discernible pattern seems to emerge. Most categories of nationality are too scarcely populated to make inferences; however, it can be noted that Bosnians specifically do not support the Left.

Question 60: Did you participate in the last local elections?
According to the responses, a plurality of respondents (who had non-missing responses) voted in all of the past local elections—roughly 44.7 percent. There were no significant differences among genders, education levels, or income levels in response to this question. Regarding age, it appears that respondents over 40 years of age are more likely to vote more often than younger respondents, whose voting patterns are much more sporadic and unpredictable. In terms of nationality, it appears that Turks vote more often than others.

Question 61: Do you agree with the following statement: I feel well represented by the elected parliamentarians?
According to the responses, the majority of persons surveyed (65.2%) strongly disagree with the statement that they feel well represented by their parliamentarians. In income categories, it appears that persons with mid-level incomes (2,000–3,000 euros) are less likely to strongly disagree with this statement, although it is impossible to test the significance of this difference empirically. Additionally, across both education and nationality categories, there also seems to be no significant differences.

Question 62: Do you agree with the following statement: Politicians and parliamentarians show interest in my worries and problems?
Again a decent majority (59.1%) of respondents strongly disagree with the above statement. Although there are some differences between genders, with women tending to disagree less than their male counterparts,

this difference is insignificant at the 0.05 level (it is, however, significant at 0.1). Again, middle-income respondents tend to disagree less with this statement—although the majority still disagree, they only slightly disagree rather than strongly disagree. Similarly, college graduates are more likely to slightly disagree rather than strongly disagree to this statement as compared to respondents in other education levels. There appears to be no significant difference among nationalities.

Question 63: Do you agree with the following statement: Parliamentarians are well reachable for me when I have a concrete problem or suggestion?
As with the previous question, the majority of respondents (70.3%) strongly disagree with the above statement. Gender appears to be unassociated with levels of agreement as men and women have a similar distribution of responses. Additionally, middle-income respondents and college graduates seem to have higher levels of agreement, although the median response is still slightly disagree among these categories. Again, there is no significant difference among nationality categories.

Question 64: Do you agree with the following statement: Politicians from my country of origin can represent me better?
Interestingly the majority of respondents (58.5%) strongly disagree with the above statement. There are no significant differences in responses among gender, income, education, or nationality divisions.

Question 65: Would you become a member of a party that calls on Islamic basic values if one existed?
According to the distribution of responses, most respondents (44.0%) would not join a party that calls on basic Islamic values if one existed, however, a large plurality (32.6%) would. In terms of gender, there is a significant difference between men and women, with women being more likely to join a political party that promotes Islamic values. Among income categories, it appears that those respondents of low-mid incomes (1,000–2,000 euros) agree with this statement more than their counterparts. Interestingly, in terms of education, those with grade school and business/vocational school educations are more likely to agree than those with higher levels of educational attainment. Finally, in terms of nationality, people from Turkish descent appear to be more likely to join a party that emphasized Islamic values than respondents from other countries.

Measures of Trust in German Society

Question 66: Do you trust the German Court system?
Looking at the distribution of responses, it appears that most respondents (65.8%) either completely or partially trust the German Court system.

However, between genders, there is a slightly significant (p. value 0.055) difference between males and females in levels of trust. Women are more likely to express high levels of trust and mistrust, while men are more likely to be neutral. Again in income categories, those with low-mid level incomes are an anomalous case, in that they tend to express higher levels of mistrust; however, it impossible to tell whether this anomaly is statistically significant. Although there is no empirical way of testing the strength of the relationship between education and trust, it appears that there is no noticeable relationship between the two and response distributions are relatively similar across education levels. Among nationalities, it appears that Bosnians and Turks are most likely to answer that they trust the German courts completely; however, it is impossible to tell whether this trend is significant.

Question 67: Do you trust democratic institutions in Germany?
The majority of respondents gave either positive or neutral reviews of their trust in German democratic institutions, with 14.1 percent claiming that they completely trust institutions, 38.7 percent claiming that they partially trust institutions, and 28.2 percent claiming neutrality. There is no significant difference between genders in response to this question, although women do appear to give negative responses at a higher rate than men. There is no particularly noticeable difference among income or education categories. Similarly, there are no large differences among nationalities, although Bosnians are slightly more likely to trust the German democratic system completely.

Question 68: Do you trust the German economic system?
Most respondents gave either positive or neutral reviews of their trust in the German economic system with 13.3 percent claiming that they completely trust institutions, 35.0 percent claiming that they partially trust institutions, and 31.5 percent claiming neutrality. There is no significant difference among gender categories in response to this question. In terms of income, those with the lowest and middle incomes tend to respond more positively to this question, though it is impossible to know whether the effect is significant. Trust appears to increase with education levels, but given small sample sizes in the highest categories of educational attainment, we cannot test the strength of this relationship. In regard to nationality, Germans and Turks have lower levels of trust, although their overall trust ratings are positive to neutral.

Question 69: Do you trust the German social system?
A large majority of respondents claim to trust the German social system—32.2 percent trust the system completely, and 38.4 percent, partially. There is no significant difference among gender, income, or education categories; however, there appears to be noticeable differences in nationality. According to the distribution of responses, it appears that Bosnian and

Lebanese respondents are more likely to completely trust the German social system while German and Turkish citizens are more likely to claim medial levels of trust.

Question 70: Do you trust German media?

In contrast to previous questions, it appears that the majority (59.7%) of individuals mistrust the German media. Although there are no significant differences among gender, income, or educational levels, it appears that in terms of nationality, Lebanese respondents are more likely to deeply distrust the German media than are the respondents from other national backgrounds.

Question 71: Do you trust the German police?

The majority of respondents (79%) gave positive or neutral reviews of their trust of the German police. Men and women differ significantly in their responses, with women being more likely to give more positive reviews (i.e., trust partially) than neutral reviews like their male counterparts. In terms of income, education, and nationality, there appear to be no significant trends.

Question 72: Do you trust the German school system?

A small majority of respondents (51.4%) claim to trust (either completely or partially) the German school system. There is no significant difference between gender categories in terms of responses, although people with mid-level incomes and high school/college degrees are less likely to give extremely positive responses than their counterparts. In terms of nationality, it appears that German and Lebanese respondents are more likely to give negative reviews than respondents from other nationalities; however, it is impossible to test the significance of this difference.

Question 73: Do you trust the German chancellor?

In contrast to previous questions, the majority of respondents (79.8%) gave neutral or negative response to this question. Between gender categories there is no significant difference in trust levels, nor does there appear to be a noticeable pattern among income or education groups. Nationality categories also appear to reflect no significant trend.

Question 74: Do you trust the German president?

A majority of persons interviewed (72.6%) gave positive or neutral response to the question of whether they trust the German president. Although there are no significant differences among gender or income categories, it appears that people of mid-level incomes are more likely to mistrust the president. Also German-born citizens reported higher levels of mistrust than did respondents from other nationalities.

Question 75: Do you trust the German parliament

Sixty-seven percent of responses claim to trust or be neutral about the German parliament. There is no significant relationship between trust and gender, income, education, or nationality.

Question 76: Do you trust the German banks?

Most respondents (48.5%) state that they trust the German banks. There are no significant relationships between trust and gender or income. However, it appears that respondents claiming the highest levels of trust dissipate as education level increases, and that Lebanese respondents are more likely to trust German banks than other German citizens.

Question 77: Do you trust Muslim organizations in Germany?

The responses are as follow: 12.9 percent completely trust Muslim organizations in Germany, 26.6 percent strongly trust them, 26.6 percent moderately trust them, 14.4 percent slightly trust them, and 19.4 percent don't trust them at all. Females tend to trust Muslims organizations in Germany more, with 19.7 percent trusting completely and 34.8 percent trusting a lot, when compared to male, who have a 6.8 percent rating of trusting completely and 19.2 percent rate of trusting a lot. There does not appear to be a very strong correlation between income and trust, though those of higher income tend to trust Muslim organizations slightly less. By education, those of the lowest level of education tended to trust Muslim organizations the most (30.8% of those with educations that did not surpass grade 8 trusted completely versus 16.7% for high school incomplete and 6.9% for high school graduates). Turks tended to trust Muslim organizations the most of any other ethnicity, with 21.4 percent trusting completely and 32.1 percent trusting a lot.

Question 78: Do you trust imams in Germany?

Of the respondents, 12.1 percent completely trust imams in Germany, 30 percent strongly, 20 percent moderately, 17.9 percent slightly, and 20 percent don't trust them at all. Females tend to trust imams more than males (among females, 19.4% trust completely and 35.8% trust a lot, as compared to 5.5% trust completely and 24.7% trust a lot among males). There is less of a distinct trend in household income versus trust in imams, but it is noteworthy that there is less trust on imams in the 2,000–3,000 euro income range. With respect to educational degrees, as one's education progresses, a population's trust on imams tends to become mollified (less "completely trust" responses and more "trust a lot" responses), though not necessarily with fewer people who holistically trust imams. Those who responded "not at all" tended to remain constant as income level changed. Bosnians were the least trustworthy of imams, with 40.9 percent responding "not at all." The Lebanese have a large number of middle-ground responses, with 40.9 percent responding "moderate trust." Turks and Germans registered 15.5

percent complete trust, 39.7 percent trust a lot, and 9.7 percent complete trust, 41.9 percent trust a lot, respectively.

Measures of Political Opinions

Question 79: Do you agree with this statement? "I am engaged because of my moral beliefs"
A little more than half of the respondents (59.7%) strongly agree that they are engaged due to their moral beliefs. In terms of gender, there is a slightly significant (p. value .052) difference between genders with more women stating that they are engaged due to their moral beliefs. In income categories, for which we can make reasonable inferences, there is no significant differences among them. However, in education, although true inferences cannot be made due to small sampling size, it appears that the lowest rates of agreement are in the high school and college graduate categories. It should be noted that the significance of this association cannot be tested empirically due to small sample populations. In nationality categories, it appears that Bosnians have the lowest rates of agreement with this statement, while Germans, Lebanese, and Turks have relatively high levels of agreement (roughly 67% on average for each).

Question 80: Do you agree with this statement? "I am engaged because of my religious beliefs"
As with the previous question, a little more than half of the respondents (54.7%) strongly agree that they are engaged due to their religious beliefs. Men tend to agree with this statement less than their female counterparts; however, this difference is insignificant. Also for income categories, for which we can make inferences, there appears to be no differences among the categories. This also holds true for educational levels in which there are few differences among them in terms of positive responses. For nationality, it appears Lebanese disagree with this statement more than their German, Turkish, and Bosnian counterparts; however, due to small sampling size it is impossible to test whether this difference is significant.

Question 81: Do you agree with this statement? "I am engaged because it is part of being a citizen"
According to the distribution of responses, a small plurality of respondents strongly agree with this statement, although roughly the same number of respondents strongly disagree with this statement as well (33.8% vs. 31.1%). There is no significant difference between gender categories in terms of agreement, although women do agree with the statement slightly more than their male counterparts. Though it is impossible to test empirically, it appears that there is no significant difference among income categories. Although those with grade school education are more likely to agree with this

statement, high school graduates are most likely to disagree. Additionally, in nationality categories, it appears that Lebanese and Turks are most likely to agree with this statement.

Question 82: Do you agree with this statement? "I am engaged because people should engage"

Over half of the respondents surveyed (52.6%) strongly agree with this statement. Between gender categories, there is a significant difference in the distribution of responses, with women being more likely to respond positively to this statement. For income categories, for which we can make accurate inferences, there seems to be a negative association between income and agreement (i.e., lower levels of income appear to have higher levels of agreement), yet it is impossible to tell whether this association is significant. In education categories, there appears to be no noticeable difference among them in regard to agreement. Finally, in nationality categories, there is no substantive difference among them, although Turks seem to have slightly lower levels of agreement than other categories.

Question 83: Do you agree with this statement? "I am engaged because it enriches my life"

According to the distribution of responses, a little over half of the respondents surveyed (55.3%) strongly agree with the above statement. The distribution of responses across gender categories is relatively equal and no significant difference exist. In regard to income, it appears that people of extremely low incomes (under 1,000 euros) agree with this statement at much higher rates than their richer counterparts. Estimates for the upper tiers of income are unavailable, however, due to small sampling sizes. By contrast, there is no significant difference among educational levels in terms of agreement, with most educational categories reporting roughly 50 percent agreement with the above statement. Finally, among nationality categories, it appears that Bosnians are more likely to agree with the above statement, although it is impossible to test whether this difference is significant.

Question 84: Do you agree with this statement? "I am engaged because people should engage"

Over half of the respondents surveyed (52.6%) strongly agree with this statement. Although women are more likely to agree with this statement than their male counterparts, there is no statistically significant relationship between gender and levels of agreement. Similarly, although lower-income respondents seem to also agree to this statement at higher rates, it is unlikely that the difference among the income categories is significant, though this cannot be tested empirically. Across education and nationality categories, there is no significant difference in agreement with the above statement.

Question 85: Why aren't you engaged?
A large plurality of respondents (47.2%) claim too busy to engage politically while a smaller minority (20.8%) claim to have other priorities that prevent them from engaging. According to the Fisher's exact test, there is no significant difference between gender categories in terms of responses. Nor is there a noticeable difference among income or education categories. In terms of nationality, it appears Turkish- and German-born citizens are more likely to respond that they do not have enough time to engage politically.

Question 86: Are you a German citizen?
Being a German citizen is correlated with the following measures of informal political participation:

- volunteering (German citizens volunteer more frequently than non-German citizens)
- feeling like you belong to a neighborhood community (German citizens feel like they belong more than non-Germans)

And the following measures of formal political behavior:

- feeling like you belong to a political or environmental initiative (German citizens feel like they belong to political and environmental initiatives more than non-Germans)
- feeling well represented by parliamentarians (German citizens are more likely to agree with this statement)
- feeling that parliamentarians are well reachable (German citizens are more likely to agree with this statement)
- feeling that politicians from your country of origin can represent you better (German citizens feel that politicians from their country of origin can represent them better)
- believing that public officials should be more religious (German citizens are more likely to agree with politicians being more religious)
- Voting in a public elections

APPENDIX 5

SURVEY OF SURVEYS

Abu Dhabi Gallup Center. 2009. "Religious Perceptions in America." Accessed January 31, 2012, http://www.abudhabigallupcenter.com/144335/religious-perceptions-america.aspx.

Association for Canadian Studies/Canadian Race Relations Foundation. 2010. *Muslims and Non-Muslims in Canada and the United States: Nine Years after 9/11*. Accessed January 30, 2012, http://www.crr.ca/content/view/744/268/lang,english/.

BBVA Foundation, 2010. *Transatlantic Trends: Immigration 2010*. Accessed February 4, 2011, http://www.affarinternazionali.it/documenti/TT-Immigr10_EN.pdf.

Centraal Bureau voor de Statistiek. 2009. *Religie aan het begin van de 21ste eeuw*. Accessed January 31, 2012, http://www.cbs.nl/nl-nl/menu/themas/vrije-tijd-cultuur/publicaties/publicaties/archief/2009/2009-e16-pub.htm.

Dabi, F., and J. Fourquet. 2010. "France and Germany's Views on Islam." *IFOP*, December 13. Accessed January 31, 2012, http://www.ifop.com/media/poll/1365-2-study_file.pdf.

European Monitoring Centre on Racism and Xenophobia (EUMC). 2006. "Muslims in the European Union. Discrimination and Islamophobia." Accessed January 31, 2012, http://eumc.europa.eu/eumc/material/pub/muslim/Manifestations_EN.pdf.

Eurostat. 2009. *Key Figures on Europe*. Accessed January 31, 2012, http://epp.eurostat.ec.europa.eu/cache/ITY_OFFPUB/KS-EI-10-001/EN/KS-EI-10-001-EN.PDF.

Gallup. 2007. *Muslims in Berlin, London, and Paris: Bridges and Gaps in Public Opinion*. Accessed January 31, 2012, http://www.gallup.com/file/se/.../WPTFMuslimsinEuropeExecSumm.pdf.

———. 2009a. *The Gallup Coexist Index 2009: A Global Study of Interfaith Relations*. Accessed January 31, 2012, http://www.euro-islam.info/wp-content/uploads/pdfs/gallup_coexist_2009_interfaith_relations_uk_france_germany.pdf.

———. 2009b. *Muslim Americans: A National Portrait. An In-Depth Analysis of America's Most Diverse Religious Community*. Accessed January 31, 2012, http://www.abudhabigallupcenter.com/144332/Muslim-Americans-National-Portrait.aspx.

Gallup. 2010. "In U.S., Religious Prejudice Stronger against Muslims." Accessed July 22, 2012, http://www.gallup.com/poll/125312/Religious-Prejudice-Stronger-Against-Muslims.aspx.

———. 2011. *Muslim Americans: Faith, Freedom and the Future. Examining U.S. Muslims' Political, Social, and Spiritual Engagement 10 Years after September 11.* Accessed January 31, 2012, http://www.abudhabigallupcenter.com/148778/report-bilingual-muslim-americans-faith-freedom-future.aspx.

IFOP. 2011. "ANALYSE: 1989–2011, *Enquête sur l'implantation et l'évolution de l'Islam de France.*" Accessed January 31, 2012, http://www.ifop.com/media/pressdocument/343-1-document_file.pdf.

Mayor of London. 2008. *Muslims in London.* Accessed January 31, 2012, http://www.islamutbildning.se/Externa_doks/Report-Muslims_in_London.pdf.

The New York Times Poll. August 27–31, 2010. Accessed January 31, 2012, http://www.nytimes.com/packages/pdf/poll_results.pdf.

Nyiri, Z. 2007. "Muslims in Europe: Basis for Greater Understanding Already Exists." *Gallup Polling.* Accessed 12 January 2011, http://www.gallup.com/corporate/115/About-Gallup.aspx.

Open Society Institute, 2007. *Muslims in the EU: Cities Report. Germany.* Accessed January 31, 2012, http://www.soros.org/initiatives/home/articles_publications/publications/museucities_20080101/museucitiesger_20080101.pdf.

———. 2009. *Muslims in Europe. A Report on 11 EU Cities.* Accessed January 31, 2012, http://www.soros.org/initiatives/home/articles_publications/publications/muslims-europe-20091215/a-muslims-europe-20110214.pdf.

———. 2010a. *Muslims in Berlin.* Accessed January 31, 2012, http://www.soros.org/initiatives/home/articles_publications/publications/berlin-muslims-report-20100427.

———. 2010b. *Muslims in Marseille.* Accessed January 31, 2012, http://www.soros.org/initiatives/home/articles_publications/publications/muslims-marseille-20110920/a-muslims-marseille-en-20110920.pdf.

———. 2010c. *Muslims in Rotterdam.* Accessed January 31, 2012, http://www.soros.org/initiatives/home/articles_publications/publications/muslims-rotterdam-20101119/a-muslims-rotterdam-report-en-20101119.pdf.

Pew. 2006. *Muslims in Europe: Economic Worries Top Concerns about Religious and Cultural Identity.* Accessed January 30, 2012, http://www.pewglobal.org/files/pdf/7-6-06.pdf.

———. 2007. *Muslim Americans: Middle Class and Mostly Mainstream.* Accessed January 30, 2012, http://pewresearch.org/assets/pdf/muslim-americans.pdf.

———. 2012. "Muslim-Western Tensions Persist." Accessed July 22, 2012, http://pewresearch.org/pubs/2066/muslims-westerners-christians-jews-islamic-extremism-september-11.

Pew Research Center. 2008. "Unfavorable Views of Both Jews and Muslims Increase in Europe." Accessed January 31, 2012, http://pewresearch.org/pubs/955/unfavorable-views-of-both-jews-and-muslims-increase-in-europe.

———. 2009. "Views of Religious Similarities and Differences. Muslims Widely Seen as Facing Discrimination." Accessed January 31, 2012, http://www.pewforum.org/uploadedfiles/Orphan_Migrated_Content/surveyo909.pdf

Religion Monitor. 2008. *Muslim Religousness in Germany*. Accessed January 30, 2012, http://www.bertelsmann-stiftung.de/bst/en/media/xcms_bst_dms_25866__2.pdf.

Tausch. 2006. *Why Europe Has to Offer a Better Deal Towards Its Muslim Communities*. Accessed January 31, 2012, http://www.caei.com.ar/ebooks/ebook16.pdf.

The Washington Post. 2010. "Washington Post-ABC Poll." Accessed January 31, 2012, http://www.washingtonpost.com/wp-srv/politics/polls/postpoll_09072010.html.

Zick, A., B. Kupper, and A. Hovermann. 2011. "Intolerance, Prejudice and Discrimination: A European Report." *Friedrich-Ebert-Stiftung*. Accessed January 31, 2012, http://www.uni-bielefeld.de/ikg/IntolerancePrejudice.pdf bielefeld.de/ikg/IntolerancePrejudice.PDF.

APPENDIX 6

MASTER LIST OF CODES

Code	Sources	References
Hijab neutral	38	407
Family neutral	41	341
Country neutral	42	299
Beliefs positive	38	286
Hijab negative	34	252
Country negative	41	248
Beliefs neutral	35	240
Community positive	37	220
Country positive	41	214
Identity neutral	39	176
Identity positive	32	170
Community neutral	33	163
Family positive	36	161
Praying positive	36	161
Vote positive	25	154
Politics negative	34	129
Beliefs negative	32	127
Praying neutral	26	118
Hijab positive	26	111
Citizenship neutral	27	110
Community negative	29	105
Politics positive	29	98
Citizenship positive	24	94
Politics neutral	25	93
Vote negative	24	92
Hard negative	18	82
Praying negative	33	82
Identity negative	29	79
Family negative	30	68
Vote neutral	17	60

(continued)

Code	Sources	References
Citizenship negative	18	56
Participation neutral	26	45
Participation positive	22	43
Government negative	22	35
Government positive	18	34
Hard neutral	16	33
Government neutral	12	26
Secularism negative	13	22
Secularism neutral	10	21
Secularism positive	8	17
Hard positive	9	15
Participation negative	8	13

TRENDS OF FORMAL POLITICAL PARTICIPATION

Muslims Have Lower Formal and Informal Political Participation Than People of Other Faiths

Formal participation includes voter registration and turnout, as well as membership in political parties and organizations, such as unions. Informal participation is a catchall phrase for those activities generally considered civic participation, including volunteering, working for NGOs, or participating in faith-based groups.

Voter eligibility requirements differ across the countries included in this survey. In several countries, non-citizens are not eligible to vote in either the national or the local elections. In the Netherlands and the United Kingdom, non-citizens are allowed to participate in just local elections. France and the United States both limit voting at the national and local levels to citizens and only in Germany are European immigrants allowed to vote in both national and local elections. Therefore, because a majority of Muslims in European countries are immigrants and have not yet been naturalized, they are almost always ineligible to participate in either national or local elections.

With the exception of the United States and Britain, few surveys dealt directly with "registration," which reflects a serious gap in current knowledge. When data on voter registration was available, it showed that Muslim voter registration was lower than non-Muslims in Europe. In the United States, there were similarly low levels of registered voters among Muslims as well as lower levels of political participation. Thus, when Muslims were eligible to vote, they tended to vote less than the rest of the population (see Figures A7.1–A7.5).

As for levels of informal participation, the results varied by country. Muslims tended to participate less in signing petitions or working with organizations and associations within Germany, France, the Netherlands, and the United Kingdom (see Figures A7.6–A7.9). This trend was also the same

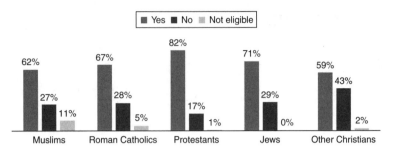

Figure A7.1   Voted in last national election (2005), United Kingdom

Source: 2010 European Social Survey

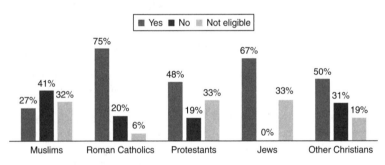

Figure A7.2   Voted in last national election (2007), France

Source: 2010 European Social Survey

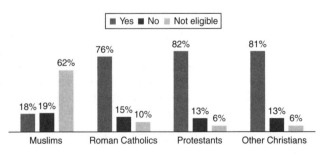

Figure A7.3   Voted in last national election (2005), Germany

Source: 2010 European Social Survey

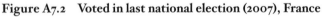

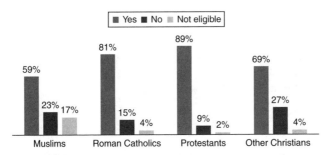

Figure A7.4 Voted in last national election (2006), the Netherlands

Source: 2010 European Social Survey

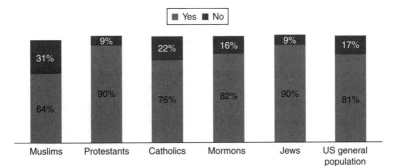

Figure A7.5 Registered to vote, United States

Source: Gallup (2009)

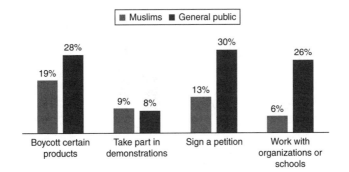

Figure A7.6 Informal participation, Germany

Source: 2010 European Social Survey

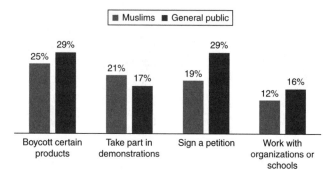

Figure A7.7   Informal participation, France

Source: 2010 European Social Survey

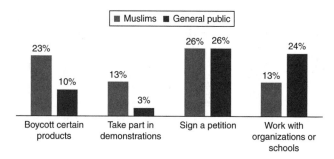

Figure A7.8   Informal participation, the Netherlands

Source: 2010 European Social Survey

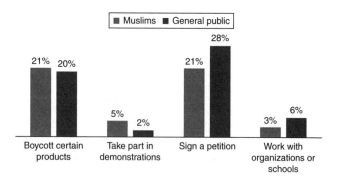

Figure A7.9   Informal participation, United Kingdom

Source: 2010 European Social Survey

for informal participation in the United States. When it came to boycotting, Muslims participated more than the general public in the Netherlands and the United Kingdom. Additionally, Muslims in Germany and France partook in demonstrations more than the general public (see Figures A7.10–A7.13).

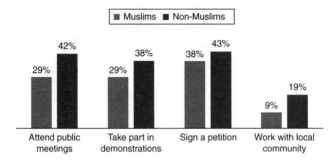

Figure A7.10   Informal political participation, Paris
Source: OSI (2010)

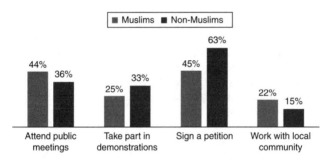

Figure A7.11   Informal political participation, Berlin
Source: OSI (2010)

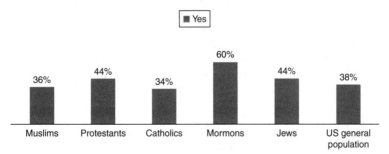

Figure A7.12   Informal participation: Volunteer time, United States
Source: Gallup (2009)

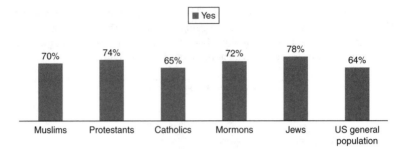

Figure A7.13   Informal participation: Given to charity, United States
Source: Gallup (2009)

Age Does Not Uniformly Influence Voting across Europe, But It Does in the United States

Generally, age influenced voting, but, in Europe, other metrics, such as class, education, or immigration status (naturalized or not), were more significant in understanding trends of voter turnout. Unfortunately, national-level data was not available on how age influences voting across Europe. Yet cities such as Paris and Berlin affirmed this trend (see Figures A7.14–A7.15).

There were two exceptions to this trend in Rotterdam and Marseille, because, as age increased, voter participation increased in both local and national elections (see Figures A7.16–A7.17).

The United States differed from the European cases, and, as the Gallup (2011) data suggested, age was a salient factor for voting in the United States. Similar to young people in the general population, less than half of eligible US Muslims (48 percent) under 30 were registered to vote. The Gallup survey further showed that among Muslim respondents, those declaring lower levels of political participation were more likely to be young (18–29 years old). While this was also true of the general sample, this trend was more accentuated among Muslims, signifying that political participation was more likely to increase sharply with age. This change in behavior with age may also come as a result of earning more money or reaching a higher level of education.

One hypothesis for young peoples' lack of political participation is that that they are more likely to hold alternative or less sophisticated understandings of the political system. Among Muslims, studies have encountered elevated concerns about political discrimination and conspiracies by the government, police, and society that may subside at more mature ages, thus, leading to a sharp increase in participation. In other words, significant Muslim political capital may exist among youths, but it is not employed—and, therefore, is not empirically measured—until later years. An additional factor may be that younger interviewees are becoming citizens at a time of

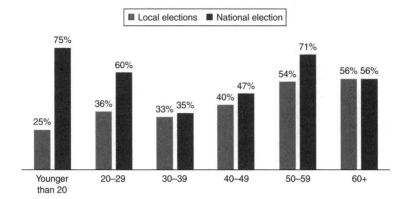

Figure A7.14   Muslims who voted, Paris

Source: OSI (2010)

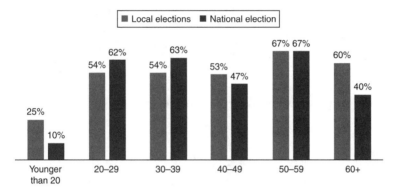

Figure A7.15   Muslims who voted, Berlin

Source: OSI (2010)

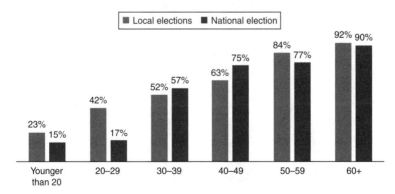

Figure A7.16   Muslims who voted, Rotterdam

Source: OSI (2010)

higher suspicion and scrutiny for Muslims, which is a very different situation than the ones experienced by the older interviewees, especially if they are from an immigrant background.

In the American context, the trend remained true, and, in every religion presented below (see Figures A7.18–A7.23), voter registration increased as age increased.[1]

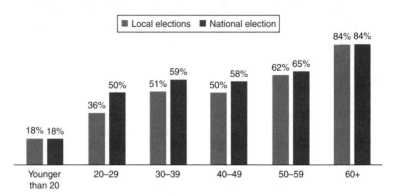

Figure A7.17   Muslims who voted, Marseille
Source: OSI (2010)

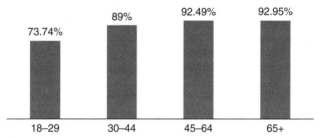

Figure A7.18   Registered to vote, Protestants
Source: Gallup (2011)

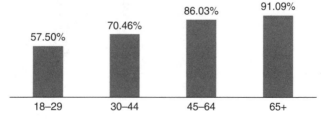

Figure A7.19   Registered to vote, Catholics
Source: Gallup (2011)

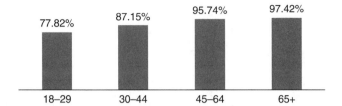

Figure A7.20   Registered to vote, Jews
Source: Gallup (2011)

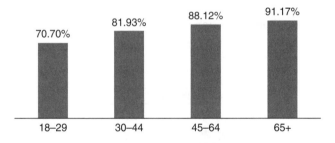

Figure A7.21   Registered to vote, Muslims
Source: Gallup (2011)

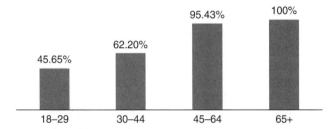

Figure A7.22   Registered to vote, Mormons
Source: Gallup (2011)

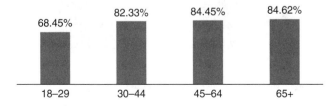

Figure A7.23   Registered to vote, other Christians
Source: Gallup (2011)

Muslims Have Left-Leaning
Political Identification in Europe

Muslims across European countries tended to align themselves with the political Left more than the general public (see Figures A7.24–A7.25).

Once again, the United States offered a slightly more mixed view of Muslim political alignment. Left-leaning political identification was not a trait specific to Muslims, because other minority groups in the United States, such as Jews and blacks, tend to lean to the Left (see Figures A7.26–A7.30).

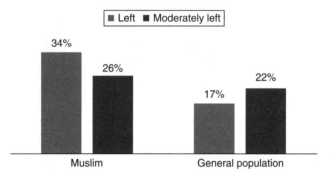

Figure A7.24   Political alignment, France
Source: Tausch (2006)

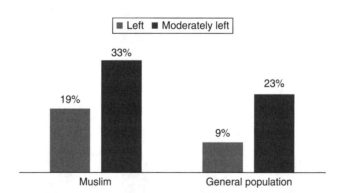

Figure A7.25   Political alignment, the Netherlands
Source: Tausch (2006)

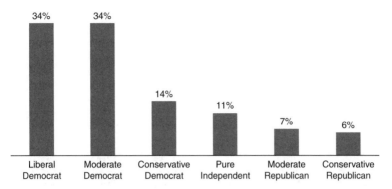

Figure A7.26   Political alignment, US Muslims

Source: Gallup (2009)

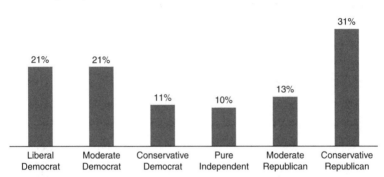

Figure A7.27   Political alignment, US Protestants

Source: Gallup (2009)

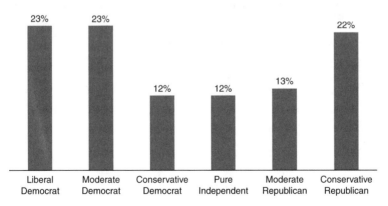

Figure A7.28   Political alignment, US Catholics

Source: Gallup (2009)

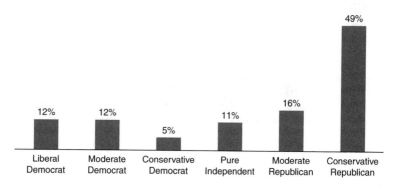

Figure A7.29   Political alignment, US Mormons

Source: Gallup (2009)

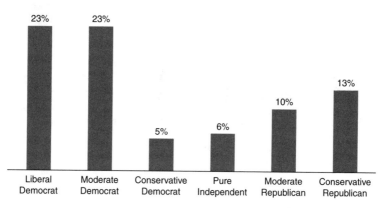

Figure A7.30   Political alignment, US Jews

Source: Gallup (2009)

APPENDIX 8

EUROPEAN REPRESENTATIVE BODIES OF ISLAM

Country	Organization	Year of Creation	Current Leader	Description
France	The French Council of the Muslim Faith	2003	Mohammed Moussaoui	The official mission statement of the organization says its purpose is to "defend the dignity and interests of the Muslim faith in France; organize and facilitate information sharing between services and places of worship; encourage dialogue between religions, the representation of Muslim places of worship within the Government."[1]
Belgium	The Muslim Council and the Executive Committee of the Muslim Council	1974	Şemsettin Uğurlu, president, is a Turkish Belgium-born Muslim with training in Islamic schools and education. Before becoming president, he was imam and professor of Islamic religion in Quaregnon. Isabelle Praile, vice-president,	Its website is http://www. embnet.be/

Country	Organization	Year of Creation	Current Leader	Description
			is originally Belgian-born but converted to be a Shiite and now wears the hijab.	
Spain	Islamic Commission of Spain	1992	Mr. Mohamed Hamed Ali is the vice president (chairman of the Muslim Community of Ceuta and president of the Spanish Federation of Islamic Religious Entities [FEERI]) and Sir Riaj Tatry is the president (commander of the Meritorious Civil Service Order and vice president of the Muslim Council for Cooperation in Europe [MCCE]).	Its website is http://ucide.org/
Germany	Central Council of Muslims in Germany	1994	Ayyub Axel Köhler and Ayman Mazyek	Its website is http://www.zentralrat.de/

ISLAMOPEDIA: A WEB-BASED RESOURCE ON CONTEMPORARY ISLAMIC THOUGHT

Islam in the West Program

Harvard University

Overview

Islamopedia Online (www.islamopediaonline.org) is a comprehensive database of Islamic thought, religious opinion, news, and analysis available to the public on the World Wide Web. From its creation, the project has sought to enhance understanding, both within academia and among the general public, about Muslim perspectives on a variety of issues relating to Islam in the contemporary world. While offering an online space for critical debate on the most contentious and disputed issues, Islamopedia Online has gathered the current debates, interpretations, and controversies—from liberalism to radicalism—concerning the Islamic religious tradition in Muslim and non-Muslim societies. Such an endeavor has assembled in one location a non-partisan presentation of the multiplicity of discourses and analyses concerning Islam. It will thus allow experts of Islam and laypeople with no expertise in Islam to better access and understand the tremendous diversity of interpretations within the field, as expressed by Islamic clerics, scholars, and activists.

Development

First Phase of Development (Fall of 2007 to Summer of 2008)

With the Carnegie grant provided in the Fall of 2007, we created a database of opinions and rulings reflecting the major concerns and religious positions across Muslim societies and set up a web forum to make this information available to a broad audience. The project was trademarked as Islamopedia Online, and the name has been copyrighted since May 2008.

The first step of this phase was to get an overview of the landscape of religious thinking and debates on the Internet. We started a comprehensive investigation of the major topics, opinions, and authorities on the Internet in order to gauge the broad landscape of work for our nascent website. Such a bird's-eye view of the Islamic thinking on the Internet allowed us to contemplate the most important topics, opinions, and religious trends currently available to Muslims and non-Muslims. We decided at this stage to focus on websites that deal with fielding questions and providing religious opinions expressed by clerics or religious leaders.

In order to complete this first phase, we created a team of ten researchers with native competency in the main relevant languages: Arabic, Farsi, Urdu, Turkish, and English. The first task of the research team was to collect information and materials from websites. In this task, the researchers were not limited by political boundaries but instead focused on the zones of influence of each of the five languages. For example, researchers explored websites originating from Turkey and other Turkish-speaking regions such as the Balkans or Turkish diasporas in the West. The websites from which materials were collected included those under the responsibility of a group, for example, Talbighi; an institution, for example, Dar al-Ifta in Cairo; or a particular cleric, for example, Sheikh Sistani. Following a thorough browsing of these websites, Islamopedia researchers catalogued their contents according to an inductive list of categories. With this web tool, Islamopedia researchers have created an extensive .csv spreadsheet describing over 44,000 entries from more than one hundred different websites around the world. Islamopediaonline.org hosts current interpretations, divergent rulings, and opinions and analyzes them within a global context.

The research team includes researchers from the broadest range of disciplines, including but not limited to anthropology, philosophy, religion, and law. Several members of this group are prominent members of the scientific community. The browsing and cataloguing process is facilitated by a purpose-built web tool where researchers submit information gathered from the websites into a central .csv data file. The web tool resembles a three-part form that first prompts researchers to enter the pertinent identifying data including their name, date and time accessed, the website name, and URL. Next, researchers are prompted to describe the content of the website they are browsing by entering its primary language and cataloging the topics and subtopics discussed along with their frequencies. Finally, the researchers are prompted to assign a geographic location to the website and enter any additional comments in a "notes" section.

Second Phase of Development (Fall of 2008 to Fall of 2009)

During this phase, the website was created and the data reformatted in order to be accessible on the online site, searchable by country, language, key word, religious authorities, and leading Muslim nonclerical scholars of the Islamic religion. Each of the nearly 2,000 text records is accessible on the site in its original language, the main points and often entire content has been translated, and information on the author of the opinion and the issuing body is also provided.

Debuting in March 2009, the initial Islamopedia website allowed researchers to independently upload and modify content, regardless of their technological expertise. The initial funding also made it possible to create Islamopedia Online's technical structure, to conduct documentary research, to hire a coordinator, and to develop valuable networks with colleagues in Muslim-majority countries. It also has allowed the project to begin collecting and analyzing legal rulings and opinions in the predominant languages of the Muslim world: Arabic, English, Persian, Turkish, and Urdu. The website has a robust database of text records, nearly 2,000 to date, categorized by language, country of origin, and topic. A section profiling current events and news was added in the summer of 2009 to further highlight how political circumstances shape religious discourses. A glossary of Arabic and religious terms was added. A general search function is also available to the browser. We are currently working to expand to a more open format where site users can interact with the rulings and analyze with content they find online.

In the summer of 2009, we also decided to create connections with Muslim scholars, activists, and religious authorities in the different countries covered by Islamopedia Online in order to ground the information and materials in different cultural contexts and be able to follow the evolution of the Islam and politics connection that we have captured in the creation of Islamopediaonline.org. We have added an advisory board, including Muna Abusulayman, executive director of the Prince Alwaleed Bin Talal Foundation and UN Goodwill Ambassador; Gary Bunt, senior lecturer in Islamic Studies at the University of Wales; John Esposito of Georgetown University's Prince Alwaleed Bin-Talal Center for Muslim-Christian Understanding; Ekmeleddin Ihsanoglu, secretary-general of the Organization of the Islamic Conference; Ruud Peters, professor of Arabic Law and Culture at the University of Amsterdam; and Tariq Ramadan, professor of Contemporary Islamic Studies at Oxford University. The Advisory Board will serve as a liaison between the Islamopedia team and the intellectual and religious resources of Muslim-majority countries.

Major Wanabi Organizations in Europe

Name of the Organization	Description
Muslim World League (MWL, *Rabitat al-'Alam al-Islami*)	The MWL was founded in Mecca in 1962. It arose out of a meeting attended by 111 Muslim intellectuals, clerics, and politicians with shared concerns over the state of the Muslim *Ummah*. The group agreed to establish a constituent council (al-Majlis al-Ta'sīsī), which, based in Mecca, was comprised of 22 Muslims of prominence who oversaw the league's activities. In 1962, the government of Saudi Arabia donated approximately $250,000 to support these endeavors.
	When the Saudi state and royal family began their proselytizing campaigns in the early 1970s, the constituent council of the MWL decided to follow suit and "concentrated on establishing a network of Islamic cultural and political organizations." In 1974, the MWL made the decision to expand its reach by increasing its efforts of "coordination *(tansīq)*, *da'wah*, jurisprudence, and social welfare," with the hopes of spreading its interpretation of Islam, often by establishing connections with local Muslim organizations. Estimations show that the MWL founded approximately "thirty-five branch offices and bureaus" during this period. In 1974, the organization made plans to form "continental councils (five existed in 1985), local Islamic councils in twenty-eight Muslim minority communities, and a coordination committee." Perhaps to commend the MWL's activism during its second decade of existence, Saudi Arabia offered the league an estimated $13 million in 1980.[1]
International Islamic Relief Organization (IIRO)	The IIRO was founded in 1979 as a joint venture by the Saudi government and the MWL. According to an article published in *Ain-al-Yaqin,* in December 2000, IIRO had built 3,800 mosques; employed 6,000 people; and spent SR 180 million ($45 million) on Islamic education/*da'wa* efforts, "from which 911 students benefited" by the year 2000. Additionally, the

(continued)

Name of the Organization	Description
	article claims that IIRO "implemented 16 training projects and more than 15,000 persons benefited from these projects." The same article in *Ain-al-Yaqin* cites figures produced by Okeil Al Okeil, director general of Al Haramein Charitable Foundation. According to Al Okeil, "the foundation [Al Haramein & Al Aqsa Charitable Foundation] had spent in 1420 H more than SR 200 million in the six continents as follows: Asia 41%, Africa 9%, Europe 21%, and projects of continuous almsgiving 11% and 6% for mosques." In addition, Al Okeil claims that the organization "printed more than 13 million book [*sic*], launched six sites on the internet, employed more than 3,000 callers, founded 1,100 mosques, schools, and cultural Islamic centers and posted more than 350,000 letter of call."
The World Assembly of Muslim Youth (WAMY)	The WAMY was established in Riyadh in 1972 under the auspices of King Faisal to "support young Muslims' personal and social development" and "enable them to fulfill their potential" in society. The assembly has different branches around the world, but its branch in Canada was stripped of its status as a charitable organization in early 2012 due to its links with Saudi-based groups that support terrorism. See the website of the assembly's branch in Britain: http://www.wamy.co.uk/ and http://news.nationalpost.com/2012/03/06/canadian-muslim-youth-organization-loses-charitable-status/.
	It now runs 18 offices in Saudi Arabia, 12 in Africa, 2 in the Americas, 26 across Asia and Oceania, 4 in Europe, and 3 in the Middle East and North Africa. An article in *Ain-al-Yaqin* cites figures produced by Dr. Mani Ibn Hammad Al Juhani, secretary general of the WAMY: "WAMY spent last year about SR 66 million and offered aids amounting to around SR 42 million which covered aids to students, founding mosques, digging water wells and other health and social projects."[2]
Holy Qur'an Memorization International Organization	The Holy Qur'an Memorization International Organization, aims to teach Muslim youth to memorize and study the Qur'an. They also set up worldwide Qur'anic recitation competitions and fund scholarships for the study of the Qur'an. The International Islamic Organization for Education, Science, and Culture takes a different approach to encouraging the study of Islamic texts. This organization coordinates between Islamic universities and other scientific institutions in the development of Islamic educational policies. See Holy Qur'an Memorization International Organization website: http://www.hqmi.org/page.php?lang=2.

Name of the Organization	Description
International Islamic Organization for Education, Makkah Al-Mukarramah Charity Foundation for Orphans	The Makkah Al-Mukarramah Charity Foundation for Orphans provides assistance to Muslim orphans and children affected by conflicts while simultaneously educating the children in the Salafi tradition.[3]
The Commission on Scientific Signs in the Qur'an and Sunnah	The Commission on Scientific Signs in the Qur'an and Sunnah is concerned with authenticating and publishing the scientific signs in the Qur'an and Sunnah, lending historical credibility to the tradition of the Prophet. See http://www.eajaz.org/eajaz/.
The World Supreme Council for Mosques	The World Supreme Council for Mosques takes a different approach and seeks to emphasize the importance of the mosque in religious and temporal life of the Muslim community. The goal of this organization is to reinvigorate the role that the mosque played in the early days of Islam in modern society. See *Rabitat al-Alam al-Islami: The Muslim World League* at: http://muslimworldalmanac.com/ver3/index2.php?option=com_content&do_pdf=1&id=123.
The Fiqh (Islamic Jurisprudence) Council	The Fiqh, or Islamic Jurisprudence Council, is an academic body consisting of Islamic scholars and jurists. It examines relevant issues and problems in the *Ummah*, seeking to find solutions to these in the Qur'an and Sunnah. See http://www.fiqhcouncil.org/node/13.

SALAFIS IN EUROPE

For the most part, the guiding principle of the life of a Salafi Muslim living in Europe is to retreat into a "purer" Muslim environment and avoid unnecessary contact with the host country. Therefore, the quietist and political trends have gained influence but sometimes the line is blurred between the political and jihadi trend. Additionally, competition between the quietist and the political trends can be quite ferocious.

Apolitical Salafi Groups in Europe

In the Netherlands, Abdelillah Bouchta, who studied in Saudi Arabia and now runs the Bouchta mosque in Tilburg, is part of the apolitical Salafi trend. In 2006, for example, the mosque leaders distributed pamphlets condemning suicide attacks.[1] The Al Waqf Islamic Foundation, a Saudi-run organization, and the Al Fourkaan mosque, connected to it (both in Eindhoven, founded in 1989 by Moroccans), are also representatives of this trend. According to a press release dated November 2, 2006, the Al Waqf Foundation estimated that the Al Fourkaan mosque had 2,000 members who come from all parts of the Muslim world and the Netherlands.[2] Despite the mosque's general apolitical approach, since 2002, many people arrested for terrorist activities had been regular attendees of Al Fourkaan mosque.[3] In 2005, several imams of the mosque were labeled as national security threats by the minister for Immigration and Integration under the Alien Law, which sought to deport radical imams.[4]

In France, there are an estimated 5,000 followers of the apolitical Salafi movement.[5] Members are usually young men of Algerian descent living in the urban areas of Paris, Lyon, Toulouse, and so on. These youth are typically unsuccessful at school and, in general, mistrust French society. In France specifically, there is a "negotiated identity" among purist Salafis. They try to escape professional careers that have the potential to corrupt them, but at the same time, they wish to maintain Western features of modernity in regard to business spirit or consumer culture.[6] For example, French Salafis approve the welfare system although they discourage political participation[7] by calling on Muslim voters to abstain from casting their ballots in the presidential elections of 2002 and 2007.[8]

In the United Kingdom, the Salafi movement had expanded during the 1980s. However, it did not become the force it is today until the 1990s when many young, second generation British Muslims, as well as non-Muslim Brits, embraced it. As elsewhere, Saudi Arabia has been a major source of support for the British Salafi movement, financing the development of numerous religious institutions including charities, mosques, schools, community centers, and more.

Apolitical Salafis emerged from a break within the group Jamiyat Ihya Minhaj al-Sunnah (JIMAS).[9] (The details of this group will be discussed later in the section on political Salafis in the UK.)[10] Abdul Wahid (Abu Khadeeja) initiated this break and created the Organization of Ahl al-Sunnah Islamic Societies (OASIS) in the 1980s because he disliked the political leaning of JIMAS. OASIS grew into several other organizations/institutions such as the SalafiPublications.com,[11] salafitalk.net,[12] and salafimanhaj.com.[13] (The OASIS organization no longer maintains its original structure and is considered a part of SalafiPublications.com.)[14] These organizations focus on correcting religious beliefs and practices of Muslims, and, thereby, they are often defined as "Super Salafis." This nickname refers to their promptitude to identify and denounce Muslims who do not adhere to their interpretation of Islam as deviants.[15]

The growth of Salafi trends in the United Kingdom has triggered a countermovement to promote and strengthen "traditional Islam" based on *madhabs* and/or Sufism. This trend is represented by figures such as American convert and scholar Hamza Yusuf,[16] Abdal Hakim Murad,[17] and Shakykh Nuh Keller.[18]

Political Salafi Groups in Europe

In the Netherlands, the trend of political Salafism is represented by Amersterdam's El-Tawheed Foundation[19] and mosque, which is closely connected with the Saudi missionary NGO Al-Haramain, and The Hague's As-Sunnah Foundation and mosque.[20] The El-Tawheed Foundation was established by Egyptians including Imam Mahmoud Shershaby in 1986. The foundation and mosque attract an array of members varying in age and ethnicity. Their primary concern is ministry and missionary work. As-Sunnah Foundation and mosque was created by Moroccans and maintains the website www.al-yaqeen.com.[21] The Institute for Teaching and Education (IOE) started by Suhayb Salam, a youth preacher from Tilburg, works with the As-Sunnah mosque to provide Islamic educational opportunities for youth. This program ultimately allows youth to become qualified to give lectures on Islamic topics and is training them to become Salafi preachers. The following at As-Sunnah mosque, estimated at 1,500 people, is again multicultural but has started to particularly attract Turkish Muslims since lessons are being offered in Turkish.

Imams Shershaby (Amsterdam), Fawaz Jneid (The Hague), and Ahmad Salam (Tilburg) are the most active leaders of the political Salafi movement in Europe. Imam Fawaz Jneid and Imam Shershaby are Syrian and were involved with the Syrian Muslim Brotherhood before immigrating to the Netherlands. Fawaz Jneid is the Imam at the As-Sunnah mosque in the Netherlands. Ahmad Salam, also Syrian, founded the Islamic Foundation for Education and Transmission of Knowledge (ISOOK)[22] in 2000.[23] This organization functions closely with the As-Sunnah mosque and IOE.[24] Salam was greatly exposed in the media when he refused to shake hands with the female Dutch minister for Immigration and Integration, Rita Verdonk, in November 2004.

Leaders of the El-Tawheed mosque, the As-Sunnah mosque, and ISOOK together established the Foundation for the Islamic Committee for Ahl-Sunnah in 2001. The chairman of the organization is Ahmed Salam and the committee works to spread Salafism by organizing *da'wa* (preaching) sessions in mosques.[25]

In France, during the 1990s, Salafism began to take on a different character as second-generation Muslims became less influenced by Algerian politics and more so by scholars from the Arabian Peninsula. These scholars came out of institutions such as the Madrasah Dar al-Hadith al-Khayriyya[26] in Dammaj, Yemen, and the al-Albani center in Amman.[27] The Saudi Arabian version of Salafism not only took hold in France via students who had studied in the region but also through Saudi-founded organizations such as the WML and the WAMY. For example, the Mantes-la-Jolie mosque was constructed and financed by the WML.[28]

The spread of political Salafism in the United Kingdom is represented by organizations such as the Green Lane Mosque[29] and Masjid Ibn Taymiyyah in Britxon.[30] The Jamiyyah Ihya' Minhaj as Sunnah (the Society for the Revival of the Prophetic Way, JIMAS)[31] was particularly effective in spreading political Salafism throughout the United Kingdom via "study circles" for Muslim youth at mosques and universities under the direction of Manwar Ali (Abu Muntasir).[32]

Another group within the United Kingdom that represents the ideas of political Salafis is the nonviolent Islamist Hizb ut-Tahir (HT).[33] This group, headquartered in London, is a transnational organization that operates in Central Asia, Pakistan, Bangladesh, and Middle Eastern countries. The main goal of HT is to establish a modern-day caliphate, and their followers view Islam as a total life system. HT uses media and community platforms—flyers, study groups, conferences, vigils, and the like—to disseminate their message on topics relevant to British Muslims. Through media-savvy spokespeople, HT has developed a sophisticated image.

Jihadi Groups in Europe

In the Netherlands, it is impossible to identify any mosque or organization that officially embraces the Jihadi trend. In the 1990s, there was a growth of Jihadi Dutch networks seeking asylum in the Netherlands who eventually settled among the long-established Muslim communities. By 1999, Jihadi networks had separated themselves from the mosques. The Internet was significant to disseminate their doctrine and, interestingly enough, Jihadi websites have included Dutch language material.[34]

Since 2006, the Jihadi networks have declined due to a decrease in their operational capabilities and government action against them. The Dutch Jihadi/Takfiri Salafis are loyal to Abu Muhammad al-Maqdisi,[35] who preaches that true Jihadists should isolate themselves from the non-Muslim world and hate those who threaten Islam. Additionally, the Jihadi/Takfi branch includes the Hofstad network, an Islamist group consisting of mostly Moroccan immigrants. This group is a violent Islamist terrorist cell consisting of Dutch Muslims of North African descent. It has links in Spain and Belgium and is connected with Abdeladim Akoudad (Naoufel) who is allegedly responsible for the Casablanca Attacks (2003). Followers of the group at different times have been suspected of terrorist plans to kill members of the Dutch parliament or initiate terrorist attacks in the Netherlands.[36]

This group was led by Mohammed Boyeri (b. 1978)[37] who killed the film director Theo Van Gogh in 2004 for directing the film *Submission* that depicts Muslim women as oppressed and abused. After stabbing Van Gogh, Boyeri attached a note to the body that threatened Jews, Ayaan Hirsi Ali,[38] and Western governments.[39] He is serving a sentence of life imprisonment without parole.

Women have played a unique role in Dutch Jihadi networks by translating Jihadi materials from Arabic websites into Dutch and by managing multiple discussion groups and forums online. Most of the Dutch Jihadi websites address the theoretical and dogmatic aspects of the Jihadi struggle.[40]

In France, the Jihadi movement emerged in the 1990s through the influence of Abdelkader Bouziane in Lyon and Abdelhadi Doudi in Marseille. Doudi was the former advisor to Mustafa Bouyali, the founder of the 1982 Algerian Armed Islamic Movement.[41] Abdelkader Bouziane moved from Algeria to France in 1979.[42] In 2004, the French government deported him for disturbing public order because of a speech he gave that condoned domestic violence against disobedient wives.[43]

Besides leaders like Abdelkader Bouziane, there are not any official Jihadi groups in France. However, the killings in March 2012 by Muhammad Merah of three French soldiers of North African origin, three Jewish children, and their teacher in Toulouse show that the ideology still attracts some individuals. Merah, a French citizen of Algerian descent, explained to police that he "wanted to avenge Palestinian children and to attack the French army because of its foreign interventions."[44] Like the assassination of Theo van Gogh, the Toulouse killings reveal that individuals can become self-radicalized and carry out deadly attacks independently.[45]

Following the March 2012 killings, the French Government expelled Muslims suspected of terrorism based on their contact with Islamic activists or their strong anti-Semitic and radical declarations.[46] Some of the statements included legitimizing hatred toward Jews,[47] calling for the killing of apostates,[48] and accusing the French authorities of trying to enslave Islam.[49] Police have stated that they arrested people that seemed to have "a similar profile to Mohamed Merah…They are isolated individuals, who are self-radicalized."[50] The police used online forums to track people who had expressed extreme views and who had said that they were planning "to travel to Afghanistan, Pakistan, and the Sahel belt to wage jihad."[51] Several of those arrested were members of Foresane Alizza, an Islamist French group with 15 to 20 members that calls for the establishment of shari'a in France and a global caliphate.[52]

The Jihadi Salafi trend in the United Kingdom was led by Abdullah al-Fasil, Abu Qatada al-Filastini, and Omar Bakri Muhammad. Abdullah al-Fasil (b. 1963 in Jamaica) is a convert to Islam who has urged his followers to act out violently against non-Muslims. He was deported back to Jamaica in 2010 after being sentenced to prison for preaching hate.[53] Abu Qatada al-Filastini is a Jordanian Palestinian who has been imprisoned in the United Kingdom for his affiliation with al-Qaeda since 2005.[54] He has been connected with the 9/11 hijackers and particularly linked as a spiritual leader to Mohamed Atta.[55] Omar Bakri Muhammad is another Jihadi who has close links to al-Qaeda. He supports violence against Western governments and, until its disbandment in 2004, was head of the Al-Muhajiroun radical group.

The crack down of the German police on jihadi-oriented groups in May 2012 put the Salafi groups in the spotlight. The minister of Internal Affairs, Hans-Peter Friedrich issued a banning order for the Solingen-based Salafi association Millatu Ibrahim. Authorities had been monitoring the Salafi group since violent clashes happened in Bonn and Solingen. Among other measures, the police have shut down the group's webpage. This, according to the minister of Interior, means an immense logistic and organizational loss for the Millatu group. Allegedly, the group's goals are to call Muslims to fight against the constitutional order of Germany, to destroy the concept of understanding among peoples, and to introduce shari'a by violent means.

Millatu Ibrahim belongs to the Jihadist arm of the Salafi movement in Germany. It has been extremely radical in its calls for violence and bloodshed. The group's leading figure is the Austrian Mohamed Mahmoud, also known as Abu Usama al-Gharib. In 2011, he was convicted for hate speech and terrorist activities by a German court. Also, he had been a founding member of the Global Islamic Media front. After his release, he had moved to Berlin and afterward to Solingen. He began preaching at the Millatu-Ibrahim-Mosque, but German authorities intervened to stop this activity. He then moved to the German state of Hessen and was finally deported from Germany. Abu Usama al-Gharib is now said to live in Egypt. His accomplice and a popular figure in the Millatu group is the former rapper Denis Cuspert, alias Deso Dogg, alias Abu Talha Al-Almani. Apparently, Cuspert has unsubscribed his Berlin apartment and is now wanted. The Ministry of Interior used videos as evidence to prove how both leaders encouraged Salafi adherents to oppose police and right-wing supporters on May 1 and May 12, 2012, demonstrations by calling for bloodshed.

Authorities have also initiated preliminary investigations against the association DawaFFM in Frankfurt-am-Main and the Cologne-based association, the True Religion. Given the lack of evidence against the groups, the ministry has not yet issued banning orders. Earlier this spring, the True Religion had initiated a campaign distributing copies of the Qur'an in German cities. The group interrupted the campaign after printing 300,000 copies, as the print shop had started attracting the public attention.

Other well-known activists have openly sympathized with the Jihadist arm of the Salafi movement and are, therefore, believed to be involved in its activities. Among them, there is the German Pierre Vogel, who converted to Islam 11 years ago. Another is the preacher and leading member of the True Religion, Ibrahim Abou Nagie, who allegedly encourages young Muslims to stand against all non-Muslims. He organizes Islamic seminars at schools and youth centers, and calls for the execution of shari'a on homosexual people.

Initially, Nagie's Qur'an distribution initiative sounded harmless. However, the German security forces became alert as soon as the radical leader Usama al-Gharib expressed his approval of the idea and offered to stand against possible attackers.

Security experts assume that the goal of Abou Nagie and Al-Gharib is to unify the Salafi scene and win more adherents in the form of converts. The Qur'an distributions and the demonstrations against the right-wing-initiated Muhammad cartoon campaigns are perceived as prestigious victories within the Salafi scene. All three associations are expected to be leading and coordinating Internet and street campaigns in Germany.

According to the Office for the Protection of the Constitution, there are more than 4,000 Salafists in Germany divided in two groups: a so-called political missionary arm and a Jihadist arm. In total, 24 Salafi members are classified as "dangerous." Although the Office for the Protection of the Constitution had issued warnings about Salafi activities and propaganda in Germany, authorities seemed little prepared for the outbreak of violence in May 2012. Salafi adherents had protested against demonstrations organized by the right-wing party Pro NRW, which had initiated a Muhammad cartoon campaign. Almost 30 police officers were injured during the clashes.

APPENDIX 12
FATWAS FROM SALAFI WEBSITES

Topic: Fertility	Sheikh/ Fatwa org	Fatwa question	Fatwa answer	Sect	Source	Sheikh Bio
Artificial Insemination						
	Yusuf Saanei, Qom (Iran)	Question: What is the status of implanting a stranger's sperm in a woman's womb, if her spouse is infertile	Insemination is in itself prohibited. To treat infertility, however, it is possible to fertilize the egg with the sperm in laboratory condition and then implant the fetus in the womb. In such a case, the woman who gave the egg is the mother, and the man who donated the sperm is the father, unless he has abandoned any claims on his sperm (for example, has deposited his sperm in a sperm bank to be used by whomever).	Shia	http://www. islamopediaonline. org/fatwa/fatwa-artificial-insemination	http://www. islamopediaonline. org/profile/ yusuf-saanei
IVF	Makarem Shirazi, Qom (Iran)	Is in vitro fertilization (IVF) permissible, and giving or selling one's sperm or embryo? Is the woman who buys the conceived	If conception occurs between the wife and husband it is allowed; and the conceived embryo may be put in a third person's uterus to develop. The child will be *mahrama* (forbidden for sexual relations) to the third person (the woman who has bought	Shia	http://www. islamopediaonline. org/fatwa/vitro-fertilization-ivf-permissible-and-giving-or-selling-ones-sperm-or-	http://www. islamopediaonline. org/profile/ makarem-shirazi

		embryo through IVF considered the mother?			
			the embryo) and her husband, even though the real mother and father are those to whom embryo belong to.		embryo-woman-who-buys-
Contraception and birth control	Makarem Shirazi	N/A	His situation is comparable to that of a hermaphrodite whose female gender has been determined. He becomes a woman and should be treated like a woman. And Allah knows best.	Sunni	http://www.islamopediaonline.org/fatwa/select-fatwas-ayatollah-makarem-shirazi-contraception-and-birth-controls	http://www.islamopediaonline.org/profile/makarem-shirazi
Artificial insemination	Mohammad Ebrahim Jannati, Qom (Iran)	N/A	Fertilizing a woman with her husband's sperm is permissible, but one has to avoid illegitimate means for that. It is impermissible to fertilize a woman with the sperm of someone other than her husband absent his consent. It is permissible to fertilize a woman with the sperm of someone other than her husband if the husband is infertile, has consent, and that this is not associated with other prohibited things. If a woman is fertilized with the sperm of someone other than her husband, the father	Shia	http://www.islamopediaonline.org/fatwa/select-fatwas-ayatollah-jannati-artificial-insemination	http://www.islamopediaonline.org/profile/mohammad-ebrahim-jannati

(continued)

Topic: Fertility	Fatwa question	Fatwa answer	Sect	Source	Sheikh Bio
Sheikh/ Fatwa org					
Muhammad Saalih al-Munajjid	Is it permissible to put the sperm of the husband and the egg from the wife in the womb of the second wife?	is the sperm donor, and the woman who gives birth is the mother. After examining the subject of artificial fertilization "test-tube babies" by studying the research presented and listening to comments of experts and doctors, and after discussion, the Council reached the following conclusions: The methods of artificial fertilization that are known nowadays are seven: i. Where fertilization occurs between the sperm taken from the husband and an egg taken from a woman who is not his wife, then the embryo is implanted in his wife's uterus. ii. Where fertilization occurs between the sperm of a man other than the husband and the wife's egg, then the embryo is implanted in the wife's uterus.	Sunni	http://www. islamopediaonline. org/fatwa/it-permissible-put-sperm-husband-and-egg-wife-womb-second-wife	http://www. islamopediaonline. org/profile/ muhammad-saalih-al-munajjid

			iii. Where fertilization occurs between the sperm and egg of the couple, and the embryo is implanted in the uterus of a woman who volunteers to carry it (surrogate motherhood). iv. Where fertilization occurs outside the womb between the sperm and egg of strangers, then the embryo is implanted in the wife's uterus. v. Where fertilization occurs outside the womb between the sperm and egg of the couple, then the embryo is implanted in the uterus of the other wife.		http://www.islamopediaonline.org/profile/ebrahim-desai
Infertility treatment	Ebrahim Desai (South Africa)	What are permissible treatments for infertility?	Infertility primarily refers to the biological inability of a man or a woman to contribute to conception. Infertility may also refer to the state of a woman who is unable to carry a pregnancy to full term. There are many biological causes of infertility, some which may be bypassed with medical intervention.	Sunni	http://www.islamopediaonline.org/fatwa/mufti-desai-south-africa-responds-question-what-are-permissible-treatments-infertility
N/A	N/A	If a woman who started the process of in vitro	1) The lady may implant any of these embryos in her uterus as long as she is still the wife	Sunni	http://www.islamopediaonline.org/fatwa/if-woman-

(continued)

Topic: Fertility	Sheikh/ Fatwa org	Fatwa question	Fatwa answer	Sect	Source	Sheikh Bio
		fertilization in Britain plans to leave that country, what should the woman with unused fertilized embryos do?	of the man from whom the sperm was taken. But if she is separated from him through death, divorce or the like and thus is no longer under the bond of marriage with him, it will be unlawful to implant any of them and she should destroy them or what remains of them.		who-started-process-invitro-fertilization-britain-plans-leave-country-what-should-wom	
Sperm banks	N/A	N/A	A woman does not have sperm like a man's, which is full of organisms [that cause pregnancy], but the available texts of the Guided Imams (upon them peace) have established that the liquid which emerges from her at the climax of sexual excitement takes the same ruling as a man's sperm. It results in major ritual impurity, as does anything that emerges from [a woman], if it is plentiful. Masturbation is forbidden for women just as it is forbidden for men.	Shia	http://www. islamopediaonline. org/ fatwa/sperm-banks	http://infad.usim. edu.my/

					Fatwa URL	Profile URL
IVF	Hatem Mohammad Al-Haj Aly	Is it permissible to have in vitro fertilization performed by a male doctor?	It is *halal* (permissible) to go to the male physician as long as it is significantly inconvenient to see an equally qualified female physician.	Sunni	http://www.islamopediaonline.org/fatwa/assembly-muslim-jurists-america-responds-question-it-permissible-have-vitro-fertilization-perf	http://www.islamopediaonline.org/profile/hatem-mohammad-al-haj-aly
	Mufti Siraj Desai (South Africa) http://darululoomabubakr.blogspot.com	Is artificial insemination allowed in Islam if it is between a legally married couple that are having trouble conceiving for unknown reasons for quite some time?	There is nothing wrong in adopting proper and permissible measures for having children however it is not permissible to adopt unlawful measures. For example, it is not right to masturbate in order to conceive children by artificial insemination. However it should be noted that if a child is born in this way from the husband's semen the child will be regarded as *sabit-un-nasab* (his father's descendant.)	Sunni	http://www.islamopediaonline.org/fatwa/artificial-insemination-allowed-islam-if-it-between-legally-married-couple-are-having-trouble-	http://www.islamopediaonline.org/profile/mufti-siraj-desai
	Makarem Shirazi	Doctors may move a conceived embryo from one's uterus to another person's	All three mentioned circumstances are permissible. But because it involves looking and touching	Shia	http://www.islamopediaonline.org/fatwa/madkarem-	http://www.islamopediaonline.org/profile/makarem-shirazi

(continued)

Topic: Fertility	Sheikh/ Fatwa org	Fatwa question	Fatwa answer	Sect	Source	Sheikh Bio
		uterus. May we do that if the second woman is also the wife of the man whose sperm was used to conceive? What if the second woman is unrelated to the man whose sperm is used for conception? Does it differ if the fetus is in a stage at which God has blown his spirit into it or not?	the body of the woman it should be done only if necessary.		sharizi-permissibility-fertility-treatments-case-multiple-wives	
Topic: Contraception						
	http://www.islamicacademy.org (US)	Is birth control allowed in Islam?	Anything in the world is being created for a special purpose, and sexual desire is to guarantee the endurance of life. Homosexuality is a sin that is forbidden by God because it is against the purpose of nature. It is necessary to guide and advice homosexuals in a friendly manner, and help them to		http://www.islamopediaonline.org/fatwa/birth-control-allowed-islam	

262

(continued)

	http://www.fatwaislam.com/	cure and recover. Religiously speaking, it is necessary and also *sharī'a*-compliant to help and guide them.			
		What is the ruling concerning the use of birth control pills by married couples?	It is not allowed for a wife to use birth control pills out of dislike for having children or out of fear of having to support the children. It is permissible to use them to prevent pregnancy due to some illness that may harm the women if she becomes pregnant or if she cannot give birth in the natural fashion but is in need of medical operation to give birth. This and other cases are permissible due to necessity. In those types of cases, she may use birth control pills unless she learns from specialized doctors that those pills may be harmful to her in some other fashion.	Sunni	For full answer click here: http://www.islamopediaonline.org/fatwa/what-ruling-concerning-use-birth-control-pills-married-couples	http://www.islamicity.com/?AspxAutoDetectCookieSupport=1
Contraception	Shaykh Khalif	I have 6 children and my husband is chronically ill, so his income is limited. Is it forbidden	Contraception is permissible whether or not one has children, so long as the fertilized egg has not implanted in the uterus.	Sunni	http://www.islamopediaonline.org/fatwa/i-have-6-children-and-my-husband-chronically-	http://www.islamopediaonline.org/profile/shaykh-khalif

Topic: Contraception	Sheikh/Fatwa org	Fatwa question	Fatwa answer	Sect	Source	Sheikh Bio
		for me to use contraception, like drinking medicine, etc.?	This matter is easier for someone who has children than for someone who has no children. However, I would like to caution that abortion, or removal of the fetus, is forbidden for any reason, unless it has been ascertained that [the pregnancy] would harm the mother in a way that would cause death (regardless of whether or not she has children). But before pregnancy all methods [of birth control] are permissible so long as the fertilized egg has not implanted.		ill-so-his-income-limited-it-forbidden-me-use-con	
Contraception and birth control	Makarem Shirazi	N/A	In order to prevent fertilization, any harmless means is permitted if it does not lead to permanent infertility of the man or the woman. However, if it is prohibited if it is associated with other prohibited things such as illegitimate touching or looking at the body of an	Shia	For full answer click here: http://www.islamopediaonline.org/fatwa/select-fatwas-ayatollah-makarem-shirazi-contraception-and-birth-control	http://www.islamopediaonline.org/profile/makarem-shirazi

| Zakir Naik (India) | What is the Islamic ruling on contraception? | opposite sex unless there is a necessity. Scholars unanimously agree that any permanent method of family planning, or even abortion, can be done if the life of the mother is in danger. For e.g., if the woman is suffering from certain diseases like heart disease or has under gone multiple caesarean operations and in her case the continuation of pregnancy or another pregnancy may be detrimental to her life, then the woman can be aborted or a permanent method of family planning can be adopted to save the life of the woman. | Sunni | For full answer click here: http://www.islamopediaonline.org/fatwa/what-islamic-ruling-contraception | http://www.islamopediaonline.org/profile/zakir-naik |
| Muhammad ibn Adam al-Kawthari | What is the Islamic ruling on female sterilization? | Under normal circumstances, female sterilization is considered to be absolutely and decidedly prohibited (haram) according to sharia. The irreversible nature associated with both the male and female sterilization clearly contradicts one of the primary purposes of | Sunni | http://www.islamopediaonline.org/fatwa/what-islamic-ruling-female-sterilization | http://www.islamopediaonline.org/profile/muhammad-ibn-adam-al-kawthari |

(continued)

Topic: Contraception	Sheikh/ Fatwa org	Fatwa question	Fatwa answer	Sect	Source	Sheikh Bio
Permanent sterilization and marrying without intent to have children	Muzammil Siddiqi	N/A	marriage — which is to have children. Permanent sterilization without any medical reason is not allowed. You should try to convince yourself to have children, unless you have some medical or psychological problems or some handicap or some other genuine reason.	Sunni	http://www.islamopediaonline.org/fatwa/dr-muzammil-siddiqi-former-president-islamic-society-north-america-marrying-no-intention-have And http://www.islamopediaonline.org/fatwa/may-woman-undergo-permanent-contraception-procedure-such-sterilization-tubal-ligation-or-vasec and http://www.islamopediaonline.org/fatwa/can-woman-undergo-any-procedure-	http://www.islamopediaonline.org/profile/muzammil-siddiqi

Source	Question	Answer	Sect	URL(s)
Mohammad Ebrahim Jannati, Qom (Iran)	N/A	A woman may use contraception without the consent of her husband, but a man may not enforce his wife to use contraception. However, it is permitted with the wife's consent.	Shia	http://www.islamopediaonline.org/fatwa/ayatollah-jannatis-female-right-decide-whether-or-not-use-contraception … make-her-permanently-sterile-surgical-contracepion-tubal-ligat http://www.islamopediaonline.org/profile/mohammad-ebrahim-jannati
Ebrahim Desai (South Africa)	Is it permissible to sterilize patients suffering from mental health conditions?	Due to the fact that unscrupulous people do tend to sometimes take advantage of mentally retarded people by having sex with them, yes, it would be permissible to deploy certain preventive measures whereby the risk of them falling thus pregnant could be reduced.	Sunni	http://www.islamopediaonline.org/fatwa/it-permissible-sterilize-patients-suffering-mental-health-conditions http://www.islamopediaonline.org/profile/ebrahim-desai
Mufti Says http://www.muftisays.com	Is it permissible for Muslims to use condoms?	It is discouraged, but not forbidden to use reversible contraceptive methods in general circumstances. However, if such contraception is practiced out of fear of not being able to provide for the child then it is forbidden.	Sunni	http://www.islamopediaonline.org/fatwa/it-permissible-muslims-use-condoms http://www.muftisays.com

(continued)

Topic: Contraception	Sheikh/ Fatwa org	Fatwa question	Fatwa answer	Sect	Source	Sheikh Bio
	Yusuf Saanei	Do you think it is suitable to educate and to encourage people to use condoms regardless of their marital status?	Yes, there is no problem.	Shia	http://www.islamopediaonline.org/fatwa/yusuf-saanei-responds-do-you-think-it-suitable-educate-and-encourage-people-use-condoms-regard And http://www.islamopediaonline.org/fatwa/it-suitable-distribute-educational-pamphlets-and-free-condoms-public-and-crowded-areas-such-bu	http://www.islamopediaonline.org/profile/yusuf-saanei
	Faraz Fareed Rabbani http://qa.sunnipath.com/	Is it permissible to sell contraception to unmarried couples?	It is permissible for you to sell condoms and other contraceptives, even if those buying may not be married. In a Muslim society, it would be the responsibility of the government to regulate	Sunni	http://www.islamopediaonline.org/fatwa/it-permissible-sell-contraception-unmarried-couples	http://www.islamopediaonline.org/profile/faraz-fareed-rabbani

	such matters in ways that promote the general good. In non-Muslim countries, one should encourage, if one can, that such matters be dealt with in positive ways that would promote the general good.		

(continued)

Topic: Dress Code

http://isgoc.com/	Is there a dress code in Islamic Law?	Sunni	http://www.islamopediaonline.org/fatwa/there-dress-code-islamic-law
	As part of submitting one's self to their creator (i.e. Islam), modesty and a sense of shyness is one of the necessary components of faith and paramount to achieving righteousness. Our body's adornments or physical features are a gift, which our creator has given us, and this gift is a trust that comes with certain responsibilities. For both males and females, God has made their physical features extremely attractive to each other for the purpose of culmination in physical union, so that the species can propagate. These physical features, by themselves, are		

Topic: Dress Code	Sheikh/Fatwa org	Fatwa question	Fatwa answer	Sect	Source	Sheikh Bio
			objects of pleasure and lust. Yet, it is when they are not manifest that the individual becomes a person.			
International details. The motivations for wearing hijab	Ghazala Hassan al-Qadri ttp://www.minhaj.org	N/A	One of the most defended actions in Islam is the head covering. Every Muslim girl, at some point in her life will have been questioned as to why a Muslim woman must cover herself and is often looked upon as being constrained in her actions.	Sunni	http://www.islamopediaonline.org/fatwa/ghazala-hassan-al-qadri-minhaj-ul-quran-international-details-motivations-wearing-hijab	http://www.islamopediaonline.org/profile/abdul-aziz-ibn-baaz
1. Darulifta http://www.darulifta-deoband.com/index.jsp 2. Salah al-Sawy		What is the ruling on women who wear jeans as they do in Arab and Western countries due to the cold climate? Female wearing jeans	1. Wearing jeans and shirt is against Shariah as it is commonly worn by *fasiq* (immoral) people and exposes the body structure. It is *makroob* (undesirable) for men also, while it is highly undesirable for women. According to the hadith of the Prophet those women who adopt the resemblance of men are cursed. 2. It is permissible for a woman to wear for her	Sunni	1. http://www.islamopediaonline.org/fatwa/what-ruling-women-who-wear-jeans-they-do-arab-and-western-countries-due-cold-climate 2. http://www.islamopediaonline.org/fatwa/what-islamic-ruling-women-wearing-jeans	2. http://www.islamopediaonline.org/profile/salah-al-sawy

	Haroon Rashid Qadri, Darul Uloom, Texas (US) http://www.islamicacademy.org	May Muslim men wear ties?	husband's jeans and anything else she would like. In front of her *maharim* (sing: mahram, non-marriageable relatives), on the other hand, what is between the navel and the knees must not be tight because this is the woman *'awrah*. To wear a tie is definitely *haram* (forbidden) and is a resemblance of *kafir* (disbelief or unbelief).	Sunni	http://www.islamopediaonline.org/fatwa/may-muslim-men-wear-ties
Improper hijab and improper dress	Lutfullah Saafi Gulpayegani	N/A	Today, unfortunately, improper hijab and improper dressing has corrupted the morals of our youth. It is incumbent upon every Muslim to prevent the evil, but the officials' responsibility is heavier given their having the means to systematically deal with the issue. Every Muslim, should he or she has the power to prevent an evil action, is obliged to do so.	Shia	http://www.islamopediaonline.org/fatwa/iranian-fatwa-condemns-improper-hijab-and-improper-dress http://www.islamopediaonline.org/profile/lutfullah-saafi-gulpayegani

(continued)

Topic: Dress Code	Sheikh/ Fatwa org	Fatwa question	Fatwa answer	Sect	Source	Sheikh Bio
	Sayyad Mohammad Hussein Fadlallah	What is the religious hijab? What is its importance?	The hijab is a protection for women and their bodies against those who have inordinate desires. It adds human value to women and restricts their sexual desire to the matrimonial bed. The hijab should cover the entire body except for the face, hands and feet. Clothes should not be suggestive in color or shape.	Shia	http://www. islamopediaonline. org/fatwa/sayyad- mohammad- hussein-fadlallah- lebanon-succinctly- answers-what- religious-hijab- what-its-imp	http://www. islamopediaonline. org/profile/ sayyad-muhammad- hussein-fadlallah
Non-obligatory character of hijab and reflections on women's dress	Javed Ahmad Ghamidi (Pakistan)	N/A	Head covering for women is a cherished part of Muslim social custom and tradition, but it is not a directive of the *shariah* (Divine law). Ghamidi believes that the Qur'an mentions *khamr* or *khumur* (an article of clothing for women) only as a 7th century Arabian dress, and gives no specific command for women to wear it.	Sunni	http://www. islamopediaonline. org/fatwa/opinion-n on-obligatory-chara cter-hijab-and-other -reflections-women s-dress	http://www. islamopediaonline. org/profile/javed- ahmad-ghamidi
	Ali al-Sistanti	What does the *sharia* say about athletes wearing short sports clothes	This is permissible in and of itself to male athletes.	Shia	http://www. islamopediaonline. org/fatwa/what- does-sharia-say-	http://www. islamopediaonline. org/profile/ ali-al-sistanti

Topic	Scholar / Source	Question	Denomination	Answer	Fatwa URL	Profile URL
		(shorts)?			about-athletes-wearing-short-sports-clothes-shorts	
Niqab (face veil)	Muhammad Ghazali II	Is niqab (complete covering of a woman in public, except for the eyes) obligatory?	Sunni	For a peaceful society free of corruption, women and men should dress appropriately and not intermingle freely. It is in women's interest to cover themselves and stay safe from the dirty element of society. Niqab is not obligatory but preferable.	http://www.islamopediaonline.org/fatwa/niqab-complete-covering-woman-public-except-eyes-obligatory	http://www.islamopediaonline.org/profile/muhammad-ghazali-ii
On the possibility of Muslim women wearing face coverings (niqab) in the United States	Ibrahim Dremali (US) http://amjaonline.com	N/A	Sunni	There is a controversy among *shariah* scholars about the status of covering face: some maintains it as obligatory, and others say it is not obligatory. And since you cover your face in your country, then there is no harm for you to wear it in U.S., and I encourage you to do so.	http://www.islamopediaonline.org/fatwa/possibility-muslim-women-wearing-face-coverings-niqab-united-states	http://www.islamopediaonline.org/profile/ibrahim-dremali
Explanation of the phrase in the Qur'an	Mufti Siraj Desai	Why is it allowed for Muslim females not to observe hijab	Sunni	According to the explanation of verse 31 in Surah Nur, great scholars including those	http://www.islamopediaonline.org/fatwa/	http://www.islamopediaonline.org/profile/

(continued)

Topic: Dress Code	Sheikh/Fatwa org	Fatwa question	Fatwa answer	Sect	Source	Sheikh Bio
dealing with female modesty, stressing that hijab is mandatory in front of male slaves but not female slaves		in front of slaves (or the slaves whom their right hands possess according to the Qur'an) [particularly as it may lead to *fitna* if the slaves are young male/men]?	from the companions and the followers have indicated that the part of the verse, "or to those owned by their right hands," applies only to female slaves, which means that hijab will be necessary in front of male slaves as it is in front of all other non-*mehrams*. Sa'id ibn al-Musayyib has advised not to be under the misconception that these particular wordings in the verse are general for both male and female slaves.		mufti-ebrahim-desai-gives-explanation-phrase-quran-dealing-female-modesty-stressing-hijab-mand	mufti-siraj-desai
	Ebrahim Desai	Is it permissible to divorce a woman because she refuses to wear a hijab, even if she is a good wife and mother otherwise?	At the outset, one should understand that it is better to make the home than break the home. The matter becomes further complicated if there are children involved in the marriage. If the wife does not wear hijab, then the husband should diplomatically encourage his wife to wear the hijab.	Sunni	http://www.islamopediaonline.org/fatwa/mufti-ebrahim-desai-south-africa-responds-question-it-permissible-divorce-woman-because-she-re	http://www.islamopediaonline.org/profile/ebrahim-desai

Head cover is not mandatory for women in Islam	Dr. Ibrahim B. Syed	Is head cover for women mandatory in Islam?	Hijab (head cover) for Muslim women is not mandated in the Qur'an. If it is, it is only the subjective interpretation of an *ayah* (verse) on the part of the reader. Hence, many Islamic scholars say that according to hadith, a woman should cover her whole body, except her face and hands. The majority of Muslims do not know in which hadith this is mentioned. A very limited number of Muslims know that this is in Sunan Abu Dawud.	Sunni	http://www.islamopediaonline.org/fatwa/dr-ibrahim-b-syed-argues-head-cover-not-mandatory-women-islam	http://www.qaradawi.net/site/topics/article.sp?cu_no=2&item_no=4955&version=1&template_id=1&parent_id=17
Burqa	Yusuf Qaradawi (Egypt)	N/A	Permissible not obligatory.	Sunni	http://www.qaradawi.net/site/topics/article.asp?cu_no=2&item_no=4955&version=1&template_id=226&parent_id=17	http://www.qaradawi.net/site/topics/article.asp?cu_no=2&item_no=1213&version=1&template_id=217&parent_id=189

Topic: Cosmetics

Cosmetic Surgery	Makarem Shirazi	N/A	It is per se permissible to undergo a cosmetic surgery, unless it is associated with	Shia	http://www.islamopediaonline.org/fatwa/ http://www.islamopediaonline.org/profile/

(continued)

Topic: Cosmetics	Sheikh/Fatwa org	Fatwa question	Fatwa answer	Sect	Source	Sheikh Bio
			another prohibited thing, like touching the body of an opposite sex, in which case the surgery is permissible solely if it is necessary.		makarem-shirazi-permissibility-cosmetic-surgery-certain-conditions	makarem-shirazi
Cosmetic Surgery	Muhammad ibn Adam al-Kawthari (UK)	Is it permissible for a Muslim surgeon to perform cosmetic surgery on a patient?	The general ruling with regards to cosmetic surgery is that of impermissibility, for it involves mutilation of one's body (*muthla*) and changing the nature created by Allah (*taghyeer khalq Allah*). However, in genuine cases of extreme abnormality, there is a dispensation of permissibility, for necessity makes prohibition lawful. Based on this, it will not be permitted for a doctor or surgeon to perform surgery for purely cosmetic reasons and merely for the purpose of beautification.	Sunni	http://www.islamopediaonline.org/fatwa/it-permissible-muslim-surgeon-perform-cosmetic-surgery-patient	http://www.islamopediaonline.org/profile/muhammad-ibn-adam-al-kawthari
Plastic surgery	IslamOnline http://www.islamonline.net	What is the resolution of the Islamic Fiqh Academy on	*[For full answer, go to the source.]*	Sunni	http://www.islamopediaonline.org/fatwa/what-	

		plastic surgery?			resolution-islamic-fiqh-academy-plastic-surgery http://www.islamopediaonline.org/fatwa/having-plastic-surgery-nose
On having plastic surgery on the nose	Ahmed Kutty	N/A	Sunni	You are allowed to undergo nasal surgery if your nose is excessively large and abnormal in size and it causes you undue psychological and emotional trauma. This permission in Islam, however, is conditional on such a procedure being considered rather safe and being recommended to you by a trustworthy and reliable specialist or specialists in the field. Having said this, however, I must caution you against resorting to this procedure simply for cosmetic purposes.	http://www.islamopediaonline.org/profile/ahmed-kutty
	Moulana Muhammad Karolia	If cosmetic surgery is forbidden, are braces permissible?	Sunni	It is permissible to wear braces (in order to line teeth as they grow) and doing this is not be a sin. It is not a deemed a "cosmetic reason for beauty" but a medicinal reason to cure an abnormality. If the teeth are left to grow without braces then there is a very high likelihood that they will cause pain and difficulty in later life.	http://www.islamopediaonline.org/fatwa/if-cosmetic-surgery-forbidden-are-braces-permissible http://www.islamopediaonline.org/profile/moulana-muhammad-karolia

(continued)

Topic: Cosmetics	Sheikh/ Fatwa org	Fatwa question	Fatwa answer	Sect	Source	Sheikh Bio
	Ibrahim Dremali (Egypt)	Is it permissible to have cosmetic reconstructive surgery to remove excess skin after weight loss?	Yes, you can do that, by Allah's Will.	Sunni	http://www.islamopediaonline.org/fatwa/assembly-muslim-jurists-america-responds-query-it-permissible-have-cosmetic-reconstructive-sur	http://www.islamopediaonline.org/profile/ibrahim-dremali
	Husayn al-Jaburi (Meccan, KSA)	Is it permissible to go to the dentist to get your teeth whitened, meaning that the dentist uses some chemicals to make the teeth white again after they have changed color due to lack of care? Is this changing the creation of Allah?	It is permissible to go to a dentist to get your teeth whitened. This is not a case of changing Allah's creation. You are only restoring your teeth to their original condition by removing extraneous stains from them. And Allah knows best.	Sunni	http://www.islamopediaonline.org/fatwa/husayn-al-jaburi-saudi-arabia-permissibility-treatments-whiten-teeth	http://www.islamopediaonline.org/profile/husayn-al-jaburi
Beautification		Botox?	Malaysia's highest Islamic authority, the National Fatwa Council, has decided	Sunni	http://www.islamopediaonline.org/news/	

Topic	Scholar	Question	Opinion	Sect	Source
			that Botox injections are not permissible for Muslims for cosmetic purposes, The New Straits Times, Malaysia's largest newspaper, reported. The council decided that substances used in Botox, a trade name for botulinum toxin A, could not be deemed *halal*, or permissible, under Islamic law. The council chairman, Shukor Husin, said that since the introduction of the cosmetic form of botulinum toxin, there have been "many fake products in the market and that is another reason why it is *haram*," or forbidden.		fatwa-malaysia-forbids-botox
Wearing perfume	Lutfullah Saafi Gulpayegani, Qom (Iran)	N/A	Perfumes and fragrances made in Muslim or non-Muslim countries are considered clean (*tayeb*), unless the person is confident that they are unclean (*najis*). Therefore, using them would not make the body or the clothes unclean.	Shia	http://www.islamopediaonline.org/fatwa/gulpayegani-iran-general-permissibility-wearing-perfumes-and-fragrances http://www.islamopediaonline. http://www.islamopediaonline.org/profile/lutfullah-saafi-gulpayegani
	Muhammad Ibn Adam al-Kawthari,	Is it impermissible to use skin or	In principle, using face-lightening creams as a		http://www.islamopediaonline.

(continued)

Topic: Cosmetics	Sheikh/ Fatwa org	Fatwa question	Fatwa answer	Sect	Source	Sheikh Bio
	Darul Iftaa (UK)	face-lightening creams?	form of adornment can not be considered unlawful (haram) according to Sharia... Using face-lightening creams does not entail mutilation (muthla) or altering Allah's creation (taghyir khalq Allah) since there is no specific operation to be undergone with a view to change the color of the skin forever. As such, using such creams is not unlawful. However, it is a kind of excessive beautification which is not warranted in Islam.	Sunni	org/fatwa/it-impermissible-use-skin-or-face-lightening-creams	org/profile/muhammad-ibn-adam-al-kawthari
	Abdul-Aziz Ibn Baaz, Fatwa Islam, Internet Catalogue, Madina (KSA)	Is it permissible for a woman to dye the hair upon her head with black dye?	It is not permissible for a woman or other than her to colour their hair with black dye, because of the statement of the Messenger sall Allaahu 'alayhi wa sallam: "Change this colour, and stay away from the black (colour)." [Reported by Muslim in his Saheeh.]	Sunni	http://www. islamopediaonline. org/fatwa/it-permissible-woman-dye-hair-upon-her-head-black-dye	http://www. islamopediaonline. org/profile/ abdul-aziz-ibn-baaz

(continued)

	Ikhwan Online (Egypt)	Is it permissible to use make-up on one's wedding day?	Women can use or wear anything on their wedding day provided they do not show their ornament to other marriageable men.	Sunni	http://www.ikhwanonline.com/
Wearing lipstick	http://www.islamicacademy.org	N/A	Lipstick is made of pork fat, so it should not be used. Nail polish does not allow water on the nails, and so *wudu* (ablutions before prayer) cannot be done completely. [*This response is credited to Bano Saira.*]	Sunni	http://www.islamopediaonline.org/fatwa/it-permissible-use-make-ones-wedding-day
				Sunni	http://www.islamopediaonline.org/fatwa/permissible-wear-lipstick-and-nail-polish
	Darul Ifta	Can women wear lipstick?	There is no wrong if it does not contain any impure ingredients and the woman applies it for her husband. But by applying lipstick generally a layer settles on the lips preventing the water of *wudu* (ablution) and *ghusl* (washing) to reach the skin, so when the *wudhu* and *ghusl* will not be valid, the *salah* (prayers) also will not be valid. Therefore, in case of applying a woman should clean it while performing *wudu*. However, if the lipstick is liquid like water, it will not carry this ruling.		http://www.islamopediaonline.org/fatwa/can-women-wear-lipstick

Topic: Cosmetics	Sheikh/ Fatwa org	Fatwa question	Fatwa answer	Sect	Source	Sheikh Bio
Tattooing	Islamic Fiqh Academy	What is the resolution of the Islamic Fiqh Academy on? plastic surgery	[For full answer, go to source (bottom half of the answer).]	Sunni	http://www.islamopediaonline.org/fatwa/what-resolution-islamic-fiqh-academy-plastic-surgery	http://www.islamonline.net
	Makarem Shirazi, Qom (Iran)	What is Islam's ruling on tattooing? Would it make any problems when making the wudhu or gusl.	If tattooing is not harmful to the body and contains no improper images, it is permissible. In any event, it is not problematic when making the wudhu or gusl.	Shia	http://www.islamopediaonline.org/fatwa/fatwa-general-permissibility-tattooing	http://www.islamopediaonline.org/profile/makarem-shirazi
	Muhammad RiDaa Al-Gulpaygaanee	Is there even any marjaa who has issued a fatwa, saying tattoos are haram?	In the name of the most high: It is best to leave from doing tattoos and if it has been done already, try to remove it if possible....	Sunni	http://www.shiachat.com/forum/index.php?/topic/234947196-what-do-you-think-of-this-tattoo-i-am-getting/page__st__75	
Women and tattooing	Abdulaziz bin othaimen (KSA)	Multiple	Impermissible and discouraged.	Sunni	http://mag030.yoo7.com/t788-topic	
Piercing	Moulana Muhammad Karolia	What kinds of body piercing are permissible in Islam?	It is not permissible to pierce the belly button, or other body parts such as the lips, tongue, eyebrows, etc.; this is		http://www.islamopediaonline.org/fatwa/what-kinds-body-	http://www.islamopediaonline.org/profile/moulana-

Topic	Scholar	Question	Ruling	Sect	Source URL
			not considered an adornment for the Muslim female in Islam. Only the ears and the nose are permissible to pierce and one can find examples of this taking place in the time of the Prophet and it was not forbidden.		piercing-are-permissible-islam / muhammad-karolia
	Faraz Fareed Rabbani, Sunni Path New Jersey (US)	Is it permissible for men to pierce their ears?	The basis—for both men and women—is that they cannot do any permanent "damage" to any part of their body, as our bodies are a trust from Allah. Piercing the ear (and nose) for women (and the like) are considered exceptions to this general rule. Other piercings (including the ear for men) remain on the original basis of impermissibility.	Sunni	http://www.islamopediaonline.org/fatwa/it-permissible-men-pierce-their-ears / http://www.islamopediaonline.org/profile/faraz-fareed-rabbani
Eyebrow shaping and hair extension	Yusuf Al-Qaradawi	N/A	Impermissible and discouraged.	Sunni	http://www.qaradawi.net/site/topics/article.asp?cu_no=2&item_no=1174&version=1&template_id=5&parent_id=12#%D8%B5%D8%A8%D8%BA

(continued)

Topic: Sports	Sheikh/ Fatwa org	Fatwa question	Sect	Fatwa answer	Source	Sheikh Bio
On the permissibility of wrestling and boxing matches without bet-placing	Ali al-Sistanti, Najaf (Iraq)	N/A		They are permissible if they do not lead to substantial bodily harm.	http://www.islamopediaonline.org/fatwa/ayatollah-sistani-permissibility-wrestling-and-boxing-matches-without-bet-placing	http://www.islamopediaonline.org/profile/ali-al-sistanti
Betting on football	Ali al-Sistanti, Najaf (Iraq)	In a football match where the winner wins some amount of money, in the view of Islam, is this money legitimate?		If this is gambling, the money is illegitimate and one may not spend it.	http://www.islamopediaonline.org/fatwa/ayatollah-sistanis-fatwa-declaring-money-earned-betting-football-soccer-matches-illegitimate	
	Yusuf Qaradawi (Egypt)	What is the ruling on sports as a profession?	Sunni	The council answered by emphasizing the rule: Taking a permissible (*mubah*) work as a profession is permissible, unless something is excepted with evidence (to the contrary). Sports per se are at least permissible if not recommended or compulsory.	http://www.islamopediaonline.org/fatwa/what-ruling-sports-profession	http://www.islamopediaonline.org/profile/yusuf-al-qaradawi

Scholar	Question	Answer		Source	Profile
Ali Gomaa (Egypt)	We have heard that some football (soccer) players don't fast during the month of Ramadan because of their hard work. What is the Islamic ruling on this?	Allah's Messenger urged the *Ummah* (Muslim community) to practice some sorts of sports that keep man healthy and the *Umma* strong unless they lead to mischief. A player who is tied to a club by contract is obliged to perform his duties and if this work is his source of income and he has to participate in matches during Ramadan and fasting affects his performance then he has the permission to break the fast. Religious scholars state that those who work difficult jobs and can become weaker as a result of fasting can break the fast. However, the practices, since its time can be controlled, should be in the evening to prevent interfering with the ability of the players on the fast.	Sunni	http://www.islamopediaonline.org/fatwa/are-professional-football-soccer-players-excused-fasting-during-month-ramadan	http://www.islamopediaonline.org/profile/ali-gomaa
Ali al-Sistanti, Najaf (Iraq)	Football [soccer] is a popular game among youths and	Although it is not forbidden to say a prayer late, it causes the person performing the	Shia	http://www.islamopediaonline.org/fatwa/	http://www.islamopediaonline.org/profile/

(continued)

Topic: Sports	Sheikh/ Fatwa org	Fatwa question	Fatwa answer	Sect	Source	Sheikh Bio
		adults, but usually it occurs during the	prayer to lose the blessing of praying on time. In some of the texts narrated by members of the Prophet's house (peace be upon them), this amounts to neglecting the prayer.		football-soccer-popular-game-among-youths-and-adults-usually-it-occurs-during-sunset-and-eveni	ali-al-sistanti
	Mufti Siraj Desai (UK)	obligatory prayers on time. Does this compound the sin [of missing the prayers]? Is it permissible to go bungy-jumping?	This is not permissible. Any act which endangers one's life and does not bring any worldly or religious benefit, is not allowed. If due to a mishap, should one die while bungy-jumping, it will be tantamount to suicide, hence from the very outset this act should be forbidden.	Sunni	http://www. islamopediaonline. org/fatwa/it-permissible-go-bungy-jumping	http://www. islamopediaonline. org/profile/ mufti-siraj-desai
Women in Sports						
Women in sports on the international platforms	Hossein Noori-Hamedani, Qom (Iran)	N/A	Ayatollah Noori-Hamadani said the presence of women at international competitions is favourable so long as that		http://www. islamopediaonline. org/fatwa/ ayatollah-noori-	http://www. islamopediaonline. org/profile/ hossein-noori-

Topic	Scholar	Question	Answer	Sect	Source
	Ali al-Sistanti, Qom (Iran)	May women participate in sporting events in front of a co-ed audience?	brings no problems with respect to their observing the Islamic hijab. No, she may not.	Shia	hamedani hamadanis-fatwa-approving-women-sports-international-platforms http://www.islamopediaonline.org/fatwa/grand-ayatollah-ali-al-sistani-forbids-womens-participation-sports-front-co-ed-audience
On the permissibility of women attending exercise classes accompanied by music	Alimah Bint S. Dhorat, Darul Uloom (UK)		It would not be permissible for a woman to attend exercise or aerobics classes accompanied by music. The Prophet… mentioned, "When singing girls and musical instruments become common, wait for red winds, earthquakes, the earth swallowing people, disfiguring and many more punishments." One can always find an alternative class whereby music is not played in the background or organize classes oneself.		http://www.islamopediaonline.org/fatwa/alimah-dorat-permissibility-women-attending-exercise-classes-accompanied-music http://www.islamopediaonline.org/profile/alimah-bint-s-dhorat
	Yusuf Qaradawi (Egypt)	Is a woman allowed to ride	Riding a bicycle or car or any other form of transportation	Sunni	http://www.islamopediaonline.

(continued)

Topic: Sports	Sheikh/ Fatwa org	Fatwa question	Fatwa answer	Sect	Source	Sheikh Bio
		a bicycle? What about teenage girls who may lose their hymen in the process?	is permissible in itself. The Arab woman during the days of ignorance as well as Islam used to ride camels. However, a woman must abide by Islamic mannerisms when riding a bicycle, such as wearing appropriate Islamic dress and avoiding physical contact with men.		org/fatwa/yusuf-qaradawi-answers-woman-allowed-ride-bicycle-what-about-teenage-girls-who-may-lose-their-	org/profile/yusuf-al-qaradawi

Topic: Sexuality	Sheikh/ Fatwa org	Fatwa question	Fatwa answer	Sect	Source	Sheikh Bio

Gender operations

Gender Change	Makarem Shirazi, Qom (Iran)	N/A	Sex change is not inherently against Islamic law and it is allowed. However, it should be done according to Islamic rules. For example, the forbidden parts should not be seen and touched unless and to the extent necessary.	Shia	http://www.islamopediaonline.org/fatwa/fatwa-permitting-sex-change-surgery-ayatollah-shirazi	http://www.islamopediaonline.org/profile/makarem-shirazi

Topic	Source	Question	Answer	Sect	References
Gender change surgery	Hossein-Ali Montazeri, Qom (Iran)	What is the ruling on gender reassignment procedures	It [sex change] is allowed unless it involves a sinful act.	Shia	http://www.islamopediaonline.org/fatwa/grand-ayatollah-hossein-ali-montazeri-permits-gender-reassignment-procedures http://www.islamopediaonline.org/profile/hossein-ali-montazeri
Gender change surgery	Salman al-Oadah, Islamtoday, Madina (KSA)	A man underwent surgery to change into a woman, being at that time a non-Muslim. He, having become a "she," has been that way for a while and has now converted to Islam. The problem is that ... "she" wants to sit with the women at the mosque but "her" niece and the women at that mosque think "she" is still a man in Islamic Law and should act as a man from now on. So what should this person do?	His situation is comparable to that of a hermaphrodite whose female gender has been determined. He becomes a woman and should be treated like a woman. And Allah knows best.	Sunni	http://www.islamopediaonline.org/fatwa/al-oadah-saudi-arabia-rulings-transgender-and-sex-change-matters http://www.islamopediaonline.org/profile/salman-al-oadah

(continued)

Topic: Sexuality	Shaikh/Fatwa org	Fatwa question	Fatwa answer	Sect	Source	Sheikh Bio
	Yusuf Saanei, Qom (Iran)	Is gender reassignment (sex change) allowed if the person is hermaphrodite?	In this situation, not only is a sex change operation permissible, but it is obligatory to do so.	Shia	http://www.islamopediaonline.org/fatwa/grand-ayatollah-saanei-mandates-sex-change-operation-hermaphrodites	http://www.islamopediaonline.org/profile/yusuf-saanei
Masturbation						
	Ali al-Sistanti, Najaf (Iraq)	Is having thoughts that lead to ejaculation considered masturbation?	Yes, it is considered masturbation, and the thoughts are not permitted.	Shia	http://www.islamopediaonline.org/fatwa/having-thoughts-lead-ejaculation-considered-masturbation	http://www.islamopediaonline.org/profile/ali-al-sistanti
	Qmaruz Zaman, daru uloom Mufti Says(UK)	May a Muslim man donate sperm?	Since this requires masturbation, it is not permissible.	Sunni	http://www.islamopediaonline.org/fatwa/may-muslim-man-donate-sperm	http://www.islamopediaonline.org/profile/qamruz-zaman
Female Masturbation	Ali Al-Sistanti, Najaf (Iraq)	Since it's established that a woman does not ejaculate sperm, may she masturbate?	A woman does not have sperm like a man's, which is full of organisms [that cause pregnancy], but the available texts of the Guided Imams	Shia	http://www.islamopediaonline.org/fatwa/its-established-woman-does-not-ejaculate-	http://www.islamopediaonline.org/profile/ali-al-sistanti

		(upon them peace) have established that the liquid which emerges from her at the climax of sexual excitement takes the same ruling as a man's sperm. It results in major ritual impurity, as does anything that emerges from [a woman], if it is plentiful. Masturbation is forbidden for women just as it is forbidden for men.		sperm-may-she-masturbate
Yusuf Al-qaradwi	I recently got married, but I am in a different town right now, away from my wife because of her job and my studies. As I get sexually frustrated, is masturbation allowed in my case? I do not want to fall into the abyss of sin, but I also want to relieve my sexual tension.	Allows masturbation under two conditions following the Hanbali school of religious thought: The Hanbali jurists permit masturbation only under two conditions: first, the fear of committing fornication or adultery, and second, not having the means to marry. Thus, we do advise you to have your wife with you and not to stay alone.	Sunni	For full answer click here: http://www.islamopediaonline.org/fatwa/yusuf-al-qaradawi-rules-permissibility-masturbation-order-avoid-adultery
				http://www.islamopediaonline.org/profile/yusuf-al-qaradawi

(continued)

Topic: Sexuality	Shaikh/ Fatwa org	Fatwa question	Fatwa answer	Sect	Source	Sheikh Bio
		Please let me know if masturbation is allowed in Islam. Is there any Islamic cure so that a Muslim could get rid of such a bad habit?				
	Mufti Siraj Desai (South Africa) http://darululoo mabubakr. blogspot.com	Is masturbation equal in sin to zina (adultery)?	Masturbation is definitely (as) a form of *zinaa* (adultery), and is *haram* (forbidden), but is lesser in gravity than the actual *zinaa* between male and female. Allah states in the Holy Quran: "And whoever seeks any other (avenue of lust) besides these (the wife and female slaves), they are the transgressors." Surah Muminoon (23) verse 7. This verse makes *haram* any form of sexual activity besides sex in marriage and sex with female slaves. The latter obviously does not exist today.	Sunni	http://www. islamopediaonline. org/fatwa/ masturbation- equal-sin- zina-adultery	http://www. islamopediaonline. org/profile/ mufti-siraj- desai

Qmaruz Zaman	Is it permissible for a husband to masturbate his wife when she is menstruating, especially if there is no physical contact and any sexual gratification would be done through clothes?	The prohibited acts during menstruation are: (a) actual intercourse; (b) skin-to-skin contact between the woman's navel and knee. Everything else is permitted, without exception, including full sexual gratification for the woman.	Sunni	http://www.islamopediaonline.org/fatwa/it-permissible-husband-masturbate-his-wife-when-she-menstruating-especially-if-there-no-physic	http://www.islamopediaonline.org/profile/muhammad-al-mukhtar-al-shinqiti
Dar Alifta http://www.darulifta-deoband.com/index.jsp	What is the ruling on committing masturbation during [Ramadan]? A 14 years old girl masturbating in [Ramadan] not knowing its sinful, would do *wudu* and do her prayers asks if she is required to fast the days that she was masturbating on and only did *wudu* and not complete *ghusul*.	First, practicing masturbation is prohibited and it is even more sinful during the day in Ramadan. Second, it is obligatory to make up for the days on which you broke your fast because masturbation invalidates fasting. You should try to estimate how many days this occurred. Third, it is also obligatory to pay *kaffarah* (expiation) which is giving a needy person half a Sa (1 Sa = 2.172 kg) of wheat and the like of the staple food of your area for each day that	Sunni	http://www.islamopediaonline.org/fatwa/committing-masturbation-while-fasting	http://www.alifta.net

(continued)

Shaikh/ Fatwa org	Fatwa question	Fatwa answer	Sect	Source	Sheikh Bio
		you missed if you delay making up for it until the next Ramadan arrives. Fourth, it is obligatory to take *Ghusl* (ritual bath) after masturbation and it is insufficient to perform ablution if you have experienced ejaculation. Fifth, it is compulsory to make up for the prayers which you offered without taking *Ghusl* because minor ritual purification (ablution and the like) does not suffice instead of major ritual purification (ritual bath).			

Homosexuality

Shaikh/ Fatwa org	Fatwa question	Fatwa answer	Sect	Source	Sheikh Bio
Hossein-Ali Montazeri, Qom (Iran)	How should we treat homosexuals? Homosexuals exist in all countries, including Muslim countries. We are an institute in Netherlands with the purpose	Anything in the world is being created for a special purpose, and sexual desire is to guarantee the endurance of life. Homosexuality is a sin that is forbidden by God because it is against the purpose of nature. It is necessary to guide and	Shia	http://www. islamopediaonline. org/fatwa/ homosexuality- and-correct- attitude-toward- homosexuals	http:// amontazeri. com/farsi/ fi.asp

of protection
of Muslim
homosexuals. As
you know, Islam
has condemned
homosexuality, not
homosexuals. The
mere homosexual
desire is not sinful;
rather, it is the
homosexual behavior
that is condemned.
Thus, we intend
to attract Muslim
homosexuals from
around the world
and aware them
of the fact that
they are not cursed
by Islam merely
because they are
homosexuals. We
wish to help them
cure and improve
their life. Our motto
is "Islam condemns
homosexuality, not
homosexuals." What
is your opinion about
this decision?

advice homosexuals in a
friendly manner, and help
them to cure and recover.
Religiously speaking,
it is necessary and also
sharia-compliant to help and
guide them.

(continued)

Topic: Sexuality	Shaikh/ Fatwa org	Fatwa question	Fatwa answer	Sect	Source	Sheikh Bio
	Islamicity	Islamicity responds to the question: What should good Muslim parents do if they have a child who is born homosexual?	Homosexual behavior (gayness and lesbianism) is prohibited because it is an assault on the humanity of a person, destruction of the family, and a clash with the aims of the Lawgiver, one of which is the establishment of sexual instincts between males and females so as to encourage the institution of marriage. Homosexuality is considered one of the most abominable sins in Islam; it is so enormous in intensity and gravity that Allah tells us in the Qur'an that because of it, an entire nation was destroyed by Allah in a most horrible way. Hence it is not correct to think about the child to be born as a homosexual.	Sunni	http://www. islamopediaonline. org/fatwa/ islamicity-responds-question-what-should-good-muslim-parents-do-if-they-have-child-who-born-ho	http://www. islamicity.com/ ?AspxAuto DetectCookie Support=1
	Abdel Khaliq Hasan al-Shareef, IslamOnline, Cairo (Egypt)	Punishments for homosexuality giving textual citations.	... committed two heinous crimes: 1) homosexuality and 2) murder. Each crime is sufficient to warrant	Sunni	For full answer, go to: http://www. islamopediaonline. org/fatwa/scholars-	http://www. islamopediaonline. org/profile/abdel-khaliq-hasan-

			al-shareef
		death penalty. In addition, this man has severed ties of kinship by seducing and killing his nephew.	debate-punishments-homosexuality-giving-textual-citations
Dar Alifta http://www.darulifta-deoband.com/index.jsp	What is the ruling on homosexuality? Is there any way to repent or offer some sort of penance (*kafara*) for it?	Undoubtedly, sodomy (homosexuality) is *haram* and forbidden in Islam. Because of this sin, the nation of Hazrat Lut (Lot) was punished by Allah in this world. There is no fixed punishment for the perpetrator of this crime, but according to Imam Abu Hanifa such people should be pushed from a mountain to death. However, this punishment should be implemented by a *qazi* (judge). In our country there is neither an Islamic government nor an Islamic *qazi* and therefore someone who commits this act should repent sincerely to Allah and ask for his forgiveness and should never return to this act.	For full answer, go to: http://www.islamopediaonline.org/fatwa/scholars-debate-punishments-homosexuality-giving-textual-citations	http://www.darulifta-deoband.com/index.jsp

(continued)

297

Topic: Sexuality	Shaikh/ Fatwa org	Fatwa question	Fatwa answer	Sect	Source	Sheikh Bio
	Tariq Ramadan	**Islam and homosexuality**	The Islamic position on homosexuality has become one of the most sensitive issues facing Muslims living in the West, particularly in Europe. It is being held up as the key to any eventual "integration" of Muslims into Western culture, as if European culture and values could be reduced to the simple fact of accepting homosexuality. *[For full answer, go to the source.]*	Sunni	http://www. islamopediaonline. org/fatwa/tariq-ramadan-comments-islam-and-homosexuality	http://www. tariqramadan. com/BIOGRAPHY, 11.html
	Dar Alifta http://www. darulifta-deoband. com/index.jsp	Is it permissible to draft a marriage contract (*nikah*) giving a virgin Muslim girl to a fornicator or homosexual man?	If the boy is Muslim then the marriage contract (*nikah*) is valid. But one should not give any virgin and virtuous girl to a fornicator and homosexual knowingly. It is injustice to the girl.		http://www. islamopediaonline. org/fatwa/it-permissible-draft-marriage-contract-nikah-giving-virgin-muslim-girl-fornicator-or-homosexua	
	Muhammad al-Mukhtar al-Shinqiti	It is reported in the news that Gambian president Yahya	I agree with president Jammeh that homosexuality is a grievous sin that	Sunni	http://www. islamopediaonline. org/fatwa/it-	http://www. islamopediaonline. org/profile/

Source	Question	Answer	School	Reference
	Jammeh threatened to behead homosexuals, and two persons were arrested and are being held for trial. What is the *shariah* stance on this?	a Muslim must find repugnant, and that its perpetrators do not deserve to be respected or accepted in the Muslim society. This sin represents retrogression in the sound and natural human disposition and destruction to the structure of family, which is the original unit in society.		reported-news-gambian-president-yahya-jammeh-threatened-behead-homosexuals-and-two-persons- / muhammad-al-mukhtar-al-shinqiti
Sunni Path, New Jersey (U.S.) http://qa.sunnipath.com	What should be the attitude of Muslims towards homosexuals?	As Muslims, our attitude towards homosexuals is that they are our fellow human beings, albeit in a state of rebellion against their *fitra*, which is the primordial state of submission to Allah that was given to every human being from the beginning of the creation of man. Guarding one's sexuality from unlawful sexual intercourse is the duty of every Muslim. If it is unlawful for a man and woman to have sexual intercourse outside of marriage, then it is even	Sunni	http://www.islamopediaonline.org/fatwa/what-should-be-attitude-muslims-towards-homosexuals / http://www.islamopediaonline.org/fatwa/what-should-be-attitude-muslims-towards-homosexuals

(continued)

Shaikh/ Fatwa org	Fatwa question	Fatwa answer	Sect	Source	Sheikh Bio
		more egregious for a man to approach another man, or a woman to approach another woman.			
Dr. Muzammil Siddiqi, president of the Fiqh Council of North America	Is homosexuality amongst Muslims something we should feel free to discuss in public or is it something we should avoid? Also what is the *adab* (Islamic manners) for dealing with homosexuals? Is the sin so grave that we should disassociate ourselves from its perpetrators?	Homosexuality is sinful and shameful. In Islamic terminology it is called *al-fahsha'* or an atrocious and obscene act. Islam teaches that believers should neither do the obscene acts, nor in any way indulge in their propagation.	Sunni	http://www. islamopediaonline. org/fatwa/dr-siddiqi-north-american-fiqh-council-responds-question-what-islamic-manner-talking-about-hom	http://www. islamopediaonline. org/profile/ muzammil-siddiqi
Ahmed Kutty (Canada)	My friend has been sexually abused in his childhood and now he only likes sex with males. Is there any treatment within Islam?	Your brother is not at all different from those who have been conditioned to fornicate or commit theft or murder or addicted to watching pornography or even television for that	Sunni	http://www. islamopediaonline. org/fatwa/my-friend-has-been-sexually-abused-his-childhood-and-now-he-only-likes-sex-	http://www. islamopediaonline. org/profile/ ahmed-kutty

Other Topics

				males-there-any-tre
Ali Gomaa	May a woman repair her hymen?	matter. All of these are destructive habits which one learns through continuous exposure or conditioning. So he must ask himself whether he would prefer to continue in this destructive behavior or change himself? If he is a Muslim, he is left with no choice but to change, for homosexuality is considered one of the most abominable sins in Islam.		
		If a woman lost her virginity on premarital sexual relations and if her actions were not known by people then it is permissible for her to repair her hymen. Moreover, the doctor has permission to do this surgery.	Sunni	http://www. islamopediaonline. org/fatwa/ali-gomaa-dar-al-ifta-al-misryah-responds-question-may-woman-repair-her-hymen
				http://www. islamopediaonline. org/profile/ ali-gomaa
Sheikh Abdullah bin Abdul Rahman Ibn Jibreen, Riyadh (KSA)	Sexual intercourse between a human being and a *jinn* [fire spirit] does occur in reality, but rarely. The question is, does	It is known that *jinn* are spirits without need for a body. However, God decreed that they would speak audibly and appear in various forms and guises, just as he decreed	Sunni	http://www. islamopediaonline. org/fatwa/ibn-jibreen-sexual-intercourse-between-human-being-and-jinn-fire-spirit
				http://www. islamopediaonline. org/profile/sheikh-abdullah-bin-abdul-rahman-ibn-jibreen

(continued)

Topic: Sexuality	Shaikh/ Fatwa org	Fatwa question	Fatwa answer	Sect	Source	Sheikh Bio
		the occurrence [of sexual intercourse] between a *jinn* and a human being require *ghusl* [washing the body to purify it after a sexual act]?	that they would enter the bodies of humans in order to overcome the souls of humans. It is usually the case that male *jinn* enter only the bodies of female humans, and female *jinns* enter the bodies of male humans, where they find pleasure and sexual desire. It has been known for sexual intercourse to occur between humans and *jinn* when *jinn* appear in human form and speak to the people they desire, then draw up an Islamic marriage contract with female humans.			
Muhammad Saalih al-Munajjid, Islam House, Riyadh (KSA)		On marrying someone who is infected and a carrier of hepatitis B.	The one who is a carrier of hepatitis B or has the disease may get married to a healthy woman or a woman who is infected with this disease, if she accepts that after he tells her about his situation. It is not permissible for him	Sunni	http://www. islamopediaonline. org/fatwa/marrying- someone-who- infected-and- carrier-hepatitis-b	http://www. islamopediaonline. org/profile/ muhammad-saalih- al-munajjid

		to get married unless he tells her about his sickness, because concealing that is deceit which is haram (forbidden). If he conceals it, then his wife finds out about that, she has the right to annul the marriage.		http://www. islamopediaonline. org/profile/abdul- aziz-ibn-baaz
Abdul-Aziz Ibn Baaz, Internet Catalogue: Fatwa Islam, Ontario Canada)	What is the ruling on having anal intercourse? Is there any atonement incumbent upon one who does so?	Anal intercourse with a woman is a major sin and a repugnant act of disobedience. Allah will not look at a man who had sex with a man or women in the anus. There is no atonement for one who has anal intercourse, according to the most correct of two opinions held by the scholars. Nor does his wife become forbidden to him due to it, rather she remains in his custody. She should not obey him in this great sin; rather she should prevent him from doing so and seek an annulment of her marriage if he does not repent.	Sunni	http://www. islamopediaonline. org/fatwa/what- ruling-having-anal- intercourse-there- any-atonement- incumbent-upon- one-who-does-so

DATA ON RELIGIOSITY AND POLITICAL PARTICIPATION OF MUSLIMS IN EUROPE AND THE UNITED STATES

Figures for Chapter 1

Figure A13.1   **Non-Muslims who have an unfavorable view of Muslims**

Source: Pew (2008)

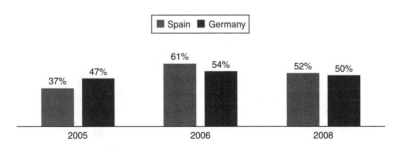

Figure A13.2   **Non-Muslims who have an unfavorable view of Muslims, Spain and Germany**

Source: Pew (2008)

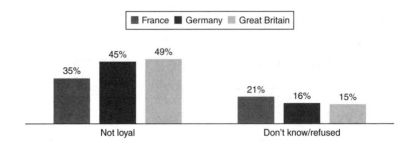

Figure A13.3   Non-Muslims' perception of Muslims' loyalty, France, Germany, and Britain

Source: Gallup (2009)

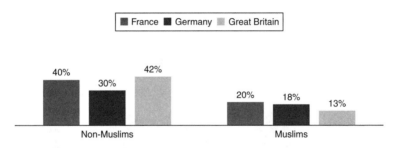

Figure A13.4   Being less expressive about one's religion is necessary for integration, France, Germany, and Britain

Source: Gallup (2009)

Figures for Chapter 2

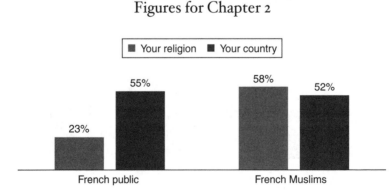

Figure A13.5   "How strongly do you identify with your country and religion?," France

Source: Gallup (2009)

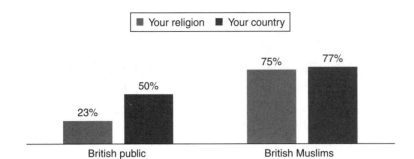

Figure A13.6 "How strongly do you identify with your country and religion?," United Kingdom

Source: Gallup (2009)

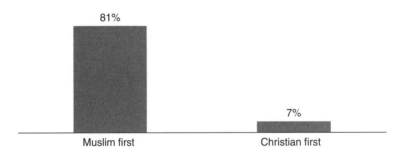

Figure A13.7 Consider themselves Muslim/Christian before their nationality, United Kingdom

Source: Pew (2006)

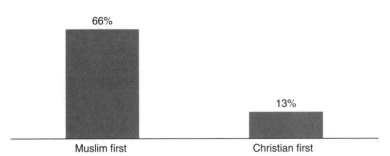

Figure A13.8 Consider themselves Muslim/Christian before their nationality, Germany

Source: Pew (2006)

Figure A13.9   Consider themselves Muslim/Christian before their nationality, France

Source: Pew (2006)

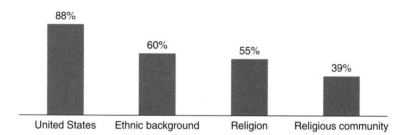

Figure A13.10   "How strongly do you identify with each of the following?," US Catholics

Source: Gallup (2011)

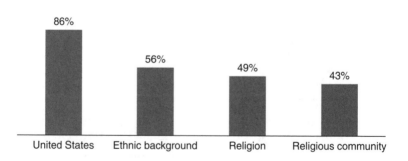

Figure A13.11   "How strongly do you identify with each of the following?," US Jews

Source: Gallup (2011)

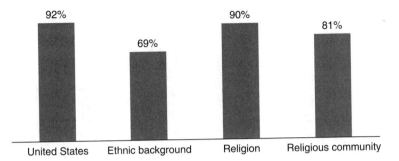

Figure A13.12 "How strongly do you identify with each of the following?," US Mormons

Source: Gallup (2011)

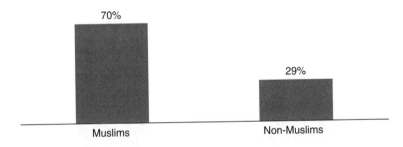

Figure A13.13 "Is religion important in your daily life?," United Kingdom

Source: Gallup (2009)

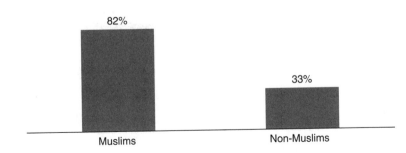

Figure A13.14 "Is religion important in your daily life?," Germany

Source: Gallup (2009)

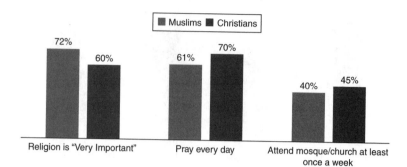

Figure A13.15   Religiosity in the United States
Source: Pew (2007)

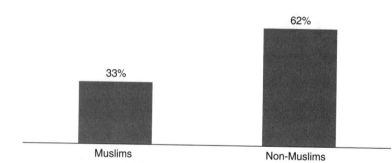

Figure A13.16   Never attended a religious service, the Netherlands
Source: CBS (2009)

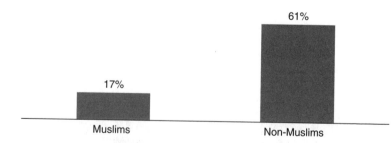

Figure A13.17   Never attended a religious service, France
Source: Tausch (2006)

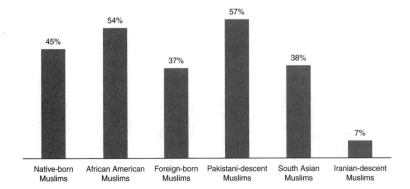

Figure A13.18   Weekly mosque attendance

Source: Pew (2007)

Figures for Chapter 3

Figure A13.19   Identifying as Moroccan/Turkish/Iraqi first and then Dutch, Amsterdam

Source: Focus Groups

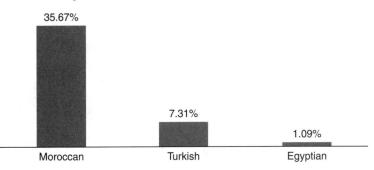

Figure A13.20   Identifying as Moroccan/Turkish/Egyptian first and then American, Boston

Source: Focus Groups

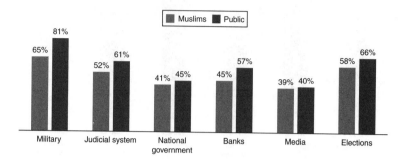

Figure A13.21 Confidence in institutions, France
Source: Gallup (2009)

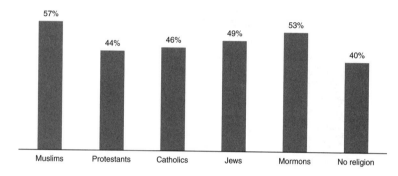

Figure A13.22 Trust in elections, United States
Source: Gallup (2011)

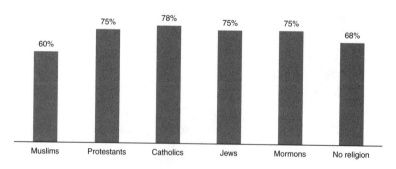

Figure A13.23 Trust in the FBI, United States
Source: Gallup (2011)

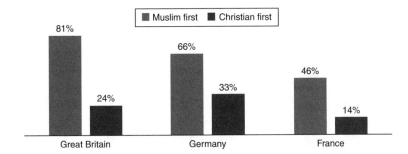

Figure A13.24   What do you consider yourself first?
Source: Pew (2006)

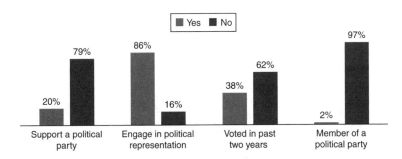

Figure A13.25   Formal political participation, Berlin survey
Source: Survey of Islam in the West Program in Berlin (2010)

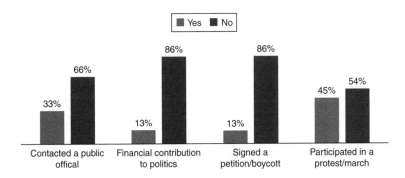

Figure A13.26   Informal political participation, Berlin survey
Source: Survey of Islam in the West Program in Berlin

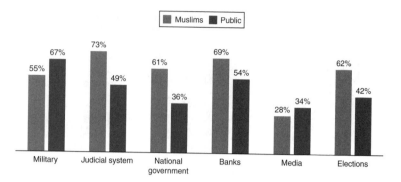

Figure A13.27 Confidence in institutions, Germany
Source: Gallup (2009)

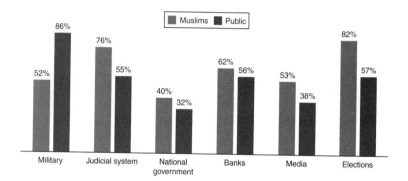

Figure A13.28 Confidence in institutions, United Kingdom
Source: Gallup (2009)

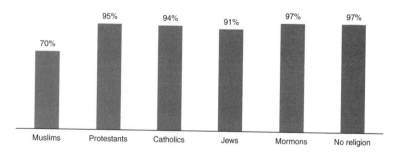

Figure A13.29 Trust in the military, United States
Source: Gallup (2011)

Figures for Chapter 4

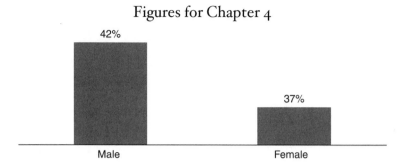

Figure A13.30   Attended mosque at least once a week, United States
Source: Pew (2007)

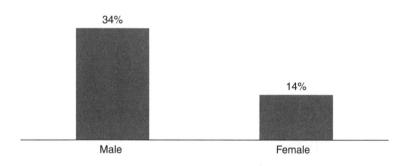

Figure A13.31   Attended mosque at least once a week, the Netherlands
Source: CBS (2009)

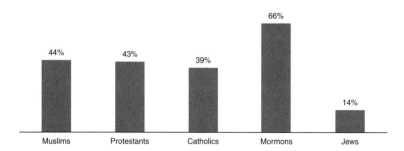

Figure A13.32   Attended a religious service at least once a week, United States
Source: Gallup (2011)

NOTES

Introduction

1. Jorgen Nielsen, *Muslims in Western Europe* (Edinburgh: Edinburgh University Press, 2004); Patrick Weil, *La France et ses immigrés* (Paris: Calmann-Lévy, 1991); Frank J. Buijs and Jan Rath, *Muslims in Europe: The State of Research* (New York: Russel Sage Foundation, 2003); Bernard Lewis and Dominique Schnapper, eds., *Muslims in Europe* (London: Pinter, 1994); and Felice Dassetto, Brigitte Maréchal, and Jorgen Nielsen, eds., *Convergences musulmanes: Aspects contemporains de l'islam dans l'Europe élargie* (Bruylant: Louvain la Neuve, 2001).

2. T. Gerholm and Y. G. Lithman, eds., *The New Islamic Presence in Western Europe* (London: Mansell, 1988); Jack Goody, *Islam in Europe* (Cambridge: Blackwell, 2004); Shireen T. Hunter, ed., *Islam, Europe's Second Religion: The New Social, Cultural and Political Landscape* (Westport: Praeger, 2002); W. A. R. Shadid and P. S. Van Koningsveld, eds., *The Integration of Islam and Hinduism in Western Europe* (Netherlands: Kampen, 1991); W. A. R. Shadid, *Religious Freedom and the Position of Islam in Western Europe* (Netherlands: Kampen, 1995); W. A. R. Shadid and P. S. Van Koningsveld, eds., *Muslims in the Margin: Political Responses to the Presence of Islam in Western Europe* (Netherlands: Kampen, 1996); Gerd Nonneman, Tim Niblock, and B. Szajkowski, eds., *Muslim Communities in the New Europe* (Berkshire: Ithaca, 1996); Steven Vertovec and C. Peach, eds., *Islam in Europe: The Politics of Religion and Community* (New York: St. Martin's, 1997); Steven Vertovec and Alisdair Rogers, *Muslim European Youth, Reproducing Ethnicity, Religion, Culture* (London: Ashgate, 1998); Iftikar H. Malik, *Islam and Modernity: Muslims in Europe and in the United States* (London: Pluto, 2004); and Hofert Alamut and Armando Salvatore, eds., *Between Europe and Islam* (Brussels: P.I.E. Peter Lang, 2000).

3. The Egerkingen Committee was the coordinating group responsible for mobilizing signatures in support of the referendum to modify Article 72 of the Swiss Gederal Constitution on Church-State religions that would prohibit minarets. See Benjaman Bruse, "Switzerland's Minaret Ban," *Euro-Islam.info,* accessed July 25, 2012, http://www.euro-islam.info/key-issues/switzerlands-minaret-ban/.

4. Kharunya Paramaguru, "German Court Bans Male Circumcision," *Time*, June 29, 2012, accessed July 27, 2012, http://newsfeed.time.com/2012/06/29/german-court-bans-male-circumcision/.

5. Henry Makow, "The Debauchery of American Womanhood: Bikini vs. Burqa," September 18, 2002, accessed July 25, 2012, http://www.henrymakow.com/180902.html.

6. "A Certain Distance to Islam," *Qantara.ed*, April 4, 2012, accessed July 25, 2012, http://en.qantara.de/wcsite.php?wc_c=18794&wc_id=19690.

7. This expression comes from the novel, *Invisible Man of Ralph Ellison*, New York, Random House, 1952.

8. Martha Nussbaum elaborates on this concept of the inner eyes to build a new approach to tolerance, see *The New Religious Intolerance, Overcoming the Politics of Fear in an Anxious Age*, Cambridge, Harvard University Press, 2012, p. 139.

9. See http://cmes.hmdc.harvard.edu/research/iw/ and http://www.euro-islam.info/.

10. See challenge program summary at http://www.euro-islam.info/2006/06/01/securitization-and-religious-divide-in-europe-muslims-in-western-europe-after-911-why-the-term-%E2%80%99islamophobia%E2%80%99-is-more-a-predicament-than-an-explanation/.

11. A. J. Bergesen, "Political Witch Hunts: The Sacred and the Subversive in Cross-National Perspective," *American Sociological Review* 42 (1977): 22–33 and T. H. Eriksen, "Formal and Informal Nationalism," *Ethnic and Racial Studies* 16 (1993): 1–25.

12. Jeffery Alexander, *The Meanings of Social Life: A Cultural Sociology* (Oxford: Oxford University Press, 2003).

13. R. Koopmans, *Contested Citizenship: Immigration and Cultural Diversity in Europe* (Minneapolis: University of Minnesota, 2005); D. J. Tichenor, *Dividing Lines: The Politics of Immigration Control in America* (Princeton: Princeton University Press, 2002); T. Givens and A. Luedtke, "The Politics of European Union Immigration Policy: Institutions, Salience, and Harmonization," *Policy Studies Journal* 32(1) (2004): 145–165; J. Money, "Defining Immigration Policy: Inventory, Quantitative Referents, and Empirical Regularities," unpublished manuscript (1999); C. Joppke, *Challenge to the Nation-State: Immigration in Western Europe and the United States* (Oxford: Oxford University Press, 1998); R. Brubaker, *Citizenship and Nationhood in France and Germany* (Cambridge: Harvard University Press, 1992); J. Rex, *Ethnic Minorities in the Modern Nation State: Working Papers in the Theory of Multiculturalism and Political Integration* (London: Macmillan, 1996); and Graham Burchell, Colin Gordon, and Peter Miller, eds., *The Foucault Effect: Studies in Governmentality; With Two Lectures by and an Interview with Michel Foucault* (Chicago: University of Chicago, 1991).

14. Raymond Taras, *Xenophobia and Islamophobia in Europe* (Edinburgh: Edinburgh University Press, 2012); George Morgan and Scott Poynting, *Global Islamophobia: Muslims and Moral Panic in the West* (Burlington, Vermont: Ashgate, 2012); Nathan Lean, *The Islamophobia Industry: How the Right Manufactures Fear of Muslims* (London: Pluto Press, 2012); and Christopher Allen, *Islamophobia* (Farnham: Ashgate, 2010).

15. D. Tichenor, *Dividing Lines: The Politics of Immigration Control in America* (Princeton, N.J.: Princeton University Press, 2002) and M. Schain, *Immigration Policy and the Politics of Immigration: A Comparative Study* (Basingstoke: Palgrave Macmillan, 2008).

16. Theodore J. Lowi, *The End of Liberalism: Ideology, Policy, and the Crisis of Public Authority* (New York: W.W. Norton, 1969).

17. T. Skocpol, *Social Revolutions in the Modern World* (Cambridge and New York: Cambridge University Press, 1994), 204.

18. Tariq Modood, *Multiculturalism* (Cambridge: Polity, 2007).

1   Muslims as the Internal and External Enemy

1. Michele Lamont and Virag Molnar, "The Study of Boundaries in the Social Sciences," *Annual Review of Sociology* 28 (2002): 167–195.

2. J. C. Alexander and P. Smith, "The Discourse of American Civil Society: A New Proposal for Cultural Studies," *Theory and Society* 22 (1993): 151–207.

3. Z. Bauman, *Intimations of Post-modernity* (London: Routledge, 1992); C. Calhoun, ed., *Habermas and the Public Sphere* (Cambridge, MA: MIT Press, 1992); and P. Smith, "Codes and Conflict towards a Theory of War as Ritual," *Theory and Society* 20 (1991): 103–138.

4. J. C. Alexander, "Citizen and Enemy as Symbolic Classification: On the Polarizing Discourse of Civil Society," in *Cultivating Differences: Symbolic Boundaries and the Making of Inequality*, ed. M. Fournier and M. Lamont (Chicago: University of Chicago Press, 1993), 289–308; Z. Bauman, "Modernity and Ambivalence," *Theory, Culture and Society* 7 (1990): 143–169; and P. Schlesinger, *Media, State and Nation: Political Violence and Collective Identities* (London: Sage, 1991).

5. Schlesinger, *Media, State and Nation*.

6. This approach builds on Georg Simmel's structural approach of the stranger, which examines an individual's twofold position as an outsider and as an insider when entering into a new group.

7. In the United States, the prototypical immigrant is a low-skilled Mexican or Central American worker rather than a conservative Muslim. Of the 15.5 million legal immigrants who entered the United States between 1989 and 2004, only 1.2 million were from predominantly Muslim countries. There was a sharp drop from more than 100,000 per year prior to 2002 down to approximately 60,000 in 2003, but this recovered somewhat to 90,000 in 2004. Immigration in the United States is thus a topic in which the issues of Islam and terrorism are at best marginal issues.

8. Ariane Chebel D'Appollonia, *Frontiers of Fear: Immigration and Insecurity in the United States and Europe* (Ithaca: Cornell University Press, 2012).

9. Although it has been rightly argued that the Muslim presence in Europe is much older, going back to Islamic Spain, this older presence has only an indirect effect on the creation of the current symbolic boundaries.

10. "Bernard Lewis: Muslims to Take Over Europe," Free Republic, February 1, 2007, accessed July 25, 2012, http://www.freerepublic.com/focus/f-news/1778003/posts.

11. For a detailed description of the socioeconomic status of Muslims across Europe, see www.euro-islam.info.

12. E. Brouwer, "Immigration, Asylum and Terrorism: A Changing Dynamic. Legal and Practical development in the EU in Response to the Terrorist Attacks of 11/09," *European Journal of Migration and Law* 4(4) (2003): 399–424 and T. Faist, "The Migrationsecurity Nexus: International Migration and Security," in *Migration, Citizenship and Ethnos: Incorporation Regimes in Germany, Western Europe and North America*, ed. Y. M. Bodemann and G. Yurdakul (Basingstoke: Palgrave Macmillan, 2005), 103–120.

13. Robert Leiken, "Europe's Angry Muslims," *Foreign Affairs* 84(4) (2005): 120–135.

14. B. Bawer, *While Europe Slept: How Radical Islam Is Destroying the West from Within* (New York: Broadway Books, 2007); M. Phillips, *Londonistan* (New York: Encounter Books, 2006); M. Steyn, *America Alone: The End of the World as We Know It* (Washington, DC: Regnery, 2006); and B. Ye'or, *Eurabia: The Euro Arab Axis* (Cranbury: Associated University Presses, 2005).

15. Arun Kundnani, "Multiculturalism and Its Discontents: Left, Right and Liberal," *European Journal of Cultural Studies* 15(2) (2010): 155–166.

16. Triadafilos Triadafilopoulos, "Illiberal Means to Liberal Ends? Understanding Recent Immigrant Integration Policies in Europe," *Journal of Ethnic and Migration Studies* 37(6) (2011): 861–880.

17. Elazar Barkan, *The Retreat of Scientific Racism: Changing Concepts of Race in Britain and the United States between the World Wars* (Cambridge: Cambridge University Press, 1992); Alan C. Cairns, "Empire, Globalization, and the Fall and Rise of Diversity," in *Citizenship, Diversity, and Pluralism: Canadian and Comparative Perspectives*, ed. Alan C. Cairns, John C. Courtney, Peter MacKinnon (Montreal and Kingston: McGill-Queen's University Press, 1999): 23–57; G. Fredrickson, *Racism: A Short History* (Princeton: Princeton University Press, 2003); and W. Kymlicka, *Multicultural Odysseys: Navigating the New International Politics of Diversity* (New York: Oxford University Press, 2007).

18. Triadafilopoulos, "Illiberal Means to Liberal Ends?"

19. Ibid.

20. Ibid., p.4; J. H. Carens, *Culture, Citizenship, and Community: A Contextual Exploration of Justice as Evenhandedness* (Oxford: Oxford University Press, 2000); W. Kymlicka, *Multicultural Citizenship: A Liberal Theory of Minority Rights* (Oxford: Oxford University Press, 1995); W. Kymlicka and K. Banting, "Immigration, Multiculturalism and the Welfare State," *Ethics & International Affairs* 20(3) (2006): 281–304; T. Modood, *Multiculturalism: A Civic Idea* (Cambridge: Polity, 2007); and B. Parekh, *Rethinking Multiculturalism: Cultural Diversity and Political Theory* (Cambridge, MA: Harvard University Press, 2002).

21. The national histories are replete with accounts of the "bad" Muslims: from the Battle of Poitiers to the Crusades. On the same note, who remembers that the French croissant was created to celebrate the battle of Lepante (1751), where a league of European countries led by the Pope won over the Ottoman Empire?

22. Roxanne Euben, *Enemy in the Mirror: Islamic Fundamentalism and the Limits of Modern Rationalism; A Work of Comparative Political Theory* (Princeton: Princeton University Press, 2012).

23. Louis Dermigny, *La Chine et L'Occident: Le Commerce a Canton au XVIIIe Siecle 1719–1833 tome II* (Paris: S.E.V.P.E.N., 1964).

24. Edward Said, *Orientalism* (New York: Pantheon, 1979); Hichem Djaït, *L'Europe Et L'Islam* (Oakland: University of California, 1985).

25. Said, *Orientalism*; Djaït, *L'Europe Et L'Islam*; Mustapha Kamal Pasha, Giorgio Shani, and Makoto Sato, *Protecting Human Security in a Post 9/11 World: Critical and Global Insights* (Hampshire: Palgrave, 2007), 114.

26. Said, *Orientalism*.

27. A. Bozeman, "The International Order in a Multicultural World. The Expansion of International Society," in *The Expansion of International Society*, ed. B. Hedley and A. Watson (Oxford: Clarendon, 1984): 161–186.

28. R. E. Rubenstein and J. Crocker, "Challenging Huntington," *Foreign Policy* 96 (1994): 113–128, as well as Said, *Orientalism*.

29. Gregor Boldt, Angelika Wolk, and Christopher Onkelbach, "Islam-Kritik empört Muslime," *Der Western*, January 2, 2011, accessed January 31, 2012, http://www.derwesten.de/nachrichten/islam-kritik-empoert-muslime-id4156145.html.

30. "Wilders Komt Met Boek Over Islam," *De Telegraaf*, December 31, 2010, accessed January 31, 2012, http://www.telegraaf.nl/binnenland/8625401/__Boek_Wilders_over_de_islam__.html?p=13,2.

31. "Wilders Wants Debate on 'Real Nature' of Mohammed," NIS News Bulletin, April 1, 2011, accessed January 31, 2012, http://www.nisnews.nl/public/010411_1.htm.

32. Bjarte Ystebo, "Kristelig Folkeparti med muslimer," *IDAG*, September 9, 2010, accessed February 18, 2012, http://www.idag.no/aktuelt-oppslag.php3?ID=18107.

33. I. Kalin, "The Slow Death of Multiculturalism in Europe," *Today's Zaman*, October 28, 2010, accessed February 18, 2012, http://www.todayszaman.com/columnist-225620-the-slow-death-of-multiculturalism-in-europe.html.

34. "Cameron: Multiculturalism Speech Not Attack on Muslim," *BBC*, February 23, 2011, accessed February 18, 2012, http://www.bbc.co.uk/news/uk-politics-12555908.

35. Keith Windschuttle, "The Cultural War on Western Civilization," *Sydney Line*, January 2002, accessed February 18, 2012, http://www.sydneyline.com/Warper cent20onper cent20Westernper cent20civilization.htm.

36. Elizabeth Sebia, "Islam in France," Euro-Islam.info, accessed January 31, 2012, http://www.euro-islam.info/country-profiles/france/.

37. Ibid.

38. "Dutch Authorities Enforce New Moroccan Laws," NIS News Bulletin, March 31, 2009, accessed February 18, 2012, http://www.nisnews.nl/public/310309_2.htm.

39. D. Motadel, "Islam in Germany," Euro-Islam.info, accessed January 31, 2012, http://www.euro-islam.info/country-profiles/germany/.

40. F. Chretienne, "À Avignon, le Père Gabriel s'interroge après un an de profanations," *Famille Chrétienne*, November 23, 2010, accessed January 31, 2012, http://www.famillechretienne.fr/agir/vie-de-l-eglise/a-avignon-le-pere-gabriel-sinterroge-apres-un-an-de-profanations_t11_s73_d58730.html.

41. Friendofmuslim, *Muslim Demographics* (Video), March 30, 2009, accessed January 29, 2012, http://www.youtube.com/watch?v=6-3X5hIFXYU and BBC, *Muslim Demographics: The Truth* (Video), August 7, 2009, accessed January 29, 2012, http://www.youtube.com/watch?v=mINChFxRXQs.

42. M. Campbell, "Nicolas Sarkozy to Target Muslim Prayers," *Australian*, December 20, 2010, accessed January 31, 2012, http://www.theaustralian.com.au/news/world/nicolas-sarkozy-to-target-muslim-prayers/story-e6frg6so-1225973565402.

43. Ferry Biedermann, "Anti-Muslim Groups Descend on Paris," *National*, December 19, 2012, accessed February 18, 2012, http://www.thenational.ae/news/world/europe/anti-muslim-groups-descend-on-paris.

44. "Islam et Occupation: Marine Le Pen provoque un tollé," *Le Figaro*, December 12, 2010, accessed January 31, 2012, http://www.lefigaro.fr/politique/2010/12/11/01002-20101211ARTFIG00475-islam-et-occupation-la-provocation-de-marine-le-pen.php.

45. E. Dugan and N. Lakhani, "Straw under Fire for Linking Race to Sex Attacks," *Independent,* January 9, 2011, accessed January 31, 2012, http://www. independent.co.uk/news/uk/crime/straw-under-fire-for-linking-race-to-sex-attacks-2179750.html.

46. "Are Women's Rights Really the Issue?," *Spiegel International,* June 24, 2012, accessed February 18, 2012, http://www.spiegel.de/international/europe/the-burqa-debate-are-women-s-rights-really-the-issue-a-702668.html.

47. Linda Woodhead, *The Muslim Veil Controversy and European Values,* accessed July 22, 2012, http://www.google.com/url?sa=t&rct=j&q=&esrc=s&source=web &cd=4&ved=0CFYQFjAD&url=http%3A%2F%2Feprints.lancs.ac. uk%2F39909%2F1%2FVeil_and_Values_-SMT.doc&ei=a3HXT4SrDdGd6A Hg-pStAw&usg=AFQjCNHaLPsNj1Ia3_zVzS_EQq4wMxN6dw.

48. Ni Putes Ni Soumises is a movement founded in 2002, which advocates against female social pressure and violence within the Muslim community, particularly in France. A website associated with the movement is http://www.npns.fr/.

49. Nacira Guénif-Souilamas and Eric Macé, *Les féministes et le Garçon Arabe* (Paris: Éditions de l'aube, 2004), 9.

50. Fadela Amara, Ni Putes Ni Soumises (Paris: La Découverte, 2003), 19.

51. Kirwan Grewal, "'The Threat from Within'—Representations of Banlieue in French Popular Discourse," in *Europe: New Voices, New Perspectives: Proceedings from the Contemporary Europe Research Centre Postgraduate Conference 2005/2006,* ed. Matt Killingsworth (Melbourne: Contemporary Europe Research Centre, University of Melbourne, 2007), 41–67.

52. Ibid.

53. Motadel, "Islam in Germany."

54. Ibid.

55. Ibid.

56. Louise Lyck Dreehsen, "Langballe Dømt for Racism," *Berlingske,* December 3, 2010, accessed June 20, 2012, http://www.b.dk/politik/langballe-doemt-racisme.

57. "Former Minister Guilty of Slander," Euro-Islam.info, October 27, 2010, accessed July 22, 2012, http://www.euro-islam.info/2010/11/02/former-minister-guilty-of-slander/.

58. She has declared several times that the twenty-first century is characterized by a battle between the values of Islam and the West. Ayaan Hirsi Ali, "The Role of Journalism Today," American Enterprise Institute for Public Policy Research, June 18, 2007, accessed July 22, 2012, http://www.aei.org/article/society-and-culture/the-role-of-journalism-today/.

59. R. Cohen, "Religion Does Its Worst," *The New York Times,* April 4, 2011, accessed January 31, 2012, http://www.nytimes.com/2011/04/05/opinion/05iht-edcohen05.html.

60. S. G. Stolberg and L. Goodstein, "Domestic Terrorism Hearing Opens with Contrasting Views on Dangers," *The New York Times,* March 10, 2011, accessed January 31, 2012, http://www.nytimes.com/2011/03/11/us/politics/11king.html.

61. L. Goodstein, "Drawing u.s. Crowd with Anti-Islam Message," *The New York Times,* March 7, 2011, accessed January 31, 2012, http://www.nytimes. com/2011/03/08/us/08gabriel.html?pagewanted=all.

62. "Juan Williams: Muslims on Planes Make Me 'Nervous,'" Huffington Post, October 19, 2010, accessed January 31, 2012, http://www.huffing-tonpost.com/2010/10/19/juan-williams-muslims-nervous_n_768719.html.

Juan Williams is an American journalist and political analyst for Fox News Channel, who had his contract terminated by National Public Radio (NPR) after he made this declaration.

63. W. Saletan, "Muslims, Keep Out," *Slate,* August 2, 2010, accessed January 31, 2012, http://www.slate.com/articles/news_and_politics/frame_game/2010/08/ muslims_keep_out.html.

64. Ibid.

65. A. Elliott, "The Man behind the Anti-Shariah Movement," *The New York Times,* July 30, 2011, accessed January 31, 2012, http://www.nytimes.com/2011/07/31/ us/31shariah.html?_r=1&adxnnl=1&pagewanted=all&adxnnlx=1325142029-Mn rhdJvFojgkqHiVpO2aJA.

66. "Pew: Some Voters Still Believe Obama is Muslim, Most Unconcerned with Candidates' Religions," Pew, July 26, 2012, accessed July 27, 2012, http://2012. talkingpointsmemo.com/2012/07/poll-pew-mormon-romney.php.

67. "Poll: Majority of GOP Believes Obama Sympathizes with Islamic Fundamentalism, Wants Worldwide Islamic Law," Huffington Post, August 20, 2010, accessed January 31, 2012, http://www.huffingtonpost.com/2010/08/30/ obama-islamic-fundamentalist-gop-polled-majority-says_n_699883.html.

68. Frank Newport, "Many Americans Can't name Obama's Religion," Gallup, June 22, 2012, accessed July 30, 2012, http://www.gallup.com/poll/155315/Many -Americans-Cant-Name-Obamas-Religion.aspx.

69. "Little Voter Discomfort with Romney's Mormon Religion," Pew Forum, July 26, 2012, accessed July 30, http://www.pewforum.org/Politics-and-Elections/ Little-Voter-Discomfort-with-Romney%E2%80%99s-Mormon-Religion-1. aspx and Carol Anne Hunt, "Many Republican Voters Still Believe Obama is Muslim," *Examiner,* July 29, 2012, accessed July 30, 2012, http://www.examiner. com/article/many-republican-voters-still-believe-obama-is-muslim.

70. The oppositions to this public discourse have mainly come from Muslim lobby groups like the Council of American Islamic Relations (CAIR). The Associated Press called United States Rep. Virgil H. Goode, Jr. (R-VA) Islamophobic for his December 2006 letter stating that Rep.-elect Keith Ellison's desire to use the Qur'an during the swearing in ceremonies was a threat to "the values and beliefs traditional to the United States of America" and for saying "I fear that in the next century we will have many more Muslims in the United States if we do not adopt the strict immigration policies."

71. These surveys, which stemmed from a plethora of sources ranging from the media to national research organizations, expressed a generally negative senti- ment toward Muslims and Islam. They were conducted at both the city and national levels, and two surveys, IFOP and Pew, compared data collected across European countries and America.

72. See Pew Research Center's Global Attitudes Project, accessed August 30, 2012, http://pewresearch.org/topics/globalattitudesforeignaffairs/.

73. "Washington Post-ABC poll," *The Washington Post,* September 7, 2010, accessed January 31, 2012, http://www.washingtonpost.com/wp-srv/politics/ polls/postpoll_09072010.html.

74. "In U.S., Religious Prejudice Stronger Against Muslims," Gallup, January 21, 2010, accessed July 22, 2012, http://www.gallup.com/poll/125312/Religious-Pr ejudice-Stronger-Against-Muslims.aspx., 2009. The report titled, "Religious Perceptions in America: With an In-Depth Analysis of U.S. Attitudes toward

Muslims and Islam" also reveals that Islam is the most negatively viewed out of the top four religions.

75. See appendix 13, table 1.2. However, in the two European countries with the most negative perspectives, Germany and Spain, unfavorable views actually declined slightly.

76. See appendix 13, table 1.3. "Gallup Coexist Index 2009: A Global Study of Interfaith Relations," Gallup, 2009, accessed January 30, 2012, http://www.gallup.com/se/ms/153578/REPORT-Gallup-Coexist-Index-2009.aspx.

77. Ibid. See appendix 13, table 1.4.

78. Pew Researdch Center, "Muslims in Europe: Economic Worries Top Concerns about Religious and Cultural Identity," 2006, accessed January 30, 2012, http://www.pewglobal.org/files/pdf/7–6–06.pdf.

79. Jérôme Forquet, "ANALYSE : 1989–2011, Enquête sur l'implantation et l'évolution de l'Islam de France," IFOP, July 2011, accessed January 31, 2012, http://www.ifop.com/media/pressdocument/343–1-document_file.pdf.

80. "Muslims in the European Union. Discrimination and Islamophobia," European Monitoring Centre on Racism and Xenophobia (EUMC), 2006, accessed January 31, 2012, http://eumc.europa.eu/eumc/material/pub/muslim/Manifestations_EN.pdf.

81. Motadel, "Islam in Germany."

82. Ibid.

83. Ibid.

84. Andreas Zick, Beate Kupper, and Andreas Hovermann, "Intolerance, Prejudice and Discrimination," accessed January 31, 2012, http://www.uni-bielefeld.de/ikg/IntolerancePrejudice.PDF.

85. P. Tevanian, "Pour 100% des musulmans, les sondages sont plutôt une menace," Les mots sont improtants, January 2011, accessed January 31, 2012, http://lmsi.net/Pour-100-des-musulmans-les.

86. Open Society Institute, "Muslims in the EU: Cities Report. Germany," 2007, accessed January 31, 2012, http://www.soros.org/initiatives/home/articles_publications/publications/museucities_20080101/museucitiesger_20080101.pdf.

87. Religion Monitor, "Muslim Religiousness in Germany," 2008, accessed January 30, 2012, http://www.bertelsmann-stiftung.de/bst/en/media/xcms_bst_dms_25866__2.pdf.

88. Ibid.

89. Jonathan Wynne-Jones, "Britons Are Suspicious towards Muslims, Study Finds," *Telegraph,* January 9, 2010, accessed January 30, 2012, http://www.telegraph.co.uk/news/religion/6958571/Britons-are-suspicious-towards-Muslims-study-finds.html.

90. Ibid.

91. Forquet, "ANALYSE."

92. Open Society Institute, "Muslims in the EU."

93. "Ad Campaign Launched in London to Improve the Image of Islam," *Free Thinker,* June 21, 2010, accessed January 31, 2012, http://freethinker.co.uk/2010/06/21/ad-campaign-launched-in-london-to-improve-the-image-of-islam/.

94. "Muslim-Western Tensions Persist," Pew, July 21, 2012, accessed July 22, 2012, http://pewresearch.org/pubs/2066/muslims-westerners-christians-jews-islamic-extremism-september-11.

95. Motadel, "Islam in Germany."
96. Ibid.
97. "Islam in the Netherlands," Euro-Islam.info, accessed January 31, 2012, http://www.euro-islam.info/country-profiles/the-netherlands/.
98. YouGov Poll, 2010.
99. "The New York Times Poll," 2001, 2002, 2003, 2010, accessed January 31, 2012, http://www.nytimes.com/packages/pdf/poll_results.pdf.
100. See Pew Forum on Religion and Public Life, http://www.pewforum.org/, 2009.
101. YouGov Poll, 2010.
102. GfK NOP, 2007.
103. "Germans Less Tolerant of Islam Than Neighbours, Study Finds," *Local*, December 2, 2010, accessed January 30, 2012, http://www.thelocal.de/society/20101202–31531.html.
104. "Islam in the Netherlands," Euro-Islam.info.
105. "Muslim-Western Tensions Persist," Pew.
106. IFOP, 2009.
107. Benjamin Bruce, "Switzerland's Minaret Ban," *Euro-Islam.info*, November 29, 2009, accessed January 30, 2012, http://www.euro-islam.info/key-issues/switzerlands-minaret-ban/.
108. "The New York Times Poll."
109. Pew, 2006.
110. "Sondage IFOP réalisé les 13 et 14 décembre auprès d'un échantillon représentatif de 970 personnes," Le Monde, December 15, 2012, accessed January 30, 2012, http://www.ifop.com/media/pressdocument/343-1-document_file.pdf. Twenty-two percent agreed with the statement, "Plutôt un facteur d'enrichissement culturel pour notre pays."
111. In these kinds of surveys, it is important to note that what "integration" might mean for the respondents is never clarified. This ultimately leaves room for multiple interpretations, which could range from socioeconomic failure to religious incompatibility.
112. "Transatlantic Trends: Immigration 2010," BBVA Foundation, 2010, accessed Feb=ruary 4, 2011, http://www.affarinternazionali.it/documenti/TT-Immigr10_EN.pdf.

Part I   In Their Own Voices:
What It Is to Be a Muslim and a Citizen in the West

1. See previous research from P. Ireland, "Immigration and Politics in the EC," *Journal of Common Market Studies* 29(5) (1991): 457–80; J. Hollifield, "Immigration and Republicanism in France: The Hidden Consensus," in *Controlling Immigration: A Global Perspective*, ed. Wayne Cornelius, Philip Martin, and James Hollifield (Stanford, CA: Stanford University Press, 1994), 143–175; J. Klausen, *The Islamic Challenge: Politics and Religion in Western Europe* (New York: Oxford University Press, 2005); and M. Schain, *Immigration Policy and the Politics of Immigration: A Comparative Study* (Basingstoke: Palgrave Macmillan, 2008).
2. I. Bagby, P. M. Perl, and B. T. Froehle, "The Mosque in America: A National Portrait," Unpublished report of the Mosque Study Project, Council of American-Islamic Relations, April, 2001.

2   Islam: Between Personal and Social Identity Markers

1. The Pew survey, however, diverges from the Gallup findings, where religion is the first choice (see appendix 13). This may be in part due to a Pew survey question that asked respondents to identify themselves by either religion or nationality while in the Gallup polling, respondents could choose more than one option. Furthermore, identifications may have had different meanings for different respondents, which could be another factor that produced disparate results between the two surveys. In the Pew survey 81 percent of Muslims in the United Kingdom, 66 percent of Muslims in Germany, and 46 percent of Muslims in France referred to themselves as Muslims first instead of their respective nationalities. Whereas only 7 percent of Christians in the United Kingdom, 13 percent of Christians in Germany, and 42 percent of Christians in France referred to themselves as Christian first.

2. S. Michelman, "Changing Old Habits: Dress of Women Religious and Its Relationship to Personal and Social Identity," *Sociological Inquiry* 67(3) (1997): 350–363 and P. Simon, *French National Identity and Integration: Who Belongs to the National Community?* (Washington, DC: Migration Policy Institute, 2012). Davis (1992) and Goffman (1959) suggest that personal and social identity tensions occur regularly, maintaining that dress serves as a kind of visual metaphor that gives off certain image and shape identity.

3. D. Snow and L. Anderson, "Identity Work among the Homeless: The Verbal Construction and Avowal of Personal Identities," *The American Journal of Sociology* 92(6) (1987): 1336–1371.

4. John F. Dovidio, Tamar Saguy, and Nurit Shnabel, "Cooperation and Conflict within Groups: Bridging Intragroup and Intergroup Processes," *Journal of Social Issues* 65(2) (2009): 429–449.

5. H. G. Koenig, "Concerns about Measuring 'Spirituality' in Research," *Journal of Nervous and Mental Disease* 196(5) (2008): 349–355; H. G. Koenig, "Research on Religion, Spirituality, and Mental Health: A Review," *Canadian Journal of Psychiatry* 54(5) (2009): 283–291; D. O. Moberg, "Assessing and Measuring Spirituality: Confronting Dilemmas of Universal and Particular Evaluative Criteria," *Journal of Adult Development* 9(1) (2002): 47–60; and Religion Monitor, "Muslim Religiousness in Germany," accessed January 30, 2012, http://www.bertelsmann-stiftung.de/bst/en/media/xcms_bst_dms_25866__2.pdf.

6. Religion Monitor, "Muslim Religiousness in Germany."

7. Another example is the IFOP polling conducted in France in 2011. It shows that fasting is especially prevalent among the 18–24 age group, which also scores highly for visits to places of worship. The picture of the French Muslim population that emerges from the survey is of a "young" (62 percent are aged under 35) and traditionally Left-leaning community. See http://www.la-croix.com/Religion/S-informer/Actualite/Tous-les-resultats-de-l-etude-Ifop-La-Croix-sur-les-musulmans-francais-_NG_-2011-08-01-694857, accessed October 23, 2012.

8. G. Davie, *Religion in Britain since 1945: Believing without Belonging* (Oxford: Blackwell, 1994) and D. Hervieu-Léger, "Religion und sozialer Zusammenhalt in Europa," *Transit* 26 (2003): 101–119.

9. Davie, *Religion in Britain since 1945,* 101–119.
10. In the Islamic tradition, the five pillars or religious duties of Muslims are:
    1. *Shahadat* (Testimony of Faith)
    2. *Salat* (ritual prayer)
    3. *Zakat* (Almsgiving)
    4. Fast of the month of Ramadan
    5. *Haj* (Pilgrimage to Mekka)
11. "Younger Americans" were those under 30 years in the Pew data and 18–24 years in the Gallup data.

3 Multiple Communities of Allegiance: How Do Muslims Say "We"?

1. According to Islamic Law, the man transmits the religion. Therefore a Muslim woman must marry a Muslim man. A Muslim man is allowed to marry Muslim, Jewish or Christian women.
2. Alawi are a sub group of the Twelver Shia.
3. This is a reference to a coup d'état by the Turkish military in September 1980.
4. French text :

   No. 7: Absolument, c'est vraiment la France profonde qui parle, donc quand on veut construire une mosquée on reproche tout de suite le financement de pays étrangers etc. Mais alors, quand il s'agit d'avoir un avis, ben y a pas de problème, on écoute. Vous rendez vous compte! C'est le ministre lui-même qui voyage en Egypte demander une, en plus à une personne je dirait controversé déjà la bas, alors que franchement il y a des tas d'autorités musulmanes qui existent en France etc. On aurait pu demander l'avis des femmes musulmanes elles mêmes.

5. Milli gazette, Zaman, Vakit, and Yeni Safak are Turkish newspapers.
6. Pew Researdch Center, "Muslims in Europe: Economic Worries Top Concerns about Religious and Cultural Identity," 2006, accessed January 30, 2012, http://www.pewglobal.org/files/pdf/7-6-06.pdf
7. Pew Research Center, "The American-Western European Values Gap," February 29, 2012, accessed October 23, 2012, http://www.pewglobal.org/2011/11/17/the-american-western-european-values-gap/.
8. As already mentioned in chapter 2, age was a salient factor for differentiation. According to the Pew data, 60 percent of younger Muslims in the United States thought of themselves as Muslims first compared to 41 percent who viewed themselves primarily as Americans. The Gallup (2011) survey reported similar findings, suggesting that the 18–24 age group tended to identify more strongly with their religion than the other age groups in the United States.
9. Informal political participation refers to voluntarism, mobilization for social causes, following up political news, reading newspapers. Formal political participation includes registration to vote, voting, membership in political parties.
10. Patrick Simon, *French National Identity and Integration: Who Belongs to the National Community?* (Washington, DC: Migration Policy Institute, 2012), 6.

4 Religiosity, Political Participation, and Civic Engagement

1. R. Putnam, *Bowling Alone: The Collapse and Revival of American Community* (New York: Simon & Schuster, 2001), 79.

2. T. Skocpol and M. P. Fiorina, *Civic Engagement in American Democracy* (Washington, DC: Brookings Institution, 2006), 344.

3. In analyzing American Protestant groups, the article by L. Beyerlein and J. R. Hipp, "From Pews to Participation: The Effect of Congregation Activity and Context on Bridging Civic Engagement," *Social Problems* 53(1) (2006): 97–117, explains a bit further that not only are religious services correlated to political and civic participation but also to the nature of the congregation. The congregation, outside of its religious function, is a social atmosphere that engenders social networks, exposes people to information, and cultivates leadership skills. The nature of the congregation and the behavior, not so much the belief of the religion, is what connects religiosity with political and civic participation in this survey.

4. A. Jamal, "The Political Participation and Engagement of Muslim Americans: Mosque Involvement and Group Consciousness," *American Politics Research* 33(4) (2005): 21–44.

5. Ibid.

6. Ibid.

7. Ibid.

8. There are a few exceptions, however, such as a German study (2011) that showed that individual religiosity and regional, religious context influence social trust. See J. Delhey and K. Newton, "Predicting Cross-National Levels of Social Trust: Global Pattern or Nordic Exceptionalism?," *European Sociological Review* 21 (2005): 311–327. Specifically, Protestant personal identity in resonance with national culture increased social trust, because the scope of the moral communities went beyond the religious in group and was embedded in the mainstream collective identity. Such a correlation between religious values and mainstream political culture has been confirmed by other surveys conducted in several countries where Protestantism is the dominant religion. Additionally, the former study demonstrates that congregational membership is a predictor of social trust in Germany, noting, "People who are actively involved in their religious community and, therefore, well integrated in religious networks display higher levels of trust." This level of social trust was highest among Catholics but Protestants still scored higher than Muslims, members of small Christian groups, and people who declared themselves nonreligious.

9. J. Solomos, "Social Capital, Political Participation and Migration in Europe: Making Multicultural Democracy Work?" *Ethnic and Racial Studies* 35(2) (2011): 363–364.

10. Ibid., 235.

11. I. Ajala, "The Muslim Vote and Muslim Lobby in France: Myths and Realities," *Journal of Islamic Law and Culture* 12(2) (2010): 84. "Voter registration is much lower for the French of African or Turkish origin, especially for younger people: 23 percent say they are not registered whereas this figure is just 7 percent for Algerians" (79).

12. Ajala, "Muslim Vote and Muslim Lobby in France," 79.
13. Interviewees who fasted during most of Ramadan were more likely to support a political party. Interviewees who more frequently participated in individual prayer were more likely to work for a campaign.
14. This is called the "Contact Theory," which states that the more contact one has, the more civically and politically engaged one becomes.
15. E. Fieldhouse and D. Cutts, "Diversity, Density, and Turnout: The Effect of Neighborhood Ethno-religious Composition on Voter Turnout in Britain Political Geography," *Political Geography* 27(5) (2008): 530–548.
16. Putnam argues that diversity "seems to trigger *not* in-group/out-group division, but anomie or social isolation," famously saying that "people living in an ethnically diverse setting appear to 'hunker down'—that is, to pull in like a turtle." He calls this the "Constrict Theory," differentiating himself from Contact Theory, defined above. Furthermore, Putnam argues that diversity does not lead to race problems or ethnically defined hostility (conflict school) but rather to a withdrawal from collective life (see R. Putnam, "E pluribus unum: Diversity and Community in the Twenty-First Century. The 2006 Johan Skytte Prize Lecture," *Scandinavian Political Studies* 30 (2007): 137–174. It should be noted, however, that Putnam limits his argument to the "short-term," as he contends that the negative effects of diversity can, and hopefully will, be countered by a gradual reconstruction of social indent itself, which in short, is a redefinition of what diversity means. Ultimately, he suggests that a new, all-encompassing identity may be created that could mesh what is now considered a variety of distinct ethnic-religious identities into one identity.
17. Bram Lancee and Jaap Dronkers, "Ethnic Diversity in Neighborhoods and Individual Trust of Immigrants and Natives: A Replication of Putnam (2007) in a West-European Country" (paper presented at the International Conference on Theoretical Perspectives on Social Cohesion and Social Capitol, Royal Flemish Academic of Belgium for Sciences and Arts, May 15, 2008).
18. C. Kesler and I. Bloemraad, "Does Immigration Erode Social Capital?," *Canadian Journal of Political Science* 43(2) (2010): 319–347.
19. Ibid., 324. Interestingly, we will show in chapter 5 that this positive effect of multicultural policies are tromped by an increasingly depreciative political discourse.
20. Ibid., 319–347. European countries included are Austria, Belgium, Denmark, Finland, France, Germany, Ireland, Italy, the Netherlands, Norway, Portugal, Spain, Sweden, Switzerland, and the United Kingdom.
21. For a critique of such generalization see Lancee and Dronkers, "Ethnic Diversity in Neighborhoods. and Individual Trust of Immigrants and Natives."

Part II Structural Conditions of the Externalization of Islam

1. Keith G. Banting, "Looking in Three Dimensions: Migration and the European Welfare State in Comparative Perspective," in *Immigration and*

Welfare: Challenging the Borders of the Welfare State, ed. Michael Bommes and Andrew Geddes (New York: Routledge, 200) 13–34; Uwe Hunger, "Temporary Transnational Labor Migration in an Integrating Europe and the Challenge to the German Welfare State," in Bommes and Geddes, *Immigration and Welfare*, 186–204; Peter Nannestad, "Immigration and Welfare States: A Survey of 15 Years of Research." *European Journal of Political Economy* 23(2) (2007): 512–532.

2. "Common Basic Principles for Integration," Council of the European Union, November 19, 2008, accessed October 21, 2012, http://www.consilium.europa. eu/uedocs/cms_data/docs/pressdata/en/jha/82745.pdf
3. Martin A. Schain, *The Politics of Immigration in France, Britain, and the United States* (New York: Palgrave Macmillan, 2008).
4. Ibid., 278.
5. Therese O'Toole, Daniel Nilsson Dehanas, Tariq Modood, Nasar Meer, and Stephen Jones, "Taking Part: Muslim Participation in Contemporary Governance, Centre for the Study of Ethnicity and Citizenship, University of Bristol, Bristol, 2013, 69 pages, p 7.
6. Ibid., 88.

5   Securitization of Islam in Europe: The Embodiment of Islam as an Exception

*The data for this chapter comes from a four-year research project of an international research team funded by the European Commission (2003–2007) (see http://www. euro-islam.info/2006/06/01/securitization-and-religious-divide-in-europe-muslims-in-western-europe-after-911-why-the-term-%E2%80%99islamophobia%E2%80%99-is-more-a-predicament-than-an-explanation/).

1. Carsten Bagge Laustsen and Ole Waever, "In Defense of Religion, Sacred Reverent Objects for Securitization" in *Religion in International Relations, the Return from Exile*, ed. Pavlos Hatzopoulos (New York: Palgrave Macmillan, 2003), 147–175.
2. D. Bigo, "Security and Immigration: Toward a Critique of the Governmentality of Unease," *Alternatives* 27 (2002): 63–92.
3. For examples, see report mentioned in note 1 as well as Lorraine Sheridan, *Effects of the Events of September 11th, 2001 on Discrimination and Implicit Racism in Five Religious and Seven Ethnic Groups: A Brief Overview* (Leicester: University of Leicester, 2002).
4. Mahmood Mamdani, *Good Muslim, Bad Muslim: America, the Cold War, and the Roots of Terror* (New York: Three Leaves Press, 2005).
5. Talal Asad, "Secularism, Nation-State, Religion," in *Formations of the Secular: Christianity, Islam Modernity*, ed. Talal Asad (Stanford: Stanford University Press, 2003).
6. Antonio Elorza, "Terrorismo islámico: Las raíces doctrinales" in *El nuevo terrorismo islamista*, ed. F. Reinares y A. Elorza (Temas de Hoy, Madrid, 2004), 156–157.
7. Fernando Reinares, "Al Qaeda, neosalafistas magrebíes y 11-M: Sobre el nuevo terrorismo islamista en España," in *El nuevo terrorismo islamista. Del 11-S al 11-M,* ed. Fernando Reinares and Antonio Elorza (Madrid: Temas de Hoy, 2004), 40–42.

8. Herman Philipse, "Stop de tribalisering van Nederland," NRC-Handelsblad, September 28, 2003, accessed July 25, 2012, http://vorige.nrc.nl/opinie/article1616396.ece/Stop_de_tribalisering_van_Nederland. Ironically, this professor was interviewed in 2003 by the French Stasi committee on *laïcité* as an expert on integration in the Netherlands. The members of the French committee concluded after an interview with the "researcher" Philipse that there was a danger of "tribalism" in the Netherlands.

9. Taylor, Jerome. "Atheists Richard Dawkings, Christopher Hitchens and Sam Harris face Islamophobia backlask." *The Independent*, April 2, 2013. Accessed April 17, 2013, available at http://www.independent.co.uk/news/uk/home-news/atheists-richard-dawkins-christopher-hitchens-and-sam-harris-face-islamophobia-backlash-8570580.html.

10. Ibid.

11. Pipes, Daniel. "Philadelphia's Burqa Crisis." *The Jewish Press.com*, February 25, 2013. Accessed April 17, 2013, available at http://www.jewishpress.com/indepth/opinions/philadelphias-burqa-crisis/2013/02/25/0/. Deustch, Anthony and Mark Hosenball. "Exclusive: U.S. groups helped fund Dutch anti-Islam politican Wilders." *Reuters*, September 10, 2012. Accessed April 17, 2013, available at http://www.reuters.com/article/2012/09/10/us-dutch-wilders-us-idUSBRE8890A720120910.

12. Reske, Henry J. and John Bachman. "Daniel Pipes: Anti-Muslim Film Did Provoke Real Outrage." *NewsMax*, October 7, 2012. Accessed April 17, 2013, available at http://www.newsmax.com/US/daniel-pipes-film-Muhammad/2012/10/07/id/459009.

13. Espoito, John L. and John O. Voll. "Tom Friedman on Muslims and Terrorism: Getting it Wrong Again." *The Huffington Post*, December 20, 2009. Accessed April 17, 2013, available at http://www.huffingtonpost.com/john-l-esposito/tom-friedman-on-muslims-a_b_398642.html.

14. He wrote in 2010 a controversial book, called, *Deutschland schafft sich ab* ("*Germany Does Away With Itself*" or "*Germany Abolishes Itself*"), where he discusses Germany's immigration policy and several other aspects of the Muslim immigration in Germany. "Sarrazin earns millions with anti-immigration book," *The Local*, December 17, 2010. Accessed January 31, 2012, http://www.thelocal.de/society/20101217-31873.html.

15. Mamdani, *Good Muslim, Bad Muslim*.

16. R. Penninx, "After the Fortuyn and Van Gogh Murders: Is the Dutch Integration Model in Disarray?" (paper read at Seminar for Experts "Integrating Migrants In Europe", at Paris, 2005), accessed August 30, 2012, http://canada.metropolis.net/events/metropolis_presents/Social_integration/Penninx_Lecture_January_2005.pdf. For example, since the new Aliens Act that was adopted in April 2001, the number of asylum requests has dropped to about a quarter of what it was during the latter half of the 1990s. J. Doomernik, "Dutch Modes of Migration Regulation" (paper for the IMISCOE cluster A1 workshop, March 2006).

17. Ibid.

18. "Islam in the Netherlands," Euro-Islam.info, accessed October 22, 2012, http://www.euro-islam.info/country-profiles/the-netherlands/.

19. "Immigrants Have to Pass a Racy Test. Netherlands Show Its Liberal Culture," Euro-Islam.info, accessed October 22, 2012, http://www.euro-islam.

info/2006/03/16/immigrants-have-to-pass-a-racy-test-netherlands-shows-its-liberal-culture/.

20. Channel 4, Special report "Troubled Dutch," March 16, 2006, accessed May 15, 2006, http://www.channel4.com/news/special-reports/special-reports-storypage.jsp?id=1964.

21. The former minister of integration (Verdonk) wanted to make the course mandatory for all *oudkomers*, including those who have Dutch citizenship. However, the advisory council on migration issues advised against this because it would have meant an unacceptable differentiation among Dutch citizens. People who have at least eight years of formal education in the Netherlands are also exempted.

22. The film's intent is similar to the purpose of the recently disseminated Flemish migration brochures in Morocco, which were created on the initiative of the Flemish nationalists (NVA) to inform potential migrants about local values and what standards to abide by when migrating. "Flemish people are punctual so be on time," and "it doesn't rain money in Belgium," are tips that are shared in the brochure. See "Ook kritiek in Vlaanderen op Marokkaanse starterskit Bourgeois," *De Standaard*, May 9, 2012, accessed October 22, 2012, http://www.standaard.be/artikel/detail.aspx?artikelid=DMF20120509_072.

23. Han Nicolaas, and Kim de Bruin, "Family Reunion and Family Formation after Immigration in the Netherlands," European Population Conference, Vienna, 1-4 September 2010. Accessed April 25 2013, http://epc2010.princeton.edu/abstracts/100670.

24. According to the CBS, this number of immigrants is the highest since the first record of immigrants dating from 1865.

25. Ethnic-based cultural activities and broadcasting were still supported by state funding, however.

26. See Focus Migration for more details at http://focus-migration.hwwi.de/The-Netherlands.2644.0.html?&L=1.

27. Initially, many feared that an immigrant might have shot him and that this could lead to large-scale unrest. It soon turned out that the shooter was a white, environmental activist.

28. "Muslims in the EU-Cities Report: The Netherlands," Open Society Institute, 2007, accessed October 22, 2012, http://dare.uva.nl/document/46997, 42.

29. "Verdonk onderzoekt verbod op Burqa," *De Volkskrant*, October 10, 2005, accessed October 22, 2012, http://www.nu.nl/algemeen/606369/verdonk-onderzoekt-verbod-op-burka.html.

30. As of March 20, 2012, the PVV only holds 23 seats since MP Hero Brinckman left the party.

31. Most Muslims in the Netherlands, however, did obtain citizenship status. Although the Central Bureau of Statistics (CBS) provides counts of the number of Muslims in the Netherlands, it is the first to acknowledge the difficulty of establishing exact figures since there is no Dutch census based on religion, nor is there any other kind of central registration of Muslims (as opposed to church registers, for instance). Counting Muslims is, therefore, based on estimates, and this has led to different calculations. In the first decade of the twenty-first century, the number of Muslims in the Netherlands was estimated by the CBS to be more than 950,000

based on the calculation of nationalities from Muslim-majority countries (Moroccans, Turks, Arabs, and Iranians were, therefore, all automatically classified as Muslim). In 2007, however, the CBS came with new calculations that lowered the number of Muslims to 825,000, a decrease of more than 10 percent. This new calculation was based on methodologies showing that, for instance, many Iraqis and most Syrians were not Muslim but Christian, and that quite some Muslims, in particular Iranians, did not identify themselves as Muslim. H. Schmeets, "Het belang van religieuze binding in sociale statistieken," *Tijdschrift voor Religie, Recht en Beleid* 1(3) (2010): 28–43.).

32. Examples include the Dutch justice minister Piet Hein Donner, who advocated a two-tier justice system according to which foreigners would be sentenced differently from Dutch nationals, and the Minister of Aliens Affairs and Integration Rita Verdonk, who in 2005 proposed to increase the possibilities to revoke the resident permits of convicted nonnationals (aliens) within certain circumstances including domestic and sexual violence.

33. Definitions available on the website of the CBS: www.cbs.nl/nl-nl/menu/methoden, under "begrippen." According to these definitions, by the way, the coming and third generation of Muslims in the Netherlands will mostly be autochthones. It appears, however, that the term allochthon has become equated with being colored

34. According to the CBS, allochthones from Japan and Indonesia are classified as "Western allochthone" based "on their social-economical and social-cultural position.... This pertains in particular to [predominantly Dutch colonial – MB] persons who have been born in the former [colony of the] Dutch Indies, and employees and their families of Japanese enterprises [in the Netherlands – MB]" (CBS, www.cbs.nl/nl-nl/menu/methoden, begrippen).

35. The Muslim Surinamese originated from Java (Indonesia) and India. In the latter case they would also call themselves "Hindu" in the ethnic meaning of the word.

36. They then have to decide whether to keep German citizenship or the nationality of their parents. Only in special cases where the country of origin does not allow renouncing its citizenship can both nationalities be kept.

37. Milli Gorus is a Turkish Islamist movement similar to the Muslim Brotherhood in Egypt.

38. Beauftragte der Bundesregierung für Migration, Flüchtlinge und Integration, *Bericht der Beauftragten der Bundesregierung für Migration, Flüchtlinge und Integration über die Lage der Ausländerinnen und Ausländer in Deutschland* (Berlin: August 2005), 345.

39. Concurrently, the coalition government (CDU/SPD) decided in August 2006 to implement a far-reaching antidiscrimination law, which goes beyond the directives of the European Commission. Not only will race, gender, and ethnic origin (like in the European directive) be protected if the law passes the Federal Council (Bundesrat), but the antidiscrimination law will also encompass measures far beyond those strictly required, such as disability, age, sexual orientation, and religion.

40. Elizabeth Sebian and Jennifer Selby, "Islam in France," Euro-Islam.info, accessed October 22, 2012, http://www.euro-islam.info/country-profiles/france/.

41. Cesari, *Securitization and Religious Divides in Europe,* 206.
42. See their website and annual reports at http://www.cncdh.fr/rubrique70f8. html?id_rubrique=27. In addition, a report on immigration submitted to the French Parliament discussing the effects of the immigration law of November 26, 2003, explicitly linked anti-immigration policies such as repatriation (or "politiques d'éloignement") to the fight against international terrorism by referring to the expulsion of 30 radical Islamist activists from France (see *Rapport au Parlement*—Les orientations de la politique de l'immigration, accessed August 30, 2012, http://www.ladocumentationfrancaise.fr/rapports-publics/054000182/index.shtml).
43. Cesari, *Securitization and Religious Divides in Europe,* 68.
44. The use of the descriptive term "asylum seeker" will from hereon be used as a representative term that includes not only asylum seekers but also political refugees and immigrants unless otherwise directed.
45. The news comes as it emerges that Omar (one of the alleged bombers) had been handed thousands of pounds in taxpayers' money. He was given £75 a week in housing benefit to pay for the one-bedroom flat where he has been the registered tenant since February 1999. His housing benefit stopped in May, but he may have been given up to £24,000 over the last five years. See "Would-be bomber was on benefits," *Breakingnews.ie,* July 26, 2005, accessed February 21, 2013, http://www.breakingnews.ie/world/would-be-bomber-was-on-benefits-213451. html.
46. Hiz Al Tahrir, which was created in 1952 in Jerusalem, advocates the return of the Caliphate by nonviolent means.
47. Bamat, Joseph. "France set to deport hard-line imams." *France 24,* January 1, 2013. Accessed April 18, 2013, available at http://www.france24.com/en/20130130-france-deport-radical-imams-islam-valls.
48. "A Lyon, débat sur les motifs de l'expulsion d'Abdelkader Bouziane," *Le Monde,* July 1, 2005.
49. "Violence contre les femmes: L'imam Bouziane relaxé," Le Figaro, June 22, 2005.
50. *Inburgering van geestelijke bedienaren: Een handleiding voor gemeenten* (The Hague: Ministerie van Binnenlandse Zaken en Koninkrijksrelaties, 2001).
51. There are currently two institutions dedicated to the training of imams, the Muslim College in London, which was established in 1981, and the Markfield Institute of Higher Education in Leicestershire, with an ambitious set of courses, which was established in 2000. "Islam in the United Kingdom," Euro-Islam.info, accessed October 22, 2012, http://www.euro-islam.info/country-profiles/united-kingdom/.
52. "Islam in the United Kingdom," Euro-Islam.info.
53. Mohamed Mukadam and Alison Scott-Baumann, *The Training and Development of Muslim Faith Leaders,* (London: Crown, 2010), 9.
54. "Councillor Shuts Down Committee for Ex-Muslims," Expatica, April 17, 2008, accessed October 22, 2012, http://www.expatica.com/nl/news/local_news/Councillor-shuts-down-committee-for-ex_Muslims.html.
55. "Berlin Muslims to Train Imams at New Islamic School," January 27, 2009, accessed October 22, 2012, http://www.dw.de/berlin-muslims-to-train-imams-at-new-islamic-school/a-3937857-1.

56. "New Program Aims to Integrate German's Foreign-Trained Imams," *Deutsche Welle World,* December 11, 2009, accessed October 22, 2012, http://www.euro-islam.info/2009/12/11/new-program-aims-to-integrate-germ any%E2%80%99s-foreign-trained-imams/.

57. "Lateral Thinkers Wanted," Qantara.de, November 8, 2010, accessed October 22, 2012, http://www.euro-islam.info/2010/09/06/islamic-theology-in-german y-poses-great-challenges-to-universities/.

58. Jonathan Fox and Yasemin Akbaba, "Securitization of Islam and Religious Discrimination: Religious Minorities in Western Democracies, 1990-2008," *Comparative European Politics,* May 13, 2013, doi: 10.1057/cep.2013.8.

59. Andrea Brandy and Guido Kleinhubbert, "Anti-Islamic Party is Playing with Fear," *Spiegel Online International,* January 3, 2008, accessed March 20, 2012, http://www.spiegel.de/international/germany/0,1518,526225,00.html.

60. Nick Cumming-Bruce and Steven Erlanger, "Swiss Ban Building of Minarets on Mosques," *The New York Times,* November 29, 2009, accessed March 20, 2012, http://www.nytimes.com/2009/11/30/world/europe/30swiss.html.

61. Laurie Goodstein, "Across Nation, Mosque Projects Meet Opposition," *The New York Times,* August 7, 2010, accessed March 20, 2012, http://www.nytimes. com/2010/08/08/us/08mosque.html?pagewanted=all.

62. "Mosque Push Back in Minnestoa and New York," Islawmix.org, accessed June 20, 2012, http://islawmix.org/news-roundup/#/2012-24/3555/Mosque-pu shback-in-Minnesota-and-New-York.

63. "Backgrounder: Stop Islamization of America (SIOA)," Anti-Defamation League, March 25, 2011, accessed March 20, 2012, http://www.adl.org/main_ Extremism/sioa.htm.

64. Sean Macloughin, "Mosques and the Public Space, Conflict and Cooperation in the Public Space," *Journal of Ethnic and Migration Studies* 31(6) (2005): 1045–1066.

65. F. Frégosi, ed., *Les conditions d'exercice du culte musulman en France: Étude de cas à partir des lieux de culte et des carrés musulmans. Etude réalisée pour le FASILD* (Paris: FASILD, 2004), 13.

66. Ministry of Interior and Kingdom Relations, Internal Security Service, "De democratische rechtsorde en islamitisch onderwijs. Buitenlandse inmeng ing en anti-integratieve tendensen," 2002, accessed October 22, 2012, https:// www.aivd.nl/actueel/@2234/democratische/.

67. Micheal S. Merry and Geert Driessen, "Islamic Schools in Three Western Countries: Policy and Procedure," *Comparative Education* 41 (4) (2005): 422.

68. Ibid., 427.

69. Geert Driessen and Micheal S. Merry, "Islamic Schools in the Netherlands: Expansion or Marginalization?," *Interchange* 37(3): 201–223,.

70. Thomas Bauer, Lamya Kaddor, and Katja Strobel, eds., *Islamischer Religionsunterricht: Hintergründe, Probleme, Perspektiven* (Münster: LIT, 2004).

71. The definition of Muslim is derived from country of origin and leaves out any notion of self-definition.

72. Harry Harun Behr, Chistoph Bochinger, and Gritt Klinkhammer, *Perspektiven für die Ausbildung muslimischer Religionslehrerinnen und Religionslehrer in Deutschland. Eine Expertise* (Bayreuth, Kulturwissenschaftliche Fakultät Universität Karlsruhe, 2003).

73. Relating to the so-called "Bremer Klausel" (clause of Bremen), Berlin has a different law according to religious teaching at public schools. Therefore, the Islamic Federation in Berlin was able to obtain the right to carry out Islamic teaching in Berlin's public schools in the year 2003.

74. The federation is linked to Milli Gorus (the Turkish Islamist group prior to the creation of the AKP, *Adalet ve Kalkınma Partisi* or Justice and Development Party). due to its "Islamist" background.

75. Freedom of religion, guaranteed by Article 4 of the German Basic Law, includes the right to believe or not to believe, to practice or not to practice one's faith in public, and to maintain religious institutions and organizations. More specifically, religious communities—as well as other ideological groups—can be recognized as corporations of public law (Körperschaften des öffentlichen Rechts) to whom the state cedes substantial parts of its sovereign rights (Article 140 of the Basic Law in combination with Article 137 of the Weimar Constitution).

76. For more information visit http://www.ams-uk.org/.

77. "Islam in the United Kingdom," Euro-Islam.info.

78. "Ecoles, collèges et lycèes musulmans de France," *Al-Kanz*, April 14, 2012, accessed May 26, 2013, available at http://www.al-kanz.org/2012/04/14/lycee-college-musulman/.

79. *Loi n° 2004-228 du 15 mars 2004 encadrant, en application du principe de laïcité, le port de signes ou de tenues manifestant une appartenance religieuse dans les écoles, collèges et lycées publics.*

80. Proposal N° 3056.

81. Alyssa Newcomb, "France to Become First European Country to Ban Burqa," April 10, 2011, accessed October 22, 2012, http://abcnews.go.com/International/burqa-ban-effect-france/story?id=13344555#.T2ooaxHpMio.

82. Official estimates put the number of women wearing the full Islamic veil in France at around 2,000. Henry Samuel, "Burqa Ban: French Women Fined for Wearing Full-Face Veil," Telegraph, September 22, 2011, accessed October 22, 2012, http://www.telegraph.co.uk/news/worldnews/europe/france/8781241/Burqa-ban-French-women-fined-for-wearing-full-face-veil.html.

83. Robert Wielaard, "Belgian Lawmakers Pass Burqa Ban," Huffington Post, April 29, 2010, accessed October 22, 2012, http://www.huffingtonpost.com/2010/04/30/belgian-lawmakers-pass-bu_n_558284.html.

84. Bruno Waterfield, "Belgian MPs Vote to Ban the Burqa," Telegraph, April 29, 2010, accessed June 22, 2012, http://www.telegraph.co.uk/news/worldnews/europe/belgium/7653814/Belgian-MPs-vote-to-ban-the-burqa.html.

85. "Dutch Unveil the Toughest Face in Europe with a Ban on the Burqa," Times Online, October 13, 2005, accessed February 21, 2013, available at http://www.religionnewsblog.com/12449/dutch-unveil-the-toughest-face-in-europe-with-a-ban-on-the-burka.

86. "Dutch Plan Ban on Muslim Face Veils Next Year," January 27, 2012, accessed October 22, 2012, http://www.reuters.com/article/2012/01/27/us-dutch-burqa-ban-idUSTRE80Q1OT20120127.

87. Ibid.

88. Ibid.

89. "CDU Fordert Burkaverbot in der Öffentlichkeit," FrankfurterRundschau, January 12, 2012, accessed October 22, 2012, http://www.fr-online.de/rhein-

main/integrationspolitik-cdu-fordert-burkaverbot-in-der-oeffentlichkeit, 1472796,11437410.html.

90. Thompson, Hannah. "Two thirds Brits want burqa ban." *YouGov*, April 14, 2011. Accessed April 28, 2013, available at http://yougov.co.uk/ news/2011/04/14/two-thirds-brits-want-burqa-ban/.

91. "U.K. Immigration Minister Opposes Ban on Face Veils," Islamtoday. net, July 20, 2010, accessed October 22, 2012, http://en.islamtoday.net/art-show-229-3722.htm.

92. "Britain Not to Ban Muslim Women from Wearing Burqa," Outlookindia. com, July 18, 2010, accessed October 22, 2012, http://news.outlookindia. com/item.aspx?687834 and "Cultural and Social affairs Department OIC islamophobia Observatory," Euro-Islam.info, July 2010, accessed October 22, 2012, http://www.euro-islam.info/2010/08/02/cultural-and-social-affairs-department-oic-islamophobia-observatory-monthly-bulletin-%E2%80%93-july-2010/.

93. Andrea Elliott, "The Man behind the Anti-Shariah Movement," The New York Times, July 30, 2011, accessed October 22, 2012, http://www.nytimes. com/2011/07/31/us/31shariah.html?_r=1&adxnnl=1&pagewanted=all&adxnnl x=1325142029-MnrhdJvFojgkqHiVpO2aJA.

94. New York City Bar Association, "The Unconstitutionality of Oklahoma Referendum 755—The 'Save our State Amendment,'" December 2010, accessed October 22, 2012, http://www.nycbar.org/pdf/report/uploads/2007 2027-UnconstitutionalityofOklahomaReferendum755.pdf.

95. Ibid.

96. For more information visit http://www.ca10.uscourts.gov/opinions/10/10–6273.pdf.

97. Including: Georgia, Indiana, Iowa, Kansas, Kentucky, Michigan, Mississippi, Missouri, Nebraska, New Hampshire, New Jersey, New Mexico, North Carolina, Oklahoma, Pennsylvania, South Carolina, South Dakota, Virginia, and West Virginia.See, Bill Raftery, "Bans on court use of sharia", Gavel to Gavel, National Center for State Courts, February 7 2913, http://gaveltogavel.us/site/2013/02/13/bans-on-court-use-of-shariainternati onal-law-heavily-modified-bills-introduced-in-2013-exempts-contracts-nat ive-american-tribes-avoids-using-word-sharia/, accessed February 21 2013

98. Elliott, "Man Behind the Anti-Shariah Movement."

99. For more information on House Bill 88, visit http://www.legis.state.ak.us/ basis/get_bill_text.asp?hsid=HB0088A&session=27.

100. For more information on SB 676, visit http://www.senate.mo.gov/12info/ BTS_Web/Bill.aspx?SessionType=R&BillID=258830.

101. Elliott, "Man Behind the Anti-Shariah Movement."

102. J. C. Alexander, "Theorizing the 'Modes of Incorporation: Assimilation, Hyphenation, and Multiculturalism as Varieties of Civil Participation,'" *Sociological Theory* 19 (3) (2001): 237–249.

103. Jonathan van Selm, "The Netherlands: Tolerance Under Pressure." Migration Policy Institute. Washington, D.C., 2003, accessed February 26, 2012, available at https://politicalscience.stanford.edu/sites/default/files/attachments/ Hagendoorn_Tolerance2011.pdf.

104. See Parliamentary Inquiry Committee (Tijdelijke Commissie Onderzoek Integratiebeleid), 5 volumes (2004).

6　How Islam Questions
the Universalism of Western Secularism

1. "Oslo's Rooftop Religious Rivalry," *BBC News,* March 30, 2000, accessed February 16, 2012, http://news.bbc.co.uk/2/hi/europe/695725.stm.

2. Usually scholars apprehend secularity as the social and political conditions that influence the ways citizens adhere to religion (see Charles Taylor, *A Secular Age* (Cambridge: Harvard University Press, 2007)). My definition emphasizes equality before the law (of all religions) and neutrality of the State (vis-à-vis all religions) as major principles that can be implemented in different legal and political ways.

3. Gerhard Robbers, "State and Church in the European Union," in *State and Church in the European Union*, ed. Gerhard Robbers (Baden-Baden: Nomos, 2005): 54–72.

4. Joel S. Fetzer and J. Christopher Soper, "Explaining and Accommodation of Muslim Religious Practices in France, Britain and Germany," paper presented at the Muslims in Western Europe Politics Conference, Bloomington, Indiana, September 22–24, 2005 and Jonathan Laurence ed., *The Emancipation of Europe's Muslims: The State's Role in Minority Integration* (Princeton: Princeton University Press, 2012).

5. Joel S. Fetzer and J. Christopher Soper, *Muslims and the State in Britain, France, and Germany* (Cambridge: Cambridge University Press, 2004).

6. See "Taking Part, Muslim participation in contemporary governance", ibid.p 17

7. Bureaucratic leaders in Islam are leaders paid by or otherwise associated with the Islamic institutions of influential Muslim countries. In Europe, this influence was exerted throughout the 1960s via national associations or other secular groups. Since the 1980s, however, religious organizations have become the primary means of keeping control over expatriate Muslim populations. This influence is exerted by countries such as Algeria, Morocco, Turkey, and Saudi Arabia through associations like the World Islamic League. Paris, Madrid, Milan, Brussels, and Geneva are all home to large mosques controlled by the governments of Algeria, Morocco, or Saudi Arabia. The most recent of these is the mosque of Berlin, which opened in December 5, 2003. This mosque is run by the DITIB (Islamic Union of Turkish Religious Affairs), the religious arm of the Turkish State in Germany.

8. Mohamed Moussaoui's website is http://www.mosquee-lyon.org/spip/spip. php?article356. The organization's official websites is http://www.embnet.be/.

9. Elizabeth Sebia, "Islam in France," Euro-Islam.info, accessed January 31, 2012, http://www.euro-islam.info/country-profiles/france/.

10. Ibid.

11. Louise Ireland, "French Muslim Council Warns Government on Veil Ban," Reuters, June 4, 2010, accessed July 22, 2012, http://in.reuters.com/article/2010/06/04/idINIndia-49050320100604.

12. Tom Heneghan, "French Muslim Councils Warns Government on Veil Ban," Reuters, June 4, 2010, accessed July 23, 2012, http://www.reuters.com/article/2010/06/04/us-france-veil-muslims-idUSTRE6532TB20100604.

13. The reaction to the burqa ban from other representative bodies in Europe was not as conciliatory. In Belgium, a 2009 law made the niqab or any type

of face veil subject to penalties, ranging from fines to jail punishment up to seven days. "Belgium First to Ban Burqa and Niqab in Public Spaces," *Daily News Egypt*, April 2, 2010, accessed July 23, 2012, http://www.the-freelibrary.com/Belgium+first+to+ban+burqa+and+niqab+in+public+spaces.-a0222856604. üemsettin Uüurlu, president of the Muslim Executive of Belgium, says the ban goes against the right to freedom to practice religion in Belgium: "We are in a democratic country and every citizen is free to act." In the same vein, Isabelle Praile, the vice president of the Muslim Executive of Belgium, warned that the law could set a dangerous precedent. "Today it's the full-face veil, tomorrow the veil, the day after it will be Sikh turbans and then perhaps it will be mini skirts," she said. "The wearing of a full-face veil is part of the individual freedoms [protected by Belgian, European and international rights laws]." Additionally, Praile Stated, "Personally, I think this law is racist and sexist, because it is again a way to stigmatize Muslims and to maintain the idea that they are dangerous, that they are some extremists or terrorists." Martin Arnold, "Multicultural Europe Blamed for Cartoon Crisis," *Financial Times*, February 26, 2006, accessed July 23, 2012, http://www.ft.com/cms/s/0/58fa26fc-a5a3-11da-bf34-0000779e2340.html#axzz1yGPpcVxT.

14. Ibid.

15. Interview with Hamideh Mohagheghi, accessed July 23, 2012, http://www.zdf.de/ZDFmediathek/beitrag/video/1613954/Erloesung-im-Islam#/beitrag/video/1613954/Erloesung-im-Islam.

16. Ibid.

17. Ibid.

18. Charles Taylor, "Rethinking Secularism: Western Secularity," Immanent Frame, 2012, accessed February 14, 2012, http://blogs.ssrc.org/tif/2011/08/10/western-secularity/.

19. Ibid.

20. Ibid.

21. Robert Audi ed., *The Cambridge Dictionary of Philosophy* (Cambridge: Cambridge University Press, 1999), 89.

22. Tariq Madood, *Multicultural Politics: Racism, Ethnicity, and Muslims in Britain* (Minneapolis: University of Minnesota Press, 2005).

23. The buffered self was separated and protected from "a world of spirits and forces which [could] cross the boundary of the mind" as a result of the reformation. In short, this separation helped develop the sense that a society itself could reform as a whole if properly disciplined. In other words, the construction of the buffered self is still a work in progress, especially in a context where religious voices and orthodoxy are transnational.

24. Jürgen Habermas, Judith Butler, Charles Taylor, Cornel West, *The Power of Religion in the Public Sphere* (New York: Columbia University Press, 2011).

25. Gert Hekma, "Imams and Homosexuality: A Post-Gay Debate in the Netherlands," *Sexualities* 5 (2002): 237.

26. "Anger Grows Over Muhammad Cartoon," *BBC News*, February 2, 2006, accessed February 18, 2012, http://news.bbc.co.uk/2/hi/europe/4673908.stm.

27. Paul Marshall and Nina Shea, *Silence: How Apostasy and Blasphemy Codes are Choking Freedom Worldwide* (New York: Oxford University Press, 2011), 186.

28. Ibid., 186.

29. Ibid., 187.

30. Paul Delien, "Jihad against Danish Newspaper," *Brussels Journal*, accessed February 25, 2012, http://www.brusselsjournal.com/node/382.

31. Interestingly, at the time of the cartoons crisis, Muslim associations in Denmark tried to use blasphemy laws to promote Muslims' rights to respect. Jytte Klausen, *The Cartoons that Shook the World* (New Haven: Yale University Press, 2009), 49.

32. "Norway: Norway Criminalizes Blasphemy," Euro-Islam.info, accessed July 23, 2012, http://www.euro-islam.info/2006/02/27/norway-norway-criminalizes -blasphemy/.

33. Interestingly, despite the existence of legislation forbidding racism and xeno-phobia prior to the cartoons crisis, it is only through the 2006 Racial and Religious Hatred Act that Muslims in the United Kingdom are protected against offenses against their faith.

34. Louis Charbonneau, "Turkish Group Accuses German Paper of Insulting Islam," Worldwide Religious News, March 16, 2006, accessed July 23, 2012, http://wwrn.org/articles/20853/?&place=germany&section=islam.

35. Article 266b prohibits the dissemination of racist statements and propaganda. Decision on possible criminal proceedings in the case of Jyllands-Posten's article "The Face of Muhammed," Director of Public Prosecutions, March 15, 2006, accessed on March 25, 2010, http://www.rigsadvokaten.dk/media/bilag/ afgorelse_Engelsk.pdf.

36. Jonathan Turley, "Judge in 'Zombie Mohammed' Case (Reportedly) Responds," Jonathan Turley, February 26, 2012, accessed July 23, 2012, http://jonathanturley. org/2012/02/26/judge-in-zombie-mohammed-case-responds/.

37. In the same vein, Dominique Colas analyzes the fight between iconoclasts and the Catholic Church in the sixteenth century and observes elements relevant to the concerns raised by Asad. Colas asserts that state power was employed to violently crush movements that refused to accept the limita-tions placed upon their religious claims in the broader public realm. He clearly illustrates that the concept of tolerance in the "civil society" of the sixteenth century was not a neutral force. Those who refused to accept the limitations for social behavior and expression were labeled "fanatics" and harshly punished. "Fanaticism," as defined by Colas, is precisely this refusal to accept the duality of the public and private realms of the social order. The tension between civil authority and particular cultural and reli-gious norms of minority communities is the crucial issue at the heart of the debate over the definition of "secularism." In twenty-first–century Europe, it is important to understand the public sphere as not only a disembodied voice but also as a product of the media and state-mediated discourses.

38. "Shari'a Law 'Could Have UK Role,'" *BBC News,* July 4, 2008, accessed July 24, 2012, http://news.bbc.co.uk/2/hi/uk_news/7488790.stm.

39. It is worth mentioning that the claim by some political actors in Muslim-majority countries that divine law is comprehensive and, therefore, a source of constitutional law diverges from the traditional perception of politics in the Islamic tradition is based on the distinction of shari'a from *siya-sah* (politics).

40. Zsolt Nyiri, "Muslims in Europe: Basis for Greater Understanding Already Exists," Gallup Polling, 2007, accessed 12 January 2011, http://www.gallup. com/corporate/115/About-Gallup.aspx.

41. Jocelyne Cesari, *Muslims in the West After 9/11: Religion, Law and Politics* (New York: Routledge, 2010).

42. Andrea Buchler, *Islamic Law in Europe? Legal Pluralism and Its Limits in European Family Laws* (Burlington: Ashgate, 2011), 16–17.

43. Ibid., 19.

44. Ibid., 13. The right to freedom of thought, as promulgated in the European Convention on Human Rights, relates to convictions and modes of behavior that "are of crucial importance in determining personal identity."

45. In this sense, the attempt to ban the shari'a in some American States (as presented in chapter 5) does not relate to this situation but is directly inspired by the security issue.

46. Jennifer Selby and Anna C. Korteweg, *Debating Shari'a: Islam, Gender Politics and Family Law Arbitration* (University of Toronto Press, 2012), 23.

47. Family Statute Law Amendment, February 2005.

48. Selby and Korteweg, *Debating Shari'a,* 66–87.

49. Limping marriages define situations where the couple is divorced according to secular civil law but the religious divorce has not be finalized for multiple reasons. Most of the time it is because the husband misuses his privilege by refusing to grant talaq (divorce) to his wife. Sonia Shah-Kazemi, *Untying the Knot: Muslim Women, Divorce and the Shari'ah* (London: Nuffield Foundation, 2001).

50. Halima Boumidienne, "African Muslim Women in France," in *God's Law versus State Law,* ed. Michael King (London: Grey Seal, 1995), 49–61.

51. In the British context, Werner Menski calls these syncretic practices, "angrezi shari'a" (Urdu term that expresses the mix of Islamic and English legal references). See Werner Menski, "Muslim Law in Britain," *Journal of Asian and African Studies* 62 (September 30, 2001), 127–163.

52. Mary E. Hess, "2010 Presidential Address: Learning Religion and Religiously Learning Amid Global Cultural Flows," *Religious Education* 106(4) (2011): 360–377.

53. These are the four major schools of jurisprudence that have codified Islamic law across the Muslim world. With the emergence of nation-states, each country has adopted the dominant school of jurisprudence as the source for civil law while continuously reforming it. See Knut S. Vikor, *Between God and the Sultan: A History of Islamic Law* (New York: Oxford University Press, 2005).

54. The bill, which was in debate in the House of Lords at the time of this writing (February 2013), is aimed at ensuring that Sharia courts operate within the realms of British law. See http://www.strategicoutlook.org/europe/news-justifying-sharia-in-britain.html, accessed October 30, 2012.

55. Bob Mitchell, "Shameful, Horrible, Evil and Barbaric," *Star,* June 17, 2010, accessed July 23, 2010, http://www.thestar.com/news/gta/crime/article/824453 – shameful-horrible-evil-and-barbaric.

56. Mark Landler, "Germany Cites Koran in Rejecting Divorce," *The New York Times,* March 22, 2007, accessed July 23, 2012, http://www.nytimes.com/2007/03/22/world/europe/22cnd-germany.html?pagewanted=all.

57. Ibid.

58. "French Appeals Court Restores Marriage in Virginity Case," *The New York Times,* October 17, 2008, accessed July 23, 2012, http://www.nytimes.com/2008/11/17/world/europe/17iht-france.4.17897832.html.

59. An annulment can be justified on the basis of trumperies used by one of the co-contractors without bringing any moral judgment on the nature of the clause, which in this case was the virginity of the wife.

60. Ibid.

61. Jorgen S. Nielsen, *"Emerging Claims of Muslim Populations in Matters of Family Law in Europe* (Birmingham: Centre for the Study of Islam and Christian-Muslim Relations, 1993).

62. Maleiha Malik, *Discrimination Law: Theory and Practice* (London: Sweet and Maxwell, 2008).

63. Bryan S. Turner and Berna Zengin Arslan, *"Shari'a* and Legal Pluralism in the West," *European Journal of Social Theory* 14(2) (2011): 139–159.

64. Pierre Mercier, *Conflits De Civilisations et Droit International Prive: Polygamie et Repudiatio* (Genève: Droz, 1972) and Jean Deprez, *"Droit international prive et conflit de civilisations. Aspects méthodologiques. Les relations entre systèmes d'Europe Occidentale et systèmes islamiques en matière de statut personnel,"* Recueil des Cours de l'Académie de la Haye* 211 (1988): 9–372.

65. Martyn Brown, "Now Muslims Demand Full Shari'a Law," *Express,* October 15, 2009, accessed July 23, 20120, http://www.express.co.uk/posts/view/134080/Now-Muslims-demand-Give-us-full-Shari'a-law.

66. "Muslim Fundamentalist Group Launched in the Netherlands," Expatica, December 22, 2010, accessed July 23, 2010, http://www.euro-islam.info/2011/01/11/shari'a4holland-founded-in-the-netherlands/. In 2012, Belkacem, the leader of Shari'a4Belgium was sentenced in Antwerp to two years imprisonment for incitement of hatred towards non-Muslims. At the same time, the Moroccan government was seeking his extradition in connection to drug trade. He was arrested and sent to Morocco in June 2012. On October 7, 2012, Shari'a4Belgium announced on their website that their organization was being dissolved.

67. Dominique Colas, *Civil Society and Fanaticism: Conjoined Histories* (Stanford: Stanford University Press, 1997).

68. Riazat Butt, "European Court of Human Rights Rules Crucifixes are Allowed in State Schools," *The Guardian,* March 18, 2011, accessed February 16, 2012, http://www.guardian.co.uk/law/2011/mar/18/european-court-human-rights-crucifixes-allowed.

69. BBC News, "Italy School Crucifixes 'Barred,'" *BBC News,* November 3, 2009, accessed February 16, 2012, http://news.bbc.co.uk/2/hi/8340411.stm.

70. "Freedom of Religion and Religious Symbols in the Public Sphere (2011–60-E)," Parliament of Canada Web Site—Site Web Du Parlement Du Canada, accessed February 16, 2012, http://www.parl.gc.ca/content/LOP/ResearchPublications/2011-60-e.htm.

71. Talal Asad, *Genealogies of Religion: Discipline and Reasons of Power in Christianity and Islam* (Baltimore: The Johns Hopkins University Press, 1993).

72. Michael E. Connolly, *Why i Am Not a Secularist* (Minneapolis: Minnesota University Press, 2000).

73. Charles Hirshkind, "Is There a Secular Body?" Religion and Ethics, April 5, 2011, accessed July 23, 2010, http://www.abc.net.au/religion/articles/2011/04/04/3182083.htm.

74. Norbert Elias, *On the Process of Civilisation: Volume 3: Collect Works of Norbert Elias* (Dublin: University College Dublin Press, 2012) and Walter Ong,

Orality and Literacy: The Technologizing of the Word (New York: Routledge, 2002).

75. French *laïcité* is an example of secularism that particularly stresses the disjunction of religious beliefs and social practices as an important part of the private/public dichotomy.

76. Due to a decision of the German Supreme Court on July 30, 2003, wearing of headscarf cannot be a reason for dismissal, yet, in many cases, it is the reason for not getting a job at all. Teachers in particular suffer from this restriction. Fereshta Ludin is a young Muslim teacher of Afghan origin whose case stood at the center of a debate on Muslim teachers' right to dress according to Islamic principles in Baden-Württemberg in 2003. According to the Ministry of Cultural Affairs, the headscarf was at odds with basic Christian values and constitutional secularism alike. As a symbol of backward and fundamentalist Islamic attitudes, the ministry stated that the hijab opposed the principles of freedom of thought and the equality of the sexes in German society. The decision of the German Supreme Court in 2003 was followed by a, still continuing, very emotional discussion among politicians, journalists, and the wider public on the reasons why some young Muslim academics maintain a strong attachment to wearing a headscarf and to what extent they are indoctrinated by extremist organizations, and how far teachers at state schools should appear "neutral" while performing their jobs. As a consequence of this ongoing discussion, 7 of the 16 states' parliaments are preoccupied with the preparation of a "law against specific religious symbols that threaten to disrupt the political or religious concord in schools" or a "law against religious symbols with a demonstrative character" or a general "law against all religious signs worn or used by teachers in state schools."

77. Asad, *Genealogies of Religion.*

78. Grace Davies, "New Approaches in the Sociology of Religion: A Western Perspective," *Social Compass* 51(1) (2005): 79.

79. Danièle Hervieu-Léger, *Religion as a Chain of Memory* (New Brunswick, NJ: Rutgers University Press, 2000), 132.

80. Ibid.

81. Majed A. Ashy, "Health and Illness from an Islamic Perspective," *Journal of Religion and Health* 38(3) (1999): 256.

82. Ibid., 257.

83. See Jocelyne Cesari, *Understanding the Arab Awakening: Islam, Modernity and Democracy* (2013 forthcoming at Cambridge University Press).

7 Salafization of Islamic Norms and Its Influence on the Externalization of Islam

1. Dale Eickelman, "Mainstreaming Islam: Taking Charge of the Faith," *Encounters* (2) (2010): 185–203.

2. Traditionally, authority was conferred according to one's theological knowledge and mastery of the methodologies used to interpret this knowledge. Only those who possessed knowledge that had been passed down through a chain of authorities or a line of recognized masters could claim legitimacy as religious leaders. Though formal education was an important component throughout much of the Muslim world, the transmission of knowledge did

not always rely on formal education, especially if the knowledge being passed down was esoteric in nature (as was the case of the Sufi masters).

3. The Hizb ut-Tahrir party is one of the most significant contemporary pan-Islamist movements that still advocates for the restoration of the Caliphate. Founded in Jerusalem in 1953, it claims branches in the Muslim world as well as Europe and the United States. In Great Britain, the party is known under the name Muhajirrun and has been active in the public sphere, particularly before September 11. Suha Taji-Farouki, *A Fundamental Quest: Hizb al-Tahrir and the Search for the Islamic Caliphate* (London: Grey Seal, 1996).

4. The initial Salafi movement in the eighteenth and nineteenth centuries was reformist in nature and contrasts with the rigid and uncompromising nature of Wahhabism. The early movement is illustrated by progressive figures such as Mohammed Abduh (1849–1905), Sayyid Jamal ad-Din al-Afghani (1838–1897), Rashid Rida (1865–1935), and Muhammad al-Shawakani (1759–1834). Their goal was to adapt ideas, laws, and institutions from the West without destroying their Islamic roots. The importance and centrality of the Islamic texts was emphasized, but they also insisted on reforming interpretation.

5. "Movements that were conceived as movements of 'renewal' were in fact more a part of the ongoing processes of Islamization of societies on the frontiers of the Islamic world. They were, in effect, part of the 'formation' of the Islamic societies rather than the 'reformation' of existing ones." John Obert Voll, "Foundations for Renewal and Reform: Islamic Movements in the Eighteenth and Nineteenth Centuries," in *The Oxford History of Islam*, ed. John L. Esposito (Oxford: Oxford University Press, 1999), 516–517.

6. John L. Esposito, *Islam: The Straight Path* (New York: Oxford University Press, 1998), 117–118.

7. The modernist and pro-Western reformism of early Salafism has been marginalized in postcolonial Muslim countries. Most Islamic reformist movements became anti-Western for two reasons, with one more readily apparent and the other more subtle. First, Western policies during colonial and postcolonial periods have supported secular, authoritarian regimes, from the Shah in Iran to Sadat and Mubarak in Egypt, while simultaneously unquestioningly backing Israel. This has resulted in Muslims associating the West with despotic, anti-Islam regimes. The second, less obvious, explanation is tied to domestic developments in Muslim nations, in which state actions have reduced the influence of Islam in social life and have disempowered Muslim clerics and religious authorities. States began to absorb and cast their influence on traditional Islamic authorities and co-opt Islamic organizations. Therefore, these religious leaders who put their Islamic expertise to the service of oppressive regimes were delegitimized in the eyes of their populations. In some ways, the Muslim Brotherhood movement has a connection to the original *salafiyya* by maintaining a contextualized and modernist interpretation of Islam.

8. Abou El Fadl, *The Great Theft: Wrestling Islam from the Extremists* (San Francisco: Harper, 2005), 73–74.

9. "Inside the Kingdom," *Time*, September 15, 2003, accessed July 25, 2012, http://www.time.com/time/magazine/article/0,9171,1005663,00.html.

10. Ibid.

11. Alexander Alexiev, "Wahhabism: State-Sponsored Extremism Worldwide," testimony before the US Senate Subcommittee on Terrorism, Technology

and Homeland Security, June 26, 2003, accessed July 25, 2012, http://kyl.sen-ate.gov/legis_center/subdocs/sc062603_alexiev.pdf.

12. Rachel Bronson, *Thicker than Oil: America's Uneasy Partnership with Saudi Arabia* (New York: Oxford University, 2006), 10. According to its website, the King Fahd Foundation has wholly or partially funded 30 such projects in Africa, 6 in South America, 23 in Asia, 6 in Australia and Oceania, 12 in Europe, and 22 in North America. (The website is http://www.kingfahdbinabdulaziz.com/main/m400.htm).

13. In addition to funds coming straight from the Saudi government, the Kingdom also supports proxy organizations that spread Wahhabism. A notable organization that depends on Saudi funding is the Muslim World League (MWL, Rabitat al-'Alam al-Islami). Today, the MWL oversees a number of nongovernmental organizations such as the International Islamic Relief Organization (IIRO), the World Assembly of Muslim Youth (WAMY), the Holy Qur'an Memorization International Organization, the International Islamic Organization for Education, Makkah Al-Mukarramah Charity Foundation for Orphans, the Commission on Scientific Signs in the Qur'an and Sunnah, World Supreme Council for Mosques, and Fiqh (Islamic Jurisprudence) Council. Although to the outside world they strongly empha-size their strong humanitarian aims (providing relief, assisting orphans, etc.), these organizations are often focused on propagating a Salafist interpretation of Islam. Many, including the IIRO and the WAMY concentrate on setting up and supporting mosque centers with an orthodox persuasion, as well as hiring, training, and subsidizing imams with Salafi/Wahhabi orientation, and publishing and disseminating Salafist literature.

14. The main website is http://www.kingfahdbinabdulaziz.com/main/m600.htm.

15. A cloth covering the face according to Wahhabi law.

16. Another group, albeit with much less financial resources, that takes a tradi-tionalist and legalistic approach to Islam is the Tabligh, sometimes referred to as the Jehovah's Witnesses of Islam. The Tabligh is usually described as a pious and proselytizing movement whose primary aim is to promote Islamic education. The essential principle of this sect within the Deobandi movement—founded in 1927 in India—is that every Muslim is responsible for spreading the values and practices of Islam. In the last two decades, this movement has gained a wide following, especially in Europe and the United States. In these conditions, competition rages in the West between Tablighis and Salafis, and anathemas rain down on both sides.

17. There are Muslim Brotherhood groups that are very active at the grass-roots level and in creating Muslim organizations to cooperate with politi-cal institutions (see Brigitte Marechal, *Les Freres Musulmans en Europe: Racines et Discours* (Muslim Brothers in Europe: Roots and Discourses) (Leuvenm: BRILL, 2008)). There are religious authorities related to some Muslim countries (Morocco, Algeria, and Turkey) who propagate a tradi-tional interpretation of Islam. Finally, there is a proliferation of indepen-dent authorities: scholars (Tariq Ramadan, Professor of Islamic Studies at Oxford University and known for his reformist thinking), social activists (Hamza Yusuf, director of the Zeytuna Institute in San Francisco), and more traditional authorities (Cheikh Qaradawi, who became global with his show on Al Jazeera called *Al Sharia wal Hayat* (Sharia and Life)). For a

typology of the different religious leaders operating in Europe and in the United States, see J. Cesari, *When Islam and Democracy Meet* (New York: Palgrave, 2006).

18. See the website http://islamopediaonline.org/.

19. Khaled M. Abou El Fadl, *And God Knows the Soldiers: The Authoritarian and Authoritative in the Islamic Tradition* (Lanham, MD: University Press of America, 2001), 125.

20. M. M. Bakhtin, *The Dialogic Imagination: Four Essays*, ed. Michael Holquist and trans. Caryl Emerson and Michael Holquist (Austin and London: University of Texas Press, 1981), 15.

21. "A distinction must be introduced here regarding the status of women in the Tabligh. Because married women are allowed to do missionary work, they get an intense Islamic education and can be taken away from the family circle and their conjugal duties. A dissonance is thus created between the theoretical vision of the ideal woman and the reality of women within Tabligh. In other words, one consequence of women's participation in Tabligh is to modernize, in a certain fashion, the condition of women and to make women more autonomous — in spite of the extremely conservative discourse on the role of the Muslim woman which dominates Tabligh." R. Collsaet, *Jihadi Terrorism and the Radicalisation Challenge in Europe* (Burlington, VT : Ashgate, 2008), 102.

22. Khaled M. Abou El Fadl, *God Knows the Soldiers.*

23. See Saleh Fawzan, "Declaration of the Negative Consequences of Women Working Outside Their Home," accessed July 30, 2012, http://www.alfawzan.ws/node/13377.

24. See "Gravity of Mixity for the Muslim Woman, Khotba Sermon of June 2011," accessed July 30, 2012, http://www.alfawzan.ws/node/13358.

25. See "Fatwa of Cheikh al Maghrawi on the Legitimacy of Hijab, " accessed July 30, 2012, http://www.maghrawi.net/?taraf=fatawi&file=displayfatawi&id=48&kalima=%C7%E1%E4%D3%C7%C1.

26. Ibid.

27. Ibid.

28. Ibid.

29. IslamQA, "Is It Permissible for a Women to Travel in an Elevator Alone with a Non-Mahram Man?," accessed July 15, 2012, http://islamqa.info/en/ref/71237.

30. See http://www.binbaz.co.uk/.

31. See http://www.maghrawi.net/?taraf=fatawi&file=displayfatawi&id=102&kalima=%C7%E1%DB%D1%C8.

32. See http://www.fatwaislam.com.

33. See http://www.binbaz.org.sa/mat/21293.

34. Salafipublications.com, "Living in Society: on Interaction with Non-Muslims," accessed July 25, 2012, http://salafipublications.com/sps/sp.cfm?secID=LSC&subsecID=LSC01&loadpage=displaysubsection.cfm.

35. See "Fatwa of Sheikh Bin Baz on the Permissibility of Social Relations with Shia," accessed July 30, 2012, http://www.binbaz.org.sa/mat/4173.

36. See "Fatwa on the Permissibility of Eating Meat Slaughtered by Shia," accessed July 30, 2012, http://www.salafvoice.com/article.php?a=5001.

37. See "Fatwa on the Fact that Shaking Hands with a Christian or a Jew Invalidates Ablution," accessed July 30, 2012, http://www.binbaz.org.sa/mat/2261.

38. IslamQA, "Is It Permissible to Swear Allegiance to a Kaafir Ruler?," accessed July 27, 2012, http://islamqa.com/en/ref/82681/Kaafir.

39. Ibid.

40. "Ahmed Salam also has no objection to political participation by Muslims in the Netherlands. The precondition is that 'this promotes the interests of Muslims' and 'the party program does not sow hatred.' Salam believes that Muslims' participation in politics will greatly improve their position. Jneid's and Salam's viewpoints are noteworthy because—as we saw in chapter one—the salafist doctrine rejects the concept of democracy." See "Salafism in the Netherlands," Nationaal Coordinator Terrorismebestijding, accessed July 25, 2012, http://www.nefafoundation.org/file/FeaturedDocs/NCTB_SalafismNetherlands0708.pdf, 46.

41. G. Starrett, "The Political Economy of Religious Commodities in Cairo," *American Anthropologist* 97(1) (1995): 51–68 and Johanna Pink, ed., *Muslim Societies in the Age of Mass Consumption* (Cambridge: Cambridge Scholars, 2009).

42. V. Miller, *Consuming Religion: Christian Faith and Practice in a Consumer Culture* (New York: Continuum International, 2005).

Conclusion

1. David Theo Goldberg, "Racial Europeanization," *Ethnic and Racial Studies* 29(2) (2006): 346 (331–364).

2. Alana Lentin and Gavin Titley, "The Crisis of 'Multiculturalism' in Europe: Mediated Minarets, Intolerable Subjects," *European Journal of Cultural Studies* 15(2) (April 2012): 123–138.

3. In the United States, "the prototypical immigrant is a low-skilled Mexican or Central American worker rather than a conservative Muslim. Of the 15.5 million legal immigrants who entered the United States between 1989 and 2004, only 1.2 million were from predominantly Muslim countries. There was a sharp drop from more than 100,000 per year prior to 2002 down to approximately 60,000 in 2003, but this recovered somewhat to 90,000 in 2004. Immigration in the United States is thus a topic in which the issues of Islam and terrorism are at best marginal issues." US Office of Immigration Statistics, 2004 Yearbook of Immigration Statistics 2004, (January 2006), 13, accessed October 27, 2012, http://www.dhs.gov/xlibrary/assets/statistics/yearbook/2004/Yearbook2004.pdf and Jocelyne Cesari, "Securitization and Religious Divides in Europe: Muslims in Western Europe After 9/11," GSRL-Paris and Harvard University, June 1, 2006.

4. Ian Buruma, "Europe's Turn to the Right," *Nation,* August 10, 2011, accessed July 27, 2012, http://www.thenation.com/article/162698/europes-turn-right.

5. Abu-Laban, Yasmeen. "Good Muslim versus Bad Muslim: The Class of Essentialisms." *Citizenship Studies* 6 (4) (2002): 459–482.

6. Mahmood Mamdani, *Good Muslim, Bad Muslim: America, the Cold War, and the Roots of Terror* (New York: Three Leaves, 2005), 24.

7. Interestingly some Muslim spokespeople are the most active advocates of this dichotomy. As members of the incriminated minority, they can voice criticisms that would seem unduly harsh or politically incorrect coming from the

majority groups. Probably the most representative figure of the good Muslims is Ayaan Hirsi Ali, who is mentioned in several chapters of this book.

8. "State Multiculturalism Has Failed, Says David Cameron," *BBC News,* February 5, 2011, accessed July 27, 2012, http://www.bbc.co.uk/news/uk-politics-12371994.

9. Martha Nussbaum, *The New Religious Intolerance, Overcoming the Politics of Fear in an Anxious Age* (Cambridge: Belknap Press of Harvard University, 2012).

10. Harris Beider, *Race, Housing & Community: Perspectives on Policy and Practice* (Hoboken, NJ: Wiely-Blackwell, 2012), 46.

11. Arun Kundani, "Multiculturalism and Its Discontents: Left, Right and Liberal," *European Journal of Cultural Studies* 15(2) (2012): 159; P. Toynbee, "Why Trevor Is Right," *The Guardian,* April 7, 2004, accessed April 8, 2004, http://www.guardian.co.uk/politics/2004/apr/07/society.immigration; and H. Young, "A Corrosive National Danger in Our Multicultural Model," *The Guardian,* November 6, 2001, accessed November 10, 2001, http://www.guardian.co.uk/world/2001/nov/06/september11.politics.

12. See Taking Part, ibid.

13. Arun Kundnani, *Spooked: How Not to Prevent Violent Extremism* (London: Institute of Race Relations, 2009).

14. Ibid., 6 and Kundani, "Multiculturalism and Its Discontents," 159.

15. Stephen Biggs, "The Monist," Liberalism, Feminism, and Group Rights, accessed July 25, 2012, http://www.readperiodicals.com/201201/2600287491.html#b.

16. Jasmine Zine, "Between Orientalism and Fundamentalism: The Politics of Muslim Women's Feminist Engagement," *Muslim World Journal of Human Rights* 3(1) (2006).

17. Danielle Celermajer, "If Islam Is Our Other, Who Are 'We'?" *Australian Journal of Social Issues* 42(1) (2007): 111.

18. Talal Asad, *Genealogies of Religion: Discipline and Reasons of Power in Christianity and Islam* (Baltimore: The Johns Hopkins University Press, 1993).

19. For an analysis of the disciplinization of Judaism in the secular European context, see Leora Faye Batnitzky, *How Judaism Became a Religion: An Introduction to Modern Jewish Thought* (Princeton, NJ: Princeton University Press, 2011).

20. Celermajer, "If Islam Is Our Other, Who Are 'We'?," 111.

21. Ibid., 113.

22. "Missed Opportunity for a Greater Inclusion of Islam in the United States," Islamopedia Online, March 17, 2011, accessed July 25, 2012, http://islamopedi-aonline.org/blog/missed-opportunity-greater-inclusion-islam-united-states.

Appendix 7   Trends of Formal Political Participation

1. Among Muslim respondents in the Gallup (2011) survey, 63 percent of low engagers were between 18 and 29 years of age. In the general sample, 37 percent of those categorized as low engagers were between 18 and 29 years of age. Such trends were of particular interest because Muslim Americans were disproportionately younger than other religious groups, which may account for the lower levels of Muslim political participation more generally in this survey. However, the amount of young people asked about their

political behavior was not equal to the amount of young people surveyed in total.

Appendix 8   European Representative Bodies of Islam

1. *"Conseil Francais du Culte Musulman,"* Journal-Officiel.Gov.Fr: Consulter Les Annonces Du JO Association. http://www.journal-officiel.gouv.fr/association/index.php?ACTION=Rechercher.

Appendix 10   Major Wanabi Organizations in Europe

1. See Reinhard Schulze and Gabriele Tecchiato, "Muslim World League," in The *Oxford Encyclopedia of the Islamic World*. *Oxford Islamic Studies Online*, accessed September 22, 2011, http://www.oxfordislamicstudies.com/article/opr/t236/e0570; "Muslim Networks and Movements in Western Europe," *Pew*, September 15, 2010, accessed July 25, 2012, http://pewforum.org/Muslim/Muslim-Networks-and-Movements-in-Western-Europe-Muslim-World-League-and-World-Assembly-of-Muslim-Youth.aspx; and Reinhard Schulze, *Islamischer Internationalismus im 20. Jahrhundert: Untersuchungen zur Geschichte der Islamischen Weltliga* (Leiden: Brill, 1990).
2. "Prince Salman Patronizes the Joint Charitable Party and Donates SR 1,5 Million," Ain-Al-Yaqeen, accessed July 25, 2012, http://www.ainalyaqeen.com/issues/20001208/feat5en.htm.
3. Rabitat al-Alam al-Islami, The Muslim World League, accessed February 23, 2013, http://muslimworldalmanac.com/ver3/index2.php?option=com_content&do_pdf=1&id=123.

Appendix 11   Salafis in Europe

1. J. Groen and A. Kranenberg, *"Salafisme: Compromisloos en rechtlijnig, maar 'niet gevaarlijk'"* (Salafism: Uncompromising and Rigidly Straightforward, but 'Not Dangerous'), De Volkskrant, July 5, 2005.
2. Ministerie von Binnenlandse Zaken en Koninkrijksrelaties, "Salafism in the Netherlands: A Passing Phenomenon or a Persistent Factor of Significance?," accessed July 25, 2012, http://www.nefafoundation.org/file/FeaturedDocs/NCTB_SalafismNetherlands0708.pdf, 65.
3. Ibid., 34.
4. Ibid., 43.
5. M. Adraoui, "Purist Salafism in France," *ISIM Review* 21 (Spring 2008): 1.
6. Ibid., 13.
7. Ibid.
8. M. Adraoui, "Salafism in France: Ideology, Practices and Contradictions," in Global Salafism: Islam's New Religious Movement, ed. Roel Mejjer (New York: Columbia University Press, 2009), 371.
9. The website http://www.jimas.org/ gives a description of their organization and has material on their opinions as well as upcoming community events.

10. S. Gillat-Ray, *Muslims in Britain: An Introduction* (New York: Cambridge University Press): 81.

11. Salafipublications.com (http://www.salafipublications.com/sps/) hosts a searchable database of written and audio scholarly opinions located on the site or linked to others with similar information. Topics covered include hadith literature, *salafiyyah, tawhid,* marriage and family, Islam for children, and so on. Salafitak.net serves mostly as a discussion forum for *hadeedah, manhaj, ibaadah, tazjutagm fiqh,* sects, innovation, and so on. Salaf.imanhaj.com also has a database of ebooks, audio, and articles discussing Salafi interpretations on Islamic issues. Albani.co.uk is yet another website formatted as database with articles and opinions, albeit specifically those of Shaikh al-Albani. Rabee.co.uk is similar except all the opinions expressed are from Rabee bin Haadee al-Madkhali. Fawzan.co.uk is just like the previous two websites expect the information is from Shaykh Saalih al-Fawzaan. FatwaIslam.com is another database focused specifically on Islamic *fatwas* that can be located by a general search or by browsing different sections on purification, prayer, fasting, charity, pilgrimage, and so on. Fatwa-online has a searchable database of *fatwas* as well as tools to facilitate Islamic education (links to learn how to read and write Arabic, etc.). Islamqa. com is another searchable *fatwa* database with commonly asked questions and several language options (English, Indonesia, Turkish, Russian, Hindi, etc.). Themadkhalis.com has information primarily on Shaykh Rabee bin Haadee al-Madkhali but also has sections on Sayyid Qutb and Hasan al-Banna.

12. The website http://salafitalk.net/st/ is a discussion forum of Salafi opinions of Islamic issues.

13. The website http://salafimanhaj.com/ is a searchable database for Salafi opinions of Islamic issues.

14. S. Hamid, "The Attraction of 'Authentic Islam': Salafism and British Muslim Youth," in *Global Salafism: Islam's New Religious Movement*, ed. Roel Mejjer (New York: Columbia University Press, 2009): 394.

15. Ibid.

16. His website is http://sandala.org/. Hamza Yusuf is the cofounder of the Zaytuna College in Berkeley, a school for educating Islamic spiritual leaders. He promotes classical learning in Islamic and teaching methodologies. In addition to being an advocate for social justice, he has been involved in several organizations that have focused on reviving Islamic studies in the West (http://sandala.org/about/hamzayusuf/).

17. Also known as Timothy John Winter (b. 1960), he is a Sufi specialist and professor of Islamic Studies at Cambridge. Not only is he a scholar of Islam and author of the eight-tape lecture series called *Understanding Islam,* but, like Hamza Yusuf, he also supports the learning of "traditional" Islam (http://www.welcome-back.org/profile/winter.shtml).

18. A convert to Islam and previous student of Al-Azhar, he is an American convert who is based in Jordan. His work concerns Islamic law and tenets of faith and supports the learning of "traditional" Islam; for more information see http://www.masud.co.uk/ISLAM/nuh/.

19. The website http://www.eltawheed.nl/ publishes the periodical *Maandblad El Tawheed* (El-Tawheed Monthly) in order to further spread its message.

20. See the website http://www.al-yaqeen.com/, a discussion forum as well as database of available *fatwas* are given on a variety of topics.

21. See http://www.al-yaqeen.com/.
22. They maintain the websites www.al-basair.com and www.isook.nl, which are not online at the time of this writing.
23. As mentioned above, neither site is online at the time of this writing.
24. Ministerie von Binnenlandse Zaken en Koninkrijksrelaties, "Salafism in the Netherlands," 31.
25. Ibid.
26. A *madrasa* focused on teaching Salafism in Dammaj, Yemen. It was founded by Muqbil bin Haadi al-Waadi'ee (d. 2001), a Sunni Muslim scholar. Thousands have studied here from all over the Muslim and Western world. See http://igitur-archive.library.uu.nl/dissertations/2006–0705–200332/c3.pdf.
27. This center is for Islamic research and methodological studies. There is strong importance placed on the spread of knowledge to non-Muslims and purification of beliefs for Muslims. See http://www.sounnah.free.fr/dawah_centreala-lbani.htm.
28. S. Amghar, "Salafism and Radicalisation of Young European Muslims," in *European Islam* (Brussels: Centre for European Policy Studies, 2007): 45–46.
29. See the main website http://www.greenlanemasjid.org/. Founded in 1979, they deliver weekly lectures, facilities for women (workshops and classes), evening *madrassah*, charitable services, Islamic Q&A, community outreach, and so on.
30. See the website http://www.brixtonmasjid.co.uk/. Established in 1990 for congregational prayers, the center has an array of Muslim attendees. It offers informational and educational services and activities to the community, youth, and women.
31. Founded in 1984, under the Manwar Ali (Abu Muntasir), it describes itself as a charitable organization on its website. Abu Muntasir studied in the United Kingdom and obtained an MA in Islamic Studies from London University. He is currently the chief executive of JIMAS.
32. He has a degree in computer science from the University of London and resides in the United Kingdom, where he continues to serve as the head of JIMAS. See the website, accessed April 15, 2012, http://www.jimas.org/manwar.htm.
33. See the website http://www.hizb.org.uk/hizb/index.php.
34. Ministerie von Binnenlandse Zaken en Koninkrijksrelaties, "Salafism in the Netherlands," 55.
35. Al-Maqdisi is a Jordanian-Palestinian jihadi theorist involved in the *Tawhed* jihadist website (http://tawhed.ws/). He is currently in the custody of the Jordanian government. He was considered a mentor to Abu Musab al-Zarqawi (d. 2006, killed by American troops in a targeted killing in Iraq), a Jordanian national who became the leader of al-Qaeda in Iraq.
36. B. de Graaf, "The Nexus between Salafism and Jihadism," Combating Terrorism Center Sentinel, March 3, 2010, accessed October 29, 2012, http://www.ctc.usma.edu/posts/the-nexus-between-salafism-and-jihadism-in-the-netherlands.
37. According to "Salafism in the Netherlands" (see note 34 Boyeri was a second-generation Moroccan who attended the El-Tawheed Mosque, where he supposedly became radicalized.

38. A Somali-born Dutch politician and writer, who wrote the scenario of the film *Submission* and gained great attention for her virulent critique of Islam as a misogynistic and backward religion.

39. E. Vermaat, "Terror on Trial in the Netherlands," Assyrian International News Agency, December 12, 2005, accessed October 29, 2012, http://www.aina.org/news/20051212121618.htm.

40. Ministerie von Binnenlandse Zaken en Koninkrijksrelaties, "Salafism in the Netherlands," 55 and Ministerie von Binnenlandse Zaken en Koninkrijksrelaties, "Jihadis and the Internet," accessed July 25, 2012, http://www.investigativeproject.org/documents/testimony/226.pdf, 65. The latter gives the following as examples of these groups: De Basis, De Basis2, MuwahhidinDeWareMoslims, ElKhatab, Al-Ansaar, Shareeah, 5434, Taheedwaljihad, Tawheedwalqital, lnoeken, and Ahloetawheed.

41. B. Thiolay, "Si certaines veulent porter le niqab, pourquoi les empêcher?," *L'Express*, January 21, 2012, accessed July 25, 2012, http://www.lexpress.fr/actualite/societe/si-certaines-veulent-porter-le-niqab-pourquoi-les-empecher_843642.html.

42. J. Sunderland, "In the Name of Prevention: Insufficient Safeguards in National Security," *Human Rights Watch* 19(3) (2007): 56.

43. "French Eject Pro-Beating Imam," *BBC*, April 21, 2004, accessed October 29, 2012, http://news.bbc.co.uk/2/hi/europe/3645145.stm.

44. "Mohamed Mehra: Toulouse Gunman's Father 'To Sue France,'" *BBC*, March 28, 2012, accessed October 29, 2012, http://www.bbc.co.uk/news/world-europe-17544154.

45. B. Riedel, "Mohamed Mehra, Who Killed 7 in France, Embodied al Qaeda's Lone Jihadist Campaign," *Daily Beast,* April 2, 2012, accessed October 29, 2012, http://www.thedailybeast.com/articles/2012/04/02/mohamed-merah-who-killed-7-in-france-embodied-al-qaeda-s-lone-jihadist-campaign.html.

46. Prior to his deportation in April 2012, Algerian imam Ali Belhadad had resumed contact with Islamic activists, which caused police to deport him. See J. Leclerc and C. Cornevin, "Prêcheurs expulsés: les mots de la haine," *LeFigaro,* April 3, 2012, accessed October 29, 2012, http://www.lefigaro.fr/actua lite-france/2012/04/02/01016-20120402ARTFIG00655-precheurs-expulses-l es-mots-de-la-haine.php and "France Launches Raids to Arrest 10 Suspected Islamist Militants," *Telegraph,* April 4, 2012, accessed October 29, 2012, http://www.telegraph.co.uk/news/worldnews/europe/france/9185023/France-launch es-raids-to-arrest-10-suspected-Islamist-suspects.html.

47. Almany Baradji, deported back to Mali in April 2012, has called Jews *kuffar* and stated that because of certain verses in the Qur'an hatred against Jews is legitimate. See Leclerc and Cornevin, "Prêcheurs expulsés."

48. Tunisian imam Malek Drine, who is scheduled to be deported, said, "The *shari'a* authorizes the murder of the brothers who turn away from Islam." See Leclerc and Cornevin, "Prêcheurs expulsés."

49. Yusuf Yuksel is a Turkish imam who is scheduled to be deported. In 2001, he called French authorities pro-Israeli and said that they attempt to enslave Islam. See Leclerc and Cornevin, "Prêcheurs expulsés."

50. "France Expels Radical Islamists after Merah Killings," *BBC*, April 2, 2012, accessed on October 29, 2012, http://www.bbc.co.uk/news/world-europe-17592569; S. Vandoorne, "France Arrests 10 Suspected Islamists

in Fresh Raids," *CNN*, April 4, 2012, accessed October 29, 2012, http://edition.cnn.com/2012/04/04/world/europe/france-arrests/; "Islamists Arrested in France Planned Kidnappings, Police Say," AFP, April 3, 2012, accessed October 29, 2012,http://ejpress.org/article/57228; and S. Heffer, "As France Summarily Kicks Out Two Extremists, What Dave Can Learn from the Ruthless and Savvy Sarko," MailOnline, April 4, 2012, accessed October 29, 2012, http://www.dailymail.co.uk/debate/article-2125286/As-France-summaril y-kicks-extremists-Dave-learn-ruthless-savvy-Sarko.html.

51. "France Launches," *Telegraph*.
52. Forsane-Alizza (Knights of Pride) was founded in 2010 by Mohammed Achamlane, a French Muslim in his 30s living in the Loire-Atlantique. The group was disassembled by French authorities in January, 2012.Mohamed Achamlane, the leader of the organization, was arrested. See J. Phelan, "French Islamist Group Forsane Alizza 'Planned to Kidnap Jewish Judge,'" GlobalPost, April 3, 2012, accessed October 29, 2012, http://www.globalpost. com/dispatch/news/regions/europe/france/120403/french-islamist-forsane-ali zza-kidnap-jewish-judge.
53. "Hate Preaching Cleric Jailed," *BBC,* March 7, 2003, accessed April 14, 2012, http://news.bbc.co.uk/2/hi/uk_news/england/2829059.stm.
54. R. Norton-Taylor, "Why Is Abu Qatada Not on Trial?" *The Guardian,* February 14, 2012, accessed April 14, 2012, http://www.guardian.co.uk/ commentisfree/2012/feb/14/abu-qatada-not-on-trial.
55. R. Booth, "Abu Qatada: Spiritual Leader for Deadly Islamist Groups?," *The Guardian*, February 7, 2012, accessed April 14, 2012, http://www.guardian. co.uk/world/2012/feb/07/abu-qatada-spiritual-leader-islamist.

BIBLIOGRAPHY

"1.277 familias de Cataluña pidieron clases de religión islámica sin obtenerlas." El País, June 9, 2003. Accessed October 22, 2012, http://elpais.com/diario/2003/06/09/ catalunya/1055120838_850215.html.

"A Certain Distance to Islam." Qantara.ed, April 4, 2012. Accessed July 25, 2012,

"A Lyon, débat sur les motifs de l'expulsion d'Abdelkader Bouziane." Le Monde, July 1, 2005.

Abou El Fadl, Khaled. *And God Knows the Soldiers: The Authoritarian and Authoritative in the Islamic Tradition*. Lanham, MD: University Press of America, 2001.

———. *The Great Theft: Wrestling Islam from the Extremists*. Harper San Francisco, 2005.

Abu Khalil, Asad, and Mahmoud Haddad. "Revival and Renewal." In *The Oxford Encyclopedia of the Islamic World*, Oxford Islamic Studies Online. Accessed November 7, 2011, http://www.oxfordislamicstudies.com/article/opr/t236/e0682.

Abu-Rabi', Ibrahim M. "Acebes acusa al ministro del Interior de miserable, indecente, mediocre e incompetente." El País, April 29, 2004.

———. "Ad campaign launched in London to improve the image of Islam." Free Thinker, June 21, 2010. Accessed January 31, 2012, http://freethinker.co.uk/2010/06/21/ad-campaign-launched-in-london-to-improve-the-image-of-islam/.

———. *Contemporary Arab Thought: Studies in Post-1967 Arab Intellectual History*. London: Pluto, 2004.

Ajala, I. "The Muslim Vote and Muslim Lobby in France: Myths and Realities." *Journal of Islamic Law and Culture* 12 (2) (2010): 77–91.

Alamut, Hofert, and Armando Salvatore, eds. *Between Europe and Islam*. Brussels: P.I.E. Peter Lang, 2000.

Alexander, J. C. "Citizen and Enemy as Symbolic Classification: On the Polarizing Discourse of Civil Society." In *Cultivating Differences: Symbolic Boundaries and the Making of Inequality*, edited by M. Fournier and M. Lamont. Chicago, University of Chicago Press, 1993, 289–308.

———. "Theorizing the Modes of Incorporation: Assimilation, Hyphenation, and Multiculturalism as Varieties of Civil Participation." *Sociological Theory* 19 (3) (2001): 237–249.

Alexander, J. C, and Smith, P. "The Discourse of American Civil Society: A New Proposal for Cultural Studies." *Theory and Society* 22 (1993): 151–207.

Alexander, Jeffery. *The Meanings of Social Life: A Cultural Sociology*. Oxford: Oxford University Press, 2003.

Allen, Christopher. *Islamophobia*. Farnham: Ashgate, 2010.

Amara, Fadela. "Anger Grows over Muhammad Cartoon." *BBC News*, February 2, 2006. Accessed February 18, 2012, http://news.bbc.co.uk/2/hi/europe/4673 908.stm.

Amara, Fadela. "Are Women's Rights Really the Issue?" Spiegel International, June 24, 2012. Accessed February 18, 2012, http://www.spiegel.de/international/europe/the-burqa-debate-are-women-s-rights-really-the-issue-a-702668.html.

———. *Ni Putes Ni Soumises*. Paris: La Découverte, 2003.

Arnold, Martin. "Multicultural Europe Blamed for Cartoon Crisis." *Financial Times*, February 26, 2006. Accessed July 23, 2012, http://www.ft.com/cms/s/0/58fa26fc-a5a3-11da-bf34-0000779e2340.html#axzz1yGPpcVxT.

Asad, Talal. *Genealogies of Religion: Discipline and Reasons of Power in Christianity and Islam* Baltimore: John Hopkins University Press, 1993.

———. "Secularism, Nation-State, Religion." In *Formations of the Secular: Christianity, Islam Modernity*, edited by Talal Asad. Stanford: Stanford University Press, 2003, 181–204.

Asens, Jaume. "Respuesta a la consejera Montserrat Tura." El País, January 24, 2006. Accessed July 25, 2012, http://elpais.com/diario/2006/01/24/catalunya/1138068442_850215.html.

Ashy, Majed A. "Health and Illness from an Islamic Perspective." *Journal of Religion and Health* 38 (3) (1999).

Audi, Robert, ed. *The Cambridge Dictionary of Philosophy*. Cambridge: Cambridge University Press, 1999.

Aznar, J. M. "Backgrounder: Stop Islamization of America (SIOA)." Anti-Defamation League, March 25, 2011. Accessed March 20, 2012, http://www.adl.org/main_Extremism/sioa.htm.

———. "Seven Theses on Today's Terrorism." Georgetown University, September 21, 2004. Accessed July 25, 2012, http://www3.georgetown.edu/president/aznar/inauguraladdress.html.

Bakhtin, M. M. *The Dialogic Imagination: Four Essays*, edited by Michael Holquist and translated by Caryl Emerson and Michael Holquist. Austin and London: University of Texas Press, 1981.

Bamforth, Nicholas, Maleiha Malik, and Colm O'Cinneide. *Discrimination Law: Theory and Context, Text and Materials*. London: Sweet and Maxwell, 2008.

Barkan, Elazar. *The Retreat of Scientific Racism: Changing Concepts of Race in Britain and the United States between the World Wars*. Cambridge: Cambridge University Press, 1992.

Basha, Adbul Salam. "Morocco Offers Helping Spain 'Monitor Mosques.'" Worldwide Religious News, May 10, 2004. Accessed March 20, 2012, http://wwrn.org/articles/8465/?&place=northern-africa&section=islam.

Batnitzky, Leora Faye. *How Judaism Became a Religion: An Introduction to Modern Jewish Thought*. Princeton, NJ: Princeton University Press, 2011.

Bauer, Thomas, Lamya Kaddor, and Katja Strobel, eds. *Islamischer Religionsunterricht: Hintergründe, Probleme, Perspektiven*. Münster: LIT, 2004.

Bauman, Z. *Intimations of Post-modernity*. London: Routledge, 1992.

———. "Modernity and Ambivalence." *Theory, Culture and Society* 7 (1990): 143–169.

Bawer, B. *While Europe Slept: How Radical Islam is Destroying the West from Within*. New York: Broadway Books, 2007.

BBC. "Beauftragte der Bundesregierung für Migration, Flüchtlinge und Integration." *Bericht der Beauftragten der Bundesregierung für Migration, Flüchtlinge und Integration über die Lage der Ausländerinnen und Ausländer in Deutschland*. Berlin: August 2005.

———. *Muslim Demographics: The Truth* [Video], August 7, 2009. Accessed January 29, 2012, http://www.youtube.com/watch?v=mINChFxRXQs.

Behr, Harry Harun, Chistoph Bochinger, and Gritt Klinkhammer. *Perspektiven für die Ausbildung muslimischer Religionslehrerinnen und Religionslehrer in Deutschland*.

Eine Expertise. Bayreuth: Kulturwissenschaftliche Fakultät Universität Karlsruhe, 2003.

Beider, Harris. "Belgian Politicians Pass Veil Ban." Al-Jazeera, April 29, 2010. Accessed July 23, 2012, http://www.aljazeera.com/news/europe/2010/04/2010429 19502798156 4.html/

———. "Belgique: Polemique autour d'une elue qui decide de porter le hijab." AJIB, January 20, 2012. Accessed July 23, 2012, http://www.ajib.fr/2012/01/elu-hijab-belgique/.

———. "Belgium First to Ban Burqa and Niqab in Public Spaces." *Daily News Egypt*, April 2, 2010. Accessed July 23, 2012, http://www.thefreelibrary.com/ Belgium+first+to+ban+burqa+and+niqab+in+public+spaces.-a0222856604.

———. *Race, Housing, & Community: Perspectives on Policy and Practice.* Hoboken, NJ: Wiley-Blackwell, 2012.

Bergesen, A. J. "Berlin Muslims to Train Imams at New Islamic School." January 27, 2009. Accessed October 22, 2012, http://www.dw.de/berlin-muslims-to-train-imams-at-new-islamic-school/a-3937857-1.

———. "Bernard Lewis: Muslims to Take Over Europe." Free Republic, February 1, 2007. Accessed July 25, 2012, http://www.freerepublic.com/focus/f-news/1778003/ posts.

———. "Political Witch Hunts: The Sacred and the Subversive in Cross-National Perspective." *American Sociological Review* 42 (1977): 22–33.

Beyerlein, L., and J. R. Hipp. "From Pews to Participation: The Effect of Congregation Activity and Context on Bridging Civic Engagement." *Social Problems* 53 (1) (2006): 97–117.

Biedermann, Ferry. "Anti-Muslim Groups Descend on Paris." National, December 19, 2012. Accessed February 18, 2012, http://www.thenational.ae/news/world/ europe/anti-muslim-groups-descend-on-paris.

Biggs, Stephen. "The Monist." *Liberalism, Feminism, and Group Rights.* Accessed July 25, 2012, http://www.readperiodicals.com/201201/2600287491.html#b.

Bigo, D. "Security and Immigration: Toward a Critique of the Governmentality of Unease." *Alternatives* 27 (2002): 63–92.

Blaschke, Jochen, and Sanela Sabanovic. "Multi-Level Discrimination of Muslim Women in Germany." In *Multi-Level Discrimination of Muslim Women in Europe*, edited by Jochen Blaschke. Berlin: Ed. Parabolis, 2000, 37–55.

Böhler, Britta. "Beseft Donner wel wat hij zegt?" De Volkskrant, November 27, 2004. Accessed July 25, 2012, http://www.volkskrant.nl/vk/nl/2664/Nieuws/archief/arti-cle/detail/715065/2004/11/27/Beseft-Donner-wat-hij-zegt.dhtml.

Boumidienne, Halima. "African Muslim Women in France." In *God's Law versus State Law,* edited Michael King. London: Grey Seal, 1995, 49–61.

Bourdieu, Pierre. "Social Space and Symbolic Power." *Sociological Theory* 7 (1) (1989): 14–25..

Boykin, William G. "Sharia Law or Constitution? America Must Choose." TexasInsider.org, February 11, 2011. Accessed October 22, 2012, http://www. texasinsider.org/?p=42440.

Bozeman, A. "The International Order in a Multicultural World. The Expansion of International Society." In *The Expansion of International Society,* edited by B. Hedley and A. Watson. Oxford: Clarendon, 1984, 161–186.

Brandy, Andrea, and Guido Kleinhubbert. "Anti-Islamic Party is Playing with Fear." Spiegel Online International, January 3, 2008. Accessed March 20, 2012, http:// www.spiegel.de/international/germany/0,1518,526225,00.html.

Brandy, Andrea, and Guido Kleinhubbert. "Britain Not to Ban Muslim Women from Wearing Burqa." Outlookindia.com, July 18, 2010. Accessed October 22, 2012, http://news.outlookindia.com/item.aspx?687834.

Bronson, Rachel. *Thicker than Oil: America's Uneasy Partnership with Saudi Arabia.* New York: Oxford University, 2006.

Brouwer, E. "Immigration, Asylum and Terrorism: A Changing Dynamic. Legal and Practical Development in the eu in Response to the Terrorist Attacks of 11/09." *European Journal of Migration and Law* 4 (4) (2003): 399–424.

Brown, Martyn. "Now Muslims Demand Full Shari'a Law." Express, October 15, 2009. Accessed July 23, 20120, http://www.express.co.uk/posts/view/134080/Now-Muslims-demand-Give-us-full-Shari'a-law.

Brubaker, R. *Citizenship and Nationhood in France and Germany.* Cambridge: Harvard University Press, 1992.

Bruce, Benjamin. "Switzerland's Minaret Ban." Euro-Islam.info, November 29, 2009. Accessed January 30, 2012, http://www.euro-islam.info/key-issues/switzerlands-minaret-ban/.

Buchler, Andrea. *Islamic Law in Europe? Legal Pluralism and Its Limits in European Family Laws.* Burlington: Ashgate, 2011.

Buijs, Frank J., and Jan Rath. *Muslims in Europe, the State of Research.* New York: Report for the Russel Sage Foundation, 2003.

Buruma, Ian. "Europe's Turn to the Right." Nation, August 10, 2011. Accessed July 27, 2012, http://www.thenation.com/article/162698/europes-turn-right.

Butt, Riazat. "European Court of Human Rights Rules Crucifixes are Allowed in State Schools." *The Guardian,* March 18, 2011. Accessed February 16, 2012, http://www.guardian.co.uk/law/2011/mar/18/european-court-human-rights-crucifixes-allowed.

Cairns, Alan C. "Empire, Globalization, and the Fall and Rise of Diversity." In *Citizenship, Diversity, and Pluralism: Canadian and Comparative Perspectives,* edited by Alan C. Cairns et al. Montreal and Kingston: McGill-Queen's University Press, 1999.

Calhoun, C. ed. *Hasbermas and the Public Sphere.* Cambridge, MA: MIT Press, 1992.

"Cameron: Multiculturalism speech not attack on Muslim," *BBC,* February 23, 2011. Accessed February 18, 2012, http://www.bbc.co.uk/news/uk-politics-12555908.

Campbell, M. "Nicolas Sarkozy to Target Muslim Prayers." Australian, December 20, 2010. Accessed January 31, 2012, http://www.theaustralian.com.au/news/world/nicolas-sarkozy-to-target-muslim-prayers/story-e6frg6so-1225973565402.

Carens, J. H. *Culture, Citizenship, and Community: A Contextual Exploration of Justice as Evenhandedness.* Oxford: Oxford University Press, 2000.

Carney, Abdel Al-Hakeem. "CDU Fordert Burkaverbot in der Öffentlichkeit." *FrankfurterRundschau,* January 12, 2012. Accessed October 22, 2012, http://www.fr-online.de/rhein-main/integrationspolitik-cdu-fordert-burkaverbot-in-der-oeffentlichkeit,1472796,11437410.html.

———. "The Desecralization of Power in Islam." *Religion, State, and Society* 31 (2003): 203–219.

Celermajer, Danielle. "If Islam Is Our Other, Who Are 'We?'" *Australian Journal of Social Issues* 42 (1) (2007):103–123.

Cesari, J. *Encyclopedia of Islam in the United States* (2 volumes). Greenwood, 2007.

———. *European Muslims and the Secular State.* Ashgate, 2005.

———. *Islam and the Arab Awakening: Religion, Modernity and Democracy.* Cambridge University Press (2013, forthcoming).

———. *Muslims in the West After 9/11: Religion, Law and Politics.* New York: Routledge, 2010.

———. "*Quand la religion aide à l'intégration: Analyse comparée des élites musulmanes en Europe et aux Etats-Unis.*" Talk presented at the conference of the Association Française de Sociologie Religieuse, Paris, February 5–7, 2001 (publication forthcoming).

———. "Securitization of Islam in Europe." *Die Welt Des Islams, International Journal for the Study of Modern Islam,* Ed Brill, Leiden, 52 (3-4) (2012): 430–449.

———. *Securitization and Religious Divides in Europe Muslims in Western Europe after 9/11: Why the Term Islamophobia IsMmore a Predicament Than an Explanation.* June 1, 2006. Accessed October 22, 2012, http://www.libertysecurity.org/IMG/pdf_Challenge_Project_report.pdf.

———. *When Islam and Democracy Meet: Muslims in Europe and in the United States.* New York: Palgrave Macmillan, 2004.

Charbonneau, Louis. "Turkish Group Accuses German Paper of Insulting Islam." *Worldwide Religious News,* March 16, 2006. Accessed July 23, 2012, http://wwrn.org/articles/20853/?&place=germany&section=islam.

Chebel D'Appollonia, Ariane. *Frontiers of Fear: Immigration and Insecurity in the United States and Europe.* Ithaca: Cornell University Press, 2012.

Chretienne, F. "À Avignon, le Père Gabriel s'interroge après un an de profanations." *Famille Chretienne,* November 23, 2010. Accessed January 31, 2012, http://www.famillechretienne.fr/agir/vie-de-l-eglise/a-avignon-le-pere-gabriel-sinterroge-apres-un-an-de-profanations_t11_s73_d58730.html.

Cohen, R. "Religion Does Its Worst." *The New York Times,* April 4, 2011. Accessed January 31, 2012, http://www.nytimes.com/2011/04/05/opinion/05iht-edcoheno5.html.

Colas, Dominique. *Civil Society and Fanaticism: Conjoined Histories.* Stanford, CA: Stanford University Press, 1997.

Connolly, William E. *Why I Am Not a Secularist.* Minneapolis: University of Minnesota Press, 1993.

Coullaut, Arantza. "Councillor Shuts Down Committee for Ex-Muslims." Expatica, April 17, 2008. Accessed October 22, 2012, http://www.expatica.com/nl/news/local_news/Councillor-shuts-down-committee-for-ex_Muslims.html.

———. "Paso oficial de la mezquita de Sevilla." El País, May 15, 2005. Accessed October 22, 2012, http://elpais.com/diario/2005/05/15/andalucia/1116109341_850215.html.

Cragg, Kenneth. "Abduh, Muhammad." In *The Oxford Encyclopedia of the Islamic World,* Oxford Islamic Studies Online. Accessed November 7, 2011, http://www.oxfordislamicstudies.com/article/opr/t236/e0011.

———. "Critics Slam 'Recycling' of Notorious Sarrazin Book." Local, January 14, 2012. Accessed January 31, 2012, http://www.thelocal.de/national/20120114-40111.html.

———. "Cultural and Social Affairs Department OIC Islamophobia Observatory." Euro-Islam.info, July 2010. Accessed October 22, 2012, http://www.euro-islam.info/2010/08/02/cultural-and-social-affairs-department-oic-islamophobia-observatory-monthly-bulletin-%E2%80%93-july-2010/.

Cumming-Bruce, Nick, and Steven Erlanger. "Swiss Ban Building of Minarets on Mosques." *The New York Times*, November 29, 2009. Accessed March 20, 2012, http://www.nytimes.com/2009/11/30/world/europe/30swiss.html.

Dassetto, Felice, Brigitte Maréchal, and Jorgen Nielsen, eds. *Convergences musulmanes, Aspects contemporains de l'islam dans l'Europe élargie*. Bruylant: Louvain la Neuve, 2001.

Davies, Grace. *Religion in Britain since 1945: Believing Without Belonging*. Oxford: Blackwell, 1994.

———. "New Approaches in the Sociology of Religion: A Western Perspective." *Social Compass* 51 (1) (2005).

Davis, Abu Hakeem Bilaal. "Fundamentals in the Manhaj of the Salaf (Part 2)." Thesalafee.wordpress.com, March 23, 2012. Accessed July 25, 2012, http://thesalafee. wordpress.com/2012/03/23/the-term-salaf-and-its-usage-in-quran-and-sunnah-by-abu-hakeem-bilaal-davis/.

Davis, F. *Fashion, Culture and Identity*. Chicago: University of Chicago Press, 1992.

Delhey, J., and K. Newton. "Predicting Cross-National Levels of Social Trust: Global Pattern or Nordic Exceptionalism?" *European Sociological Review* 21 (2005): 311–327.

Delien, Paul. "Jihad against Danish Newspaper." *Brussels Journal*, October 22, 2005. Accessed February 25, 2012, http://www.brusselsjournal.com/node/382.

Deprez, Jean. "*Droit international prive et conflit de civilisations. Aspects méthodologiques. Les relations entre systèmes d'Europe Occidentale et systèmes islamiques en matière de statut personnel.*" In *Recueil des Cours de l'Académie de la Haye*, 211 (1988-IV) 9–372.

Djaït, Hichem. *L'Europe Et L'Islam*. Oakland: University of California, 1985.

Dolz, Patricia Ortega. "La mezquita del barrio. La actividad en los centros de oración islámicos que proliferan en España se ha convertido en foco de atención para el Gobierno." El País, May 9, 2004. Accessed October 22, 2012, http://elpais.com/diario/2004/05/09/espana/1084053602_850215.html.

Doomernik, J. "Dutch Modes of Migration Regulation." Paper for the IMISCOE cluster A1 workshop, March 2006.

Dovidio, J. F., T. Saguy, and N. Shnabel. "Cooperation and Conflict within Groups: Bridging Intragroup and Intergroup Processes." *Journal of Social Issues* 65 (2009): 429–449.

Driessen, Geert, and Micheal S. Merry. "Islamic Schools in the Netherlands: Expansion or Marginalization?" *Interchange* 37 (3) (2006): 201–223.

Dugan, E., and N. Lakhani. "Dutch Authorities Enforce New Moroccan Laws." NIS News Bulletin, March 31, 2009. Accessed February 18, 2012, http://www.nisnews. nl/public/310309_2.htm.

———. "Dutch Compromise on Jews and Muslims Ritual Slaughter." Ahlul Bayt News Agency, June 7, 2012. Accessed October 22, 2012, http://abna.ir/data. asp?lang=3&Id=320472.

———. "Dutch Plan Ban on Muslim Face Veils Next Year." January 27, 2012. Accessed October 22, 2012, http://www.reuters.com/article/2012/01/27/us-dutch-burqa-ban-idUSTRE80Q1OT20120127.

———. "Dutch Unveil the Toughest Face in Europe with a Ban on the Burqa." *Times Online*, October 2005.

———. "Straw Under Fire for Linking Race to Sex Attacks." *Independent*, January 9, 2011. Accessed January 31, 2012, http://www.independent.co.uk/news/uk/crime/straw-under-fire-for-linking-race-to-sex-attacks-2179750.html.

Eickelman, Dale. "Mainstreaming Islam: Taking Charge of the Faith." *Encounters* (2) (2010): 185–203.

Elias, Norbert. *On the Process of Civilisation: Volume 3: Collect Works of Norbert Elias.* Dublin: University College Dublin Press, 2012.

Elliott, Andrea. "The Man behind the Anti-Shariah Movement." *The New York Times,* July 30, 2011. Accessed January 31, 2012, http://www.nytimes.com/2011/07/31/us/31shariah.html?_r=1&adxnnl=1&pagewanted=all&adxnnlx=1325142029-MnrhdJ vFojgkqHiVpO2aJA.

Elorza, Antonio. "Terrorismo islámico: Las raíces doctrinales." In *El nuevo terrorismo islamista. Del 11-S al 11-M,* edited by F. Reinares and A. Elorza. Madrid: Temas de Hoy, 2004, 149–176.

Eriksen, T. H. "Formal and Informal Nationalism." *Ethnic and Racial Studies* 16 (1993): 1–25.

Esman, Abigail. "Burqa Ban Comes to the Netherlands. Finally." *Forbes,* January 27, 2012. Accessed July 23, 2012, http://www.forbes.com/sites/abigailesman/2012/01/27/burqa-ban-comes-to-the-netherlands-finally/.

Esposito, John L. *Islam: The Straight Path.* New York: Oxford University Press, 1998.

———., ed. "Salafi." In *The Islamic World: Past and Present, Oxford Islamic Studies Online.* Accessed September 7, 2011, http://www.oxfordislamicstudies.com/article/opr/t243/e294.

Euben, Roxanne. *Enemy in the Mirror: Islamic Fundamentalism and the Limits of Modern Rationalism: A Work of Comparative Political Theory.* Princeton: Princeton University Press, 1999.

———. "Excarcelados tres islamistas tras ser absueltos por el Supremo." El País, April 8, 2006. Accessed July 25, 2012, http://elpais.com/diario/2006/04/08/espana/1144447232_850215.html.

Faist, T. "The Migrationsecurity Nexus: International Migration and Security." In *Migration, Citizenship and Ethnos: Incorporation Regimes in Germany, Western Europe and North America,* edited by Y. M. Bodemann and G. Yurdakul. Basingstoke: Palgrave Macmillan, 2005.

———. "Fátima acude al instituto con su pañuelo en medio de una gran expectación." El País, February 18, 2002. Accessed October 22, 2012, http://sociedad.elpais.com/sociedad/2002/02/18/actualidad/1013986801_850215.html.

Ferrara, Alessandro. "The Separation of Religion and Politics in a Post-Secular Society." *Philosophy & Social Criticism* 35 (1–2): 77–91.

Fetzer, Joel S., and J. Christopher Soper. "Explaining and Accommodation of Muslim Religious Practices in France, Britain and Germany." Paper presented at the Muslims in Western Europe Politics Conference, Bloomington, Indiana, September 22–24, 2005.

———. *Muslims and the State in Britain, France, and Germany.* Cambridge: Cambridge University Press, 2004.

Fieldhouse, E., and D. Cutts. "Diversity, Density, and Turnout: The Effect of Neighborhood Ethno-religious Composition on Voter Turnout in Britain Political Geography." *Political Geography* 27 (5) (2008): 530–48.

———. "Former Minister Guilty of Slander." Euro-Islam.info, October 27, 2010. Accessed July 22, 2012, http://www.euro-islam.info/2010/11/02/former-minister-guilty-of-slander/.

Foucault, M., G. Burchell, C. Gordon, and P. Miller. *The Foucault Effect: Studies in Governmentality.* Two Lectures and an Interview with Michel Foucault. Chicago: University of Chicago, 1991.

Fourquet, Jérôme. "ANALYSE : 1989–2011, Enquête sur l'implantation et l'évolution de l'Islam de France. " IFOP, July 2011. Accessed January 31, 2012, http://www. ifop.com/media/pressdocument/343-1-document_file.pdf.

Fox, Jonathan, and Yasemin Akbaba. "France and its Muslims: Riots, Jihadis, and Depoliticisation." *International Crisis Group,* March 9, 2006. Accessed July 25, 2012, http://www.crisisgroup.org/en/regions/europe/172-france-and-its-muslims-riots-jihadism-and-depoliticisation.aspx.

———. "Religious Discrimination against Religious Minorities in Western Democracies from 1990 to 2008." Paper presented at the annual meeting of the International Studies Association Annual Conference "Global Governance: Political Authority in Transition," Montreal, Quebec, Canada March 16, 2011. Accessed March 20, 2012, http://www.allacademic.com/meta/p501549_index.html.

Fredrickson, G. *Racism: A Short History.* Princeton: Princeton University Press, 2003.

———. "Freedom of Religion and Religious Symbols in the Public Sphere (2011–60-E)." *Parliament of Canada Web Site— Site Web Du Parlement Du Canada.* Accessed February 16, 2012, http://www.parl.gc.ca/content/LOP/ResearchPublications/2011–60-e. htm.

Frégosi, F. "French appeals court restores marriage in virginity case." *The New York Times,* October 17, 2008. Accessed July 23, 2012, http://www.nytimes. com/2008/11/17/world/europe/17iht-france.4.17897832.html.

———, ed. *Les conditions d'exercice du culte musulman en France: Étude de cas à partir des lieux de culte et des carrés musulmans. Etude réalisée pour le FASILD.* Paris: FASILD, 2004.

Friendofmuslim, *Muslim Demographics.* [Video], March 30, 2009. Accessed January 29, 2012, http://www.youtube.com/watch?v=6-3X5hIFXYU.

"Gallup Coexist Index 2009: A Global Study of Interfaith Relations." *Gallup,* 2009. Accessed January 30, 2012, http://www.gallup.com/se/ms/153578/REPORT-Gallup-Coexist-Index-2009.aspx.

———. "Muslim Americans: A National Portrait." 2009. Accessed on October 20, 2012, http://www.gallup.com/strategicconsulting/153572/REPORT-Muslim-Ame ricans-National-Portrait.aspx.

———. "The Gallup Coexist Index 2009: A Global Study of Interfaith Relations." 2009. Accessed October 23, 2012, http://www.euro-islam.info/2009/05/15/the-gallup-coexist-index-2009-a-global-study-of-interfaith-relations/.

Gallup. "Muslim Americans: Faith, Freedom and the Future." 2011. Accessed October 20, 2012, http://www.gallup.com/strategicconsulting/153611/REPORT-Muslim-A mericans-Faith-Freedom-Future.aspx.

Gerholm, T., and Y. G. Lithman. "Germans Less Tolerant of Islam Than Neighbours, Study Finds." Local, December 2, 2010. Accessed January 30, 012, http://www. thelocal.de/society/20101202-31531.html.

———, eds. *The New Islamic Presence in Western Europe.* London: Mansell, 1988.

Givens, T., and A. Luedtke. "The Politics of European Union Immigration Policy: Institutions, Salience, and Harmonization." *Policy Studies Journal* 32 (1) (2004): 145–165.

Glasse, Cyril. *The New Encyclopedia of Islam.* Walnut Creek, CA: AltaMira, 2001.

Goffman, E. *The Presentation of Self in Everyday Life.* New York: Anchor, 1959.

Goldberg, David Theo . "Racial Europeanization." *Ethnic and Racial Studies* 29 (2) (2006): 331–364.

Goodstein, Laurie. "Across Nation, Mosque Projects Meet Opposition." *The New York Times,* August 7, 2010. Accessed March 20, 2012, http://www.nytimes.com/2010/08/08/us/08mosque.html?pagewanted=all.

———. "Drawing U.S. Crowd with Anti-Islam Message." *The New York Times,* March 07, 2011. Accessed January 31, 2012, http://www.nytimes.com/2011/03/08/us/08gabriel.html?pagewanted=all.

Goody, Jack. *Islam in Europe.* Cambridge: Blackwell, 2004.

Govan, Fiona. "Spain Considers Burka Ban." July 20, 2012. Accessed October 22, 2012, http://www.telegraph.co.uk/news/worldnews/europe/spain/7898629/Spain-considers-burqa-ban.html.

Granda, Elsa. "La Comisión Islámica califica de disparate el control de los imames." El País, May 3, 2004. Accessed October 22, 2012, http://elpais.com/diario/2004/05/03/espana/1083535211_850215.html.

Grewal, Kirwan. "'The Threat from Within'—Representations of Banlieue in French Popular Discourse." In *Europe: New Voices, New Perspectives: Proceedings from the Contemporary Europe Research Centre Postgraduate Conference 2005/2006,* edited by Matt Killingsworth. Melbourne: Contemporary Europe Research Centre, the University of Melbourne, 2007, 41–67.

Guénif-Souilamas, Nacira, and Eric Macé. *Les féministes et le Garçon Arabe.* Paris: Éditions de l'aube, 2004.

Habermas, Jürgen, Judith Butler, Charles Taylor, and Cornel West. *The Power of Religion in the Public Sphere.* New York: Columbia University Press, 2011.

Haykel, Bernard. "On the Nature of Salafi Thought and Action." In *Global Salafism: Islam's New Religious Movement,* edited by Roel Meijer. London: Hurst, 2009, 33–58.

Heine, P., and R. Spielhaus. "Sunnis and Shiites in Germany: A Brief Analysis of the Results of the Study by the Bertelsmann Stiftung." In *Religion Monitor,* edited by Liz Mohn. Gütersloh, GER: Bertelsmann Stiftung, 2008, 24–30.

Hekma, Gert. "Imams and Homosexuality: A Post-Gay Debate in the Netherlands." *Sexualities* 5 (2002): 237–248.

Heneghan, Tom. "French Muslim Councils Warns Government on Veil Ban." *Reuters,* June 4, 2010. Accessed July 23, 2012, http://www.reuters.com/article/2010/06/04/us-france-veil-muslims-idUSTRE6532TB20100604.

Hervieu-Léger, D. *Religion as a Chain of Memory.* New Brunswick, NJ: Rutgers University Press, 2000.

———. "Religion und sozialer Zusammenhalt in Europa." *Transit* 26 (2003): 101–119.

Hess, Mary. "2010 Presidential Address: Learning Religion and religiously Learning Amid Global Cultural Flows," *Religious Education* 106(4) (2011): 360–377.

Hirshkind, Charles. "Is There a Secular Body?" Religion and Ethics, April 5, 2011. Accessed July 23, 2010, http://www.abc.net.au/religion/articles/2011/04/04/3182083.htm.

Hirsi Ali, Ayaan. "The Role of Journalism Today." American Enterprise Institute for Public Policy Research, June 18, 2007. Accessed July 22, 2012, http://www.aei.org/article/society-and-culture/the-role-of-journalism-today/.

Hourani, Albert. *Arabic Thought in the Liberal Age.* London: Oxford University Press, 1962.

Hunt, Carol Anne. "Many Republican Voters Still Believe Obama Is Muslim." Examiner, July 29, 2012. Accessed July 30, 2012, http://www.examiner.com/article/many-republican-voters-still-believe-obama-is-muslim.

Hunter, Shireen. ed. *Islam, Europe's Second Religion: The New Social, Cultural and Political Landscape*. Westport: Praeger, 2002.

IFOP. "France and Germany's Views on Islam," 2011. Accessed October 22, 2012, http://www.ifop.com/?option=com_publication&type=poll&id=1365

———. "Immigrants and Natives: A Replication of Putnam (2007) in a West-European Country." Paper presented at the International Conference on Theoretical Perspectives on Social Cohesion and Social Capitol, Royal Flemish Academic of Belgium for Sciences and Arts. May 15, 2008.

———. "Immigrants Have to Pass a Racy Test. Netherlands Show Its Liberal Culture." Euro-Islam.info. Accessed October 22, 2012, http://www.euro-islam.info/2006/03/16/immigrants-have-to-pass-a-racy-test-netherlands-shows-its-liberal-culture/.

———. "In U.S., Religious Prejudice Stronger against Muslims." Gallup, January 21, 2010. Accessed July 22, 2012, http://www.gallup.com/poll/125312/Religious-Prejudice-Stronger-Against-Muslims.aspx.

IFOP. *Inburgering van geestelijke bedienaren: Een handleiding voor gemeenten*. The Hague: Ministerie van Binnenlandse Zaken en Koninkrijksrelaties, 2001.

———. "Inside the Kingdom." *Time*, September 15, 2003. Accessed July 25, 2012, http://www.time.com/time/magazine/article/0,9171,1005663,00.html.

Ireland, Louise. "Is It Permissible for a Women to Travel in An Elevator Alone with a Non-Mahram Man?" IslamQA. Accessed July 15, 2012. http://islamqa.info/en/ref/71237.

———. "Is It Permissible to Swear Allegiance to a Kaafir Ruler?" IslamQA. Accessed July 27, 2012, http://islamqa.com/en/ref/82681/Kaafir.

Isherwood, Julian. "Danes Restrict Imams to Stiffly Muslim Radicals." *The Telegraph*, February 19, 2004. Accessed March 20, 2012, http://www.telegraph.co.uk/news/worldnews/europe/denmark/1454816/Danes-restrict-imams-to-stifle-Muslim-radicals.html.

———. "Islam et Occupation : Marine Le Pen provoque un tollé." Le Figaro, December 12, 2010. Accessed January 31, 2012, http://www.lefigaro.fr/politique/2010/12/11/01002-20101211ARTFIG00475-islam-et-occupation-la-provocation-de-marine-le-pen.php.

———. "Islam in the Netherlands." Euro-Islam.info. Accessed January 31, 2012, http://www.euro-islam.info/country-profiles/the-netherlands/.

———. "Islam in the United Kingdom." Euro-Islam.info. Accessed October 22, 2012, http://www.euro-islam.info/country-profiles/united-kingdom/.

Islamopedia Online. "Missed Opportunity for a Greater Inclusion of Islam in the United States," March 17, 2011. Accessed July 25, 2012, http://islamopediaonline.org/blog/missed-opportunity-greater-inclusion-islam-united-states.

———. "Italy School Crucifixes 'Barred.'" *BBC News*, November 3, 2009. Accessed February 16, 2012, http://news.bbc.co.uk/2/hi/8340411.stm.

Jamal, A. "The Political Participation and Engagement of Muslim Americans: Mosque Involvement and Group Consciousness." *American Politics Research* 33 (4) (2005): 21–44.

Joppke, C. *Challenge to the Nation-State: Immigration in Western Europe and the United States*. Oxford: Oxford University Press, 1998.

———. "Juan Williams: Muslims on Planes Make Me 'Nervous.'" Huffington Post, October 19, 2010. Accessed January 31, 2012, http://www.huffingtonpost.com/2010/10/19/juan-williams-muslims-nervous_n_768719.html.

Kainz, Howard. "Islam and the Definition of Religion." Catholic Thing, July 13, 2010. Accessed October 22, 2012, http://www.thecatholicthing.org/columns/2010/islam -and-the-definition-of-religion.html.

Kalin, I. "The Slow Death of Multiculturalism in Europe." Today's Zaman, October 28, 2010. Accessed February 18, 2012, http://www.todayszaman.com/columnist-22 5620-the-slow-death-of-multiculturalism-in-europe.html.

Kern, Soeren. "Muslim Hijab Sparks New Islam-Related Controversy in Spain." October 13, 2011. Accessed October 22, 2012, http://www.gatestoneinstitute. org/2502/muslim-hijab-sparks-new-islam-related-controversy.

Kesler, C., and I. Bloemraad. "Does Immigration Erode Social Capital?" *Canadian Journal of Political Science* 43 (2) (2010): 319–347.

Klausen, Jytte. *The Cartoons That Shook the World.* New Haven: Yale University Press, 2009.

Koenig, H. G. "Concerns about Measuring 'Spirituality' in Research." *Journal of Nervous and Mental Disease* 196 (5) (2008): 349–355.

Koopmans, R. *Contested Citizenship: Immigration and Cultural Diversity in Europe.* Minneapolis: University of Minnesota, 2005.

Krebs, R., and P. Jackson. "Twisting Tongues and Twisting Arms: The Power of Political Rhetoric." *European Journal of International Relations* 13 (1) (2007).

Kundani, Arun. "Multiculturalism and Its Discontents: Left, Right and liberal." *European Journal of Cultural Studies* 15 (2) (2012): 159 (155–166).

——. *Spooked: How Not to Prevent Violent Extremism.* London: Institute of Race Relations, 2009.

——. "Stop and Search: Police Step up Targeting of Blacks and Asians." Institute of Race Relations, March 26, 2003. Accessed July 25, 2012, http://www.irr.org.uk/ news/stop-and-search-police-step-up-targetting-of-blacks-and-asians/.

Kymlicka, W. *Multicultural Citizenship: A Liberal Theory of Minority Rights.* Oxford: Oxford, 1995.

——. *Multicultural Odysseys: Navigating the New International Politics of Diversity.* New York: Oxford University Press, 2007.

Kymlicka, W., and K. Banting. "Immigration, Multiculturalism and the Welfare State." *Ethics & International Affairs* 20 (3) (2006): 281–304.

Lamont, Michele, and Virag Molnar. "The Study of Boundaries in the Social Sciences." *Annual Review of Sociology* 28 (2002): 167–195.

Lancee, B., and J. Dronkers. "Ethnic Diversity in Neighborhoods and Individual Trust of Immigrants and Natives: A Replication of Putnam (2007) in a West-European Country." Paper presented at the International Conference on Theoretical Perspectives on Social Cohesion and Social Capitol, Royal Flemish Academic of Belgium for Sciences and Arts. May 15, 2008.

Landler, Mark. "Germany Cites Koran in Rejecting Divorce." *The New York Times,* March 22, 2007. Accessed July 23, 2012, http://www.nytimes.com/2007/03/22/ world/europe/22cnd-germany.html?pagewanted=all.

——. "Lateral Thinkers Wanted." Qantara.de, November 8, 2010. Accessed October 22, 2012, http://www.euro-islam.info/2010/09/06/islamic-theology-in-germany-po ses-great-challenges-to-universities/.

Laurence, Jonathan, ed. *The Emancipation of Europe's Muslims: The State's Role in Minority Integration.* Princeton: Princeton University Press, 2012.

Laustsen, Carsten Bagge, and Ole Waever. "In Defense of Religion, Sacred Reverent Objects for Securitization." In *Religion in International Relations, the Return from*

Exile, edited by Pavlos Hatzopoulos. New York: Palgrave Macmillan, 2003, 147–175.

Lean, Nathan. *The Islamophobia Industry: How the Right Manufactures Fear of Muslims*. London: Pluto, 2012.

Leiken, Robert. "Europe's Angry Muslims." *Foreign Affairs* 84 (4) (2005): 120–135.

Lentin, Alana, and Gavin Titley. "The Crisis of 'Multiculturalism' in Europe: Mediated Minarets, Intolerable Subjects." *European Journal of Cultural Studies* 15 (2) (April 2012): 123–138.

Lewis, Bernard, and Dominique Schnapper, eds. *Muslims in Europe*. London: Pinter, 1994.

——. "Little Voter Discomfort with Romney's Mormon Religion." Pew Forum, July 26, 2012. Accessed July 30, 2012, http://www.pewforum.org/Politics-and-Elections/Little-Voter-Discomfort-with-Romney%E2%80%99s-Mormon-Religion-1.aspx.

Lowi, Theodore J. *The End of Liberalism: Ideology, Policy, and the Crisis of Public Authority*. New York: W.W. Norton, 1969.

Lyck Dreehsen, Louise. "Langballe Dømt for Racism." Berlingske, December 3, 2010. Accessed June 20, 2012, http://www.b.dk/politik/langballe-doemt-racisme.

Macloughin, Sean. "Mosques and the Public Space, Conflict and Cooperation in the Public Space." *Journal of Ethnic and Migration Studies* 31 (6) (2005): 1045–1066.

Madood, Tariq. *Multicultural Politics: Racism, Ethnicity, and Muslims in Britain*. Minneapolis: University of Minnesota Press, 2005.

Makow, Henry. "The Debauchery of American Womanhood: Bikinivs. Burqa." September 18, 2002. Accessed February 18, 2012, http://www.henrymakow.com/180902.html.

Malik, Iftikar H. *Islam and Modernity: Muslims in Europe and in the United States*. London: Pluto, 2004.

Mamdani, Mahmood. *Good Muslim, Bad Muslim: America, the Cold War, and the Roots of Terror*. New York: Three Leaves, 2005.

Maréchal, Brigitte. *The Muslim Brothers in Europe: Roots and Discourse*. Leiden: Brill, 2008.

Marshall, Paul, and Nina Shea. *Silence: How Apostasy and Blasphemy Codes Are Choking Freedom Worldwide*. New York: Oxford University Press, 2011.

——. "Más de 150 musulmanes protestan en Badalona contra el cierre de su mezquita." *La Vanguardia*, February 26, 2005.

Mercier, Pierre. *Conflits De Civilisations Et Droit International Prive: Polygamie Et Repudiatio*. Genève: Droz, 1972.

Merry, Michael S., and Geert Driessen, "Islamic Schools in Three Western Countries: Policy and Procedure." *Comparative Education* 41 (4) (2005): 411–432.

Michelman, S. "Changing Old Habits: Dress of Women Religious and Its Relationship to Personal and Social Identity." *Sociological Inquiry* 67 (3) (1997): 350–363.

Ministry of the Interior and Kingdom Relations, Internal Security Service. *De democratische rechtsorde en islamitisch onderwijs. Buitenlandse inmenging en anti-integratieve tendensen*. 2002. Accessed October 22, 2012, https://www.aivd.nl/actueel/@2234/democratische/.

Mitchell, Bob. "Shameful, Horrible, Evil and Barbaric." Star, June 17, 2010. Accessed July 23, 2010, http://www.thestar.com/news/gta/crime/article/824453 – shameful-horrible-evil-and-barbaric.

Moberg, D. O. "Assessing and Measuring Spirituality: Confronting Dilemmas of Universal and Particular Evaluative Criteria." *Journal of Adult Development* 9 (1) (2002): 47–60.

Modood, T. *Multiculturalism: A Civic Idea*. Cambridge: Polity, 2007.

Mohn, Liz, ed. *Religion Monitor 2008 Muslim Religiousness in Germany*. Gütersloh: Bertelsmann Stiftung, 2008.

Money, J. "Defining Immigration Policy: Inventory, Quantitative Referents, and Empirical Regularities." unpublished manuscript (1999).

Morgan, George, and Scott Poynting. *Global Islamophobia: Muslims and Moral Panic in the West*. Burlington, VT: Ashgate, 2012.

———. "Mosque Push Back in Minnesota and New York." Islawmix.org. Accessed June 20, 2012, http://islawmix.org/news-roundup/#/2012–24/3555/Mosque-pushback -in-Minnesota-and-New-York.

Motadel, D. "Islam in Germany." Euro-Islam.info. Accessed January 31, 2012, http://www.euro-islam.info/country-profiles/germany/.

Movimiento contra la Intolerancia. *Estudio sobre actitudes sociales ante la inmigración y minorías étnicas de los jóvenes valencianos*. Valencia, 2004.

Mukadam, Mohamed, and Alison Scott-Baumann. *Muslim Americans: Faith, Freedom and the Future*. 2011. Accessed October 20, 2012, http://www.gallup.com/strategic-consulting/153611/REPORT-Muslim-Americans-Faith-Freedom-Future.aspx.

———. "Muslim Fundamentalist Group Launched in the Netherlands." Expatica, December 22, 2010. Accessed July 23, 2010, http://www.euro-islam.info/2011/01/11/shari'a4holland-founded-in-the-netherlands/.

———. "Muslims in the EU-Cities Report: The Netherlands." Open Society Institute, 2007. Accessed October 22, 2012, http://dare.uva.nl/document/46997, 42.

———. "Muslims in the European Union. Discrimination and Islamophobia." European Monitoring Centre on Racism and Xenophobia (EUMC), 2006. Accessed January 31, 2012, http://eumc.europa.eu/eumc/material/pub/muslim/Manifestations_EN.pdf.

———. "Muslim Networks and Movements in Western Europe." Pew, September 15, 2010. Accessed July 25, 2012, http://pewforum.org/Muslim/Muslim-Net works-and-Movements-in-Western-Europe-Muslim-World-League-and-World-Assembly-of-Muslim-Youth.aspx.

———. "Muslim-Western Tensions Persist." Pew, July 21, 2012. Accessed July 22, 2012, http://pewresearch.org/pubs/2066/muslims-westerners-christians-jews-islamic-extremism-september-11.

———. *The Training and Development of Muslim Faith Leaders*. London: Crown, 2010.

Natalicchio, Nick. "Netherlands Ritual Slaughter Ban Canceled, Cabinent Adopts New Guidelines." December 21, 2012. Accessed October 22, 2012, http://www.huffingtonpost.com/2011/12/21/netherlands-ritual-slaughter-ban_n_1162675.html.

———. "New Program Aims to Integrate German's Foreign-Trained Imams." Deutsche Welle World, December 11, 2009. Accessed October 22, 2012, http://www.euro-islam.info/2009/12/11/new-program-aims-to-integrate-germany%E2%80%99s-foreign-trained-imams/.

———. "Robertson: 'Islam Is Not a Religion. It Is a Worldwide Political Movement Meant on Domination.'." Media Matters for America, June 12, 2007. Accessed October 22, 2012, http://mediamatters.org/research/2007/06/12/robertson-islam-is-not-a-religion-it-is-a-world/139073.

New York City Bar Association. *The Unconstitutionality of Oklahoma Referendum 755—the "Save our State Amendment."* December 2010. Accessed October 22, 2012, http://www.nycbar.org/pdf/report/uploads/20072027-Unconstitutiona lityofOklahomaReferendum755.pdf.

The New York Times Poll, 2001, 2002, 2003, 2010. Accessed January 31, 2012, http://www.nytimes.com/packages/pdf/poll_results.pdf.

The New York Times Poll. "The Unconstitutionality of Oklahoma Referendum 755—The 'Save our State Amendment.'" Committee on Foreign & Comparative Law, New York City Bar, December 2010. Accessed July 22, 2012, http://www.nycbar.org/pdf/ report/uploads/20072027-UnconstitutionalityofOklahomaReferendum755.pdf.

Newcomb, Alyssa. "France to Become First European Country to Ban Burqa." April 10, 2011. Accessed October 22, 2012, http://abcnews.go.com/International/ burqa-ban-effect-france/story?id=13344555#.T2ooaxHpMio.

Newport, Frank. "Many Americans Can't Name Obama's Religion." Gallup, June 22, 2012. Accessed July 30, 2012, http://www.gallup.com/poll/155315/Many-Americans -Cant-Name-Obamas-Religion.aspx.

Nielsen, Jorgen S. *Emerging Claims of Muslim Populations in Matters of Family Law in Europe.* Birmingham: Centre for the Study of Islam and Christian-Muslim Relations, 1993.

Nielsen, Jorgen S. *Muslims in Western Europe.* Edinburgh: Edinburgh University Press, 2004.

Nonneman, Gerd, Tim Niblock, and B. Szajkowski, eds. *Muslim Communities in the New Europe.* Berkshire: Ithaca Press, 1996.

———. "Norway: Norway Criminalizes Blasphemy." Euro-Islam.info. Accessed July 23, 2012, http://www.euro-islam.info/2006/02/27/norway-norway-criminalize s-blasphemy/.

Nussbaum, Martha C. *The New Religious Intolerance: Overcoming the Politics of Fear in an Anxious Age.* Cambridge: Harvard University, 2012.

Nyiri, Zsolt. "Muslims in Europe: Basis for Greater Understanding Already Exists." Gallup Polling, 2007. Accessed 12 January 2011, http://www.gallup.com/ corporate/115/About-Gallup.aspx.

Ong, Walter. *Orality and Literacy: The Technologizing of the Word.* New York: Routledge, 2002.

Open Society Institute. *Muslims in the EU: Cities Report, Germany,* 2007. Accessed January 31, 2012, http://www.soros.org/initiatives/home/articles_publications/ publications/museucities_20080101/museucitiesger_20080101.pdf.

"Oslo's Rooftop Religious Rivalry." *BBC News,* March 30, 2000. Accessed February 16, 2012, http://news.bbc.co.uk/2/hi/europe/695725.stm.

Paramaguru, Kharunya. "German Court Bans Male Circumcision." *Time,* June 29, 2012.

Parekh, B. *Rethinking Multiculturalism: Cultural Diversity and Political Theory.* Cambridge: Harvard University Press, 2000.

Pasha, Mustapha Kamal, Giorgio Shani, and Makoto Sato. *Protecting Human Security in a Post 9/11 World: Critical and Global Insights.* Hampshire: Palgrave, 2007.

Penninx, R. "After the Fortuyn and Van Gogh Murders: Is the Dutch Integration Model in Disarray?" Paper read at Seminar for Experts "Integrating Migrants in Europe," at Paris, 2005. Accessed April 18, 2013, http://canada.metropolis.net/ events/metropolis_presents/Social_integration/Penninx_Lecture_January_2005. pdf.

Pew Global Attitudes Project. "Muslims in Europe: Economic Worries Top Concerns about Religious and Cultural Identity." 2006. Accessed January 30, 2012, http:// pewglobal.org/files/pdf/7-6-06.pdf.

Pew Research Center. "Muslim Americans: Middle Class and Mostly Mainstream." 2007. Accessed January 30, 2012, http://pewresearch.org/assets/pdf/muslim- americans.pdf.

———. "The American-Western European Values Gap." February 29, 2012. Accessed October 23, 2012, http://www.pewglobal.org/2011/11/17/the-american-western-european-values-gap/.

———. "Pew: Some voters Still Believer Obama is Muslim, Most Unconcerned with Candidates' Religions." Pew, July 26, 2012. Accessed July 27, 2012, http://2012.talkingpointsmemo.com/2012/07/poll-pew-mormon-romney.php.

Philipse, Herman. "Stop De Tribalisering van Nederland." NRC-Handelsblad, September 28, 2003. Accessed July 25, 2012, http://vorige.nrc.nl/opinie/article1616396.ece/Stop_de_tribalisering_van_Nederland.

Phillips, M. *Londonistan*. New York: Encounter Books, 2006.

———. "Poll: Majority Of GOP Believes Obama Sympathizes with Islamic Fundamentalism, Wants Worldwide Islamic Law." Huffington Post, August 20, 2010. Accessed January 31, 2012, http://www.huffingtonpost.com/2010/08/30/obama-islamic-fundamentalist-gop-polled-majority-says_n_699883.html.

Putnam, R. *Bowling Alone: The Collapse and Revival of American Community*. New York: Simon & Schuster, 2001.

———. "E pluribus unum: Diversity and Community in the Twenty-first Century. The 2006 Johan Skytte Prize Lecture." *Scandinavian Political Studies* 30 (2007): 137–174.

"Rapport Commission nationale consultative des droits de l'homme." Accessed October 22, 2012, http://www.ladocumentationfrancaise.fr/var/storage/rapports-publics/074000226/0000.pdf, 101–124.

Reinares, Fernando. "Al Qaeda, neosalafistas magrebíes y 11-M: sobre el nuevo terrorismo islamista en España." In *El nuevo terrorismo islamista. Del 11-S al 11-M,* edited by Fernando Reinares and Antonio Elorza. Madrid: Temas de Hoy, 2004, 15–43.

"Research on Religion, Spirituality, and Mental Health: A Review." *Canadian Journal of Psychiatry* 54 (5) (2009): 283–291.

Rex, J. *Ethnic Minorities in the Modern Nation State: Working Papers in the Theory of Multiculturalism and Political Integration*. London: MacMillan, 1996.

Rincon, Reyes. "Vecinos de Sevilla intentan crear alarma por la mezquita." El País, November 28, 2004. Accessed October 22, 2012, http://elpais.com/diario/2004/11/28/andalucia/1101597726_850215.html.

Robbers, Gerhard. "State and Church in the European Union." In *State and Church in the European Union*, edited by Gerhard Robbers. Baden-Baden: Nomos, 2005, 577–589.

Rubenstein, R. E., and J. Crocker. "Challenging Huntington." *Foreign Policy* 96 (1994): 113–128.

Sacks, Jonathan. *The Dignity of Difference: How to Avoid the Clash of Civilizations*. London: Continuum, 2003.

Said, Edward. *Orientalism*. New York: Pantheon, 1979.

Salafipublications.com. "Living in Society: On Interaction with Non-Muslims." Accessed July 25, 2012. http://salafipublications.com/sps/sp.cfm?secID=LSC&subsecID=LSC01&loadpage=displaysubsection.cfm

———. "Salafism in the Netherlands." National Coordinator Terrorismebestijding. Accessed July 25, 2012, http://www.nefafoundation.org/file/FeaturedDocs/NCTB_SalafismNetherlands0708.pdf.

Saletan, W. "Muslims, Keep Out." Slate, August 2, 2010. Accessed January 31, 2012, http://www.slate.com/articles/news_and_politics/frame_game/2010/08/muslims_keep_out.html.

Samuel, Henry. "Burqa Ban: French Women Fined for Wearing Full-Face Veil." *The Telegraph*, September 22, 2011. Accessed October 22, 2012, http://www.telegraph. co.uk/news/worldnews/europe/france/8781241/Burqa-ban-French-women-fined-for-wearing-full-face-veil.html.

———. "Sarrazin Earns Millions with Anti-Immigration Book." Local, December 17, 2010. Accessed January 31, 2012, http://www.thelocal.de/society/20101217-31873. html.

Savage, T. M. "Europe and Islam: Crescent Waxing, Cultures Clashing." *Washington Quarterly*, 27 (3) (2004): 25–50.

Schain, M. *Immigration Policy and the Politics of Immigration: A Comparative Study.* Basingstoke: Palgrave Macmillan, 2008.

Schlesinger, P. *Media, State and Nation: Political Violence and Collective Identities.* London: Sage, 1991.

Schmeets, H. "Het belang van religieuze binding in sociale statistieken." *Tijdschrift voor Religie, Recht en Beleid* 1 (3) (2010): 29–41.

Schmitt, C. *El concepto de lo político.* Accessed October 22, 2012, http://www.laeditorialvirtual.com.ar/pages/CarlSchmitt/CarlSchmitt_ElConceptoDeLoPolitico.htm.

Schulze, Reinhard. *Islamischer Internationalismus im 20. Jahrhundert: Untersuchungen zur Geschichte der Islamischen Weltliga.* Leiden: Brill, 1990.

Schulze, Reinhard, and Gabriele Tecchiato. "Muslim World League." In The *Oxford Encyclopedia of the Islamic World,* Oxford Islamic Studies Online. Accessed September 22, 2011, http://www.oxfordislamicstudies.com/article/opr/t236/e0570.

Sebian, Elizabeth, and Jennifer Selby, "Islam in France." Euro-Islam.info. Accessed October 22, 2012, http://www.euro-islam.info/country-profiles/france/.

Selby, Jennifer, and Anna C. Korteweg. *Debating Shari'a: Islam, Gender Politics and Family Law Arbitration.* Toronto: University of Toronto Press, 2012.

Shadid, W. A. R., and P. S. Van Koningsveld, eds. *The Integration of Islam and Hinduism in Western Europe.* Netherlands: Kampen, 1991.

———. *Muslims in the Margin: Political Responses to the Presence of Islam in Western Europe.* Netherlands: Kampen, 1996

———. *Religious Freedom and the Position of Islam in Western Europe.* Netherlands: Kampen, 1995.

Shahin, Emad Eldin. "Salafiyah." In *The Oxford Encyclopedia of the Modern Islamic World,* edited by John L. Esposito. Oxford Islamic Studies Online. Accessed September 7, 2011, http://www.oxfordislamicstudies.com/article/opr/t236/e0700/version/1.

Shah-Kazemi, Sonia. *Untying the Knot: Muslim Women, Divorce and the Shari'ah.* London: Nuffield Foundation, 2001

———. "Shari'a Law 'Could Have uk Role,'" *BBC News,* July 4, 2008. Accessed July 24, 2012, http://news.bbc.co.uk/2/hi/uk_news/7488790.stm.

Sheridan, Lorraine. *Effects of the Events of September 11th 2001 on Discrimination and Implicit Racism in Five Religious and Seven Ethnic Groups: A Brief Overview.* Leicester: University of Leicester, 2002.

Simmel, Georg, and Wolf, Kurt H. *The Sociology of Georg Simmel,* edited and translated by Kurt H. Wolf. New York: Free Press, 1950, 402–403.

Simon, P. *French National Identity and Integration: Who Belongs to the National Community?* Washington, DC: Migration Policy Institute, 2012.

Skocpol, T. *Social Revolutions in the Modern World.* Cambridge and New York: Cambridge University Press, 1994.

Skocpol, T., and M. P. Fiorina. *Civic Engagement in American Democracy.* Washington, DC: Brookings Institution, 2006.

Smith, P. "Codes and Conflict towards a Theory of War as Ritual." *Theory and Society* 20 (1991): 103–138.

Snow, D., and L. Anderson. "Identity Work Among the Homeless: the Verbal Construction and Avowal of Personal Identities." *The American Journal of Sociology* 92 (6) (1987): 1336–1371.

Solomos, J. "Social Capital, Political Participation, and Migration in Europe: Making Multicultural Democracy Work?" *Ethnic and Racial Studies* 35 (2) (2011): 363–364.

———. "Sondage IFOP réalisé les 13 et 14 décembre auprès d'un échantillon représentatif de 970 personnes." Le Monde, December 15, 2012. Accessed January 30, 2012, http://www.ifop.com/media/pressdocument/343-1-document_file.pdf.

Spanish to monitor Friday sermons." Middle East Online, May 3, 2004. Accessed March 20, 2012, http://www.middle-east-online.com/english/?id=9873.

———. "State Multiculturalism Has Failed, Says David Cameron." *BBC News,* February 5, 2011. Accessed July 27, 2012, http://www.bbc.co.uk/news/uk-politics-12371994.

Stewart, Elizabeth. *Catastrophe and Survival: Walter Benhamin and Psychoanalysis.* New York: Continuum, 2010.

Steyn, M. *America Alone: The End of the World as We Know It* . Washington, DC: Regnery, 2006.

Stolberg, S. G., and L. Goodstein, "Domestic Terrorism Hearing Opens with Contrasting Views on Dangers," *The New York Times,* March 10, 2011, accessed January 31, 2012, http://www.nytimes.com/2011/03/11/us/politics/11king.html.

Taji-Farouki, Suha. *A Fundamental Quest: Hizb al-Tahrir and the Search for the Islamic Caliphate.* London: Grey Seal, 1996.

Taras, Raymond. *Xenophobia and Islamophobia in Europe.* Edinburgh: Edinburgh University Press, 2012.

Taylor, Charles. "Rethinking Secularism: Western Secularity." The Immanent Frame, 2012. Accessed February 14, 2012, http://blogs.ssrc.org/tif/2011/08/10/western-secularity/.

———. "Teilnehmer des Plenums der DIK in der zweiten Phase." Deutsche Islam Konferenz, May 17, 2010. Accessed July 23, 2012, http://www.deutsche-islam-konferenz.de/cln_101/nn_2026762/SubSites/DIK/DE/TeilnehmerStruktur/Teilnehmer/teilnehmer-node.html?__nnn=true

Tevanian, P. "Pour 100% des musulmans, les sondages sont plutôt une menace." Les mots sont improtants, January 2011. Accessed January 31, 2012, http://lmsi.net/Pour-100-des-musulmans-les.

———. "Texto aprobado por el Pleno del Congreso de los Diputados, en su sesión del día 30 de junio de 2005, resultante del Dictamen de la Comisión de Investigación sobre el 11 de marzo de 2004 y de los votos particulares incorporados al mismo." Boletín Oficial de las Cortes Generales, Congreso de los Diputados 242, April 14, 2005. Accessed October 22, 2012, http://www.congreso.es/portal/page/portal/Congreso/PopUpCGI?CMD=VERLST&BASE=puw8&DOCS=1–1&DOCORDER=LIFO&QUERY=(CDD200507140242.CODI.).

Tichenor, D. J. *Dividing Lines: The Politics of Immigration Control in America.* Princeton: Princeton University Press, 2002.

Toynbee, P. "Why Trevor Is Right." *Guardian,* April 7, 2004. Accessed April 8, 2004, http://www.guardian.co.uk/politics/2004/apr/07/society.immigration.

———. "Transatlantic Trends: Immigration 2010." BBVA Foundation, 2010. Accessed February 4, 2011, http://www.affarinternazionali.it/documenti/TT-Immigr10_EN.pdf.

Triadafilopoulos, Triadafilos. "Illiberal Means to Liberal Ends? Understanding Recent Immigrant Integration Policies in Europe." *Journal of Ethnic and Migration Studies* 37 (6) (2011): 861–880.

Tura, M. "Las huellas del 'chacal.'" El País, January 19, 2006. Accessed July 25, 2012, http://elpais.com/diario/2006/01/19/catalunya/1137636443_850215.html.

Turley, Jonathan. "Judge in 'Zombie Mohammed' Case (Reportedly) Responds." Jonathan Turley, February 26, 2012. Accessed July 23, 2012, http://jonathanturley.org/2012/02/26/judge-in-zombie-mohammed-case-responds/.

Turner, Bryan S., and Berna Zengin Arslan. "*Shari'a* and Legal Pluralism in the West." *European Journal of Social Theory* 14 (2) (2011): 139–159.

———. "U.K. Immigration Minister Opposes Ban on Face Veils." Islamtoday.net, July 20, 2010. Accessed October 22, 2012, http://en.islamtoday.net/artshow-229-3722.htm.

US Office of Immigration Statistics. *2004 Yearbook of Immigration Statistics.* January 2006. Accessed October 27, 2012, http://www.dhs.gov/xlibrary/assets/statistics/yearbook/2004/Yearbook2004.pdf.

van Selm, Joanne. "The Netherlands: Death of a Filmmaker Shakes a Nation." *Migration Policy Institute*, October 2003. Accessed April 14, 2013, available at http://www.migrationinformation.org/Profiles/display.cfm?ID=341.

———. "Verdonk onderzoekt verbod op Burqa." De Volkskrant, October 10, 2005. Accessed October 22, 2012, http://www.nu.nl/algemeen/606369/verdonk-onderzoekt-verbod-op-burka.html.

Vertovec, Steven, and Alisdair Rogers, eds. *Muslim European Youth, Reproducing Ethnicity, Religion, Culture.* London: Ashgate, 1998.

Vertovec, Steven, and C. Peach, eds. *Islam in Europe: The Politics of Religion and Community.* New York: St. Martin's, 1997.

———. "Violence contre les femmes: l'imam Bouziane relaxé." Le Figaro, June 22, 2005.

Voll, John Obert. "Foundations for Renewal and Reform: Islamic Movements in the Eighteenth and Nineteenth Centuries." In *The Oxford History of Islam*, edited by John L. Esposito. Oxford: Oxford University Press, 1999, 509–548.

———. "Washington Post-ABC poll." *The Washington Post,* September 7, 2010. Accessed January 31, 2012, http://www.washingtonpost.com/wp-srv/politics/polls/postpoll_09072010.html.

Waterfield, Bruno. "Belgian MPs Vote to Ban the Burqa," *The Telegraph*, April 29, 2010. Accessed June 22, 2012, http://www.telegraph.co.uk/news/worldnews/europe/belgium/7653814/Belgian-MPs-vote-to-ban-the-burqa.html.

Weil, Patrick. *La France et ses immigrés.* Paris: Calmann-Lévy, 1991.

Wielaard, Robert. "Belgian Lawmakers Pass Burqa Ban." Huffington Post, April 29, 2010. Accessed October 22, 2012, http://www.huffingtonpost.com/2010/04/30/belgian-lawmakers-pass-bu_n_558284.html.

———. "Wilders komt met boek over islam." De Telegraaf, December 31, 2010. Accessed January 31, 2012, http://www.telegraaf.nl/binnenland/8625401/__Boek_Wilders_over_de_islam__.html?p=13,2.

———. "Wilders Wants Debate on 'Real Nature' of Mohammed." *NIS News Bulletin*, April 1, 2011. Accessed January 31, 2012, http://www.nisnews.nl/public/010411_1.htm.

Willsher, Kim. "France's Muslim Hit Back at Nicolas Sarkozy's Policy on Halal Meat." *The Guardian*, March 10, 2012. Accessed June 19, 201, http://www.guardian.co.uk/world/2012/mar/10/nicolas-sarkozy-halal-meat-france-election.

Windschuttle, Keith. "The Cultural War on Western Civilization." The Sydney Line, January 2002. Accessed February 18, 2012, http://www.sydneyline.com/Warper cent2oonper cent2oWesternper cent2ocivilization.htm.

Wolk, Boldt, and Onkelbach. "Islam-Kritik empört Muslime." Der Western, January 2, 2011. Accessed January 31, 2012, http://www.derwesten.de/nachrichten/ islam-kritik-empoert-muslime-id4156145.html.

Woodhead, Linda. "The Muslim Veil Controversy and European Values." Accessed July 22, 2012, http://www.google.com/url?sa=t&rct=j&q=&esrc=s&source=web &cd=4&ved=0CFYQFjAD&url=http%3A%2F%2Feprints.lancs.ac.uk%2 F39909%2F1%2FVeil_and_Values_-SMT.doc&ei=a3HXT4SrDdGd6AHg-pStAw &usg=AFQjCNHaLPsNj1Ia3_zVzS_eQq4wMxN6dw.

Woolls, Daniel. "Spanish Govt Wants to Monitor Mosques." *Mail and Guardian online*, May 3, 2004. Accessed March 20, 2012, http://mg.co.za/article/2004–05–03-spanish-govt-wants-to-monitor-mosques.

Wynne-Jones, Jonthan. "Britons Are Suspicious towards Muslims, Study Finds." *The Telegraph*, January 9, 2010. Accessed January 30, 2012, http://www.telegraph.co.uk/ news/religion/6958571/Britons-are-suspicious-towards-Muslims-study-finds.html.

Ye'or, B. *Eurabia: The Euro Arab Axis*. Cranbury: Associated University Presses, 2005.

Young, H. "A Corrosive National Danger in Our Multicultural Model." *Guardian*, November 6, 2001. Accessed November 10, 2001, http://www.guardian.co.uk/ world/2001/nov/06/september11.politics.

Ystebo, Bjarte. "Kristelig Folkeparti med muslimer." IDAG, September 9, 2010. Accessed February 18, 2012, http://www.idag.no/aktuelt-oppslag.php3?ID=18107.

———. "Zapatero respalda el control de los sermones." El País, May 5, 2004. Accessed October 22, 2012, http://elpais.com/diario/2004/05/05/espana/1083708008_850215. html

Zick, Andreas, Beate Kupper, and Andreas Hovermann. "Intolerance, Prejudice and Discrimination." Accessed January 31, 2012, http://www.uni-bielefeld.de/ikg/ IntolerancePrejudice.PDF.

Zine, Jasmin. "Between Orientalism and Fundamentalism: The Politics of Muslim Women's Feminist Engagement." *Muslim World Journal of Human Rights* (Special Issue: Post-September 11th Developments in Human Rights in the Muslim World) 3 (1) (2006), doi: 10.2202/1554-4419.1080.

INDEX

Abduh, Mohammed, 344
Abu Laban, Ahmed, 113
Afghanistan, 5, 34, 84, 94, 115, 253
African Americans, 22, 44
Age, 74, 88, 91, 135
Ahmad, Salman, 145, 251
Ajala, Imèn, 74–75, 329
Akbaba, Yasemin, 96, 335
Akkari, Ahmed, 113
Al Qaradawi, Yusuf, 345
Alabama, 103
al-Afghani, Sayyid Jamal
    ad-Din, 344
Al-Albani, 131, 350
Alaoui, Fouad, 109
Alaska, 103
Al-Azhar, 129, 350
Alexander, Jeffery, xvi, 102, 318–319, 337
Algeria, Algerians, 56, 63, 118, 329, 338,
    345, 352
Ali, Ayaan Hirsi, 10, 86, 99, 322, 348
al-Shawakani, Muhammad, 344
Amara, Fadela, 9–10, 322
Amendment, First, 12–13, 103, 115
Amsterdam, viii, xv, 3, 21, 22, 24, 33–36,
    39, 41, 43, 46, 50, 52, 56, 58–59, 63,
    67–68, 102
Anti-Semitism, 15, 253
Apostasy, 253
Arabs, 7, 13, 333
Arjomand, Homa, 117
Asad, Talal, 115, 122, 125, 144, 330,
    342, 348
Austria, 2, 97, 329

Bacquelaine, Daniel, 101
Badawi, Zaki, 119
Battle of Poitiers, 320
Bauer, Alexander, 102, 336

Behaving, 37–42
Belgium, xiv, 107–110, 120, 329, 332,
    336, 339
Believing, 38–39, 327
Belonging, 23, 37–40, 73–74, 327
Berger, Maurits, 102
Berlin, vii, ix, xv, 21, 33–34, 42–43, 46–47,
    49–50, 52, 54, 56–57, 62–66, 72, 75,
    96, 99, 322, 333, 335, 336, 338
    focus groups, xv, xvii, 21
    survey, ix, xv, 23–24
Berlusconi, Silvio, 7
Bin Baz, Abd al-Aziz ibn Abd Allah,
    135, 346
Birmingham, 100, 342
Blunkett, David, 93
Body, xiv, 81, 109, 121–124, 125–127, 134
Bombings,
    London, 3, 14, 55–56, 94
    Madrid, 3
Bosnia, Bosnian(s), 5, 22, 24, 33–34,
    52–53, 65
Boston, viii, xv, 22, 24, 33, 35, 41–42, 45,
    52, 56–57, 65
Boubakeur, Dalil, 109–110
Boutih, Malek, 92
Bouyeri, Mohammed, 11
Bouziane, Adbelkader, 94–95, 334
Boykin, William (General), 12
Bradford, 100
Bremen, 99, 336
Burlingame, Debra, 12, 97

Cameron, David, 7, 141, 321, 348
Cartoons, xviii, 8, 29, 110, 113–114, 340
Catholic, vii, viii, 26, 32, 44, 108, 125,
    144–145, 328, 340
Cattenoz, Pierre, 8
Celermajer, Danielle, 144, 348

Central Bureau of Statistics (CBS), 332
Chirac, Jacques, 9, 109
Christianity, 39, 122, 125, 144, 330,
    342, 348
Christians, viii, 16, 35, 38, 39, 50, 52,
    60–61, 133, 136, 325–326
Church, 6, 35, 37, 64, 71, 73–75, 89,
    99–100, 108, 111, 125, 333, 340
  attendance, 71
  and state, 99, 108, 117, 143, 317, 338
CIA, 11–12
Citizen, 1, 4, 8, 11, 13, 15–16, 20, 29, 51,
    61–63, 65, 72, 74–75, 88–90, 97,
    104, 107, 109, 112, 117, 120, 121,
    126, 139, 141, 143–144, 319, 326,
    332, 339
Citizenship, xvi, 8, 10, 26, 51, 57, 61–63,
    87, 89–92, 94, 104, 115, 124, 318–320,
    330, 332–334
Civic engagement, xiv, 23, 61, 66–68,
    71, 328
Civilization (s), 3, 7, 141–142, 321
  clash, 3, 5, 86
Class, xviii, 1, 40, 76–78, 81–82, 92,
    139–140, 351
Cliteur, Paul, 84
Cohesion, 329
  social, 76–78, 98, 329
Colas, Dominique, 340
Colonial, 134, 143, 333, 344
  postcolonial, 116, 126, 134, 143, 344
Commission on Scientific Signs in the
    Qur'an and Sunnah, 345
Community,
  country of residence, 50, 60–61, 63,
    72, 87, 118
  ethnic, 49
  local, 50–51, 66
  national, xvi, 1, 34–35, 62, 66,
    326, 327
  religious, 30, 50, 51–52, 108, 137, 328
Connolly, Michael, 122, 342
Constrict Theory, 77, 329
Council of American Islamic Religions
    (CAIR), 323
Court,
  administrative, 103
  European Court of Human Rights,
    121, 342
Crusades, 320

Dawkins, Richard, 85, 331
de Krom, Paul, 8
Democracy (ies), 4, 5, 74, 84, 86, 96–97,
    113–115, 120, 124, 139, 141, 328–329,
    343, 346–347
Democrat, 82, 89, 92, 95, 102, 115, 339
  party, 7, 10, 14, 64, 82, 91
Demonstration, 92, 102, 328
Denmark, 10, 113–114, 329, 340
Diet, 34, 126
  dietary rules, 42–43, 71, 124, 144
Discrimination, xvi, xviii, 50, 55–58, 74,
    84, 96, 98, 105, 108, 324, 330, 333, 342
  religious, 335
Diversity, 76–78, 90, 96, 98, 104, 118,
    141, 320, 329–330
  cultural, 89, 104, 130, 142, 318, 320
Donner, Piet Hein, 333
Doxa (*see* orthodoxy)
Dress code, xiii, 9, 34, 45, 47, 72, 84,
    96, 100, 107, 121–123, 124, 132, 134,
    135, 144
Driessen, Geert, 98, 335

Education, 332, 334–335, 343–344, 351
  Islamic, 95–96, 98, 345–346, 350
  religious, 94, 98–100, 111, 132, 341
Egerkingen Committee, 317
El Fadl, Khaled Abou, 133
Elias, Norbert, 122, 342
Ellison, Keith, 145, 323
Elorza, Antonio, 84, 331
Enemy,
  external, xviii, 1, 3, 5–6, 10, 15, 19,
    77, 319
  internal, xviii, 1, 5, 15, 19, 77, 319
Enlightenment, 4, 6, 122
Equality, 4, 9, 10, 89, 91, 99, 105, 107,
    116, 118–119, 134–135, 137, 141–143,
    319, 338
  gender, 93, 110, 117, 122, 142
Essentialism,
  clash, 141
Ethics, 41, 53, 112, 115, 320, 342
Ethnicity, 22, 25, 33, 41–42, 44, 49, 51–52,
    53, 56, 58, 61, 76–78, 79, 139–140,
    317, 330, 339
Europe,
  Western, 2, 8, 17, 26, 61, 75, 81, 88, 98,
    317–319, 326, 327, 330, 338, 347, 349

European Union, 2–3, 93–94, 318, 324, 330, 338
Evangelicals, 73

Fallaci, Oriana, 84
Fast (*see* Ramadan)
FBI, ix, 11, 68
Feminism, 141, 348
Fiqh Council, 345
Florida, 11, 103
Focus groups, xv, xvii, 21–27, 31–32, 39, 42, 45, 47, 51, 55, 60–63, 64–65, 84, 126, 129
Fortuyn, Pim, 89–90, 104, 331, 368
Fourest, Caroline, 85
Fox, Jonathan, 96, 323, 335
France, vii, viii, xiii, 2, 7–8, 13–19, 30–31, 35, 37, 57, 60–61, 63, 68, 74–75, 81, 84–85, 92–93, 94–95, 98, 100, 101–102, 105, 107–110, 123, 125, 317–318, 321–322, 324, 326–330, 334
Freedom,
    expression, 91, 113, 142
    religion, 97, 121, 336, 342
    speech, 16, 85, 110, 113–114
Friedman, Thomas, 85

Gabriel, Brigitte, 11, 321–322, 349
Gallup, 12–13, 26, 29–32, 42, 44, 61, 68, 71, 73, 323–324, 326–327, 341, 348
Gauck, Joachim, xiv
Gender, xiv, xv, xvi, 9, 22, 23, 25, 38, 42, 43, 46, 51, 63, 71, 73, 93, 110, 117, 121–124, 134, 141–142, 328, 333, 341
Generation, xiii, xv, 21–22, 44, 51–52, 54, 64, 126, 333, 351
Georgia, 337
Germany, vii, viii, ix, xiv, 2, 6, 7, 8, 10, 13–14, 15–19, 26, 30–31, 33, 35, 37–38, 44, 60–61, 65–66, 68, 81, 84, 91–92, 95–97, 99, 102, 108, 111, 118, 123, 318–319, 321–322, 324–327, 329–331, 335, 338, 340–341
Ghettoization, 3, 98
Goldberg, David Theo, 139, 347
Goode, Virgil H., 323
Green, Damian, 102

Hadith, 41, 130, 350
Halat-Mec, Gönül, 111

Harris, Sam, 85
Hedegaar, Lars, 10
Hervieu-Leger, Daniele, 125
Higgins, Brian, 145
Hijab, xiii, xvi, 9–10, 42, 45–47, 55–56, 58, 72, 100–101, 123, 126, 134–135, 141, 346
Hirshkind, Charles, 122, 342
Hitchens, Christopher, 85
Hizb ut-Tahrir, 94, 344
Hlayhel, Raed, 113
Holland, Francois, 93
Holy Qur'an Memorization International Organization, 345
Homeland Security, 11, 345
Homosexuality, 42, 91, 113, 125, 339
Huntington, Samuel, 3, 321
Hussain, Zubair Butt, 10

Ibn Baaz, Abdul Aziz, 131
Identification, 3, 14, 23, 27–29, 30, 31–35, 37, 39, 42, 49, 58–59, 60–61, 66, 72–74, 120, 129, 141, 326
Identity(ies),
    marker, 29–30, 33, 47
    national, 15, 29, 34, 58, 60
    personal, 33, 39, 328
    political, 4
    religious, 20, 27, 60, 75
    social, 32–33, 45, 326
Immigration,
    policy, xviii, 91, 92–93, 104, 318, 323, 326
Indian Subcontinent, 45
Indiana, 103, 337, 338
Individual, xiii, xvi, xvii, 3–5, 12, 14–15, 22, 24–26, 29, 32, 37, 38, 43, 51, 73, 75–77, 79, 91–92, 94, 105, 110, 112, 115–116, 119–122, 124–127, 131, 133, 134–135, 142, 144, 319, 328, 329, 339
Individualism,
    religious, 124–125
Institut Français d'Opinion Publique (IFOP), 13, 16–19, 53, 323–325, 327
Institutionalization, 104
Institutions, 1, 23, 26, 68–69, 73, 77–78, 81–82, 95, 108–111, 116, 120, 126, 131–132, 135, 143, 318, 334, 336, 338, 344–345

Integration, viii, xii, xiv–xv, xvii–xviii,
    3–4, 7, 10–11, 13, 14–19, 25, 38, 57, 81,
    83, 86–92, 95–96, 98, 100, 104, 109,
    111, 123–125, 130, 140, 142–145, 249,
    251, 298, 306, 317–318, 320, 325–327,
    330–333, 337–338
  political, 81–82, 142, 318
  socioeconomic, 81–82
International Islamic Organization for
    Education, 345
Iowa, 103, 337
Iran, 3, 44, 117, 333, 344
Iraq, viii, 5, 21, 41, 53, 57, 59, 64, 84,
    94–95, 333, 351
Islamic,
  communities, 18, 68
  organizations, 99–100, 109, 344
  religiosity, 23, 29, 72–73, 139
Islamization, 7, 11, 90, 98, 130, 335, 344
Islamophobia, xvi, 15, 84, 318, 324,
    330, 337

Jamal, Amaney, 73
Jespersen, Karen, 10
Jewish, xiv, 32, 51–52, 100, 348, 353
Jews, vii, viii, 13, 39, 44, 50, 133,
    136, 352
Jihad, 11, 340, 346, 351–352
Jneid, Fawaz, 137, 347
Jones (Pastor), 11, 114
Judaism, 144, 348

Kansas, 103, 337
Kelek, Necla, 9, 86
Kentucky, 337
Khotbas, 109, 346
King, Peter, 11, 97
Kundani, Arun, 142, 348

Laïcité, 10, 93, 100, 101, 123, 144, 331,
    336, 343
Langballe, Jesper, 10
Lazio, Rock, 12, 97
Le Pen, Jean-Marie, 92
Le Pen, Marine, 9, 106, 321
Lewis, Bernard, 85
Liberalism, 318, 348
  neoliberal, 140
  Schmittian Liberalism, 6, 93

London, xv, 3, 14, 18, 21–22, 24, 33, 41, 45,
    49–51, 53–57, 60, 61, 64, 74, 94–95,
    100, 119, 317–319, 325, 334
Lowi, Theodore, xvi, 318

Makkah Al-Mukarramah Charity
    Foundation for Orphans, 345
Manji, Irshad, 86
Marriage, 42, 50, 51–54, 86, 88, 91–92,
    116–119, 135, 341342, 350
Mehra, 352
Merkel, Angela, 7, 8
Merry, Michael, 98, 335
Michigan, 337
Middle East, 14, 19, 134
Minarets, xiii, xvi, 18, 84, 97–98, 124, 143,
    317, 335, 347
Minority (ies),
  ethnic, 63, 318
  religious, 76, 96, 335
Mississippi, 337
Missouri, 103, 337
Modernity, 84, 124–126, 130, 137, 317, 319,
    330, 343
Modernization, 3, 121, 126
Modood, Tariq, xvii, 318, 320, 330
Mohammed Moussaoui, 109–110, 338
Mohammad, Omar Bakri, 94
Morality, 114, 134
Morocco, 8, 35–36, 54, 56, 109, 118, 130,
    332, 338, 345
  Moroccans, viii, 21–22, 53, 61,
    89, 90
Mosque,
  attendance, viii, ix, 23, 29, 37, 42,
    44–45, 71–75
  building, 9, 14, 18–19, 98
  ground zero, xiii, 11–12, 18–19, 97
Moussaoui, Mohammed, 109–110, 338
Mubarak, Gamal, 344
Multicultural,
  policies, 77, 142, 329
  societies, 85
Multiculturalism, xvii, 3, 7, 16, 78, 87,
    100, 104, 140, 142, 318–320,
    347–348
Muslim Brotherhood, 110, 130, 333,
    344–345
Muslim College in London, 95, 334

Muslim World League (MWL), 345, 349
Myard, Jacques, 101, 104

Nationalism, 4, 8, 142, 318, 349
Nebraska, 337
The Netherlands, vii, viii, ix, xvii, 2, 6,
    17–18, 26–27, 30, 35–37, 62, 75, 77,
    84, 87–90, 95, 98–99, 101, 102–104,
    108, 120, 123, 137, 142, 325, 329–331,
    335, 339, 342, 347, 349, 351–352
New Hampshire, 337
New Jersey, 337
New Mexico, 103, 337
New York City, 11, 337
Niqab, 100–101, 107, 110, 123–124, 132,
    134, 339, 352
North Africa, 2, 14, 19, 22, 63
North Carolina, 337
Nussbaum, xiv, 348

Obama, Barak, 11–12, 323
Oklahoma, 12, 103, 337
Ong, Walter, 122, 124, 342, 344
Opinion (public), xvii, 5, 13, 19, 85, 350
Orthodoxy, 42, 126, 133, 135, 141, 339
Orthopraxis, 42
Oslo, 107, 338
Ottoman Empire, 5, 130
Oudkomers, 88, 332

Pakistan, 9, 21, 41, 44, 118, 130
Paris, vii, xv, 21, 22, 24, 33, 57–58,
    63, 148
Party,
    extreme-right, 6, 10, 62, 140
    membership, 60, 73–74, 91, 100, 328
    parties, 10, 65–66, 96, 97, 103, 114, 116
Pennsylvania, 337
Petition, 9, 82, 115–116, 328
Pew, 12–14, 15, 17–19, 26–27, 29–30, 37,
    42, 44, 61, 323–328, 349
Philipse, Herman, 84, 331
Pipes, Daniel, 85
Pluralism,
    legal, 116, 341–342
    religious, 144
Political participation, 21, 23–24, 26,
    61, 64, 65, 68, 71–74, 76–79, 81,
    135, 137, 139, 328–329, 347

formal, vi, ix, 348–349
informal, vii, ix
Politics, xiv, 5, 22, 25, 36, 57–60, 62–64,
    78, 82–83, 103, 107, 116, 123, 137, 140,
    317–318, 320, 325–327, 328, 339–341,
    348–349
Polling(s), xv, 326–327, 341
Polls, 6, 13–14, 16, 18, 40
Polygamy, 8, 93
Praile, Isabelle, 109, 339
Prayer, 9, 14, 29, 37, 39–40, 42–44, 54, 71,
    73, 75–76, 107, 321, 350–351
Prophet Mohammed, 85, 113
Protestants, 6, 12, 26, 31–32, 44, 73, 99,
    122, 124–126, 144, 328–329
Putnam, Robert, 328–330

Qur'an,
    burning, 114
    interpretation(s), 118, 130–134

Racism, 15, 93, 320, 322, 324, 330, 340
Radical, 11, 84, 85, 97, 99, 141, 320,
    334, 352
Radicalism, 110
    Islamic, 108
    political, 104
Radicalization, xiii, 11, 144, 351
Ramadan (month), 42, 75–76
Ramadan, Tariq, 345
Rasmussen, Anders Fogh (Danish Prime
    Minister), 113
Rawls, John, 113–114
Reformism, 344
Reid, Jen'nan, 73
Reinares, Fernando, 84, 331
Religion, viii, xvi, xviii, 6–7, 9–14, 17,
    24–25, 26, 29–38, 41–42, 46, 50–55,
    57, 58, 60–61, 66–67, 72–76, 78,
    84, 85–87, 89, 92, 96–97, 99–100,
    102, 103, 107–109, 111–114, 121–122,
    124–126, 133, 136, 137, 139, 143–145,
    317, 322–328, 330, 333, 334–343,
    347–348, 351
Republican, party, 12, 14, 97
Revivalist, 130–132
Rida, Rashid, 344
Rights,
    collective, 112

Rights—*Continued*
    human rights, 7, 59, 64, 93, 101, 111,
        113–114, 117, 120–121, 341, 342,
        348, 352
    individual, xvii, 112, 115, 120, 134
Rituals, 1, 72, 120, 133
Rushdie Affair, 104, 112–113

Sadat, Anwar, 344
Salafi, vi, xiv, xvi, xvii, xviii, 49, 94,
        110, 120, 130–135, 137, 141, 344,
        345, 350
Salafization, 47, 129–137, 139, 343
Salat (*see* prayer)
Sarkozy, Nicolas, 7–9, 92, 321
Sarrazin, Thilo, 86
Saudi Arabia, 131–132, 134, 338, 345
Schain, Martin, 82, 318, 326, 330
Scheffer, Paul, 85
Schools,
    Islamic, 96, 98–100, 131, 335
    private, 100
    public, 57, 98–100, 108–109, 111, 121,
        122, 123, 336
Schüble, Wolfgang, 95
Secular,
    culture, 82, 107, 143
    principles, 107, 116, 123, 143–144
Secularism, xvii, xviii, 10, 26, 84, 93,
        99, 100, 107–109, 113–114,
        121–122, 140, 143–144, 330, 339,
        340, 343
Secularity, 9, 107, 144, 338, 339
Securitization, xvii, xviii, 83–84, 87, 89,
        94, 101, 103, 117, 330, 334, 347
Security, xvii, 3–4, 9, 10–11, 18, 20, 77,
        83, 87, 93–95, 101, 116, 123–124,
        140–141, 319–320, 330, 335, 341,
        345, 352
Self, declaration, 31–32, 37
September 11 2001, 25, 55, 85, 140
Sexuality, 124, 135–136
Shari'a, xiii, xvi, xvii, 11–12, 15, 94–95,
        98–99, 103, 110, 114–120, 142,
        340–341, 352
    angrezi, 341
    courts, 117, 142
Shi'ism, 109
Shia, 96, 327, 346

Simmel, Georg, 319
South Asians, 44
South Carolina, 337
South Dakota, 103, 337
Spain, 13, 15, 18, 61, 62, 84, 102,
        107–108, 123, 319, 324, 329
Straw, Jack, 9, 322
Sunna (*see* Hadith)
Switzerland, xiii, 18, 88, 97, 107, 317,
        325, 329
Symbolic,
    boundaries, xv, xvi, xvii, xviii, 1, 319
Symbolism, 35

Tabligh, 130, 134, 345
Taylor, Charles, 111–112, 338, 339
Tennessee, 97, 103
Terrorism, 1–5, 10–11, 14, 17–18, 20, 67,
        83–84, 86–87, 91, 94, 95, 104, 124,
        319, 322, 331, 334, 346–347, 351
Terrorists, 3, 10–11, 13, 17–18, 25, 84–85,
        94, 97, 339
Tolerance, 3, 10, 17, 40, 96, 121, 141–142,
        338, 340
Topos, 4, 133
Toynbee, Polly, 9, 348
Trefidopoulos, Triadafilos, 4
Trust, vii, viii, ix, 17, 23, 26, 50–51, 55,
        68–69, 76–79, 82, 99, 328–329
Tunisia, 36, 118, 352
Turkey, 3, 34, 54, 58–60, 62, 96, 118, 130,
        338, 345

Ummah, 49, 60, 130, 136
United Kingdom, vii, viii, ix, xiii, 2, 7, 17,
        30, 60, 68, 81, 84–85, 93–95, 98, 100,
        103, 104, 108–110, 117–118, 120, 123,
        142, 326, 329, 334, 336, 340, 351
United States, vi, vii, viii, ix, xiii, xv,
        xvi, xvii, 2, 3, 5–6, 11–13, 17, 18–20,
        25, 26, 29–32, 38, 42, 44, 55, 61, 66,
        68, 71–75, 76–79, 84, 86, 88, 97, 103,
        107–108, 114, 116, 130–131, 139–140,
        317–320, 323, 327, 330, 344–348

Values,
    civic, 62
    political, 11, 141
Van Gogh, Theo, 86, 99, 331

Verdonk, 88, 89, 101, 332–333
Virginia, 98, 103, 337
Vote,
  eligibility to, 64
  registration, 74, 329

Wahab, Abdel, 130
Wahhabism, 130–132, 344–345
West Virginia, 337
Wilders, Geert, 6, 62, 90, 101, 140, 321
Williams, Juan, 11, 323

World Assembly of Muslim Youth, 345
World Supreme Council for
  Mosques, 345
Worship, 19, 26, 36, 39, 71–72, 75, 98, 327
Wulf, Christian, xvi

Yusuf, Hamza, 345, 350

Zaytuna College, 350
Zine, Jasmine, 143, 348
Zypries, Brigitte, 95

Printed in the United States of America